Mathematical Modeling and Simulation in Mechanics and Dynamic Systems, 2nd Edition

Mathematical Modeling and Simulation in Mechanics and Dynamic Systems, 2nd Edition

Editors

Maria Luminița Scutaru
Catalin I. Pruncu

Basel • Beijing • Wuhan • Barcelona • Belgrade • Novi Sad • Cluj • Manchester

Editors
Maria Luminița Scutaru
Transilvania University of Brașov
Brașov
Romania

Catalin I. Pruncu
Politecnico di Bari
Bari
Italy

Editorial Office
MDPI
St. Alban-Anlage 66
4052 Basel, Switzerland

This is a reprint of articles from the Special Issue published online in the open access journal *Mathematics* (ISSN 2227-7390) (available at: https://www.mdpi.com/si/mathematics/Math_Model_Simul_Mech_Dyn_Syst_II).

For citation purposes, cite each article independently as indicated on the article page online and as indicated below:

Lastname, A.A.; Lastname, B.B. Article Title. *Journal Name* **Year**, *Volume Number*, Page Range.

ISBN 978-3-7258-0209-8 (Hbk)
ISBN 978-3-7258-0210-4 (PDF)
doi.org/10.3390/books978-3-7258-0210-4

© 2024 by the authors. Articles in this book are Open Access and distributed under the Creative Commons Attribution (CC BY) license. The book as a whole is distributed by MDPI under the terms and conditions of the Creative Commons Attribution-NonCommercial-NoDerivs (CC BY-NC-ND) license.

Contents

Maria Luminita Scutaru and Catalin-Iulian Pruncu
Mathematical Modeling and Simulation in Mechanics and Dynamic Systems, 2nd Edition
Reprinted from: *Mathematics* **2024**, *12*, 341, doi:10.3390/math12020341 1

Sorin Vlase, Marin Marin and Negrean Iuliu
Finite Element Method-Based Elastic Analysis of Multibody Systems: A Review
Reprinted from: *Mathematics* **2022**, *10*, 257, doi:10.3390/math10020257 4

Shiqi Xia, Yimin Xia and Jiawei Xiang
Modelling and Fault Detection for Specific Cavitation Damage Based on the Discharge Pressure of Axial Piston Pumps
Reprinted from: *Mathematics* **2022**, *10*, 2461, doi:10.3390/math10142461 19

Muhammad Faizan, Farhan Ali, Karuppusamy Loganathan, Aurang Zaib, Ch Achi Reddy and Sara I. Abdelsalam
Entropy Analysis of Sutterby Nanofluid Flow over a Riga Sheet with Gyrotactic Microorganisms and Cattaneo–Christov Double Diffusion
Reprinted from: *Mathematics* **2022**, *10*, 3157, doi:10.3390/math10173157 32

Andronikos Paliathanasis, Genly Leon and PeterG. L. Leach
Lie Symmetry Classification and Qualitative Analysis for the Fourth-Order Schrödinger Equation
Reprinted from: *Mathematics* **2022**, *10*, 3204, doi:10.3390/math10173204 54

Lahcen El Ouadefli, Abdeslam El Akkad, Omar El Moutea, Hassan Moustabchir, Ahmed Elkhalfi, Maria Luminița Scutaru and Radu Muntean
Numerical Simulation for Brinkman System with Varied Permeability Tensor [†]
Reprinted from: *Mathematics* **2022**, *10*, 3242, doi:10.3390/math10183242 69

Yunnan Teng, Quan Wen, Liyang Xie and Bangchun Wen
Study on Vibration Friction Reducing Mechanism of Materials
Reprinted from: *Mathematics* **2022**, *10*, 3529, doi:10.3390/math10193529 81

Magdalena Tutak, Jarosław Brodny, Antoni John, Janos Száva, Sorin Vlase and Maria Luminita Scutaru
CFD Model Studies of Dust Dispersion in Driven Dog Headings
Reprinted from: *Mathematics* **2022**, *10*, 3798, doi:10.3390/math10203798 91

Maria Luminita Scutaru, Marin Marin and Sorin Vlase
Dynamic Absorption of Vibration in a Multi Degree of Freedom Elastic System
Reprinted from: *Mathematics* **2022**, *10*, 4045, doi:10.3390/math10214045 103

Constantin Fetecau, Abdul Rauf, Tahir Mushtaq Qureshi and Dumitru Vieru
Steady-State Solutions for MHD Motions of Burgers' Fluids through Porous Media with Differential Expressions of Shear on Boundary and Applications
Reprinted from: *Mathematics* **2022**, *10*, 4228, doi:10.3390/math10224228 118

Jesús Alfonso Medrano-Hermosillo, Ricardo Lozoya-Ponce, Abraham Efraím Rodriguez-Mata and Rogelio Baray-Arana
Phase-Space Modeling and Control of Robots in the Screw Theory Framework Using Geometric Algebra
Reprinted from: *Mathematics* **2023**, *11*, 572, doi:10.3390/math11030572 133

Ioan Száva, Sorin Vlase, Ildikó-Renáta Száva, Gábor Turzó, Violeta Mihaela Munteanu, Teofil Gălățanu, et al.
Modern Dimensional Analysis-Based Heat Transfer Analysis: Normalized Heat Transfer Curves
Reprinted from: *Mathematics* **2023**, *11*, 741, doi:10.3390/math11030741 150

Omar El Moutea, Lahcen El Ouadefli, Abdeslam El Akkad, Nadia Nakbi, Ahmed Elkhalfi, Maria Luminita Scutaru and Sorin Vlase
A Posteriori Error Estimators for the Quasi-Newtonian Stokes Problem with a General Boundary Condition
Reprinted from: *Mathematics* **2023**, *11*, 1943, doi:10.3390/math11081943 . . . . **183**

Jianing Cao and Hua Chen
Mathematical Model for Fault Handling of Singular Nonlinear Time-Varying Delay Systems Based on T-S Fuzzy Model
Reprinted from: *Mathematics* **2023**, *11*, 2547, doi:10.3390/math11112547 . . . . **203**

Editorial

Mathematical Modeling and Simulation in Mechanics and Dynamic Systems, 2nd Edition

Maria Luminita Scutaru [1,*] and Catalin-Iulian Pruncu [2,*]

1 Department of Mechanical Engineering, Faculty of Mechanical Engineering, Transilvania University of Brașov, 500036 Brașov, Romania
2 Departimento di Meccanica, Matematica e Management, Politecnico di Bari, 70126 Bari, Italy
* Correspondence: lscutaru@unitbv.ro (M.L.S.); catalin.pruncu@gmail.com (C.-I.P.)

1. Introduction

Although it has been considered difficult to make further contributions in the field of mechanics, the spectacular evolution of technology and numerical calculation techniques has made these opinions shift, and increasingly sophisticated models have been developed, which should predict, as accurately as possible, the phenomena that take place in dynamic systems. Therefore, researchers have come to study mechanical systems with complicated behavior using experiments and computer models [1–3]. The key requirement is that the system is nonlinear in its form. The impetus in mechanics and dynamical systems has come from many sources: computer simulation, experimental science, mathematics, and modeling [4–7]. There is a wide range of influences. Computer experiments change the way in which we analyze these systems. Topics of interest include, but are not limited to, modeling mechanical systems, new methods in dynamic systems, the behavior simulation of a mechanical system, nonlinear systems, multibody systems with elastic elements, multi-degrees of freedom, mechanical systems, experimental modal analysis, and mechanics of materials.

2. Statistics of the Special Issue

There were 28 total submissions to this Special Issue, of which 13 were published (46.4%) and 15 rejected (63.6%). The authors' geographical distribution is shown in Table 1, and it can be seen that the 67 authors are from 13 different countries. Note that it is usual for a paper to be written by more than one author and for authors to collaborate with authors with different affiliations or multiple affiliations.

Table 1. Geographic distribution of authors by country.

Country	Number of Authors
Romania	13
China	9
Spania	1
India	2
Pakistan	5
Egypt	1
Morocco	6
South Africa	3
Chile	2
Poland	3
Mexico	4
Hungary	1

The following papers were published in this Special Issue:

1. Vlase, S.; Marin, M.; Negrean, I.N. Finite Element Method-Based Elastic Analysis of Multibody Systems: A Review. *Mathematics* **2022**, *10*, 257. https://doi.org/10.3390/math10020257.
2. Xia, S.; Xia, Y.; Xiang, J. Modelling and Fault Detection for Specific Cavitation Damage Based on the Discharge Pressure of Axial Piston Pumps. *Mathematics* **2022**, *10*, 2461. https://doi.org/10.3390/math10142461.
3. Faizan, M.; Ali, F.; Loganathan, K.; Zaib, A.; Reddy, C.A.; Abdelsalam, S.I. Entropy Analysis of Sutterby Nanofluid Flow over a Riga Sheet with Gyrotactic Microorganisms and Cattaneo–Christov Double Diffusion. *Mathematics* **2022**, *10*, 3157. https://doi.org/10.3390/math10173157.
4. Paliathanasis, A.; Leon, G.; Leach, P.G.L. Lie Symmetry Classification and Qualitative Analysis for the Fourth-Order Schrödinger Equation. *Mathematics* **2022**, *10*, 3204. https://doi.org/10.3390/math10173204.
5. El Ouadefli, L.; El Akkad, A.; El Moutea, O.; Moustabchir, H.; Elkhalfi, A.; Scutaru, L.M.; Muntean, R. Numerical Simulation for Brinkman System with Varied Permeability Tensor. *Mathematics* **2022**, *10*, 3242. https://doi.org/10.3390/math10183242.
6. Teng, Y.; Wen, Q.; Xie, L.; Wen, B. Study on Vibration Friction Reducing Mechanism of Materials. *Mathematics* **2022**, *10*, 3529. https://doi.org/10.3390/math10193529.
7. Tutak, M.; Brodny, J.; John, A.; Száva, J.; Vlase, S.; Scutaru, M.L. CFD Model Studies of Dust Dispersion in Driven Dog Headings. *Mathematics* **2022**, *10*, 3798. https://doi.org/10.3390/math10203798.
8. Scutaru, M.L.; Marin, M.; Vlase, S. Dynamic Absorption of Vibration in a Multi Degree of Freedom Elastic System. *Mathematics* **2022**, *10*, 4045. https://doi.org/10.3390/math10214045.
9. Fetecau, C.; Rauf, A.; Qureshi, T.M.; Vieru, D. Steady-State Solutions for MHD Motions of Burgers' Fluids through Porous Media with Differential Expressions of Shear on Boundary and Applications. *Mathematics* **2022**, *10*, 4228. https://doi.org/10.3390/math10224228.
10. Medrano-Hermosillo, J.A.; Lozoya-Ponce, R.; Rodriguez-Mata, A.E.; Baray-Arana, R. Phase-Space Modeling and Control of Robots in the Screw Theory Framework Using Geometric Algebra. *Mathematics* **2023**, *11*, 572. https://doi.org/10.3390/math11030572.
11. Száva, I.; Vlase, S.; Száva, I.-R.; Turzó, G.; Munteanu, V.M.; Gălățanu, T.; Asztalos, Z.; Gálfi, B.-P. Modern Dimensional Analysis-Based Heat Transfer Analysis: Normalized Heat Transfer Curves. *Mathematics* **2023**, *11*, 741. https://doi.org/10.3390/math11030741.
12. El Moutea, O.; El Ouadefli, L.; El Akkad, A.; Nakbi, N.; Elkhalfi, A.; Scutaru, M.L.; Vlase, S. A Posteriori Error Estimators for the Quasi-Newtonian Stokes Problem with a General Boundary Condition. *Mathematics* **2023**, *11*, 1943. https://doi.org/10.3390/math11081943.
13. Cao, J.; Chen, H. Mathematical Model for Fault Handling of Singular Nonlinear Time-Varying Delay Systems Based on T-S Fuzzy Model. *Mathematics* **2023**, *11*, 2547. https://doi.org/10.3390/math11112547.

3. Authors of the Special Issue

For the publications in this Special Issue, there was an average of four authors per manuscript.

A list of papers published in this Special Issue can be found in Section 2. It can be seen that most of the articles adhere very well to the theme of the Special Issue. The research was carried out by well-constituted teams of researchers in appropriately equipped laboratories from universities in several countries. Authors from different universities collaborated to achieve common objectives. Each paper includes original results developed by groups of researchers. We note the high number of researchers who have been involved in this project, and we thank them for participating in this Special Issue.

4. Brief Overview of the Contributions to the Special Issue

In this Special Issue, three topics were dominant, namely modeling of the multibody system using the Finite Element Method, applied mathematics in dynamic systems, and analytical methods in multibody systems.

Author Contributions: Conceptualization, M.L.S. and C.-I.P.; methodology, M.L.S. and C.-I.P.; software, M.L.S. and C.-I.P.; validation, M.L.S. and C.-I.P.; formal analysis, M.L.S. and C.-I.P.; investigation, M.L.S. and C.-I.P.; resources, M.L.S. and C.-I.P.; data curation, M.L.S. and C.-I.P.; writing—original draft preparation, M.L.S. and C.-I.P.; writing—review and editing, M.L.S. and C.-I.P.; visualization, M.L.S. and C.-I.P.; supervision, M.L.S. and C.-I.P.; project administration, M.L.S. and C.-I.P. All authors have read and agreed to the published version of the manuscript.

Conflicts of Interest: The authors declare no conflicts of interest.

References

1. Marin, M.; Seadawy, A.; Vlase, S.; Chirila, A. On mixed problem in thermoelasticity of type III for Cosserat media. *J. Taibah Univ. Sci.* **2022**, *16*, 1264–1274. [CrossRef]
2. Vlase, S.; Negrean, I.; Marin, M.; Scutaru, M.L. Energy of Accelerations Used to Obtain the Motion Equations of a Three-Dimensional Finite Element. *Symmetry* **2020**, *12*, 321. [CrossRef]
3. Vlase, S.; Marin, M.; Öchsner, A. Considerations of the transverse vibration of a mechanical system with two identical bars. *Proc. Inst. Mech. Eng. Part L—J. Mater.—Des. Appl.* **2019**, *233*, 1318–1323. [CrossRef]
4. Vlase, S.; Teodorescu, P.P.; Itu, C.; Scutaru, M.L. Elasto-Dynamics of a Solid with a General "Rigid" Motion using FEM Model. Part II. Analysis of a Double Cardan Joint. *Rom. J. Phys.* **2013**, *58*, 882–892.
5. Negrean, I.; Crisan, A.V.; Vlase, S. A New Approach in Analytical Dynamics of Mechanical Systems. *Symmetry* **2020**, *12*, 95. [CrossRef]
6. Marin, M.; Chirila, A.; Öchsner, A.; Vlase, S. About finite energy solutions in thermoelasticity of micropolar bodies with voids. *Bound. Value Probl.* **2019**, *2019*, 89. [CrossRef]
7. Vlase, S.; Negrean, I.; Marin, M.; Nastac, S. Kane's Method-Based Simulation and Modeling Robots with Elastic Elements, Using Finite Element Method. *Mathematics* **2020**, *8*, 805. [CrossRef]

Disclaimer/Publisher's Note: The statements, opinions and data contained in all publications are solely those of the individual author(s) and contributor(s) and not of MDPI and/or the editor(s). MDPI and/or the editor(s) disclaim responsibility for any injury to people or property resulting from any ideas, methods, instructions or products referred to in the content.

Review

Finite Element Method-Based Elastic Analysis of Multibody Systems: A Review

Sorin Vlase [1,2,*], Marin Marin [3,*] and Negrean Iuliu [2,4]

1. Department of Mechanical Engineering, Transilvania University of Brașov, 500036 Brașov, Romania
2. Romanian Academy of Technical Sciences, B-dul Dacia 26, 030167 Bucharest, Romania; iuliu.negrean@mep.utcluj.ro
3. Department of Mathematics and Informatics, Transilvania University of Brașov, B-dul Eroilor 20, 500036 Brașov, Romania
4. Department of Mechanical Systems Engineering, Faculty of Machine Building, Technical University of Cluj-Napoca, 400641 Cluj-Napoca, Romania
* Correspondence: svlase@unitbv.ro (S.V.); m.marin@unitbv.ro (M.M.)

Abstract: This paper presents the main analytical methods, in the context of current developments in the study of complex multibody systems, to obtain evolution equations for a multibody system with deformable elements. The method used for analysis is the finite element method. To write the equations of motion, the most used methods are presented, namely the Lagrange equations method, the Gibbs–Appell equations, Maggi's formalism and Hamilton's equations. While the method of Lagrange's equations is well documented, other methods have only begun to show their potential in recent times, when complex technical applications have revealed some of their advantages. This paper aims to present, in parallel, all these methods, which are more often used together with some of their engineering applications. The main advantages and disadvantages are comparatively presented. For a mechanical system that has certain peculiarities, it is possible that the alternative methods offered by analytical mechanics such as Lagrange's equations have some advantages. These advantages can lead to computer time savings for concrete engineering applications. All these methods are alternative ways to obtain the equations of motion and response time of the studied systems. The difference between them consists only in the way of describing the systems and the application of the fundamental theorems of mechanics. However, this difference can be used to save time in modeling and analyzing systems, which is important in designing current engineering complex systems. The specifics of the analyzed mechanical system can guide us to use one of the methods presented in order to benefit from the advantages offered.

Keywords: Maggi's equations; Lagrange method; Gibbs–Appell equations; Hamilton formalism; analytical mechanics

Citation: Vlase, S.; Marin, M.; Iuliu, N. Finite Element Method-Based Elastic Analysis of Multibody Systems: A Review. *Mathematics* **2022**, *10*, 257. https://doi.org/10.3390/math10020257

Academic Editor: Athanasios Tzavaras

Received: 22 December 2021
Accepted: 12 January 2022
Published: 15 January 2022

Publisher's Note: MDPI stays neutral with regard to jurisdictional claims in published maps and institutional affiliations.

Copyright: © 2022 by the authors. Licensee MDPI, Basel, Switzerland. This article is an open access article distributed under the terms and conditions of the Creative Commons Attribution (CC BY) license (https://creativecommons.org/licenses/by/4.0/).

1. Introduction

In recent years, research, led by practical applications in engineering, and which uses increasingly complex equipment, operates at higher speeds in difficult environmental conditions, and which is subjected to intense loads, has driven the development of methods for analyzing large deformable mechanical systems. Studies determined by these developments in technology have led to the analysis of multibody systems with deformable elements. In order to perform this analysis, the researchers developed and reinvented the existing methods to apply them to the new situations that has arisen. The development of this field is based on the numerical techniques related to the finite element method (FEM) as well as on the application of classical methods used in analytical mechanics (the latter representing the best way to approach such systems). Analytical mechanics has the advantage of general methods in which the procedures that apply follow a certain order, the same in which all cases may occur. These methods can be easily algorithmized. The methods of analytical mechanics fit well with such an analysis because of the problems of complexity and the possibility to study a mechanical system with a large number of degrees of freedom (DOF). Such an analysis avoids the study of each element and the assembly of the obtained systems of equations, and it allows for the obtainment of the evolution equations, starting from the fundamental notions written for the whole system (kinetic energy, potential energy, work, acceleration energy, momentum, Hamiltonian, etc.). This is possible due to the tools used by analytical mechanics, which generalize the way of presentation of motion. The constraints that occur in engineering systems (due to the connections between the elements and the connection to the fixed space) that reduce the DOF number of the system are best described in the analytical mechanics, regardless of the method applied. Analytical mechanics has proven to be a powerful tool for analyzing complex systems, providing a set of equivalent formulations from which the most appropriate formulation can be selected.

The basic notions from the analytical descriptions stated above allow for a complete description of the mechanical system and can easily obtain the solution.

The main advantage of using Lagrange's equations in engineering is that it allows for a unitary solution of the problems of the dynamics of mechanical systems, according to a well-established itinerary and by moving through the same stages each time. Thus, the method is well suited for algorithms. Another advantage is that only scalar quantities are used instead of the vector quantities used in Newton's equations. Lagrange's equations can also highlight the existence of motion constants, which in some cases, can simplify solving the problem [1].

However, analytical mechanics offers other alternatives for writing the equations of motion of a dynamic system that, in some situations, may have advantages over Lagrange's classical approach. For this reason, during the development of the elastic MBS study, different methods were applied, identifying the advantages and disadvantages. The engineering requirements for the study of high speed and high load systems have driven the development of research for the application of MEF in the case of multibody systems (MBS), and there are many papers that address such a problem in order to obtain immediate practical results [2–9].

The practical applications for solving concrete problems, immediate in the industry, were supported by theoretical works that developed the mathematical bases of the numerical modeling of such problems. The aim of these works is to develop wide possibilities of computer simulations for the analysis of more accurate models, which will capture significant details in the operation of mechanical systems. The development of such appropriate algorithms allows for the modeling and analysis of systems that cannot be solved with existing computer codes. The main problem is that the procedures used in MEF differ from the procedures used in flexible multibody system codes.

Three ways of approaching such problems are used. The first of these approaches uses algorithms that involve successful simulations by establishing an interface between existing codes. The second way is to implement algorithms aimed at studying MBS in existing finite element algorithms. The third way used is the finite element formulation of the behavior of MBS with elastic elements, which requires a great effort for implementation in computer algorithms. A number of papers presents these methods [10–12].

Works dealing with the effective integration of equations of motion show results obtained to facilitate this step in [13]. Precise modeling of such systems is an important contribution to the development of engineering, but the potential is low due to the numerical calculation involved. The integration of the equations of motion of a complex multibody system is a time consuming computation. For example, simulating the behavior of a crankshaft that interacts with the surrounding elements requires a processing time for the CPU of several hours and determines the total time required for such a calculation. Methods for improving this step are presented in [13].

In addition, the use of symbolic calculus allows for a faster simulation code. A general integration procedure using the symbolic calculation was presented in [14]. A comparison with other models used in the literature highlighted the advantages of this approach.

In this theoretical development, multibody codes proved to be powerful tools for studying the nonlinear response of MBS with elastic elements. These systems might have had rigid movements over which small elastic deformations overlapped. For example, Refs. [15,16] presented a unitary approach and an overview of how to prepare the necessary data for dynamic models. The determination and writing of the matrix coefficients that intervened in the equations of motion were performed outside the code of the finite element. These data were then stored in a standardized object-oriented structure, and thus the dataset became independent of the wording of the MBS code.

Interesting methods of analysis and calculation simplification and some engineering applications are presented in the literature. A computational system framework was introduced in [17] using the finite element absolute nodal coordinate formulation. In that paper, they created the geometry of the system that made the analysis of the system possible. These two methods of analysis, MBS and FEM, were used to analyze a rocket sled, and the main problem was to establish the boundary conditions [18]. Using, in conjunction, these two methods, the simulation became more effective than those previously made using classical analyses.

Some issues regarding the harmonization of the two MBS and FEM analysis methods are presented in [19,20]. After developing a formalism that allows for the simultaneous analysis of systems using the two methods, the authors present engineering applications confirming the validity of the analysis and the models used. A successful application for a complex mechanical system is made in [21], where railway vehicles were analyzed using flexible tracks models. The study proposed a model that has flexible railway tracks. Classical theory of Timoshenko curved beam was used for modeling. The paper presented new aspects concerning the computation procedures applied in this analysis. Applications for the study of composites were developed in [22,23], and mathematical methods of solving with practical applications justifying the applicability and advantages were studied in [24–26].

Modeling a flexible multibody system used in parallel with MEF requires significant computing resources. One strategy used by researchers is the use of reduced-order models (ROMs). For plane systems, an approach using classical Lagrange equations is presented in [27]. The method can be extended to three-dimensional systems. This method helps to significantly reduce the effort and computation time required.

Topological representations and models have been used to simplify the symbolic writing of equations of motion within these systems in order to reduce the time required for modeling. An example showing this mode of analysis is presented in [28].

Mathematical methods for solving MBS problems with elastic elements have been continuously developed in order to find the best way to deal with this type of problem, which involves considerable modeling and calculation effort. In this sense, the reduced transfer matrix method for a multibody system (MSRTMM) was developed. An application of this method, along with the Riccati transformation, is presented in [29]. Three case studies were analyzed: a thin rectangular plane plate, a parallelogram thin plane plate and a multibody system with two-dimensional elements. MSRTMM has the advantage of high computing speed, ease of writing algorithms and numerical stability.

Specific methods have been developed for systems with certain features. An exact calculation method using dynamic stiffness was used to analyze vibrations of multibody systems with flexible beams connecting rigid bodies [30]. Rigid bodies can have any geometry and can have connections between them by means of elastic beams. The results were compared with other published results. This method is a powerful tool for optimizing such systems or for identifying modal parameters. A mathematical framework for calculating the mass matrix of a rigid–flexible multibody system with parameters is presented in [31]. The proposed method of analysis was applied to the calculation of a parallel Delta robot. In the field of mathematics involved in solving these complex problems, different models and ways of approaching systems have been proposed. For example, in [32], the well-known Ritz method was applied, which is especially known for its computational efficiency and is used extensively by engineers. It was proposed to use a generalized version of the MBS study method with a general topology. The numerical examples developed illustrate the advantages of the method.

The evaluation of inertial forces is a central and complicated task for the dynamic analysis of flexible multibody systems (FMS). A high-precision formulation for a 3D problem of flexible multibody systems is presented in [33]. The novelty is that the equations of motion were obtained with the principles of virtual power, without having to use the differentiation of the rotation matrix. Some numerical examples support the method proposed in that paper.

A practical method for numerically solving problems related to eigenvalues is presented in [34].

This paper presents, critically, the main methods of analytical mechanics used for the analysis of MBS with linear elastic components. To achieve this, a brief review of the use of MEF in this type of analysis is made.

2. FEA of Elastic MBS

To analyze an MBS having elastic components and to use FEM to consider the elastic behavior, the most used method thus far is the method of Lagrange equations, which will be highlighted in the future presentation. The purpose of an analysis of this type is to obtain, in a first step, the evolution equations for a single finite element from the studied system, if shape functions are known (thus, the type of finite element). These shape functions will determine the matrix coefficients of differential equations obtained. The equations are expressed in a local reference frame related to the finite element analyzed in rigid motion, together with the whole body that it discretizes. They must be reported, as a whole, to a global reference system against which the movement of the whole system will be analyzed. After this transition is made, it is necessary to assemble the obtained systems of equations. In this way, we finally obtain the system of evolution equations. All these presented procedures are performed according to the classical and well-known methods applied in FEM. By introducing boundary conditions and loads, one can then proceed to solve the system of equations and determine the answer to the system. In this analysis, the deformations are considered small enough such that the general movement of the system (rigid movement) is not influenced in any way by these deformations. The main problem remains regarding the harmonization of the two methods, which both use different procedures.

The analyzed works present the evolution in the study of these problems, starting from simple, one-dimensional elements and gradually moving to more and more complex finite elements. In the first studies of such problems, one-dimensional finite elements were studied, and the movement of the system was considered plane [35–37]. Complex, bi- and three-dimensional finite elements have been studied and applied in [38]. Recently, methods of analysis have been developed, and more sophisticated models have been studied. For example, the damping issues in such systems are presented in [39–41]. The contributions in these papers refer to the development of different types of finite elements that serve the purpose. Iterative methods and the Newton–Raphson algorithm can be used to solve the equations of motion. The analysis of the effects of temperature in the study of MBS with flexible elements is presented in [42]. The paper proposes a sandwich beam element that is convenient for describing large displacements and rotations. As in the cases mentioned above, an incremental–iterative method is used to solve the evolution equations together with the Grünwald approximation and the Newton–Raphson algorithm. The use of composite materials in flexible multibody systems is presented in [43], and a systematic presentation of the results obtained in FEM applied to the study of elastic MBS is made in [44].

Lagrange's equations are the main tools to obtain motion equations for a finite element that discretizes an MBS system, regardless of whether one-, two-, or three-dimensional finite elements or the type of motion of the elements of the MBS system are used. This method has proven to be, over time, useful and has been relatively convenient in the application and verification of the countless applications studied within it. The major advantage of this method is the use of notions with which researchers are familiar. At this time, in the studies, Lagrange's equations are the most widely used method for studying such problems.

However, analytical mechanics offers alternative methods of analysis equivalent to the method of Lagrange's equations. These methods use less commonly used concepts, which distances researchers from using these alternative methods. At the moment, the diversity of the approached problems and the needs for analysis imposed by the development of technology make it necessary to re-evaluate these methods, as they can show their advantages in certain situations. This paper will show an analysis of the main methods of analysis in analytical mechanics and will try to point out the advantages and disadvantages involved. The methods presented and analyzed in the paper are Lagrange's equations, Gibbs–Appell equations, Maggi's formalism and Hamilton's equations. These methods are the most used methods in application. There are, of course, other equivalent or alternative methods, but they are much less used and we do not present them here, especially since there are only a few papers that use them, and they do not seem to have obvious advantages.

We observe here that the Lagrangian has, in its component, physical quantities with which we are well acquainted (kinetic energy, potential energy, work)—a strong reason is that it is frequently used. Another reason can be represented by the fact that the generalized coordinates allow for the unitary treatment of such a system and the representations used allow for an easy application of numerical methods. Another advantage is represented by the fact that the liaison forces (or Lagrange's multipliers) are eliminated in writing these equations such that the number of unknowns is reduced and limited to the generalized coordinates in the first instance. FEM, where the number of DOFs used is high, can lead to a significant decrease in working time, and it is a major advantage for the user.

The energy of accelerations is a notion little used by researchers. A disadvantage is that the expression for velocity contains four matrix terms, while the acceleration contains five such terms [45,46]. For this reason, the number of operations for determining the energy of accelerations is slightly higher than for obtaining kinetic energy. This disadvantage is offset by the significantly lower number of differentiation operations required compared to Lagrange's equations. The method is little used, although in recent years, the need for calculations has led to reconsideration of the method [47–51]. The main advantage is the lower number of differentiation operations required to obtain the final equations of motion.

Hamilton's equations were less frequently used in the dynamic analysis of mechanical systems. There is little literature to present the advantages or disadvantages of this method. However, if we take into account that the system of second-order equations is replaced by a system of first-order equations, the use of this method may show its advantages for suitable applications [52–55].

Recent contributions to the development of this field are presented in [56–59].

3. Kinematics

A brief recapitulation of basic notions in analytical mechanics is necessary [60]. In the following, the element will relate to a local (mobile) reference frame. The mobile reference system participates in the general movement of the MBS system. This element is known via the angular velocity $\overline{\omega}$, angular acceleration $\overline{\varepsilon}$, velocity $\overline{v}_o$ and acceleration $\overline{a}_o$ of the origin of the local reference system. We use two indices L (from local) and G (from global) to denote the sizes corresponding to the local and global coordinate systems. The orthonormal operator $[ROT]$ makes the transformation of the components from the local system to the global one, $\{a\}_G = [ROT]\{a\}_L$.

By differentiating the transformation operator $[ROT]$, it is now possible to obtain the angular velocity and acceleration operator [61].

An arbitrary point M becomes, after deformation, M'. In this case, the deformation process is expressed by:

$$\{r_{M'}\}_G = \{r_O\}_G + [ROT](\{r\}_L + \{u\}_L). \tag{1}$$

The linear dependence between nodal displacement and vector displacement of the current point of the element is expressed in FEA through a linear relation:

$$\{u\}_L = [N]\{\delta\}_L. \tag{2}$$

Here, $\{\delta\}_L$ is denoted by the vector of the independent coordinates. With this assumption, the velocity vector of M' becomes:

$$\{v_{M'}\}_G = \{\dot{r}_{M'}\}_G = \{\dot{r}_O\}_G + [\dot{ROT}]\{r\}_L + [\dot{ROT}][N]\{\delta\}_L + [ROT][N]\{\dot{\delta}\}_L. \tag{3}$$

and the acceleration vector:

$$\{a_{M'}\}_G = \{\ddot{r}_O\}_G + [\ddot{ROT}]\{r\}_L + [\ddot{ROT}][N]\{\delta\}_L + 2[\dot{ROT}][N]\{\dot{\delta}\}_L + [ROT][N]\{\ddot{\delta}\}_L. \tag{4}$$

We can observe that some of these sizes are expressed in the local system coordinate and others in a global system coordinate. Passing to the local frame, we have:

$$\{v_{M'}\}_L = [ROT]^T \{v_{M'}\}_G = \{\dot{r}_O\}_L + [ROT]^T[\dot{ROT}]\{r\}_L + [ROT]^T[\dot{ROT}][N]\{\delta\}_L + [N]\{\dot{\delta}\}_L$$

$$= \begin{bmatrix} [E] & [ROT]^T[\dot{ROT}] & [ROT]^T[\dot{ROT}][N] & [N] \end{bmatrix} \begin{Bmatrix} \{\dot{r}_O\}_L \\ \{r\}_L \\ \{\delta\}_L \\ \{\dot{\delta}\}_L \end{Bmatrix}. \tag{5}$$

$$\{a_{M'}\}_L = [ROT]^T \{a_{M'}\}_G = \{\ddot{r}_O\}_L + [ROT]^T[\ddot{ROT}]\{r\}_L + [ROT]^T[\ddot{ROT}][N]\{\delta\}_L + 2[ROT]^T[\dot{ROT}][N]\{\dot{\delta}\}_L + [N]\{\ddot{\delta}\}_L$$

$$= \begin{bmatrix} [E] & [ROT]^T[\ddot{ROT}] & [ROT]^T[\ddot{ROT}][N] & 2[ROT]^T[\dot{ROT}][N] & [N] \end{bmatrix} \begin{Bmatrix} \{\ddot{r}_O\}_L \\ \{r\}_L \\ \{\delta\}_L \\ \{\dot{\delta}\}_L \\ \{\ddot{\delta}\}_L \end{Bmatrix}. \tag{6}$$

4. Fundamental Notions in Dynamics of FEA of MBS

4.1. Kinetic Energy

The kinetic energy plays an important role in an analytical description. Its expression is given by the equation:

$$E_c = \frac{1}{2} \int_V \rho \{v_{M'}\}_G^T \{v_{M'}\}_G dV. \tag{7}$$

Considering Equation (5), it obtains, for kinetic energy, the complete expression:

$$E_c = \begin{bmatrix} \{\dot{r}_O\}_L & \{r\}_L & \{\delta\}_L & \{\dot{\delta}\}_L \end{bmatrix}$$

$$\begin{bmatrix} [E] & [ROT]^T[\dot{ROT}] & [ROT]^T[\dot{ROT}][N] & [N] \\ [\dot{ROT}]^T[ROT] & [\dot{ROT}]^T[\dot{ROT}] & [\dot{ROT}]^T[\dot{ROT}] & [\dot{ROT}]^T[ROT][N] \\ [N]^T[\dot{ROT}]^T[ROT] & [N]^T[\dot{ROT}]^T[\dot{ROT}] & [N]^T[\dot{ROT}]^T[\dot{ROT}] & [N]^T[\dot{ROT}]^T[ROT][N] \\ [N]^T & [N]^T[ROT]^T[\dot{ROT}] & [N]^T[ROT]^T[\dot{ROT}][N] & [N]^T[N] \end{bmatrix} \begin{Bmatrix} \{\dot{r}_O\}_L \\ \{r\}_L \\ \{\delta\}_L \\ \{\dot{\delta}\}_L \end{Bmatrix} \quad (8)$$

We denote:

$$[m] = \int_V \rho[N]^T[N]\,dV; \quad (9)$$

$$[m_O^i] = \int_V \rho[N]^T dV; \quad \{q^i(\varepsilon)\}_L = \int_V \rho[N]^T[\varepsilon]_L\{r\}_L dV; \quad (10)$$

$$\{q^i(\omega)\}_L = \int_V \rho[N]^T[\omega]_L[\omega]_L\{r\}_L dV; \quad (11)$$

$$[k(\varepsilon)] = \int_V \rho[N]^T[\varepsilon][N]dV; \quad (12)$$

$$[k(\omega)] = \int_V \rho[N]^T[\omega]_L[\omega]_L[N]dV; \quad (13)$$

$$[c] = \int_V \rho[N]^T[\omega]_L[N]dV; \quad (14)$$

$$\{m_{ix}\} = \int_V \rho\big[S_{(i)}\big]^T x\,dV \;;\; \{m_{iy}\} = \int_V \rho\big[N_{(i)}\big]^T y\,dV \;;\; \{m_{iz}\} = \int_V \rho\big[N_{(i)}\big]^T z\,dV. \quad (15)$$

4.2. Potential Energy

The classic expression for the internal work (potential energy) is:

$$E_p = \frac{1}{2}\int_V \{\sigma\}^T\{\varepsilon\}dV, \quad (16)$$

where $\{\varepsilon\}$ is the strain vector and $\{\sigma\}$ is the stress vector;
The generalized Hooke law has the well-known form:

$$\{\sigma\} = [H]\{\varepsilon\}. \quad (17)$$

The strains can be expressed as [6]:

$$\{\varepsilon\} = [b]\{u\} = [b][N]\{\delta\}_L. \quad (18)$$

Using Equations (17) and (18), we obtain:

$$E_p = \frac{1}{2}\{\delta\}_L^T \left(\int_V [N]^T[b]^T[H]^T[b][N]dV\right)\{\delta\}_L. \quad (19)$$

Matrix $[k]$ is the stiffness matrix:

$$[k] = \int_V [N]^T[b]^T[H]^T[b][N]dV. \quad (20)$$

Equation (19) has the traditional form:

$$E_p = \frac{1}{2}\int_V \{\delta\}_L^T[k]\{\delta\}_L dV. \tag{21}$$

4.3. Work

The concentrated forces $\{q\}_L$ and volume forces $\{p\} = \{p(x,y,z)\}$ produce mechanical work:

$$W^c = \{q\}_L^T\{\delta\}_L, \tag{22}$$

and:

$$W = \int_V \{p\}_L^T\{f\}_L dV = \left(\int_V \{p\}_L^T[N]dV\right)\{\delta\}_L = \{q^*\}_L^T\{\delta\}_L, \tag{23}$$

4.4. Lagrangian

The expression of the Lagrangian is [60]:

$$L = E_c - E_p + W + W^c, \tag{24}$$

Using Equations (21)–(23), the Lagrangian takes the form:

$$L = E_c - \frac{1}{2}\int_V \{\delta\}_L^T[k]\{\delta\}_L dV + \{q^*\}_L^T\{\delta\}_L + \{q\}_L^T\{\delta\}_L. \tag{25}$$

4.5. Momentum

The momentum for a finite element is:

$$\begin{aligned}\{p\}_G &= \int_V \rho\{v_{M'}\}_G dV \\ &= \int_V \rho\left(\{\dot{r}_O\}_G + \left[\dot{ROT}\right]\{r\}_L + \left[\dot{ROT}\right][N]\{\delta\}_L + [ROT][N]\{\dot{\delta}\}_L\right)dV \\ &= m\{\dot{r}_O\}_G + \left[\dot{ROT}\right]\{\bar{s}\}_L + \left[\dot{ROT}\right]\left(\int_V \rho[N]dV\right)\{\delta\}_L + [ROT]\left(\int_V \rho[N]dV\right)\{\dot{\delta}\}_L \\ &= m\{\dot{r}_O\}_G + m\left[\dot{ROT}\right]\{\bar{r}_C\}_L + \left[\dot{ROT}\right][m_O^i]\{\delta\}_L + [ROT][m_O^i]\{\dot{\delta}\}_L \end{aligned} \tag{26}$$

The notation $m = \int_V \rho dV$ represents the total mass of the finite element, $\{\bar{s}\}_L$ is the static moment and $[m_O^i] = \int_V \rho[N]dV$ is the matrix of the inertia of the element (see Equation (11)).

In the local system, there is the relation:

$$\begin{aligned}\{p\}_L &= [ROT]^T\{p\}_G = \\ &= m\{\dot{r}_O\}_L + m[ROT]^T\left[\dot{ROT}\right]\{\bar{r}_C\}_L + [ROT]^T\left[\dot{ROT}\right][m_O^i]\{\delta\}_L + [m_O^i]\{\dot{\delta}\}_L.\end{aligned} \tag{27}$$

In an alternative way, the momentum can be calculated with the relation:

$$\{p\}_L = \left\{\frac{\partial L}{\partial\{\dot{d}\}_L}\right\}. \tag{28}$$

From (27), the vector of velocities $\{\dot{\delta}\}_L$ can be obtained:

$$\{\dot{\delta}\}_L = [m_O^i]^{-1}\left(\{p\}_L - m\{\dot{r}_O\}_L - m[ROT]^T\left[\dot{ROT}\right]\{\bar{r}_C\}_L - [ROT]^T\left[\dot{ROT}\right][m_O^i]\{\delta\}_L\right). \tag{29}$$

4.6. Hamiltonian

Using the previous notations, the Hamiltonian becomes:

$$H = \left\{\frac{\partial L}{\partial \{\dot\delta\}_L}\right\}^T \{\dot\delta\}_L - L = \{p\}^T \left[m_O^i\right]^{-1}\left(\{p\}_L - m\{\dot r_O\}_L - m[ROT]^T\left[R\dot OT\right]\{\bar r_C\}_L - [ROT]^T\left[R\dot OT\right]\left[m_O^i\right]\{\delta\}_L\right) - L. \quad (30)$$

where, for the Lagrangian, Equation (25) is used.

4.7. Energy of Accelerations

We introduce the notion of energy of acceleration. The expression of this is, for N material points, [61]:

$$E_a = \frac{1}{2}\sum_{i=1}^{N} m_i a_i^2. \quad (31)$$

For a solid body, the expression becomes:

$$E_a = \frac{1}{2}\int_V \rho a^2 dV. \quad (32)$$

Using Equation (4) for acceleration, Equation (32) becomes:

$$E_a = \tfrac{1}{2}\int_V \rho a_{M'}^2 dV = \tfrac{1}{2}\int_V \rho \{a_{M'}\}^T\{a_{M'}\}dV$$

$$= \tfrac{1}{2}\int_V \rho \left(\{\ddot r_O\}_G^T + \{r\}_L^T\left[R\ddot OT\right]^T + \{\delta\}_L^T[N]^T\left[R\ddot OT\right]^T + 2\{\dot\delta\}_L^T[N]^T\left[R\dot OT\right]^T + \{\ddot\delta\}_L^T[N]^T[ROT]^T\right) \times \quad (33)$$

$$\times\left(\{\ddot r_O\}_G + \left[R\ddot OT\right]\{r\}_L + \left[R\ddot OT\right][N]\{\delta\}_L + 2\left[R\dot OT\right][N]\{\dot\delta\}_L + [ROT][N]\{\ddot\delta\}_L\right)dV$$

More comments concerning this notion are presented in [62].

5. Analytical Method in FEA of MBS

5.1. Lagrange's Equations

The classic Lagrange's equations are:

$$\frac{d}{dt}\left\{\frac{\partial L}{\partial \dot\delta}\right\}_L - \left\{\frac{\partial L}{\partial \delta}\right\}_L = 0. \quad (34)$$

By $\left\{\frac{\partial E}{\partial X}\right\}$, it is denoted as:

$$\left\{\frac{\partial E}{\partial X}\right\} = \begin{Bmatrix}\frac{\partial E}{\partial x_1}\\ \frac{\partial E}{\partial x_2}\\ \vdots \\ \frac{\partial E}{\partial x_n}\end{Bmatrix} \text{ and: } \{X\} = \begin{Bmatrix}x_1\\ x_2\\ \vdots\\ x_n\end{Bmatrix}. \quad (35)$$

Using the Lagrangian previously obtained in Equation (25) results in:

$$[m]\{\ddot\delta\}_L + [c]\{\dot\delta\}_L + ([k] + [k(\varepsilon)] + [k(\omega)])\{\delta\}_L = \{q\}_L + \{q^*\}_L - \{q^i(\varepsilon)\}_L - \{q^i(\omega)\}_L - \left[m_O^i\right]\{\ddot r_O\}_L. \quad (36)$$

We mention here the difference between the application of Lagrange's equations (three differentiations $\left\{\frac{\partial L}{\partial d}\right\}, \frac{d}{dt}\left\{\frac{\partial L}{\partial \dot{d}}\right\}, \left\{\frac{\partial L}{\partial \dot{d}}\right\}$) and the application of the Gibbs–Appell equations (when it is necessary to make only a single differentiation $\left\{\frac{\partial E_a}{\partial \ddot{d}}\right\}$) [61].

5.2. Gibbs–Appell Formalism

The Gibbs–Appell equation represents an alternative to Lagrange's equations. To use these, it is necessary to know the energy of acceleration, obtained in Equation (33). The Gibbs–Appell equations are [62]:

$$\frac{\partial E_a}{\partial \ddot{q}_j} = Q_j \quad j = \overline{1,n}. \tag{37}$$

Equation (33) has, in its component, the following terms [22]:

- E_{a2} containing the quadratic terms in accelerations:

$$E_{a2} = \frac{1}{2}\int_V \rho\left(\{\ddot{\delta}\}_L^T [N]^T [N] \{\ddot{\delta}\}_L\right) dV; \tag{38}$$

- E_{a1} containing the linear terms in accelerations:

$$E_{a1} = \int_V \rho\left(\{\ddot{\delta}\}_L^T [N]^T [ROT]^T \{\ddot{r}_O\} + \{\ddot{\delta}\}_L^T [N]^T [ROT]^T [R\ddot{O}T] \{r\}_L + \{\ddot{\delta}\}_L^T [N]^T [ROT]^T [R\ddot{O}T] [N]\{d\}_L + 2\{\ddot{\delta}\}_L^T [N]^T [ROT]^T [R\dot{O}T] [N]\{\dot{\delta}\}_L\right) dV \tag{39}$$

- The terms E_{a0} without any term with accelerations that play no role in obtaining the equations.

Equation (37) can be written if we take into account our notations as:

$$\left\{\frac{\partial E_a}{\partial \ddot{d}}\right\}_L - \{Q\}_L = 0; \tag{40}$$

The term E_a is:

$$E_a = E_{a0}(\dot{q}) + E_{a1}(\dot{q}, \ddot{q}) + E_{a2}(\ddot{q}); \tag{41}$$

and:

$$\{Q\}_L = [k]\{\delta\}_L + \{q\}_L + \{q^*\}_L; \tag{42}$$

If we differentiate it, we obtain:

$$\frac{\partial E_{a2}}{\partial\{\ddot{d}\}_L} = \left(\int_V \rho[N]^T [S] dV\right)\{\ddot{d}\}_L = [m]\{\ddot{d}\}_L; \tag{43}$$

$$\frac{\partial E_{a1}}{\partial\{\ddot{d}\}_L} = -[m_O^i]\{\ddot{r}_O\}_L - \{q^i(\omega)\} - \{q^i(\varepsilon)\} + ([k(\omega)] + [k(\varepsilon)])\{d\}_L + [c]\{\dot{d}\}_L; \tag{44}$$

$$\frac{\partial E_{a0}}{\partial\{\ddot{d}\}_L} = 0. \tag{45}$$

Performing the calculations in the end, we obtain Equation (36).

Compared to Lagrange's method, this method requires a smaller number of differentiations. In this way, the number of calculations decreases and thus the time required to solve such problems. If we take into account that finite element models involve a large number of DOFs and thus a large number of calculations, reducing the number of operations offered by this method can lead to significant savings in computer time.

5.3. Hamilton's Method

The use of the Lagrange formalism (or Gibbs-Appell) leads to the obtaining of a system of second-order differential equations. Technically, solving this system of second-order equations is achieved by transforming it into a system of first-order differential equations of double dimension. Hamiltonian mechanics use unknown $2n$, and the system of differential equations obtained is from the beginning a system of differential equations of the first order of size $2n$. The unknowns are the generalized coordinates $\{\delta\}_L$ and canonically conjugated moment:

$$\{p\}_L = -\left\{\frac{\partial L}{\partial \{\delta\}_L}\right\}. \quad (46)$$

Thus, the main difference between Lagrange's and Hamilton's method is the use of the canonical conjugated moment instead of the generalized velocities. The major advantage of applying this method could precisely be the direct obtainment of a system of first-order equations, which can be solved directly using the usual commercial software.

Hamilton's equations are a first-order system of differential equations [62]. They are:

$$\{\dot{\delta}\}_L = \left\{\frac{\partial H}{\partial \{p\}_L}\right\}; \{\dot{p}\}_L = -\left\{\frac{\partial H}{\partial \{\delta\}_L}\right\}. \quad (47)$$

From Equations (27)–(29), we obtain:

$$\{\dot{\delta}\}_L = [m_O^i]^{-1}\left(\{p\}_L - m\{\dot{r}_O\}_L - m[ROT]^T[\dot{ROT}]\{\bar{r}_C\}_L - [ROT]^T[\dot{ROT}][m_O^i]\{\delta\}_L\right);$$

$$\{\dot{p}\}_L = \{p\}^T[m_O^i]^{-1}[ROT]^T[\dot{ROT}][m_O^i] + \int_V \rho\left(\{\dot{r}_O\}_L^T[ROT]^T[\dot{ROT}][N]\right)dV$$

$$+ \int_V \rho\left(\{r\}_L^T[\dot{ROT}]^T[\dot{ROT}][S]\right)dV + \int_V \rho\left([N]^T[\dot{ROT}]^T[\dot{ROT}][N]\{\delta\}_L + [N]^T[\dot{ROT}]^T[ROT][N]\{\delta\}_L\right)dV \quad (48)$$

$$- \int_V [k]\{d\}_L dV + \{q^*\}_L^T + \{q\}_L^T$$

These represent the equations of motion sought.

The main advantage of Hamilton's method is that it provides us with a system of first-order differential equations. However, the number of unknowns to be found is doubled. In the case of using other methods, the differential equations obtained are of the second order. Solving techniques require for their transformation into first-order differential systems by introducing new variables. In the case of Hamilton's method, these new variables are obtained directly and have physical significance.

5.4. Maggi's Equations

The form of these equations are [63]:

$$\sum_{k=1}^{n} a_{kj}\left[\left(\frac{d}{dt}\left(\frac{\partial E_c}{\partial \dot{q}_k}\right) - \frac{\partial E_c}{\partial q_k}\right) - Q_k\right] = 0 \; ; \; j = \overline{1, n-m}, \quad (49)$$

representing a number of $n - m$ independent equations called Maggi's equations.

Using these equations makes it simpler to analyze such a system from the point of view of a formal description. In this case, only the kinetic energy is necessary to compute. The liaisons between elements offer us the possibility to eliminate the liaison forces and thus to simplify the calculus.

6. Conclusions and Discussion

The most important step in the dynamic analysis of an elastic MBS is to write the equations of evolution. The next steps that follow, namely, the assembly of the equations of motion and their solution, will be performed according to the classical methods used in the commercial software of FEM. To obtain the equations is the most difficult problem to solve, given the multitude of terms that appear in such a description. As a result, finding a formalism that would make it possible to write these equations as easily as possible is an important step in this analysis. The method used almost exclusively in this type of analysis, until now, was the Lagrange's equations. This is primarily due to the fact that researchers are familiar with this method, and they use fundamental notions currently used by researchers (kinetic energy, potential, work, ...). However, analytical mechanics offer several formulations that are equivalent to each other and to Lagrange's equations. Gibbs–Appell equations, Hamilton equations, Maggi equations, Jacobs equations and other equivalent forms can be used in this way. With such a multitude of methods that can be used that are equivalent to each other, the question arises as to which of these methods can be applied more easily than the method of Lagrange's equations. The paper analyzes several analytical forms used to determine the equations of motion of MBS systems with elastic elements to identify and analyze the advantages and disadvantages of these methods, which could allow for a more economical result. Lagrange's equations have the advantage of being a method widely used by researchers due to a familiarity of researchers with it. The Gibbs–Appell equations prove to be easy to write by skipping some steps related to the derivation of the equations. This turns out to be a more economical method in terms of the time required to write the equations. In this method, the number of differentiations of terms decreases, and as a result, the total number of calculations required decreases. However, we mention that Lagrange's method has the advantage of using kinetic energy, a well-known notion with which we operate easily. The Gibbs–Appell equations use the energy of accelerations, a notion that most engineers are less familiar with. Not many papers contain applications of the Gibbs–Appell equations. Generally, the papers present the Gibbs–Appell formalism as a secondary method to solve a problem (useful but not necessary) [62].

These equations are formally more elegant and simpler, and the necessary number of differentiations is smaller. Using this method, a system with a holonomic constraint can be handled in an economical manner, as with Lagrange's equations.

Maggi's method also has the advantages of simplicity in approaching problems, being essentially equivalent to the Gibbs–Appell method [64]. It is proven that this formulation is a simple and stable method for determining the dynamic response of constrained multibody systems [65].

Hamilton's method of equations proves to be the least profitable for the type of problems studied; in general, the time required to obtain the equations is not economical, and the complexity of the intermediate calculations is high. However, we do not deny that this approach could prove useful in certain applications because the system of differential equations obtained is first order and thus avoids a computational step, used in the classical solution of these systems, where systems of equations obtained are second-order differentials.

If we take into account all these considerations, we can reasonably assume that the alternative and equivalent methods developed in analytical mechanics (and which, for the moment, do not seem to have practical applicability) will be reevaluated and developed due to more faithful modeling requirements imposed by technology.

Funding: This research received no external funding. The APC was funded by Transilvania University of Brasov.

Institutional Review Board Statement: Not applicable.

Informed Consent Statement: Not applicable.

Conflicts of Interest: The authors declare no conflict of interest.

Notations

$\{r_{M'}\}_G$	position vector of point M';
$\{r_M\}_G$	position vectors of point M;
$\{u\}_L$	displacement vector;
$\{r_O\}_G$	position vector of origin O (of the mobile reference frame)
index G	vector with components express in the global reference frame;
index L	vector with components express in the local reference frame;
$[ROT]$	rotation matrix;
$[N]$	shape functions matrix;
$\{v_{M'}\}$	velocity of point M';
$\{a_{M'}\}$	acceleration of point M';
$\{\delta\}$	nodal displacement vector;
E_c	kinetic energy;
E_p	potential energy;
L	Lagrangian;
H	Hamiltonian;
$\{\sigma\}$	stress vector;
$\{\varepsilon\}$	strain vector;
$\{v\}^T\{w\}$	dot product between the vectors $\{v\}$ and $\{w\}$;
$\{p\}$	conjugated moment;
E_a	energy of acceleration;
W^c	work of the concentrated forces;
W	work of the volume forces.

References

1. Gans, F.R. *Engineering Dynamics: From the Lagrangian to Simulation*; Springer: New York, NY, USA, 2013; ISBN 978-1-4614-3929-5.
2. Shi, Z.; Meacci, M.; Meli, E.; Wang, K.Y.; Rindi, A. Validation of a Finite Element Multibody System Model for Vehicle-Slab Track Application. In *Advances in Dynamics of Vehicles on Roads and Tracks, Iavsd 2019, Proceedings of the 26th Symposium of the International Association of Vehicle System Dynamics (IAVSD), Gothenburg, Sweden, 12–16 August 2019*; Proceedings Paper in Book Series: Lecture Notes in Mechanical Engineering; Springer: Cham, Switzerland, 2020; pp. 407–414. [CrossRef]
3. Tokarczyk, J. Migration of Computational Models in Virtual Prototyping of Complex Mechanical Systems. In *Book Group Author IAENG, Proceedings of the World Congress on Engineering and Computer Science, WCECS 2012, San Francisco, CA, USA, 24–26 October 2012*; Proceedings Paper, Book Series: Lecture Notes in Engineering and Computer Science; Newswood Limited: Hong Kong, China, 2012; Volume II, pp. 1334–1337.
4. Marce-Nogue, J.; Klodowski, A.; Sanchez, M.; Gil, L. Coupling finite element analysis and multibody system dynamics for biological research. *Palaeontol. Electron.* 2015, *18*, 5T.
5. Miao, B.R.; Zhang, W.H.; Huang, G.H.; Wu, S.C.; Zhao, Y.X. Research of High Speed Train Carbody Structure Vibration Behaviors and Structure Fatigue Strength Characteristic Technology. In *Advanced Materials Research*; Advanced in Product Development and Reliability III 2012; Proceedings Paper; Trans Tech Publications Ltd.: Freienbach, Switzerland, 2012; Volume 544, pp. 256–261. [CrossRef]
6. Ding, J.G.; Dai, Y.W.; Qiao, Z.; Huang, H.J.; Zhuang, W. Analysis of the Response of a Frame Structure during an Earthquake Using the Transfer Matrix Method of a Multibody System. *J. Eng. Mech.* 2015, *141*, 04015020. [CrossRef]
7. Wallrapp, O.; Sachau, D. Space Flight Dynamic Simulations using Finite Element Results in Multibody System Codes. In *Advances in Computational Mechanics, Proceedings of the 2nd International Conference on Computational Structures Technology, CST' 94, Athens, Greece, 30 August–1 September 1994*; Proceedings Paper; Greece; 1994; pp. 149–158. Available online: https://elib.dlr.de/28194/ (accessed on 10 October 2021).
8. Zhang, J.H.; Jiang, S.S. Definition of Boundary Conditions and Dynamic Analysis of Rocket Sled and Turntable. In *Applied Mechanics and Materials, Proceedings of the 1st International Conference on Mechanical Engineering, Phuket, Thailand, 2 March 2011*; Proceedings Paper; Trans Tech Publications Ltd.: Freienbach, Switzerland, 2011; Volume 52–54, pp. 261–268. [CrossRef]
9. Scutaru, M.L.; Chircan, E.; Marin, M.; Grif, H.S. Liaison Forces Eliminating and Assembling of the Motion Equation in the Study of Multibody System with Elastic Elements. In *Procedia Manufacturing, Proceedings of the 13th International Conference Interdisciplinarity in Engineering (Inter-Eng. 2019), Targu Mures, Romania, 3–4 October 2019*; Proceedings Paper; Elsevier B.V.: Amsterdam, The Netherlands, 2020; Volume 46, pp. 78–86. [CrossRef]
10. Shabana, A.A. *Dynamics of Multibody Systems*, 4th ed.; Cambridge University Press: Cambridge, UK, 2013.
11. Shabana, A.A.; Bauchau, O.A.; Hulbert, G.M. Integration of Large Deformation Finite Element and Multibody System Algorithms. *J. Comput. Nonlinear Dyn.* 2007, *2*, 351–359. [CrossRef]

12. Rui, X.; Rong, B.; Wang, G. New Method for Dynamics Modeling and Simulation of Flexible Multibody System. In Proceedings of the Third International Conference on Mechanical Engineering and Mechanics, Beijing, China, 21–23 October 2009; Volumes 1 and 2, pp. 17–23.
13. Witteveen, W.; Stefan, P.; Pichler, F. On the Projection of a Flexible Bodies Modal Coordinates onto Another Finite Element Model with Local Modifications. *J. Comput. Nonlinear Dyn.* **2019**, *14*, 074501. [CrossRef]
14. Liang, Y.T.; McPhee, J. Symbolic integration of multibody system dynamics with the finite element method. *Multibody Syst. Dyn.* **2018**, *43*, 387–405. [CrossRef]
15. Wallrapp, O. Flexible bodies in multibody system codes. *Veh. Syst. Dyn.* **1998**, *30*, 237–256. [CrossRef]
16. Wallrapp, O. Standardization of Flexible Body Modeling in Multibody System Codes, Part I: Definition of Standard Input Data. *Mech. Struct. Mach.* **1994**, *22*, 283–304. [CrossRef]
17. Patel, M.; Orzechowski, G.; Tian, Q.; Shabana, A.A. A new multibody system approach for tire modeling using ANCF finite elements. *Proc. Inst. Mech. Engineers. Part K-J. Multibody Dyn.* **2016**, *230*, 69–84. [CrossRef]
18. Zhang, J.H.; Jiang, S.S. Rigid-Flexible Coupling Model and Dynamic Analysis of Rocket Sled. International Conference on Sustainable Construction Materials and Computer Engineering (ICSCMCE 2011). In *Advanced Materials Research, Proceedings of the Sustainable Construction Materials and Computer Engineering, Kunming, China, 24–25 September 2011*; Proceedings Paper; Trans Tech Publications Ltd.: Freienbach, Switzerland, 2012; Volume 346, pp. 447–454. [CrossRef]
19. Lu, H.J.; Rui, X.T.; Ding, Y.Y.; Chang, Y.; Chen, Y.H.; Ding, J.G.; Zhang, X.P. A hybrid numerical method for vibration analysis of linear multibody systems with flexible components. *Appl. Math. Model.* **2022**, *101*, 748–771. [CrossRef]
20. You, T.W.; Gong, D.; Zhou, J.S.; Sun, Y.; Chen, J.X. Frequency response function-based model updating of flexible vehicle body using experiment modal parameter. *Veh. Syst. Dyn.* **2021**. [CrossRef]
21. Costa, J.N.; Antunes, P.; Magalhaes, H.; Pombo, J.; Ambrosio, J. A finite element methodology to model flexible tracks with arbitrary geometry for railway dynamics applications. *Comput. Struct.* **2021**, *254*, 106519. [CrossRef]
22. Krauklis, A.E.; Gagani, A.I.; Echtermeyer, A.T. Prediction of Orthotropic Hygroscopic Swelling of Fiber-Reinforced Composites from Isotropic Swelling of Matrix Polymer. *J. Compos. Sci.* **2019**, *3*, 10. [CrossRef]
23. Krauklis, A.E.; Gagani, A.I.; Echtermeyer, A.T. Near-Infrared Spectroscopic Method for Monitoring Water Content in Epoxy Resins and Fiber-Reinforced Composites. *Materials* **2018**, *11*, 586. [CrossRef] [PubMed]
24. Gagani, A.I.; Monsås, A.B.; Krauklis, A.E.; Echtermeyer, A.T. The effect of temperature and water immersion on the interlaminar shear fatigue of glass fiber epoxy composites using the I-beam method. *Compos. Sci. Technol.* **2019**, *181*, 107703. [CrossRef]
25. Rocha, A.V.M.; Akhavan-Safar, A.; Carbas, R.; Marques, E.A.S.; Goyal, R.; El-zein, M.; da Silva, L.F.M. Numerical analysis of mixed-mode fatigue crack growth of adhesive joints using CZM. *Theor. Appl. Fract. Mechanics.* **2020**, *106*, 102493. [CrossRef]
26. Rocha, A.V.M.; Akhavan-Safar, A.; Carbas, R.; Marques, E.A.S.; Goyal, R.; El-zein, M.; da Silva, L.F.M. Fatigue crack growth analysis of different adhesive systems: Effects of mode mixity and load level. *Fatigue Fract. Eng. Mater. Struct.* **2020**, *43*, 330–341. [CrossRef]
27. Cammarata, A. Global modes for the reduction of flexible multibody systems Methodology and complexity. *Multibody Syst. Dyn.* **2021**, *53*, 59–83. [CrossRef]
28. Manca, A.G.; Pappalardo, C.M. Topology Optimization Procedure of Aircraft Mechanical Components Based on Computer-Aided Design, Multibody Dynamics, and Finite Element Analysis. In *Advances in Design, Simulation and Manufacturing III: Mechanical and Chemical Engineering, Proceedings of the 3rd International Conference on Design, Simulation, Manufacturing-(DSMIE), Kharkiv, Ukraine, 9–12 June 2020*; Book Series: Lecture Notes in Mechanical Engineering; Springer: Cham, Swizerland, 2020; Volume 2, pp. 159–168. [CrossRef]
29. Lu, H.J.; Rui, X.T.; Zhang, X.P. A computationally efficient modeling method for the vibration analyses of two-dimensional system structures using reduce transfer matrix method for multibody system. *J. Sound Vib.* **2021**, *502*, 116096. [CrossRef]
30. Liu, X.; Sun, C.L.; Banerjee, J.R.; Dan, H.C.; Chang, L. An exact dynamic stiffness method for multibody systems consisting of beams and rigid-bodies. *Mech. Syst. Signal Processing* **2021**, *150*, 107264. [CrossRef]
31. Raoofian, A.; Taghvaeipour, A.; Kamali, E.A. Elastodynamic analysis of multibody systems and parametric mass matrix derivation. *Mech. Based Des. Struct. Mach.* **2020**; early access. [CrossRef]
32. Jeong, S.; Yoo, H.H. Generalized classical Ritz method for modeling geometrically nonlinear flexible multibody systems having a general topology. *Int. J. Mech. Sci.* **2020**, *181*, 105687. [CrossRef]
33. Wang, G.; Qi, Z.H.; Xu, J.S. A high-precision co-rotational formulation of 3D beam elements for dynamic analysis of flexible multibody systems. *Comput. Methods Appl. Mech. Eng.* **2020**, *360*, 112701. [CrossRef]
34. Hou, Y.S.; Liu, C.; Hu, H.Y. Component-level proper orthogonal decomposition for flexible multibody systems. *Comput. Methods Appl. Mech. Eng.* **2020**, *361*, 112690. [CrossRef]
35. Bagci, C. Elastodynamic Response of Mechanical Systems using Matrix Exponential Mode Uncoupling and Incremental Forcing Techniques with Finite Element Method. In Proceedings of the Sixth Word Congress on Theory of Machines and Mechanisms, India, Delhi, 15–20 December 1983; p. 472.
36. Bahgat, B.M.; Willmert, K.D. Finite Element Vibrational Analysis of Planar Mechanisms. *Mech. Mach. Theory* **1976**, *11*, 47. [CrossRef]
37. Cleghorn, W.L.; Fenton, E.G.; Tabarrok, K.B. Finite Element Analysis of High-Speed Flexible Mechanisms. *Mech. Mach. Theory* **1981**, *16*, 407. [CrossRef]

38. Vlase, S.; Dănăşel, C.; Scutaru, M.L.; Mihălcică, M. Finite Element Analysis of a Two-Dimensional Linear Elastic Systems with a Plane "rigid Motion. *Rom. Journ. Phys.* **2014**, *59*, 476–487.
39. Deü, J.-F.; Galucio, A.C.; Ohayon, R. Dynamic responses of flexible-link mechanisms with passive/active damping treatment. *Comput. Struct.* **2008**, *86*, 258–265. [CrossRef]
40. Zhang, X.; Erdman, A.G. Dynamic responses of flexible linkage mechanisms with viscoelastic constrained layer damping treatment. *Comput. Struct.* **2001**, *79*, 1265–1274. [CrossRef]
41. Shi, Y.M.; Li, Z.F.; Hua, H.X.; Fu, Z.F.; Liu, T.X. The Modeling and Vibration Control of Beams with Active Constrained Layer Damping. *J. Sound Vib.* **2001**, *245*, 785–800. [CrossRef]
42. Hou, W.; Zhang, X. Dynamic analysis of flexible linkage mechanisms under uniform temperature change. *J. Sound Vib.* **2009**, *319*, 570–592. [CrossRef]
43. Neto, M.A.; Ambrósio, J.A.C.; Leal, R.P. Composite materials in flexible multibody systems. *Comput. Methods Appl. Mech. Eng.* **2006**, *195*, 6860–6873. [CrossRef]
44. Piras, G.; Cleghorn, W.L.; Mills, J.K. Dynamic finite-element analysis of a planar high-speed, high-precision parallel manipulator with flexible links. *Mech. Mach. Theory* **2005**, *40*, 849–862. [CrossRef]
45. Gibbs, J.W. On the fundamental formulae of dynamics. *Am. J. Math.* **1879**, *2*, 49–64. [CrossRef]
46. Appell, P. Sur une forme générale des equations de la dynamique. *J. Reine Angew. Math.* **1900**, *121*, 310–319.
47. Mirtaheri, S.M.; Zohoor, H. The Explicit Gibbs-Appell Equations of Motion for Rigid-Body Constrained Mechanical System. In Proceedings of the RSI International Conference on Robotics and Mechatronics ICRoM, Tehran, Iran, 23–25 October 2018; pp. 304–309.
48. Korayem, M.H.; Dehkordi, S.F. Motion equations of cooperative multi flexible mobile manipulator via recursive Gibbs-Appell formulation. *Appl. Math. Model.* **2019**, *65*, 443–463. [CrossRef]
49. Shafei, A.M.; Shafei, H.R. A systematic method for the hybrid dynamic modeling of open kinematic chains confined in a closed environment. *Multibody Syst. Dyn.* **2017**, *38*, 21–42. [CrossRef]
50. Korayem, M.H.; Dehkordi, S.F. Derivation of dynamic equation of viscoelastic manipulator with revolute-prismatic joint using recursive Gibbs-Appell formulation. *Nonlinear Dyn.* **2017**, *89*, 2041–2064. [CrossRef]
51. Marin, M.; Ellahi, R.; Chirilă, A. On solutions of Saint-Venant's problem for elastic dipolar bodies with voids. *Carpathian J. Math.* **2017**, *33*, 219–232. [CrossRef]
52. Cheng, Y.D.; Wang, Z.X. A new discontinuous Galerkin finite element method for directly solving the Hamilton-Jacobi equations. *J. Comput. Phys.* **2014**, *268*, 134–153. [CrossRef]
53. Zheng, F.; Qiu, J.X. Directly solving the Hamilton-Jacobi equations by Hermite WENO Schemes. *J. Comput. Phys.* **2016**, *307*, 423–445. [CrossRef]
54. Anguelov, R.; Lubuma, J.M.S.; Minani, F. A monotone scheme for Hamilton-Jacobi equations via the nonstandard finite difference method. *Math. Methods Appl. Sci.* **2010**, *33*, 41–48. [CrossRef]
55. Liu, H.L.; Pollack, M.; Saran, H. Alternating Evolution Schemes for Hamilton-Jacobi Equations. *SIAM J. Sci. Comput.* **2013**, *35*, A122–A149. [CrossRef]
56. Rong, B.; Rui, X.T.; Tao, L.; Wang, G.P. Theoretical modeling and numerical solution methods for flexible multibody system dynamics. *Nonlinear Dyn.* **2019**, *98*, 1519–1553. [CrossRef]
57. Vlase, S.; Teodorescu, P.P. Elasto-Dynamics of a Solid with a General "RIGID" Motion using FEM Model. Part I. Theoretical Approach. *Rom. J. Phys.* **2013**, *58*, 872–881.
58. Vlase, S.; Negrean, I.; Marin, M.; Nastac, S. Kane's Method-Based Simulation and Modeling Robots with Elastic Elements, Using Finite Element Method. *Mathematics* **2020**, *8*, 805. [CrossRef]
59. Mitu, G.L.; Chircan, E.; Scutaru, M.L.; Vlase, S. Kane's Formalism Used to the Vibration Analysis of a Wind Water Pump. *Symmetry* **2020**, *12*, 1030. [CrossRef]
60. Ursu-Fisher, N. *Elements of Analytical Mechanics*; House of Science Book Press: Cluj-Napoca, Romania, 2015.
61. Vlase, S.; Negrean, I.; Marin, M.; Scutaru, M.L. Energy of Accelerations Used to Obtain the Motion Equations of a Three-Dimensional Finite Element. *Symmetry* **2020**, *12*, 321. [CrossRef]
62. Negrean, I.; Kacso, K.; Schonstein, C.; Duca, A. *Mechanics*; UTPESS: Cluj Napoca, Romania, 2012.
63. Vlase, S.; Marin, M.; Scutaru, M.L. Maggi's equations used in the finite element analysis of the multibody systems with elastic elements. *Mathematics* **2020**, *8*, 399. [CrossRef]
64. de Jalón, J.G.; Callejo, A.; Hidalgo, A. Efficient Solution of Maggi's Equations. *J. Comput. Nonlinear Dyn.* **2012**, *7*, 021003. [CrossRef]
65. Desloge, E. The Gibbs–Appell equations of motion. *Am. J. Phys. Am. Assoc. Phys. Teach.* **1988**, *56*, 841–847. [CrossRef]

Article

Modelling and Fault Detection for Specific Cavitation Damage Based on the Discharge Pressure of Axial Piston Pumps

Shiqi Xia [1,*], Yimin Xia [1] and Jiawei Xiang [2]

1. State Key Laboratory of High Performance Complex Manufacturing, Central South University, Changsha 410017, China; xiaymj@csu.edu.cn
2. College of Mechanical and Electrical Engineering, Wenzhou University, Wenzhou 325035, China; jwxiang@wzu.edu.cn
* Correspondence: shiqixia@csu.edu.cn

Abstract: Cavitation will increase the leakage and discharge pressure fluctuation of axial piston pumps. In particular, specific cavitation damage may aggravate the pressure impact and performance degradation. The influence of the specific cavitation damage on the discharge pressure is unclear, and the need for fault detection of this damage is urgent. In this paper, we propose a discharge pressure-based model and fault detection methodology for the specific cavitation damage of axial piston pumps. The discharge pressure model with specific damage is constructed using a slender hole. The simulation model is solved through numerical integration. Experimental investigation of cavitation damage detection is carried out. Discharge pressure features in the time domain and frequency domain are compared. The results show that waveform distortions, spectrum energy relocation, generation of new frequencies and sidebands can be used as features for fault detection regarding the specific cavitation damage of axial piston pumps.

Keywords: modelling; fault detection; cavitation damage; discharge pressure; axial piston pump

MSC: 76A02

1. Introduction

Axial piston pumps are key power components of hydraulic systems applied in the industrial equipment and construction machinery [1,2]. They can convert mechanical energy into fluid power energy with a high efficiency and compact structure. The fluid with high pressure and a high flow rate can accomplish the power transmission and energy output in these applications.

Structures of an axial piston pump consist of three main interfaces: the interface between the slipper and a swash plate, the interface between the piston and a cylinder block, and the interface between the cylinder block and a valve plate [3,4]. These interfaces with the oil film work as bearings and sealings in the pump [5]. The output flow and pressure of piston pumps are discontinuous and fluctuate. The transformation from low pressure to high pressure is achieved through the valve plate. The cylinder block is subject to unbalanced forces from the low-pressure area and high-pressure area. Therefore, the interface between the cylinder block and valve plate plays an important role in improving the pump's efficiency and lifetime [6].

The pressure transformation in the valve plate will result in a huge variation gradient. In addition, flow passages in the cylinder block are irregular and complex. They exacerbate oil cavitation [7–9]. The pressure of some places in the interface between the cylinder block and valve plate is less than the gas separation pressure. The separated bubbles will be crushed when they arrive at the high-pressure area of the valve plate. Energies released by the bubbles can damage this interface and decrease the volumetric efficiency [10,11].

Numerous studies on the cavitation of axial piston pumps have been carried out. In terms of the analysis of the cavitation mechanism, the centrifugal effect of fluid in the cylinder block can result in pressure differences between the outside wall and inside wall, and the cavitation is more likely to appear in the inside wall [12]. The effect of the fluid temperature on the cavitation is analyzed. The high viscosity caused by the low temperature will aggravate the cavitation [13]. Throttling structures of the valve plate have an important influence on the pressure transformation. An unreasonable structure design causes the pressure variation gradient to increase [14]. Triangular grooves of the spherical valve plate cause special cavitation [15]. Low suction pressure of the inlet will induce insufficient inlet flow [16]. In addition, the effect of a long pipeline for the inlet on wave propagation is investigated [17].

The above-mentioned factors can exacerbate the cavitation problems of axial piston pumps. In order to reduce the intensity of cavitation, methods for improving these factors are proposed. Anti-cavitation throttling structures of the valve plate [18,19], a higher back pressure of the inlet [20,21], an optimized suction duct [22], and an improved unloading outlet [23] are utilized for cavitation suppression. During the analysis of the cavitation mechanism and cavitation suppression, computational fluid dynamics (CFD) models are built. Four CFD models, based on the cavitation [3] and a CFD model based on the full cavitation [22] are proposed for the modelling of pumps' cavitation. A full CFD model is developed from the fluid compressibility, gaseous dynamics, and cavitation damage [24]. The vapor cavitation [25] based CFD model is presented to identify the critical inlet pressure [26]. Apart from the CFD model, an analytical cavitation model is used to determine the pump's speed limitations [27].

For the detection of cavitation for axial piston pumps, the vibration signal is widely used as an indicator for the machine learning model. The denoised time frequency images [28] and multi-channel signals [29] are put into the convolutional neural networks model. Time domain analysis and frequency spectral analysis of the vibration signal are carried out to detect the pumps' cavitation on line [30].

Pumps' cavitation will increase the flow leakage and pressure impact. Therefore, the discharge pressure has a strong correlation with the cavitation, in contrast to the vibration signal [31,32]. In particular, specific cavitation can damage the surface of the cylinder block and valve plate. The specific cavitation damage is shown in Figure 1. This damage is located between the two adjacent piston holes of the cylinder block. It should be pointed out that there is little research on the modelling and fault diagnosis of cavitation damage based on the pressure signal. In addition, the effects of the specific cavitation damage on the discharge pressure are unclear.

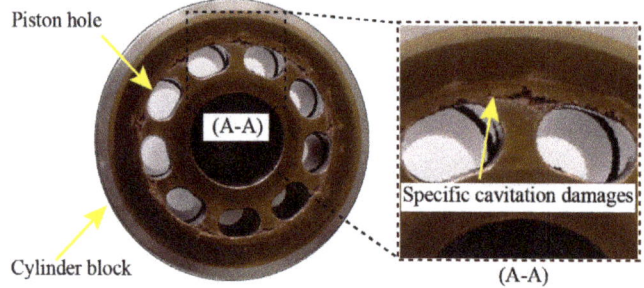

Figure 1. Specific cavitation damage to axial piston pumps.

In this paper, a model of the discharge pressure is built, which takes into account effects of the specific cavitation damage. Fault detection, based on the discharge pressure model, is accomplished. The remainder of this paper is structured as follows. Section 2 describes the simulation model of the pump's discharge pressure. Section 3 presents the experimental investigation on the cavitation damage. Section 4 shows the results and discussions of the simulation model and experimental investigation. Conclusions are summarized in Section 5.

2. Simulation Model

2.1. Discharge Pressure

The typical structure of an axial piston pump is shown in Figure 2. The pump rotor system mainly includes the shaft, cylinder block, piston, slipper, and retainer. The shaft is supported by the large and small bearings at both ends. The cylinder block is in splined connection with the shaft. Pistons are at equal distance around the cylinder block center. Slippers and pistons are linked by spherical hinges. When the rotor system rotates, pistons reciprocate along the cylinder block hole under the action of the retainer and inclined swash plate. Oil suction and extrusion are accomplished by the pistons' reciprocating motions and valve plate with the high-pressure area and low-pressure area.

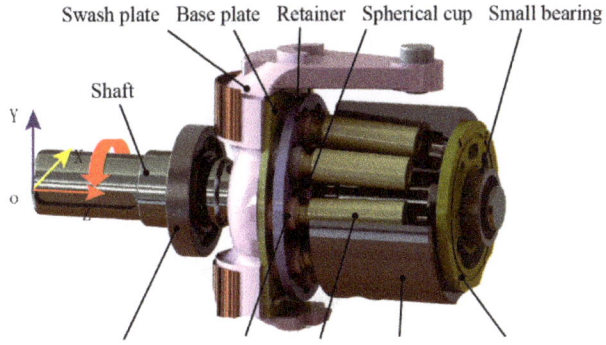

Figure 2. Typical structure of an axial piston pump.

The discharge pressure of an axial piston pump is a key parameter during the oil extrusion process. It depends on the pump's kinematics. The kinematic diagram of the piston pump is shown in Figure 3. The coordinate systems O-xyz and O'-x'y'z' represent the positions when the inclined angles of the swash plate are 0 and β, respectively. The angle γ is the inclined angle of pistons in the cylinder block hole. The point M' represents the piston's position when the shaft rotates clockwise by an angle φ. Assuming $OO'' = x_0$, $OM = R$, $O''M_x = x$, $MM' = h$, $MM'' = r$, $MM_z = n$, one can obtain the following equations:

$$h = (x - x_0)/\cos \gamma, \ x = n \tan \beta = (R + r) \tan \beta \cos \varphi, \ r = (x - x_0) \tan \gamma. \tag{1}$$

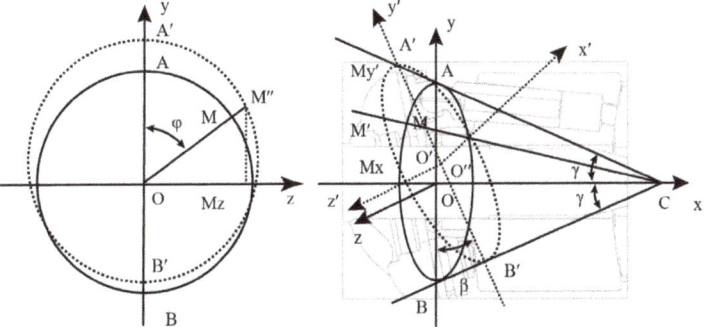

Figure 3. Kinematic diagram of an axial piston pump.

By substituting parameters r and x in the parameter h, one can obtain the following equation:

$$h = \frac{R \tan\beta \cos\varphi - x_0}{\cos\gamma(1 - \cos\varphi \tan\beta \tan\gamma)} \tag{2}$$

The piston displacement of the reciprocating motions along the cylinder block hole is calculated as:

$$x_p(1) = \frac{(R - x_0 \tan\gamma)\tan\beta(1 - \cos\varphi)}{\cos\gamma(1 - \tan\beta \tan\gamma)(1 - \cos\varphi\tan\beta\tan\gamma)}, \tag{3}$$

where $x_p(1)$ refers to the piston displacement of the first piston when the shaft rotates clockwise by an angle φ. The piston displacement of the kth piston is $x_p(k)$:

$$x_p(k) = \frac{(R - x_0 \tan\gamma)\tan\beta[1 - \cos(\varphi + 2\pi k/Z)]}{\cos\gamma(1 - \tan\beta \tan\gamma)[1 - \cos(\varphi + 2\pi k/Z)\tan\beta\tan\gamma]}, \tag{4}$$

where Z is the number of pistons distributed in the cylinder block. The axial piston pump presented in this paper has an odd number of pistons.

The piston velocity of the reciprocating motions along the cylinder block hole is calculated as:

$$v_p(1) = \frac{dx_p(1)}{dt} = \frac{\omega_s \sin\varphi \tan\beta(R - x_0 \tan\gamma)}{\cos\gamma(1 - \cos\varphi \tan\beta \tan\gamma)^2}$$

$$\vdots$$

$$v_p(k) = \frac{dx_p(k)}{dt} = \frac{\omega_s \sin(\varphi + 2\pi k/Z) \tan\beta(R - x_0 \tan\gamma)}{\cos\gamma[(1 - \cos(\varphi + 2\pi k/Z))\tan\beta \tan\gamma]^2} \tag{5}$$

$$\vdots$$

$$v_p(Z) = \frac{dx_p(Z)}{dt} = \frac{\omega_s \sin(\varphi + 2\pi) \tan\beta(R - x_0 \tan\gamma)}{\cos\gamma[(1 - \cos(\varphi + 2\pi))\tan\beta \tan\gamma]^2},$$

where ω_s is the rotating speed of the cylinder block.

The output flow rate of an axial piston pump depends on the flow of a single piston located in the high-pressure area. The flow of the kth piston is calculated as:

$$Q_p(k) = \pi r_p^2 v_p(k) - Q_{c1}(k) - Q_{c2}(k) - Q_{c3}(k), \tag{6}$$

where r_p refers to the radius of the piston. $Q_{c1}(k)$, $Q_{c2}(k)$, and $Q_{c3}(k)$ are leakage flows of the slipper pair, the piston pair, and the valve plate pair, respectively.

$$Q_{c1}(k) = \frac{\pi h_{c1}^3 \lambda [P_p(k) - P_{le}]}{6\mu(\ln r_s - \ln R_s)}, \tag{7}$$

where h_{c1} is the clearance between the slipper and a base plate. λ refers to the pressure ratio coefficient. $P_p(k)$ represents the pressure of the kth piston. P_{le} is the pressure of the leakage port. μ refers to the dynamic viscosity. r_s and R_s are radius of the sealing belt for slippers.

$$Q_{c2}(k) = \frac{2\pi r_p h_{c2}^3 + 3\varepsilon^2 \pi r_p h_{c2}^3}{12\mu l_p}[P_p(k) - P_{le}], \tag{8}$$

where h_{c2} and l_p represent the clearance and contact length between the piston and cylinder block, respectively. ε refers to the eccentricity.

$$Q_{c3}(k) = \frac{\pi \lambda h_{c3}^3}{6\mu}\left(\frac{\varphi_2 - \varphi_1}{\ln R_2 - \ln R_1} + \frac{\varphi_2 - \varphi_1}{\ln R_4 - \ln R_3}\right)[P_p(k) - P_{le}], \tag{9}$$

where h_{c3} is the clearance between the cylinder block and a valve plate. R_1, R_2, R_3, and R_4 represent the radius of the sealing belt for the valve plate. φ_1 and φ_2 are the distribution angles of the damping grooves.

The output flow rate Q_{out} is the sum of instantaneous flows of pistons distributed in the high-pressure area:

$$\begin{aligned} Q_{out} &= Q_p(1) + Q_p(2) + \cdots + Q_p(K) \\ &= \pi r_p^2 \sum_1^K v_p(k) + \sum_1^K Q_{c1}(k) - \sum_1^K Q_{c2}(k) - \sum_1^K Q_{c3}(k), \end{aligned} \quad (10)$$

where the number K of pistons distributed in the high-pressure area is calculated as:

$$K = \begin{cases} \frac{Z+1}{2} & 0 < \varphi \leq \frac{\pi}{Z} \\ \frac{Z-1}{2} & \frac{\pi}{Z} < \varphi \leq \frac{2\pi}{Z}. \end{cases} \quad (11)$$

The time derivative of the discharge pressure P_{out} is given by:

$$\begin{aligned} \frac{dP_{out}}{dt} &= \frac{Q_{out} B_f}{V_{out}} \\ &= \frac{\pi r_p^2 B_f}{V_{out}} \sum_1^K v_p(k) + \frac{B_f}{V_{out}} \sum_1^K Q_{c1}(k) - \frac{B_f}{V_{out}} \sum_1^K Q_{c2}(k) - \frac{B_f}{V_{out}} \sum_1^K Q_{c3}(k), \end{aligned} \quad (12)$$

where B_f is the fluid bulk modulus. V_{out} refers to the volume of the output port.

The time derivative of the pressure $P_p(k)$ for the kth piston is calculated as:

$$\begin{aligned} \frac{dP_p(k)}{dt} &= \frac{Q_p(k) B_f}{V(k)} \\ &= \frac{\pi r_p^2 B_f}{V(k)} v_p(k) - \frac{B_f}{V(k)} Q_{c1}(k) - \frac{B_f}{V(k)} Q_{c2}(k) - \frac{B_f}{V(k)} Q_{c3}(k), \end{aligned} \quad (13)$$

where $V(k)$ refers to the volume of the kth piston.

2.2. Input of the Specific Cavitation Damage

As shown in Figure 1, the specific cavitation damage will lead to internal leakage flows between the adjacent pistons [33]. The size of the cavitation damage is approximately a slender hole. Therefore, the flow model of the slender hole is utilized as an input of the specific cavitation damage in the discharge pressure model. It is assumed that a specific cavitation damage is located between the kth piston and $k + 1$th piston. The leakage flow of the specific cavitation damage Q_{scd} is given by the flow model of the slender hole:

$$Q_{scd} = \frac{\pi d_{scd}^3 \left[P_{p\text{-}scd}(k) - P_{p\text{-}scd}(k+1) \right]}{128 \mu l_{scd}}, \quad (14)$$

where d_{scd} and l_{scd} are the diameter and length of the slender hole, respectively. $P_{p\text{-}scd}(k)$ and $P_{p\text{-}scd}(k+1)$ represent the pressures of the kth piston and $k + 1$th piston with the input of the specific cavitation damage. The flows of the adjacent pistons are given by the following equations:

$$Q_{p\text{-}scd}(k) = \pi r_p^2 v_p(k) - Q_{c1}(k) - Q_{c2}(k) - Q_{c3}(k) - Q_{scd} \quad (15)$$

$$Q_{p\text{-}scd}(k+1) = \pi r_p^2 v_p(k+1) - Q_{c1}(k+1) - Q_{c2}(k+1) - Q_{c3}(k+1) + Q_{scd}. \quad (16)$$

The output flow rate $Q_{out\text{-}scd}$ with the input of the specific cavitation damage is the difference between the output flow rate Q_{out} and the internal leakage flow Q_{scd}:

$$\begin{aligned} Q_{out\text{-}scd} &= Q_p(1) + Q_p(2) + \cdots + Q_p(K) - Q_{scd} \\ &= \pi r_p^2 \sum_1^K v_p(k) + \sum_1^K Q_{c1}(k) - \sum_1^K Q_{c2}(k) - \sum_1^K Q_{c3}(k) - Q_{scd}. \end{aligned} \quad (17)$$

The time derivative of the discharge pressure $P_{out\text{-}scd}$ with the input of the specific cavitation damage is given by:

23

$$\frac{dP_{\text{out-scd}}}{dt} = \frac{Q_{\text{out-scd}} B_f}{V_{\text{out}}}$$

$$= \frac{\pi r_p^2 B_f}{V_{\text{out}}} \sum_1^K v_p(k) + \frac{B_f}{V_{\text{out}}} \sum_1^K Q_{c1}(k) - \frac{B_f}{V_{\text{out}}} \sum_1^K Q_{c2}(k) - \quad (18)$$

$$\frac{B_f}{V_{\text{out}}} \sum_1^K Q_{c3}(k) - \frac{B_f Q_{\text{scd}}}{V_{\text{out}}}.$$

The time derivative of the pressures $P_{\text{p-scd}}(k)$ and $P_{\text{p-scd}}(k+1)$ for the kth piston and mboxemph$k$ + 1th piston is calculated as:

$$\frac{dP_{\text{p-scd}}(k)}{dt} = \frac{Q_{\text{p-scd}}(k) B_f}{V(k)}$$

$$= \frac{\pi r_p^2 B_f v_p(k)}{V(k)} - \frac{B_f Q_{c1}(k)}{V(k)} - \frac{B_f Q_{c2}(k)}{V(k)} - \quad (19)$$

$$\frac{B_f Q_{c3}(k)}{V(k)} - \frac{B_f Q_{\text{scd}}}{V(k)}$$

$$\frac{dP_{\text{p-scd}}(k+1)}{dt} = \frac{Q_{\text{p-scd}}(k+1) B_f}{V(k+1)}$$

$$= \frac{\pi r_p^2 B_f v_p(k+1)}{V(k+1)} - \frac{B_f Q_{c1}(k+1)}{V(k+1)} - \frac{B_f Q_{c2}(k+1)}{V(k+1)} - \quad (20)$$

$$\frac{B_f Q_{c3}(k+1)}{V(k+1)} + \frac{B_f Q_{\text{scd}}}{V(k+1)}.$$

2.3. Model Properties

Simulation models with the specific cavitation damage are constructed based on the flow continuity and pressure derivative equation. The main parameters of the pump simulation models are listed in Table 1.

Table 1. Simulation model properties.

Parameters	Values	Parameters	Values
γ	5°	β	14°
R	36.75 mm	Z	9
ω_s	1500 r/min	r_p	8.50 mm
h_{c1}	0.01 mm	x_0	8.89 mm
P_{le}	0.10 MPa	λ	0.9
r_s	7.70 mm	μ	46 cP
h_{c2}	0.02 mm	R_s	9.10 mm
h_{c3}	0.01 mm	ε	0.01 mm
R_2	23.50 mm	R_1	20.00 mm
R_4	34.75 mm	R_3	31.50 mm
φ_2	154°	φ_1	26°
V_{out}	48.60 mm³	B_f	1.7×10^{-2} MPa
d_{scd}	0.5 mm/0.8 mm	l_{scd}	6.0 mm

The normal pump model and simulation models with specific cavitation damage input (case 1: $d_{\text{scd}} = 0.5$ mm, case 2: $d_{\text{scd}} = 0.8$ mm) are constructed. The rotating speed of the cylinder block is 1500 r/min. The initial pressure of the discharge pressure is 21.0 MPa. The simulation models are solved through the Runge–Kutta numerical integration algorithm. The fixed time step valve is 1×10^{-4} s. The order of the integration algorithm is 4. The total simulation time is 0.2 s.

3. Experimental Investigation
3.1. Layout of the Test Rig

Experimental investigation on the axial piston pump was carried out. The test rig of the pump is shown in Figure 4a. The system schematic diagram of this test rig is presented in Figure 4b. The power of the electric motor as supplied to the pump through the torque-speed sensor. The pump converted mechanical energy into fluid power. The discharge pressure of the pump was measured through the pressure gauge and pressure sensor. A relief valve was used as the regulator of the discharge pressure. A flow sensor was placed between the pump and relief valve. Detailed descriptions of the test rig are shown in Table 2.

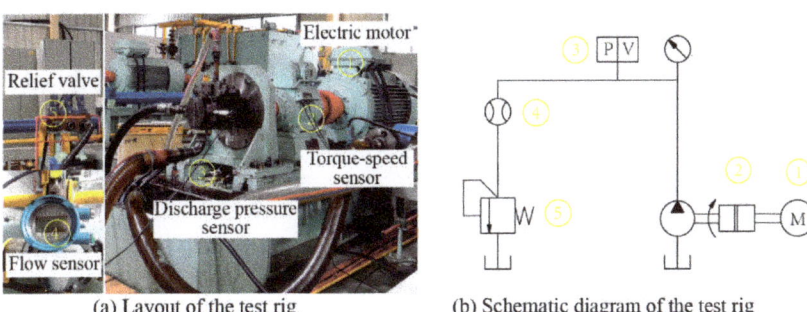

Figure 4. Layout and schematic diagram of the test rig.

Table 2. Detailed descriptions of the test rig.

No.	Components	Descriptions
1	Electric motor	ABB-IEL-280M75
2	Torque-speed sensor	ZJ-5000/3000-120-02
3	Discharge pressure sensor	HM90-0~35MPa-H3V2F1
4	Flow sensor	LXB-1
5	Relief valve	DBW30B-1-50B/350

3.2. Testing Pump with Cavitation Damage

The valve plate pair of the testing pump is shown in Figure 5. Specific cavitation damage was applied between the adjacent piston holes of the cylinder block. The size of the specific damage was 6.0 mm × 2.0 mm × 1.0 mm. An axial piston pump with specific cavitation damage and a normal pump was tested on the test rig. The motor speed was 1500 r/min. The discharge pressure was regulated at around 21.0 MPa. All the pumps had full displacements. The discharge pressures of the tested pumps were measured for 10 s with a sampling frequency of 48,000 Hz.

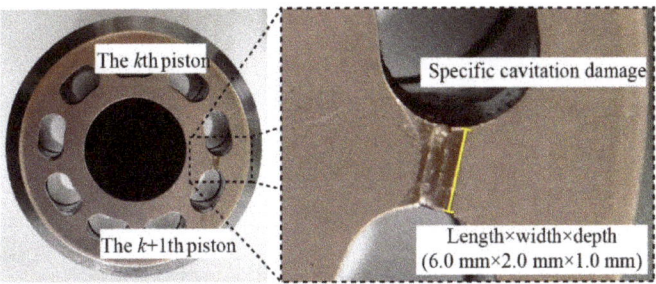

Figure 5. Valve plate pair with specific cavitation damage.

4. Results and Discussion

4.1. Simulations

The discharge pressure of the simulation model with no specific cavitation damage is shown in Figure 6. It can be seen that the pressure oscillation is due to the iterative calculation during the initial stage. The discharge pressure becomes convergent after 6.5×10^{-4} s. The pressure cure fluctuates around 21.0 MPa. The fluctuation range is ±0.2 MPa. This means that the simulation model is effectively solved through the numerical integration.

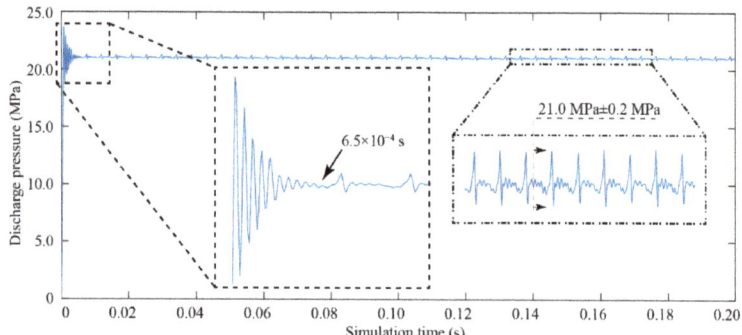

Figure 6. Simulated discharge pressure during the iterative process (normal pump model, rotational speed: 1500 r/min, discharge pressure: 21 MPa).

Discharge pressures of the normal pump model and pump models with specific cavitation damage (case 1: 0.5 mm, case 2: 0.8 mm) are shown in Figure 7. Considering that the discharge pressure fluctuates periodically, pressures under different model cases are compared during two cycles (0.08 s). It can be seen that the pressure curve of case 1 has nearly uniform spikes. There are a lot of signal burrs in case 1 and case 2. The burrs occur at 0 s, 0.2 s, 0.4 s, 0.6 s, and 0.8 s. In addition, the amplitudes of burrs in case 2 are higher than those in case 1. The results show that specific cavitation damages in the valve plate pair cause the discharge pressure to become distorted. On average, there are two signal distortions in a cycle. The greater the damage, the greater the signal distortion.

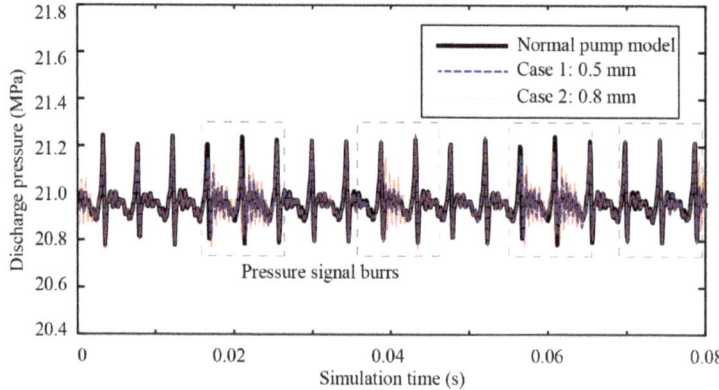

Figure 7. Comparisons of the simulated discharge pressures under different model cases.

Spectra of the discharge pressures under three cases are shown in Figure 8. The spectral energy of the pressure is mainly concentrated in the 1st, 2nd, 3rd, and 4th pumping frequencies. The amplitudes of these frequencies for case 1 and case 2 are lower than those in the normal pump model. In addition, the amplitudes in case 2 are less than the amplitudes in case 1. This shows that specific cavitation damage will decrease the amplitudes of the pumping frequencies in the spectra. As the damage increases, the amplitudes become smaller. The spectral energies of the pumping frequencies in case 1 and case 2 are allocated to other sidebands around themselves. It can be seen that the spectrum of the normal pump model has almost no 25 Hz sideband, while the amplitudes of this sideband for case 1 and case 2 increase gradually. In addition, amplitudes of the sideband around the 4th pumping frequency are larger than those around the 2nd and 3rd pumping frequency. No sideband can be found around the 1st pumping frequency. Moreover, the spectra of case 1 and case 2 have frequencies (50 Hz, 100 Hz, 150 Hz, and 200 Hz) below the 1st pump frequency. The amplitudes of these frequencies increase as damage increases.

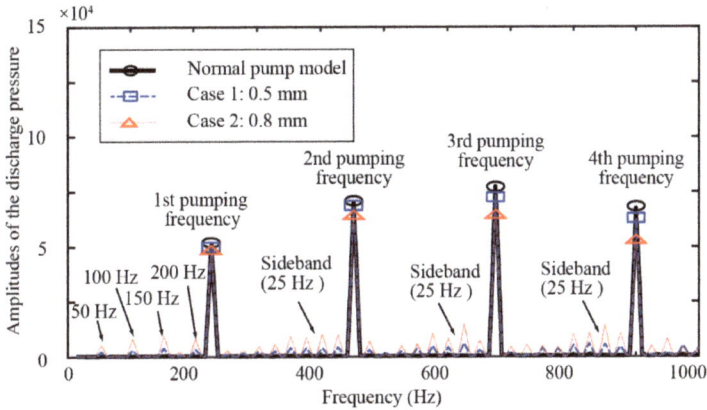

Figure 8. Spectra of the discharge pressures under different model cases.

Comparisons of the simulated discharge pressures and their spectra show that the specific cavitation damage will lead to waveform distortions, spectrum energy relocation, and the generation of new frequencies and sidebands. In order to study the effects of these influence mechanisms on the discharge pressure, internal leakage flow rates of the slender hole are shown in Figure 9. We define the flow rates as positive flows and negative flows. Positive flow occurs when the pressure of the $k + 1$th piston is larger than the pressure of the kth piston. In the opposite case, it is called negative flow. It can be seen that flow rates alternately appear at 0 s, 0.2 s, 0.4 s, 0.6 s, and 0.8 s. The absolute values of flow rates for case 1 and case 2 are 1.83 L/min and 4.69 L/min, respectively. This means that high specific damage will lead to more leakage flows between the adjacent pistons. In addition, backflows occur at the start and end of the positive flows and negative flows. The specific cavitation damage in the valve plate pair exacerbates the backflows in axial piston pumps. Backflows in case 2 are higher than those in case 1. The maximum backflows of case 1 and case 2 are -0.91 L/min and -0.40 L/min, respectively.

The internal pressures of the kth piston and $k + 1$th piston are shown in Figure 10. The initial pressures in the kth piston and $k + 1$th piston are the inlet pressures (0.1 MPa) due to the fact that two pistons are located in the low-pressure area. The pressure of the kth piston and the $k + 1$th piston becomes the discharge pressure (21.0 MPa) when the shaft rotates by an angle of $2\pi(k-1)/Z$ and $2\pi k/Z$, respectively. At this time, backflows appear, and the pressure difference results in the negative flow rate. Then, the two adjacent pistons are both located in the high-pressure area and no flow is found with no pressure difference. Positive flow rates appear when the pressure of the kth piston becomes the inlet pressure. It is also found that the amplitudes of the pressure spikes decrease when the pump has specific cavitation. The maximum pressure spikes for the normal pump model, case 1 and case

2 are 23.0 MPa, 22.6 MPa and 22.1 MPa, respectively. The results show that the pressure difference between the two adjacent pistons leads to leakage flow and discharge pressure distortions of axial piston pumps.

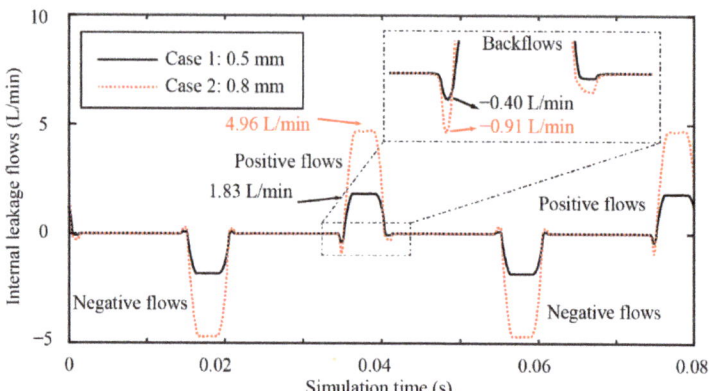

Figure 9. Internal leakage flows of the slender hole.

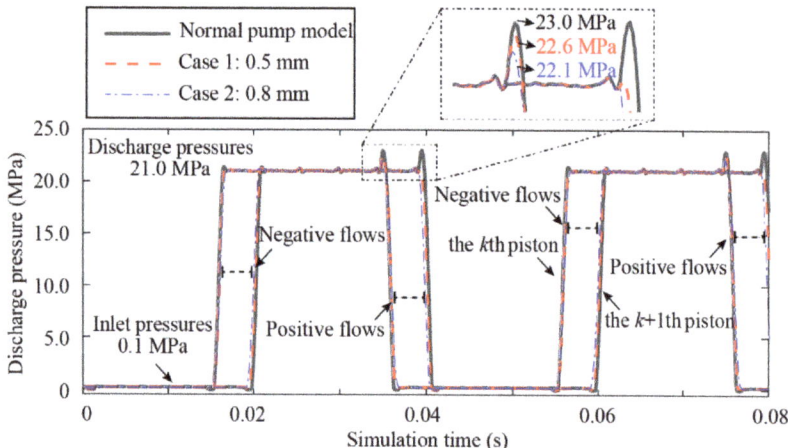

Figure 10. Internal pressures of the kth piston and the $k + 1$th piston.

4.2. Cavitation Damage Detection

The experimental results of discharge pressures for the normal pump and the testing pump with cavitation damage are shown in Figure 11. Measured discharge pressures during the two cycles are shown in Figure 11a. The tested pressure of the normal pump fluctuates around 21.0 MPa. It ranges from 20.8 MPa to 21.2 MPa. The variations of the tested pressures are consistent with the simulation results shown in Figure 7. Some signal distortions of the tested pressure for the testing pump with cavitation damage are found at 0.2 s and 0.4 s during one cycle. This is because internal leakage flows appear in the corresponding time due to the specific cavitation damages, as shown in Figure 9.

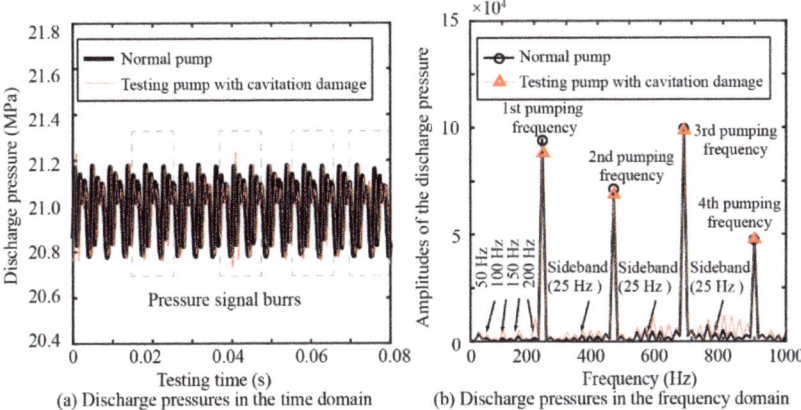

Figure 11. Comparisons of the tested discharge pressures and their spectra.

Frequency spectra of the tested discharge pressures for the normal pump and the testing pump with cavitation damage are shown in Figure 11b. Spectral energies are mostly located in the first four pumping frequencies. The 3rd pumping frequency has the maximum amplitudes. It can be seen that the specific cavitation damage results in amplitude decreases for these pumping frequencies. Sidebands with a frequency of 25 Hz appear in the spectra. In particular, the amplitudes of the sideband around the 4th pumping frequency are larger than the sidebands around the 2nd and 3rd pumping frequency. In addition, the 50 Hz frequency and its harmonics also occur below the 1st pumping frequency. The experimental results show that the waveform distortions, spectrum energy relocation, and the generation of new frequencies and sidebands can be used as features for the fault detection of the specific cavitation damage of axial piston pumps.

5. Conclusions

This paper proposes a discharge pressure-based model and a fault detection methodology for the specific cavitation damage of axial piston pumps. A slender hole is used as the input of the simulated discharge pressure model with specific damage. An experimental investigation on the fault detection of cavitation damage is carried out. The following conclusions are drawn. First, the modelling methodology based on the pressure and slender hole is applicable for the cavitation damage detection. Second, the internal leakage flow leads to waveform distortions of the adjacent piston pressure and discharge pressure. Third, specific cavitation damage gives rise to new frequency of 50 Hz and its harmonics, 25 Hz sidebands around the 4th pumping frequency. These frequencies and sidebands in the spectra can be used as fault features for the specific cavitation damage detection of axial piston pumps.

Author Contributions: Conceptualization, S.X. and Y.X.; methodology, S.X.; software, S.X.; validation, S.X., Y.X. and J.X.; formal analysis, S.X.; investigation, S.X.; resources, Y.X.; data curation, S.X.; writing—original draft preparation, S.X.; writing—review and editing, S.X.; visualization, S.X.; supervision, Y.X.; project administration, J.X.; funding acquisition, Y.X. All authors have read and agreed to the published version of the manuscript.

Funding: This research was funded by the National Key Research and Development Program of China (Grant No. 2020YFB2007101), the Project of State Key Laboratory of High Performance Complex Manufacturing (Grant No. ZZYJKT2021-16), and the Open Foundation of the State Key Laboratory of Fluid Power and Mechatronic Systems (Grant No. GZKF-202007).

Institutional Review Board Statement: Not applicable.

Informed Consent Statement: Not applicable.

Data Availability Statement: The data presented in this study are available on request from the corresponding author. The data are not publicly available due to an ongoing study.

Acknowledgments: The authors would like to thank the following people: Zhihua Ye, Huaijun Shi and Ping Wu in Ningbo Hilead Hydraulic Co., Ltd., for their help in preparing the pumps and performing the tests.

Conflicts of Interest: The authors declare no conflict of interest.

References

1. Suh, S.; Kim, W. Nonlinear Position Control Using Differential Flatness Concept with Load Torque Observer for Electro Hydraulic Actuators with Sinusoidal Load Torque. *Mathematics* **2020**, *8*, 1484. [CrossRef]
2. Xu, H.G.; Zhang, J.H.; Sun, G.M.; Huang, W.D.; Huang, X.C.; Lyu, F.; Xu, B.; Su, Q. The direct measurement of the cylinder block dynamic characteristics based on a non-contact method in an axial piston pump. *Measurement* **2021**, *167*, 108279. [CrossRef]
3. Casoli, P.; Vacca, A.; Franzoni, G.; Berta, G.L. Modelling of fluid properties in hydraulic positive displacement machines. *Simul. Model. Pract. Theory* **2006**, *14*, 1059–1072. [CrossRef]
4. He, Y.; Tang, H.; Ren, Y.; Kumar, A. A deep multi-signal fusion adversarial model based transfer learning and residual network for axial piston pump fault diagnosis. *Measurement* **2022**, *192*, 110889. [CrossRef]
5. Chao, Q.; Zhang, J.; Xu, B.; Wang, Q. Multi-position measurement of oil film thickness within the slipper bearing in axial piston pumps. *Measurement* **2018**, *122*, 66–72. [CrossRef]
6. Richardson, D.; Sadeghi, F.; Rateick, R.G.; Rowan, S. Experimental and Analytical Investigation of Floating Valve Plate Motion in an Axial Piston Pump. *Tribol. Trans.* **2017**, *60*, 537–547. [CrossRef]
7. Zhang, C.C.; Zhu, C.H.; Meng, B.; Li, S. Challenges and Solutions for High-Speed Aviation Piston Pumps: A Review. *Aerospace* **2021**, *8*, 392. [CrossRef]
8. Brijkishore; Khare, R.; Prasad, V. Prediction of cavitation and its mitigation techniques in hydraulic turbines-A review. *Ocean Eng.* **2021**, *221*, 108512. [CrossRef]
9. Wang, X.; Zhou, S.; Shan, Z.; Yin, M. Investigation of Cavitation Bubble Dynamics Considering Pressure Fluctuation Induced by Slap Forces. *Mathematics* **2021**, *9*, 2064. [CrossRef]
10. Yun, L.; Yan, Z.; Jianping, C.; Rongsheng, Z.; Dezhong, W. A cavitation performance prediction method for pumps: Part2-sensitivity and accuracy. *Nucl. Eng. Technol.* **2021**, *53*, 3612–3624. [CrossRef]
11. Osterland, S.; Muller, L.; Weber, J. Influence of Air Dissolved in Hydraulic Oil on Cavitation Erosion. *Int. J. Fluid Power* **2021**, *22*, 373–392. [CrossRef]
12. Chao, Q.; Zhang, J.H.; Xu, B.; Huang, H.P.; Zhai, J. Centrifugal effects on cavitation in the cylinder chambers for high-speed axial piston pumps. *Meccanica* **2019**, *54*, 815–829. [CrossRef]
13. Chao, Q.; Xu, Z.; Tao, J.F.; Liu, C.L.; Zhai, J. Cavitation in a high-speed aviation axial piston pump over a wide range of fluid temperatures. *Proc. Inst. Mech. Eng. Part A J. Power Energy* **2021**, *236*, 727–737. [CrossRef]
14. Sun, Z.G.; Li, Y.D.; Liang, N.; Zhong, H.M. Study on Restraining Cavitation of Axial Piston Pump Based on Structure of Cylinder Block and Valve Plate Triangular Throttling Groove. *Shock Vib.* **2022**, *1*, 6918936.
15. Zhao, B.; Guo, W.W.; Quan, L. Cavitation of a Submerged Jet at the Spherical Valve Plate/Cylinder Block Interface for Axial Piston Pump. *Chin. J. Mech. Eng.* **2020**, *33*, 67. [CrossRef]
16. Sachdeva, A.; Borkar, K.; Bhansali, A.; Salutagi, S. Critical Inlet Pressure Prediction for Inline Piston Pumps Using Multiphase Computational Fluid Dynamics Modelling. *SAE Int. J. Aerosp.* **2021**, *14*, 117–126. [CrossRef]
17. Manhartsgruber, B. Non-linear dynamics of a hydraulic piston pump model with long suction line and cavitation. In Proceedings of the International Workshop on Power Transmission and Motion Control, Bath, UK, 15 August 2003.
18. Shi, Y.X.; Lin, T.R.; Meng, G.Y.; Huang, J.X. A Study on the Suppression of Cavitation Flow Inside an Axial Piston Pump. In Proceedings of the Prognostics and System Health Management Conference, Chengdu, China, 19 January 2017.
19. Ye, S.G.; Zhang, J.H.; Xu, B.; Song, W.; Chen, L.; Shi, H.Y.; Zhu, S.Q. Experimental and numerical studies on erosion damage in damping holes on the valve plate of an axial piston pump. *J. Mech. Sci. Technol.* **2017**, *31*, 4285–4295. [CrossRef]
20. Lu, L.; Fu, X.; Ryu, S.; Yin, Y.B.; Shen, Z.X. Comprehensive discussions on higher back pressure system performance with cavitation suppression using high back pressure. *Proc. Inst. Mech. Eng. Part C J. Mech. Eng. Sci.* **2018**, *233*, 2442–2455. [CrossRef]
21. Manhartsgruber, B. A novel concept for boosting the suction line of piston pumps by piezo-actuated pipe walls. In Proceedings of the Bath/Asme Symposium on Fluid Power and Motion Control, Bath, UK, 12 September 2018.
22. Fang, Y.; Zhang, J.H.; Xu, B.; Mao, Z.B.; Li, C.M.; Huang, C.S.; Lyu, F.; Guo, Z.M. Raising the Speed Limit of Axial Piston Pumps by Optimizing the Suction Duct. *Chin. J. Mech. Eng.* **2021**, *34*, 105–117. [CrossRef]
23. Zhang, B.; Zhao, C.X.; Hong, H.C.; Cheng, G.Z.; Yang, H.Y.; Feng, S.B.; Zhai, J.; Xiao, W.H. Optimization of the outlet unloading structure to prevent gaseous cavitation in a high-pressure axial piston pump. *Proc. Inst. Mech. Eng. Part C J. Mech. Eng. Sci.* **2022**, *236*, 3459–3473. [CrossRef]
24. Yin, F.L.; Nie, S.L.; Xiao, S.H.; Hou, W. Numerical and experimental study of cavitation performance in sea water hydraulic axial piston pump. *Proc. Inst. Mech. Eng. Part I J. Syst. Control. Eng.* **2016**, *230*, 716–735. [CrossRef]

25. Jablonska, J.; Kozubkova, M.; Mahdal, M.; Marcalik, P.; Tuma, J.; Bojko, M.; Hruzik, L. Spectral analysis of gaseous cavitation in water through multiphase mathematical and acoustic methods. *Phys. Fluids* **2021**, *33*, 085128. [CrossRef]
26. Dong, H.K.; Wang, Y.; Chen, J.H. First attempt to determine the critical inlet pressure for aircraft pumps with a numerical approach that considers vapor cavitation and air aeration. *Proc. Inst. Mech. Eng. Part G J. Aerosp. Eng.* **2020**, *234*, 1926–1938. [CrossRef]
27. Chao, Q.; Tao, J.F.; Lei, J.B.; Wei, X.L.; Liu, C.L.; Wang, Y.H.; Meng, L.H. Fast scaling approach based on cavitation conditions to estimate the speed limitation for axial piston pump design. *Front. Mech. Eng.* **2021**, *16*, 176–185. [CrossRef]
28. Chao, Q.; Wei, X.; Lei, J.; Tao, J.; Liu, C. Improving accuracy of cavitation severity recognition in axial piston pumps by denoising time–frequency images. *Meas. Sci. Technol.* **2022**, *33*, 055116. [CrossRef]
29. Chao, Q.; Tao, J.F.; Wei, X.L.; Wang, Y.H.; Meng, L.H.; Liu, C.L. Cavitation intensity recognition for high-speed axial piston pumps using 1-D convolutional neural networks with multi-channel inputs of vibration signals. *Alex. Eng. J.* **2020**, *59*, 4463–4473. [CrossRef]
30. Siano, D.; Panza, M.A. Diagnostic method by using vibration analysis for pump fault detection. *Energy Procedia* **2018**, *148*, 10–17. [CrossRef]
31. Zhai, J.; Zhou, H. Model and Simulation on Flow and Pressure Characteristics of Axial Piston Pump for Seawater Desalination. In Proceedings of the International Conference on Mechatronics and Applied Mechanics, Hong Kong, China, 27 December 2011.
32. Guo, M.; Liu, C.; Liu, S.Q.; Ke, Z.F.; Wei, W.; Yan, Q.D.; Khoo, B.C. Detection and evaluation of cavitation in the stator of a torque converter using pressure measurement. *Phys. Fluids* **2022**, *34*, 045124. [CrossRef]
33. Xia, S.; Zhang, J.; Ye, S.; Xu, B.; Xiang, J.; Tang, H. A mechanical fault detection strategy based on the doubly iterative empirical mode decomposition. *Appl. Acoust.* **2019**, *155*, 346–357. [CrossRef]

Article

Entropy Analysis of Sutterby Nanofluid Flow over a Riga Sheet with Gyrotactic Microorganisms and Cattaneo–Christov Double Diffusion

Muhammad Faizan [1], Farhan Ali [1], Karuppusamy Loganathan [2,3,*], Aurang Zaib [1], Ch Achi Reddy [4] and Sara I. Abdelsalam [5,6,*]

[1] Department of Mathematical Sciences, Federal Urdu University of Arts, Sciences & Technology, Karachi 75300, Pakistan
[2] Research and Development Wing, Live4Research, Tiruppur 638106, India
[3] Department of Mathematics and Statistics, Manipal University Jaipur, Jaipur-303007, India
[4] Department of Science and Humanities, MLR Institute of Technology, Hyderabad 500043, India
[5] Instituto de Ciencias Matemáticas (ICMAT) (CSIC-UAM-UCM-UC3M), 28049 Madrid, Spain
[6] Basic Science, Faculty of Engineering, The British University in Egypt, Al-Shorouk City, Cairo 11837, Egypt
* Correspondence: loganathankaruppusamy304@gmail.com (K.L.); sara.abdelsalam@bue.edu.eg (S.I.A.)

Abstract: In this article, a Riga plate is exhibited with an electric magnetization actuator consisting of permanent magnets and electrodes assembled alternatively. This exhibition produces electromagnetic hydrodynamic phenomena over a fluid flow. A new study model is formed with the Sutterby nanofluid flow through the Riga plate, which is crucial to the structure of several industrial and entering advancements, including thermal nuclear reactors, flow metres and nuclear reactor design. This article addresses the entropy analysis of Sutterby nanofluid flow over the Riga plate. The Cattaneo–Christov heat and mass flux were used to examine the behaviour of heat and mass relaxation time. The bioconvective motile microorganisms and nanoparticles are taken into consideration. The system of equations for the current flow problems is converted from a highly non-linear partial system to an ordinary system through an appropriate transformation. The effect of the obtained variables on velocity, temperature, concentration and motile microorganism distributions are elaborated through the plots in detail. Further, the velocity distribution is enhanced for a greater Deborah number value and it is reduced for a higher Reynolds number for the two cases of pseudoplastic and dilatant flows. Microorganism distribution decreases with the increased magnitude of Peclet number, Bioconvection Lewis number and microorganism concentration difference number. Two types of graphical outputs are presented for the Sutterby fluid parameter ($\beta = -2.5$, $\beta = 2.5$). Finally, the validation of the present model is achieved with the previously available literature.

Keywords: Sutterby nanofluid; Riga plate; entropy analysis; bioconvection; microorganisms; HAM

MSC: 76D05; 35Q79; 76A05

Citation: Faizan, M.; Ali, F.; Loganathan, K.; Zaib, A.; Reddy, C.A.; Abdelsalam, S.I. Entropy Analysis of Sutterby Nanofluid Flow over a Riga Sheet with Gyrotactic Microorganisms and Cattaneo–Christov Double Diffusion. *Mathematics* **2022**, *10*, 3157. https://doi.org/10.3390/math10173157

Academic Editors: Maria Luminița Scutaru, Catalin I. Pruncu, Vasily Novozhilov, Marco Pedroni and Xiangmin Jiao

Received: 12 July 2022
Accepted: 30 August 2022
Published: 2 September 2022

Publisher's Note: MDPI stays neutral with regard to jurisdictional claims in published maps and institutional affiliations.

Copyright: © 2022 by the authors. Licensee MDPI, Basel, Switzerland. This article is an open access article distributed under the terms and conditions of the Creative Commons Attribution (CC BY) license (https://creativecommons.org/licenses/by/4.0/).

1. Introduction

The rate of heat transport characteristics has received increasing attention from various scientists owing to its tremendous industrial features, for example, in mechanical, optical, electrical and cooling instruments. The rate of heat transport increment is very crucial in depositing energy. Therefore, researchers have focused on the investigation of a new type of fluid that is a mixture of nanoparticles with a size of 100 nm and larger thermophysical properties than ordinary fluids, known as nanoliquids. A nanoliquid is a colloidal suspension of the nanoparticle's thermal behaviour in the ordinary fluid. The first attempt was conducted by Choi et al. [1] in 1995. They showed the thermal conductivity of nanoliquids by adding nanosized particles. Later, Buongiorno [2] used this understanding of nanofluid to achieve a mathematical form by adding Brownian and Thermophoretic terms. A mixed convection nanofluid flow with different geometries was presented by Hussain et al. [3,4]. Haq et al. [5] studied the second law analysis on a cross nanofluid. The MHD mixed convective flow of CNTs/Al_2O_3 nanofluid in water past a heated flexible plate with injection/suction and radiation was studied by Prabakaran et al. [6]. Mankiw et al. [7] analysed the MHD time-dependent flow of nanofluid with variable properties due to an inclined stretching sheet under thermal radiation. Shahid [8] studied the effect of an upper convective Maxwell fluid over a permeable surface near the stagnation point. Rafique et al. [9] addressed the stratified micropolar nanofluid flow past the Riga surface. The unsteady viscous flow of the nanofluid flow over the Riga plate using a rotating system was investigated by Parvine et al. [10]. Abbas et al. [11] studied entropy production over the Riga plate with the suction case. Mohamed et al. [12] using a non-homogeneous dynamic model, which is physically more accurate in describing nanofluids than homogeneous ones. They numerically examined the free convective flow in a cubical cavity filled with a copper–water nanofluid. Aziz et al. [13] discussed the characteristics of nanoparticles with Lorentz and Coriolis forces. More developments of nanofluids are in [14–17].

Different fluid forms, such as polymer melts, colloidal suspensions and organic chain mixes, are used in a wide range of industrial and production processes. The rheological behaviour of these fluids cannot be described well by the Naiver–Stokes equation. Therefore, several nonlinear fluid models have been proposed to represent the rheological characteristics of complicated fluids. One of the non-Newtonian fluid models is used to examine the key characteristics of pseudoplastic and dilatant fluids, which is known as Sutterby fluid model. Numerous experts have studied the flow of the Sutterby liquid extensively. Waqas et al. [18] inspected the Sutterby nanofluid flow using two rotating disks. Yahya et al. [19] investigated Williamson Sutterby nanoparticles under the Cattaneo–Christov heat flux. The effect of MHD on Sutterby nanoparticles due to porous movable sheets was discovered by Fayydh et al. [20]. Gowda et al. [21] examined the Cattaneo–Christof theory of heat diffusion in a Sutterby nanofluid. The thermal aspect of Sutterby nanofluid containing the microorganisms due the stretched cylinder was examined by Aldabesh et al. [22]. Hayat et al. [23] investigated the Sutterby fluid with thermal radiation due to a rotating disk. Fujii et al. [24] addressed a Sutterby fluid with natural convection flow due to a vertical plate. Darcy surface with MHD flow of Sutterby fluid was reported by Bilal et al. [25]. The bioconvection flow of a Sutterby nanofluid due to a rotating disk is described by Khan et al. [26]. Sohail et al. [27] designed the free convection flow of a Sutterby fluid with Cattaneo–Christov theory. The heat generation/absorption in the thermally stratified flow of a Sutterby fluid through a linearly stretched plate is analysed by Saif et al. [28]. Usman et al. [29] investigated the two-dimensional stagnant flow of a Sutterby nanofluid across a stretching wedge with porous media. Ali et al. [30] discussed the heat and mass transportation of a Sutterby nanofluid due to a horizontally stretching surface with bioconvection of microorganisms. The influence of homogeneous–heterogeneous reaction on Sutterby fluid flow through a disk with Cattaneo–Christov heat flux was studied by Khan et al. [31].

In the modern period, research on bioconvection exists due to the upwards motion of microorganisms, whose microorganisms are denser than water. The upward surface of the fluid develops thickness due to the collection of the microorganisms. Because of this, the upper surface becomes disturbed and microorganisms are fall down, which develops the bioconvection. Bioconvection phenomena have been continuously researched due to their applications in the clinical area, manufacturing process and biofuel production. Bioconvection can be organised in the motion of direction with enormous microorganism species. In this way, gyrotactic microorganisms are among those whose swimming directional is based on viscous and gravitational force. Kuznetsov et al. [32,33] reported the investigation of bioconvection in a mixed suspension of nanoparticles with gyrotactic microorganisms. Kotha et al. [34] examined the MHD flow of nanofluids with motile gyrotactic microorganisms over a vertical plate. Siddiq et al. [35] analysed numerically, through the bvp4c method, the bioconvection of micropolar nanofluid flow through a stretchable disk. Ali et al. [36] studied the effect of bioconvection and Cattaneo–Christov heat flux effects of a micropolar-type nanofluid past a vertical stretching sheet. Azam et al. [37] investigated the effect of bioconvection flow for a Sutterby nanoliquid with nonlinear radiation. Khashi'ie et al. [38] studied a hybrid nanofluid having bioconvection with gyrotactic microorganisms. Azam [39] explored the time-dependent flow of the chemically reactive Sutterby nanofluid and the influence of gyrotactic microorganisms. Hayat et al. [40] operated the bioconvection flow of nanomaterial subject to the melting effect. They addressed thermal nonlinear radiation and Joule heating for heat distribution characteristics. Reddy et al. [41] analysed the time-dependent flow of a cross nanofluid comprising the gyrostatic microorganisms due to slip velocity. Sarkar et al. [42] defined a Sutterby nanofluid flow having motile gyrotactic microorganisms over the Riga plate. Syed et al. [43] described the biocovective phenomena of a Prandtl hybrid nanofluid over a stretched surface.

The current investigation aims to express the Sutterby nanofluid flow over a Riga plate with Cattaneo–Christov double diffusion and gyrotactic microorganisms. Chemical reactions and heat source-sink are considered. The main intention of this work is the inclusive analysis of this flow problem. The governing systems are designed as a coupled partial system. The flow problems are altered into the nonlinear ordinary system by applying suitable transformations. Further, the solution of ordinary differential equations is computed via the homotopy analysis method (HAM). The novel outcomes of the current work are obtained through different parameters and explained in detail with graphs and tables.

2. Description of the Physical Model

Consider the incompressible and steady flow of a Sutterby nanofluid over the Riga plate containing gyrotactic microorganisms. Cattaneo–Christov with heat and mass flux were also incorporated into the temperature and concentration equation. The x-axis is considered along with the sheet and the y-axis is taken perpendicular to the sheet. Moreover, the velocity of the sheet is taken as $U_w = ax$. The temperature of the surface, the concentration of the surface and the microorganism of the surface are represented by T_w, C_w and χ_w, respectively. Furthermore, it was assumed that the fluid contains gyrotactic bacteria. The fluids' microorganisms gravitate towards the light. Gyrotactic phenomena, or movement against gravity, are made possible by the "bottom heavy" bulk microorganism, which orients their bodies. The existence of microorganisms is advantageous for the suspension of the nanoparticles. The motion of microorganisms is taken, irrespective of that of the nanoparticles, to ensure the stability of convection. The flow of a double-diffusive fluid across a Riga plate containing gyrotactic microorganisms has not been investigated, and this study aims to fill that gap with the simplification of unsteady boundary layer approximation expressions provided in [22]. Figure 1 describes the physical model of the present problem.

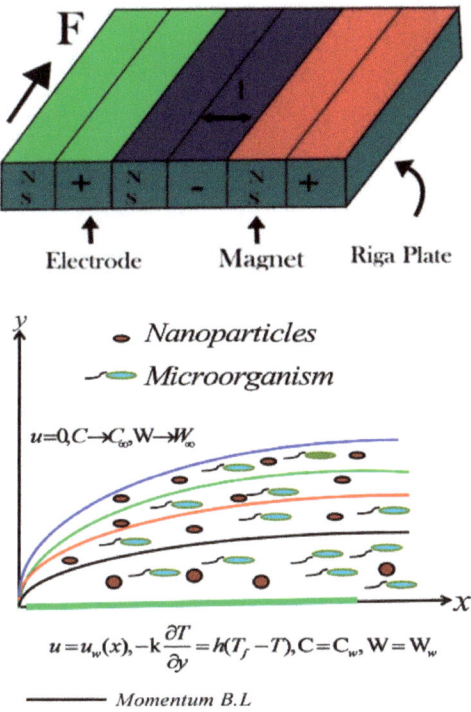

Figure 1. Physical configuration of the flow problem.

Fluid Model

The Cauchy stress tensor τ for the Sutterby fluid [44] is defined as

$$\tau = \mu(\dot{\gamma})A_1 - pI, \tag{1}$$

where the Sutterby viscosity model is represented as

$$\mu = \mu_\circ \left[\left(\frac{\sinh^{-1}(\dot{\beta}\dot{\gamma})}{(\dot{\beta}\dot{\gamma})}\right)\right]^n, \tag{2}$$

where n, $\mu_\circ$ and $\dot{\beta}$ are the power law index, zero share rate viscosity and time material constant. Introducing Equation (2) into Equation (1), then we have

$$\tau = \mu_\circ \left[\left(\frac{\sinh^{-1}(\dot{\beta}\dot{\gamma})}{(\dot{\beta}\dot{\gamma})}\right)\right]^n A_1 - p. \tag{3}$$

The governing equations are illustrated in the following form [21]:

$$\frac{\partial u}{\partial x} + \frac{\partial v}{\partial y} = 0 \tag{4}$$

$$u\frac{\partial u}{\partial x}+v\frac{\partial u}{\partial y}=\frac{\mu_0}{\rho}\left[\frac{\partial^2 u}{\partial y^2}+\frac{\beta B^2}{2}\left(\frac{\partial u}{\partial y}\right)^2\frac{\partial^2 u}{\partial y^2}\right]+\frac{\pi j_0 M_0}{8\rho}\exp\left(-\frac{\pi}{d}y\right) \quad (5)$$

$$u\frac{\partial T}{\partial x}+v\frac{\partial T}{\partial y}+\Phi_E\Omega_E=\frac{k}{\rho C_p}\left(\frac{\partial^2 T}{\partial y^2}\right)+\tau\left(D_B\frac{\partial C}{\partial y}\frac{\partial T}{\partial y}+\frac{D_T}{T_\infty}\left(\frac{\partial T}{\partial y}\right)^2\right)-\frac{1}{\rho C_p}\frac{\partial q_r}{\partial y}+\frac{Q_0}{\rho C_p}(T-T_\infty), \quad (6)$$

$$u\frac{\partial C}{\partial x}+v\frac{\partial C}{\partial y}+\Phi_C\Omega_C=D_B\frac{\partial^2 c}{\partial y^2}+\frac{D_T}{T_\infty}\left(\frac{\partial^2 T}{\partial y^2}\right)-K_0(C-C_\infty), \quad (7)$$

$$u\frac{\partial \chi}{\partial x}+v\frac{\partial \chi}{\partial y}+\frac{b\chi_c}{(C_w-C_\infty)}\frac{\partial}{\partial y}\left(\chi\frac{\partial C}{\partial y}\right)=D_m\frac{\partial^2 \chi}{\partial y^2}, \quad (8)$$

where u and v are velocity components in the x and y directions. v represents the kinematic viscosity of the fluid, ρ represents the density of the fluid, α represents the thermal diffusivity, C is the concentration, D_B and D_t represent Brownian diffusion and thermophoretic diffusion (respectively), C_p denotes volumetric expansion, D_m represents microorganism coefficient, and Ω_E and Ω_C are the fluid relaxation time.

In the above equations, the terms Ω_E and Ω_C are stated as

$$\Omega_E = u\frac{\partial u}{\partial x}\frac{\partial T}{\partial x}+v\frac{\partial u}{\partial y}\frac{\partial T}{\partial x}+u\frac{\partial v}{\partial x}\frac{\partial T}{\partial y}+v\frac{\partial v}{\partial y}\frac{\partial T}{\partial y}+u^2\frac{\partial^2 T}{\partial x^2}+2uv\frac{\partial^2 T}{\partial x \partial y}+v^2\frac{\partial^2 T}{\partial y^2} \quad (9)$$

$$\Omega_C = u\frac{\partial u}{\partial x}\frac{\partial C}{\partial x}+v\frac{\partial u}{\partial y}\frac{\partial C}{\partial x}+u\frac{\partial v}{\partial x}\frac{\partial C}{\partial y}+v\frac{\partial v}{\partial y}\frac{\partial C}{\partial y}+u^2\frac{\partial^2 C}{\partial x^2}+2uv\frac{\partial^2 C}{\partial x \partial y}+v^2\frac{\partial^2 C}{\partial y^2} \quad (10)$$

The relevant boundary conditions are assumed to be:

$$\left.\begin{array}{l}u=u_w(x),\ v=0,\ -k\frac{\partial T}{\partial y}=h(T_w-T_\infty),\ C=C_w,\ \chi=\chi_w\ \text{as}\ y=0,\\ u\to 0,\ T\to T_\infty,\ C\to C_\infty,\ \chi\to\chi_\infty\ \text{at}\ y\to\infty.\end{array}\right\} \quad (11)$$

$$q_r=\frac{4\sigma_1}{3k^*}\frac{\partial T^4}{\partial y}=-\frac{16\sigma^*}{3k^*}T^3\frac{\partial T^4}{\partial y}, \quad (12)$$

where T^4 can be expanded as follows:

$$T^4 \cong 4T^3_\infty T-3T^4_\infty. \quad (13)$$

Replacing Equation (12) into Equation (13),

$$q_r=\frac{16\sigma * T^3_\infty}{3k^*}\frac{\partial T}{\partial y}. \quad (14)$$

Introducing the variables [14]

$$\left.\begin{array}{l}u=axf'(\eta),\ v=-\sqrt{av}f(\eta),\ \eta=y\sqrt{\frac{a}{v}},\\ \theta=\frac{T-T_\infty}{T_w-T_\infty},\ \phi=\frac{C-C_\infty}{C_w-C_\infty},\ W=\frac{\chi-\chi_\infty}{\chi_w-\chi_\infty},\end{array}\right\} \quad (15)$$

Using Equation (15), Equations (4)–(6) become

$$f''' + ff'' - f'^2 + \frac{1}{2}\beta\delta Re_\gamma f''^2 f''' + Ze^{-A\eta} = 0, \quad (16)$$

$$\theta''\left(1+\frac{4}{3}Rd\right)+PrNt\,\theta'^2+PrNb\,\theta'\phi'-Pr\lambda_1\left(ff'\theta'+f^2\theta''\right)+Pr\Upsilon\theta=0 \quad (17)$$

$$\phi''+Scf\phi'+\left(\frac{Nt}{Nb}\right)\theta''-PrSc\lambda_2\left(ff'\phi'+f^2\phi''\right)-ScCr\phi=0, \quad (18)$$

$$W'''-Pe[\phi''(W+\omega)+\phi'W']-Lbf W'=0, \quad (19)$$

The corresponding boundary conditions are

$$f(0) = 0, f'(0) = 1, \theta'(0) = Bi(\theta(0)) - Bi, \phi(0) = 1 \\ f'(\infty) = 0, \theta(\infty) = 0, \phi(\infty) = 0, W(\infty) = 0. \quad \} \quad (20)$$

where $Z = \frac{\pi J_o M_o h}{8\rho U_o^2}$ is the modified Hartmann number; $Re_\gamma = \frac{ax^2}{v}$ is the Reynolds number; $\delta = \frac{B^2 a^2}{v}$ is the Deborah number; $Rd = \frac{4\sigma^* T_\infty^3}{kk^*}$ is the radiation parameter; $Pr = \frac{v}{a}$ is the Prandtl number; $Nb = \frac{\tau D_B(C_w - C_\infty)}{v}$ is the Brownian motion parameter; $Nt = \frac{\tau D_t(T_w - T_\infty)}{T_\infty v}$ is the thermophoresis parameter; $Sc = \frac{v}{D_B}$ is the Schmidt number; $Bi = \frac{h_f}{k}\sqrt{\frac{v}{a}}$ is the Biot number; $Pe = \frac{bW_c}{D_m}$ is the Peclet number; $Lb = \frac{v}{D_m}$ is the bioconvection Lewis number; and $Cr = \frac{K_o}{c}$ is the chemical reaction.

The thermofluidic quantities of engineering interest in this study are skin friction, Cf_x, heat transfer rate, Nu_x, mass transfer rate, Sh_x, and motile density, Wh_x.

$$Cf_x = \frac{\tau_w}{\rho u_w^2}, Nu_x = \frac{xq_w}{k(T_w - T_\infty)}, Sh_x = \frac{xq_m}{D_b(C_w - C_\infty)} \text{ and } Wh_x = \frac{xq_n}{D_m(X_w - X_\infty)} \quad (21)$$

where τ_w is the surface shear stress, q_w is the surface heat flux, q_m is the surface mass flux and q_n is the motile density, which are presented by the following expressions:

$$\tau_w = -\mu_0 \left[\frac{\partial u}{\partial y} + \frac{1}{6}\beta\delta Re_\gamma \left(\frac{\partial u}{\partial y}\right)^3\right]_{y=0}, q_w = -k\left(\frac{\partial T}{\partial y}\right)\Big|_{y=0}, \\ q_m = -k\left(\frac{\partial C}{\partial y}\right)\Big|_{y=0} \text{ and } q_n = -D_m\left(\frac{\partial \chi}{\partial y}\right)\Big|_{y=0}. \quad \} \quad (22)$$

The dimensionless form of the above parameters is expressed as

$$Cf_x Re_x^{0.5} = \left[f''(0) + \frac{1}{6}\beta\delta Re_\gamma (f''(0))^3\right], \frac{Nu_x}{Re_x^{1/2}} = -\left[1 + \frac{4}{3}Rd\right]\theta'(0), \\ \frac{Sh_x}{Re_x^{1/2}} = -\phi'(0) \text{ and } \frac{Wh_x}{Re_x^{1/2}} = -W'(0). \quad \} \quad (23)$$

where $Re_x = \frac{xU_w}{v}$ is the local Reynolds number.

3. Entropy Generation Analysis

The entropy generation with a Sutterby nanofluid is communicated as [37]:

$$S'''_{gen} = \frac{k}{T_o}\left(\left[\frac{\partial T}{\partial x}\right]^2 + \left[\frac{\partial T}{\partial y}\right]^2 + \frac{16\sigma^* T_\infty^3}{3kk^*}\left(\frac{\partial T}{\partial y}\right)^2\right) + \frac{\mu}{T_\infty}\left(\frac{\partial u}{\partial y}\right)^2\left[1 + \frac{\beta\delta Re_\gamma}{6}\left(\frac{\partial u}{\partial y}\right)^2\right] \\ + \frac{RD_m}{C_\infty}\left(\frac{\partial C}{\partial y}\right)^2 + \frac{RD_m}{T_\infty}\left(\frac{\partial T}{\partial y}\right)\left(\frac{\partial C}{\partial y}\right) + \frac{RD_m}{X_\infty}\left(\frac{\partial \chi}{\partial y}\right)^2 + \frac{RD_m}{T_\infty}\left(\frac{\partial \chi}{\partial y}\right)\left(\frac{\partial T}{\partial y}\right). \quad (24)$$

The significance of the entropy production can be written as

$$S'''_o = \frac{\kappa(\Delta T)^2}{L^2 T_\infty^2} \quad (25)$$

Using Equation (15), the rate of entropy Equation (24) can be converted as:

$$N_G = \frac{S'''_{gen}}{S'''_o} = Re_\gamma(1 + Rd)\theta'^2 + Re_\gamma \frac{Br}{\Pi}\left[1 + \frac{\beta\delta Re_\gamma}{3}(f'')^2\right] + Re_\gamma\left(\frac{\Gamma}{\Pi}\right)^2 \phi'^2 \\ + Re_\gamma\left(\frac{\Gamma}{\Pi}\right)\phi'\theta' + Re_\gamma\left(\frac{\xi}{\Pi}\right)^2 W'^2 + Re_\gamma\left(\frac{\xi}{\Pi}\right)W'\theta'. \quad (26)$$

The Bejan number Be is defined as the ratio over the entropy generation with heat transport, S_T, and the total entropy production, N_G, and it can be written as:

$$Be = \frac{S_T}{N_G}$$

$$Be = \frac{Re_\gamma(1+Rd)\theta'^2 + Re_\gamma\left(\frac{\Gamma}{\Pi}\right)^2\phi'^2 + Re_\gamma\left(\frac{\Gamma}{\Pi}\right)\phi'\theta' + Re_\gamma\left(\frac{\xi}{\Pi}\right)^2 W'^2 + Re_\gamma\left(\frac{\xi}{\Pi}\right)W'\theta'}{Re_\gamma(1+Rd)\theta'^2 + Re_\gamma\frac{Br}{\Pi}\left[1+\frac{\beta\delta Re_\gamma}{3}(f'')^2\right] + Re_\gamma\left(\frac{\Gamma}{\Pi}\right)^2\phi'^2}$$

$$+ Re_\gamma\left(\frac{\Gamma}{\Pi}\right)\phi'\theta' + Re_\gamma\left(\frac{\xi}{\Pi}\right)^2 W'^2 + Re_\gamma\left(\frac{\xi}{\Pi}\right)W'\theta' \tag{27}$$

4. Homotopy Expression

Nonlinearity issues are solved using a variety of numerical approaches. The HAM [45–52] technique, which is the most successful semi-analytically approach and applied to utilize these greatly nonlinear equations. These variables are used to calculate the approximation rate of this solution. The flow map of HAM process is given in Chart 1. Furthermore, the user can select the starting assumptions for the solutions. The higher order non-linear ODE Equations (16)–(20) are solved through this HAM technique.

$$f_\circ(\eta) = (1-e^{-\eta}), \theta_\circ(\eta) = \left[\frac{Bi}{1+Bi}\right]e^{-\eta}, \phi_\circ(\eta) = e^{-\eta}, W_\circ(\eta) = e^{-\eta}, \tag{28}$$

$$\hat{L}_f = f''' - f', \hat{L}_\theta = \theta'' - \theta, \hat{L}_\phi = \phi'' - \phi, \hat{L}_W = W'' - W, \tag{29}$$

with the property

$$\left.\begin{array}{l}\hat{L}_f(R_1 + R_2 e^{-\eta} + R_3 e^{-\eta}) = 0, \\ \hat{L}_\theta(R_4 + R_5 e^{-\eta}) = 0, \\ \hat{L}_\phi(R_6 + R_7 e^{-\eta}) = 0, \\ \hat{L}_W(R_8 + R_9 e^{-\eta}) = 0,\end{array}\right\} \tag{30}$$

in which $Bi(i = 1\text{–}9)$ are the constants.

Zeroth order formulation

$$\left.\begin{array}{l}(1-s)\hat{L}_f[f(\eta;s) - f_\circ(\eta)] = s\hbar_f N_f[f(\eta;s), \theta(\eta,s), \phi(\eta,s), W(\eta,s)], \\ (1-s)\hat{L}_\theta[\theta(\eta;s) - \theta_\circ(\eta)] = s\hbar_\theta N_\theta[f(\eta;s), \theta(\eta,s), \phi(\eta,s)], \\ (1-s)\hat{L}_\phi[\phi(\eta;s) - \phi_\circ(\eta)] = s\hbar_\phi N_\phi[f(\eta;s), \theta(\eta,s), \phi(\eta,s)], \\ (1-s)\hat{L}_W[W(\eta;s) - W_\circ(\eta)] = s\hbar_W N_W[f(\eta;s), \theta(\eta,s), \phi(\eta,s), W(\eta,s)].\end{array}\right\} \tag{31}$$

$$\left.\begin{array}{l}f(0,s) = 0, \ f'(0,s) = 1, \ f'(\infty,s) = 0, \\ \theta'(0,s) = Bi[\theta(0,s) - 1], \ \theta(\infty,s) = 0, \\ \phi(0,s) = 1, \ \phi(\infty,s) = 0, \\ W(0,s) = 0, \ W(\infty,s) = 0,\end{array}\right\} \tag{32}$$

where N_f, N_θ, N_ϕ and N_W are defined below:

$$N_f[f(\eta,s)] = \frac{\partial^3 f(\eta,s)}{\partial \eta^3} + f(\eta,s)\frac{\partial^2 f(\eta,s)}{\partial \eta^2} - \left[\frac{\partial f(\eta,s)}{\partial \eta}\right]^2$$
$$+ \frac{1}{2}\beta\delta Re_\gamma\left[\frac{\partial f(\eta,s)}{\partial \eta}\right]^2\left[\frac{\partial^3 f(\eta,s)}{\partial \eta^3}\right] + Ze^{-A\eta}, \tag{33}$$

$$N_\theta[f(\eta,s),\theta(\eta,s)] = \frac{\partial^2\theta(\eta,s)}{\partial\eta^2}\left(1+\frac{4}{3}Rd\right) + \text{Pr}Nt\left[\frac{\partial\theta(\eta,s)}{\partial\eta}\right]^2$$
$$+\text{Pr}Nb\left[\frac{\partial\theta(\eta,s)}{\partial\eta}\right]\left[\frac{\partial\phi(\eta,s)}{\partial\eta}\right] - \text{Pr}\lambda_1\left(\begin{array}{c}f(\eta,s)\left[\frac{\partial f(\eta,s)}{\partial\eta}\right]\left[\frac{\partial\theta(\eta,s)}{\partial\eta}\right]\\+[f(\eta,s)]^2\frac{\partial^2\theta(\eta,s)}{\partial\eta^2}\end{array}\right) \quad (34)$$
$$+\text{Pr}\Upsilon\theta(\eta,s),$$

$$N_\phi[f(\eta,s),\theta(\eta,s),\phi(\eta,s)] = \frac{\partial^2\phi(\eta,s)}{\partial\eta^2} + Scf(\eta,s)\left[\frac{\partial\phi(\eta,s)}{\partial\eta}\right]$$
$$+\left(\frac{Nt}{Nb}\right)\left[\frac{\partial^2\theta(\eta,s)}{\partial\eta^2}\right] - \text{Pr}Sc\lambda_2\left(\begin{array}{c}f(\eta,s)\frac{\partial f(\eta,s)}{\partial\eta}\frac{\partial\phi(\eta,s)}{\partial\eta}\\+f^2(\eta,s)\frac{\partial^2\phi(\eta,s)}{\partial\eta^2}\end{array}\right) - ScCr\phi(\eta,s), \quad (35)$$

$$N_W[f(\eta,s),\phi(\eta,s),W(\eta,s),] = \frac{\partial^2 W(\eta,s)}{\partial\eta^2} - Pe\left[\begin{array}{c}\frac{\partial^2\phi(\eta,s)}{\partial\eta^2}(W+\omega)\\+\frac{\partial\phi(\eta,s)}{\partial\eta}\frac{\partial W(\eta,s)}{\partial\eta}\end{array}\right] - Lbf(\eta,s)\frac{\partial W(\eta,s)}{\partial\eta}. \quad (36)$$

For $s=0$ and $s=1$, the results are achieved:

$$\left.\begin{array}{l}f(\eta;0)=f_0(\eta),\ \theta(\eta;0)=\theta_0(\eta),\ \phi(\eta;0)=\phi_0(\eta),\ W(\eta;0)=W_0(\eta)\\ f(\eta;1)=f(\eta),\ \theta(\eta;1)=\theta(\eta),\ \phi(\eta;1)=\phi(\eta),\ W(\eta;1)=W(\eta)\end{array}\right\} \quad (37)$$

m^{th} **order formulation**

The mth order deformation can be presented in the following forms:

$$\left.\begin{array}{l}\hat{L}_f[f_m(\eta,s)-\chi_m f_{m-1}(\eta)] = \hbar_f R_{f,m}(\eta),\\ \hat{L}_\theta[\theta_m(\eta,s)-\chi_m\theta_{m-1}(\eta)] = \hbar_\theta R_{\theta,m}(\eta),\\ \hat{L}_\phi[\phi_m(\eta,s)-\chi_m\phi_{m-1}(\eta)] = \hbar_\phi R_{\phi,m}(\eta),\\ \hat{L}_W[\theta_m(\eta,s)-\chi_m W_{m-1}(\eta)] = \hbar_W R_{W,m}(\eta).\end{array}\right\} \quad (38)$$

Boundary conditions are:

$$\left.\begin{array}{l}f'_m(0)=f_m(0)=f'_m(\infty)=\theta'_m(0)-Bi\theta_m(0)=\theta_m(\infty)=0,\\ \phi_m(0)=\phi_m(\infty)=W(0)=W(\infty)=0.\end{array}\right\} \quad (39)$$

where

$$R_{f,m}(\eta) = f'''_{m-1}(\eta) + \sum_{k=0}^{m-1} f_{m-1-k}f''_k - \sum_{k=0}^{m-1} f'_{m-1-k}f'_k + \frac{1}{2}\beta\delta Re_\gamma \sum_{k=0}^{m-1} f''_{m-1-k}f''_k f'''_k + Ze^{-A\eta} \quad (40)$$

$$R_{\theta,m}(\eta) = \theta''_{m-1}(\eta)\left(1+\frac{4}{3}Rd\right) + \text{Pr}Nt\sum_{k=0}^{m-1}\theta'_{m-1-k}\theta'_k + \text{Pr}Nb\sum_{k=0}^{m-1}\phi'_{m-1-k}\theta'_k$$
$$-\text{Pr}\lambda_1\left(\sum_{k=0}^{m-1}\left(\sum_{r=0}^k f_{m-1-k}f'_{k-r}\right)\theta'_k + \sum_{k=0}^{m-1}f'_{m-1-k}f'_k\theta'_k\right) + \text{Pr}\Upsilon\theta_{m-1} \quad (41)$$

$$R_{\phi,m}(\eta) = \phi''_{m-1}(\eta) + Sc\sum_{k=0}^{m-1}f'_{m-1-k}\phi_k + \left(\frac{Nt}{Nb}\right)\theta''_{m-1}$$
$$-\text{Pr}Sc\lambda_2\left(\sum_{k=0}^{m-1}\left(\sum_{r=0}^k f_{m-1-k}f'_{k-r}\right)\phi'_k + \sum_{k=0}^{m-1}f'_{m-1-k}f'_k\phi''_k\right) - ScCr\phi_{m-1} \quad (42)$$

$$R_{W,m}(\eta) = W''_{m-1}(\eta) - Pe\left(\sum_{k=0}^{m-1}\phi''_{m-1-k}W_k + \phi''_{m-1}\omega + \sum_{k=0}^{m-1}\phi'_{m-1-k}W'_k\right) - $$
$$Lb\sum_{k=0}^{m-1}W'_{m-1-k}f_k \quad (43)$$

$$\eta_m = \left\{\begin{array}{l}0, m\leq 1\\ 1, m>1\end{array}\right\}. \quad (44)$$

The general solutions are

$$\left.\begin{array}{l} f_m = f_m^* + R_1 + R_2 e^\eta + R_3 e^{-\eta} \\ \theta_m = \theta_m^* + R_4 e^\eta + R_5 e^{-\eta} \\ \phi_m = \phi_m^* + R_6 e^\eta + R_7 e^{-\eta} \\ W_m = W_m^* + R_8 e^\eta + R_9 e^{-\eta} \end{array}\right\} \quad (45)$$

where $f_m^*, \theta_m^*, \phi_m^*, W_m^*$ are the special solutions.

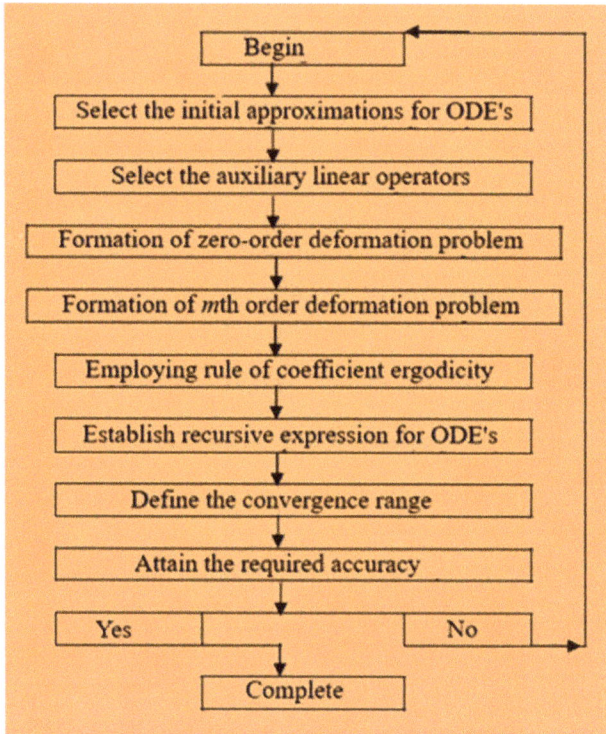

Chart 1. Flow chart of HAM expression.

Convergence of Homotopy Solutions

The parameters $\hbar_f, \hbar_\theta, \hbar_\phi$ and $\hbar_W$ are the converging control of the desired series solution. For the function $f''(0), \theta'(0), \phi'(0), W'(0)$ seek the permissible values to obtain the 25th and 30th order. Figures 1–4 specify that the range of $\hbar_f, \hbar_\theta, \hbar_\phi$ and $\hbar_W$ as $-2.0 < \hbar_f < -0.1, -2.0 < \hbar_\theta < -1.0, -1.7 < \hbar_\phi < -1.0$ and $-2.0 < \hbar_W < -1.0$. The series converges in the entire region of η when $\hbar_f = -0.65, \hbar_\theta = \hbar_\phi = -0.55$ and $\hbar_W = -0.7$. The order of approximation for HAM is denoted in Table 1.

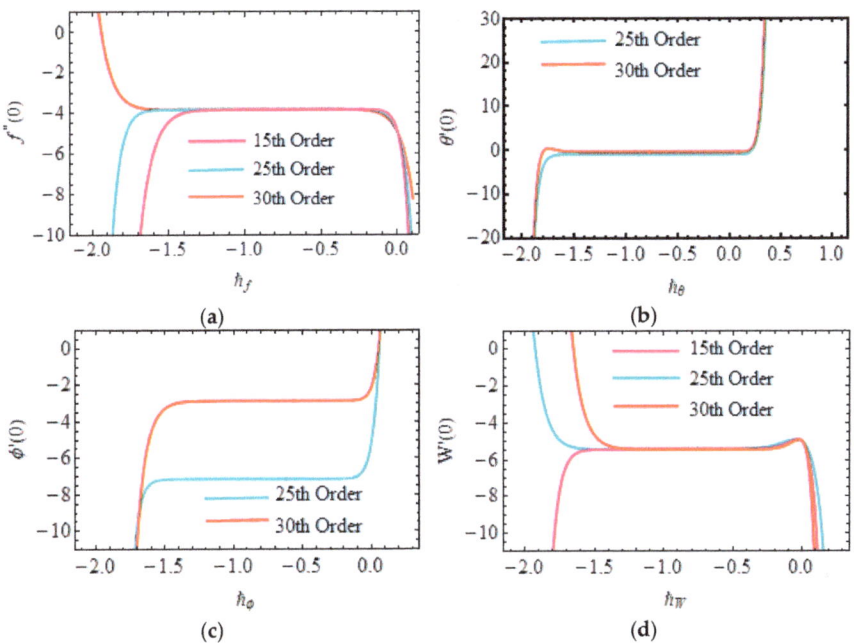

Figure 2. Plots of (**a**) $\hbar_f$—curve of $f''(0)$, (**b**) $\hbar_\theta$—curve of $\theta'(0)$, (**c**) $\hbar_\phi$—curve of $\phi'(0)$ and (**d**) $\hbar_w$—curve of $W'(0)$.

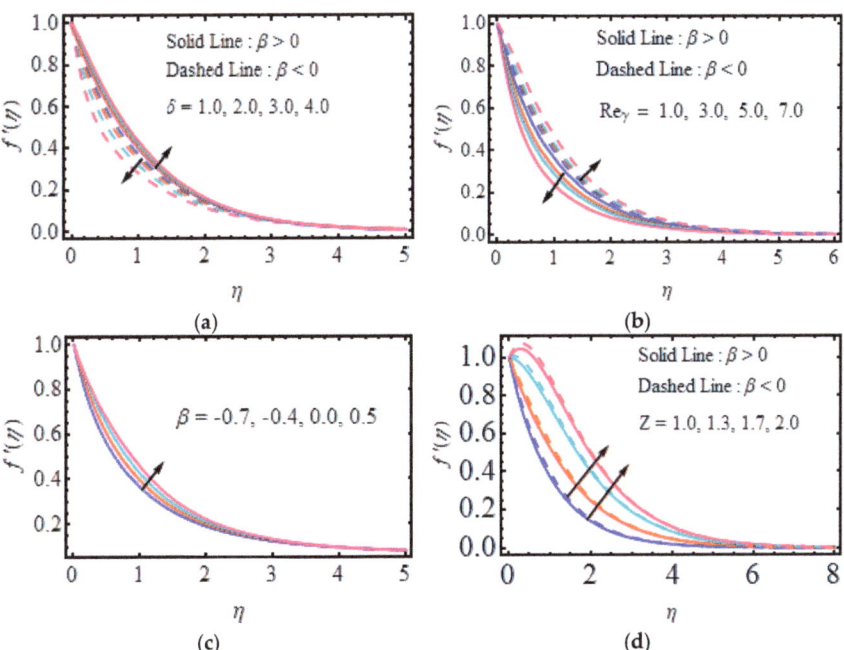

Figure 3. (**a**–**d**). The impact of the numerous variables of $f'(\eta)$: (**a**) δ, (**b**) Re_γ, (**c**) β and (**d**) Z.

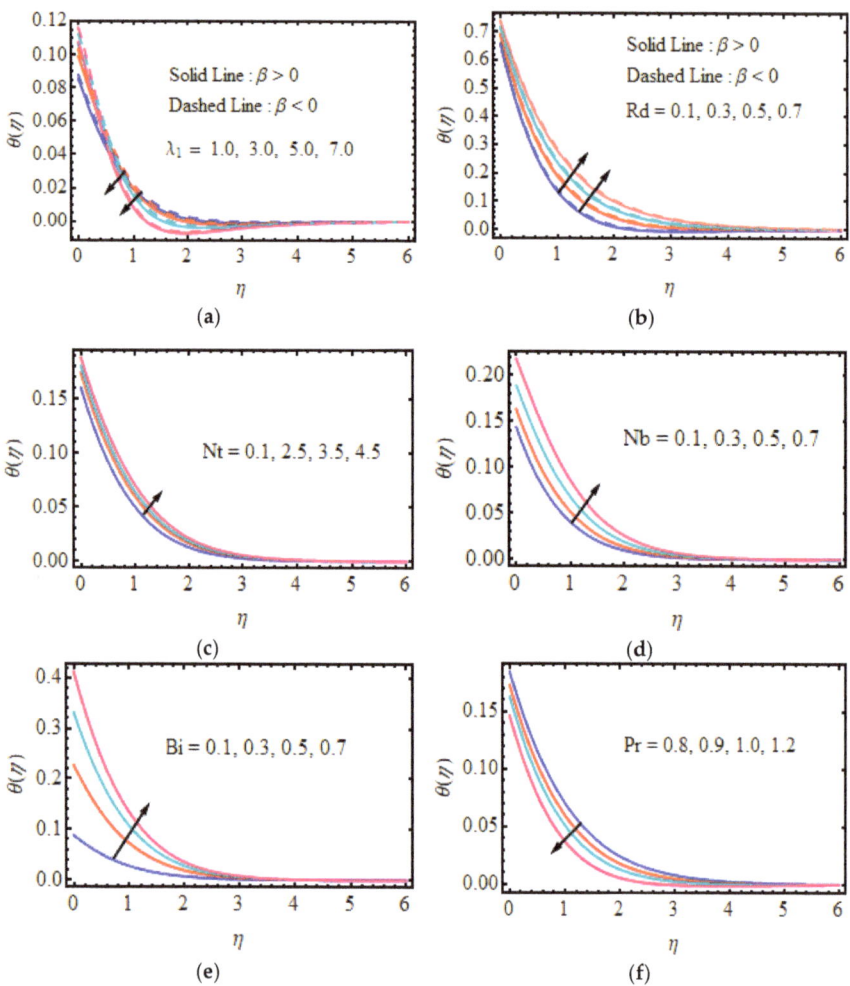

Figure 4. (**a**–**f**). The impact of the numerous variables of $\theta(\eta)$: (**a**) λ_1, (**b**) Rd, (**c**) Nt, (**d**) Nb, (**e**) Bi and (**f**) Pr.

Table 1. Convergence solution of HAM.

	Order of HAM			
Approximation	$-f''(0)$	$-\theta'(0)$	$-\phi'(0)$	$-W'(0)$
1	0.874702	0.166821	1.21667	0.955833
5	0.768677	0.167973	1.41759	1.038657
10	0.765186	0.168223	1.42596	1.07814
15	0.765357	0.168144	1.42606	1.08236
20	0.765347	0.168158	1.42609	1.08264
25	0.765341	0.168158	1.42608	1.08261
30	0.765341	0.168157	1.42608	1.08258
35	0.765341	0.168157	1.42608	1.08258
40	0.765341	0.168157	1.42608	1.08258

5. Results and Discussion

The system of Equations (16)–(19) subject to the boundary condition (20) was addressed through the homotopy analysis method (HAM). To discuss the performance of the physical significance against the velocity field $f'(\eta)$, temperature distribution $\theta(\eta)$, concentration field $\phi(\eta)$, motile microorganism profile $W(\eta)$, entropy production N_G, Bejan number Be, as well as skin friction, Nusselt number, Sherwood number and motile density microorganism were delineated, as seen in Figures 3–9. Table 2 verifies $-\theta(0)$ in accordance with Wang [52], Gorla and Sidawi [53], and Khan and Pop [54], with the limiting case $Nt = Nb = Rd = \lambda_1 = \Upsilon = 0$ and found a good agreement.

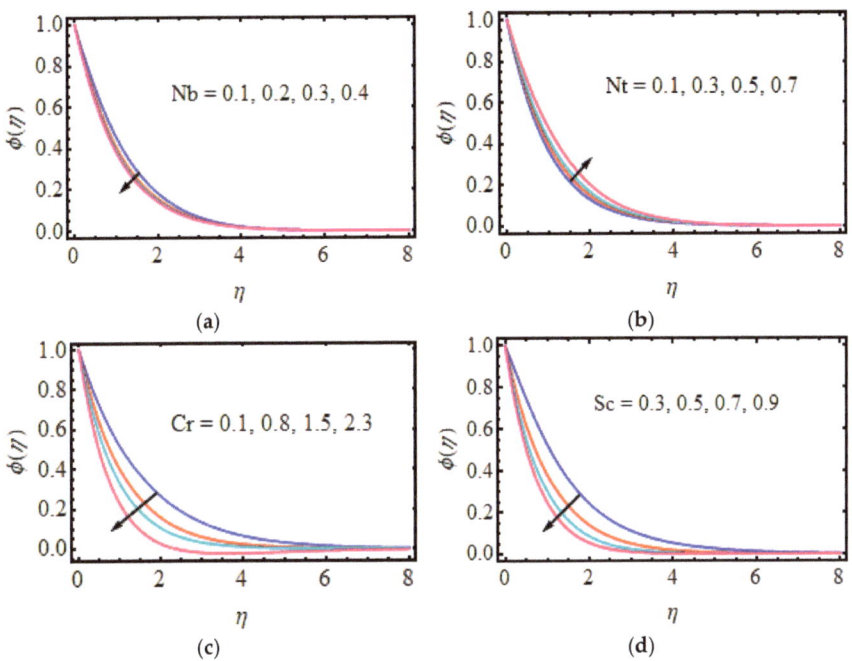

Figure 5. (a–d) The impact of the numerous variables of $\phi(\eta)$: (a), (b) Nt, (c) Cr and (d) Sc.

Table 2. Comparison of the obtained values of the Nusselt number $-\theta(0)$ with those of Wang [52], Gorla and Sidawi [53], and Khan and Pop 45 [54], when $Nt = Nb = Rd = \lambda_1 = \Upsilon = 0$.

Pr	Wang [52]	Gorla and Sidawi [53]	Khan and Pop [54]	Present
0.07	0.0663	0.0663	0.0663	0.0663
0.20	0.1691	0.1691	0.1691	0.1691
0.70	0.4539	0.4539	0.4539	0.4539
2.00	0.9113	0.9113	0.9113	0.9113

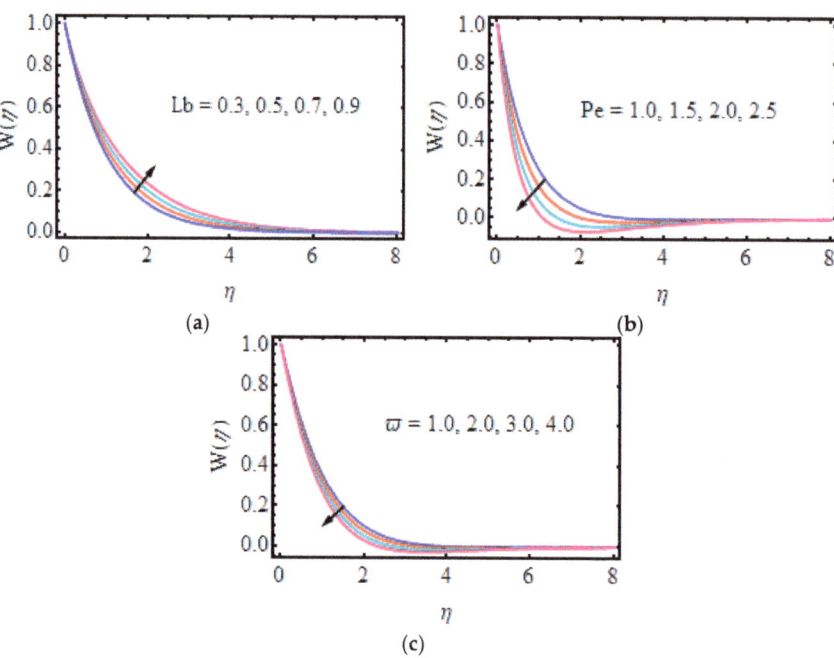

Figure 6. (a–c) The impact of the numerous variables of $\phi(\eta)$: (a) Nb, (b) Nb and (c) Cr.

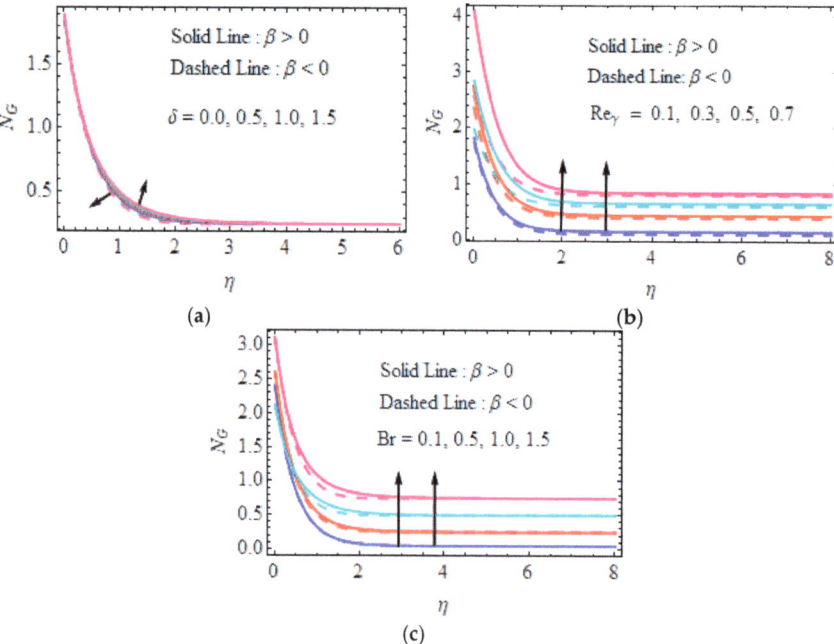

Figure 7. (a–c) The impact of the numerous variables of N_G: (a) δ, (b) Re_γ and (c) Br.

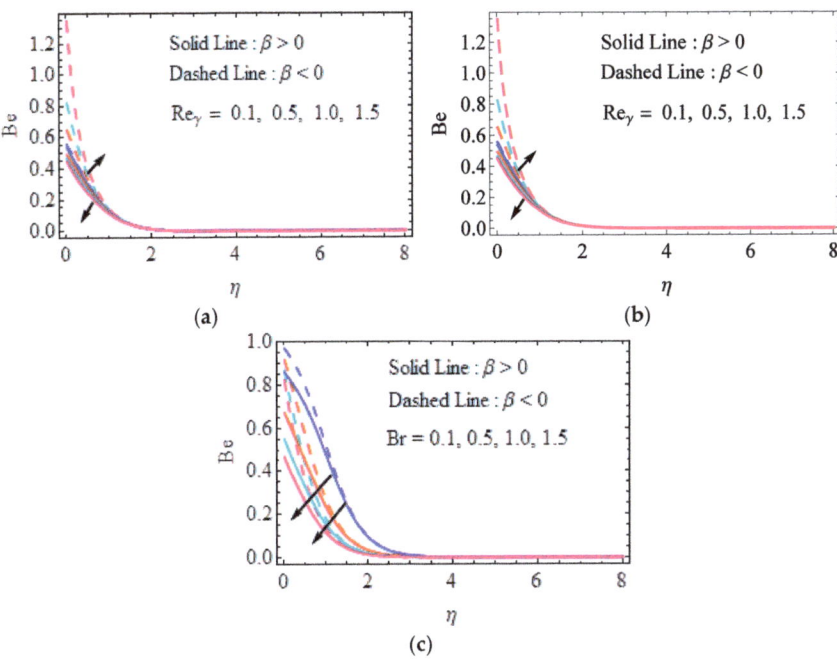

Figure 8. (a–c) The impact of the numerous variables of Be : (a) δ, (b) Re_γ and (c) Br.

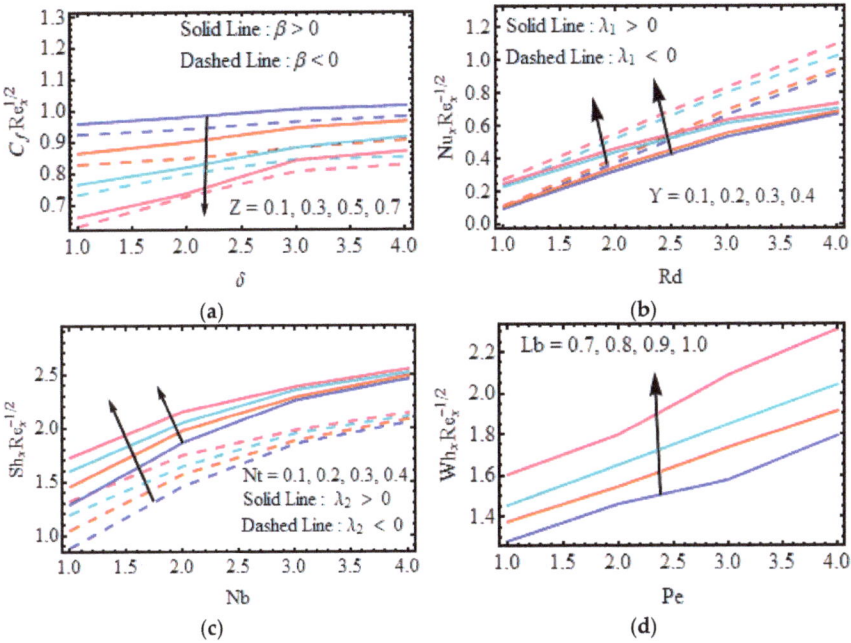

Figure 9. (a–d) Variation in the numerous variables of $Re_x^{1/2}Cf, Re_x^{-1/2}Nu, Re_x^{-1/2}Sh, Re_x^{-1/2}Wh_x$: (a) Z, δ, (b) Nb, Υ, (c) Nb, Nt and (d) Lb, Pe.

5.1. Velocity Profile

The effects of different numerous parameters over the velocity distribution $f'(\eta)$ are discussed in Figure 3a–d. Figure 3a shows that the velocity of the fluid diminishes with the superior values of Deborah number δ, for the case of $\beta < 0$, and the velocity field is enhanced for the rising value of Deborah number δ, for the case of $\beta > 0$. Figure 3b shows that the velocity field $f'(\eta)$ is reduced for higher Reynolds number Re_γ values, in the case of $\beta < 0$; a higher Re_γ tends to diminish the viscous force and the fluidity decreases for the pseudoplastic fluid. For shear thicking fluid, the velocity field enhances as Re_γ increases, for the $\beta < 0$ case. Figure 3c shows that the effect of the augmentation in the power law index parameter β causes that the velocity profile rises for shear thickening fluid. Figure 3d demonstrates the significance of the Hartmann number Z on the velocity field, for the two cases of $\beta < 0$ and $\beta > 0$. It was revealed that the strength of Z changes and the velocity of the fluid escalates in both cases. Physically, an increment in Z corresponds to enhancing the external electric field that constructs the wall-parallel Lorentz force. Therefore, $f'(\eta)$ increases.

5.2. Temperature Profile

Figure 4a–f plot the consequences of temperature $\theta(\eta)$ against different values of the involved parameters over the temperature field. The thermal relaxation time parameter impacts on $\theta(\eta)$ are demonstrated in Figure 4a. It can be noted that the thermal relaxation parameter tends to decrease the temperature profile for both the dilatants and pseudoplastic cases. Figure 4b reveals the inclination of $\theta(\eta)$ for specific values of the thermal radiation parameter, for $\beta > 0$ and $\beta < 0$. The temperature of the fluid increases due to the enlargement in the radiation parameter Rd in both cases. Figure 4c reports the variation of thermophoresis Nt over temperature. This is due to the nanoparticles move from the hotter surface to the colder surface. Figure 4d demonstrates the influence of the Brownian motion parameter Nb on the temperature profile. This is due to Brownian motion, which is the erratic movement of the particles suspended in the fluid. The random collision of particles suspended in the fluid increases the temperature of the fluid, which further contributes to the anticipated improvement in the temperature profile $\theta(\eta)$. Figure 4e depicts the impact of the Biot number $\theta(\eta)$. From the figure, it can be seen that the temperature field is boosted by enhancing the value of Bi. Actually, the Biot number Bi means the ratio of convection proportion of conducting the inner side of the boundary at the surface. Figure 4f displays variations of the Prandtl number against $\theta(\eta)$. The temperature is maintained in light of a higher Pr.

5.3. Nanoparticle Concentration Profile

The outcomes of the different leading parameters $\phi(\eta)$ are presented in Figure 5a–d. Figure 5a shows the characteristics of Nb on $\phi(\eta)$. The concentration distribution depletes with a rising Nb. Brownian motion's relationship with the Brownian diffusion coefficient, which causes the concentration field to decrease, is the cause of this phenomenon. The influence of the thermophoresis variable on $\phi(\eta)$ is rendered in Figure 5b. An augmentation in Nt leads to a reduction in concentration. One can notice, from that graph, the upsurge in Nt improves the mass transfer. The chemical reaction influences the profile of concentration, as seen in Figure 5c. The enhanced values Cr result in a fluid particle break near the surface, which reduces the concentration and the corresponding boundary layer thickness. The Schmidt number effect against the concentration profile is displayed in Figure 5d. Clearly, a depreciation in concentration is noted for the greater Sc, due to the reduction in mass diffusion.

5.4. Microorganism Profile

The effect of different influential variables on the microorganism's field is shown in Figure 6a–c. Variations in motile microorganisms against the biocovection Lewis number Lb for various values are seen in Figure 6a. Therefore, the greater values of Lb reduces the microorganism field. Actually, Lb has an opposite trend with thermal diffusivity as an escalation in Lb decreases the thermal diffusivity in regards to a decline in motile density. From Figure 6b, it can be seen that the higher Peclet number in the microorganism field produces a reduction in $W(\eta)$. It has a direct relation with cell swimming speed; therefore, the climbing Pe improves the cell speed of micro-best stumbling microorganism diffusivity. As a result, $W(\eta)$ declines with the rising values of Pe. Figure 6c examines the characteristics of $W(\eta)$, the opposite ω. It can be seen that the motile density shrinks for the larger ω. In fact, improving the values of ω escalates the concentration of microorganisms in ambient concentration. Finally, $W(\eta)$ declines.

5.5. Entropy Generation Profile

Figure 7a–c examine the performance of numerous variable parameters δ, Re_γ and Br entropy production N_G. Figure 7a sketched the effect of Deborah number δ over N_G. This shows the enhancement in entropy production close to the wall for dilatant $\beta > 0$ and deduction close to the wall for pseudoplastic fluid $\beta < 0$. Increasing the influence in the Reynolds number Re_γ entropy generation is studied for dilatant and pseudoplastic fluid fluids plots in Figure 7b. The disparity in N_G against Br is plotted in Figure 7c. Entropy generation increases with increasing value Br in both cases. Subsequently, Br attributes the proportion of free heat through viscous heating with the molecular condition. Therefore, heat is created in the system for increased values of Br as well as disorder increasing in the system, which explains the upsurges in the entropy of the system.

5.6. Bejan Number Profile

The performance Be is opposite to the variations in the variables δ, Re_γ and Br; the plots Be are shown in Figure 8a–c. Figure 8a,b show the behaviour of the physical parameters of the Deborah and Reynolds numbers on the Bejan number. It examined that the Bejan number declines with the larger values of Deborah and Reynolds numbers for shear thickening and increases for both numbers for the shear-thinning fluid. Furthermore, Figure 8c shows that the influence of the Bejan number Be reduces ($\beta > 0$, $\beta < 0$) with the growing values of Br.

5.7. Physical Entitles

Figure 9a reports that the skin friction coefficient $Re_x^{1/2} Cf_x$ is deformed in both cases for the larger values of the parameters Z and δ for $\beta < 0$ and $\beta > 0$. The influence of the non-Newtonian nanofluid parameter on the Nusselt number $Re_x^{-1/2} Nu$ against the thermal radiation Rd is highlighted in Figure 9b. The heat transport gradient increases when rising the Rd and Υ. The significance of Nt and Nb on the Sherwood number is shown in Figure 9c. It is determined that there is amplification in the Sherwood number $Re_x^{-1/2} Sh$ for raised values of fluid parameters. Figure 9d elucidates the substantial rescaled density number of motile microorganisms. The rescaled density number of motile microorganisms is voluminous for higher variations of Pe and Lb. Figure 10a–d shows the 3D representation of skin friction, Nusselt number, Sherwood number and motile density, respectively.

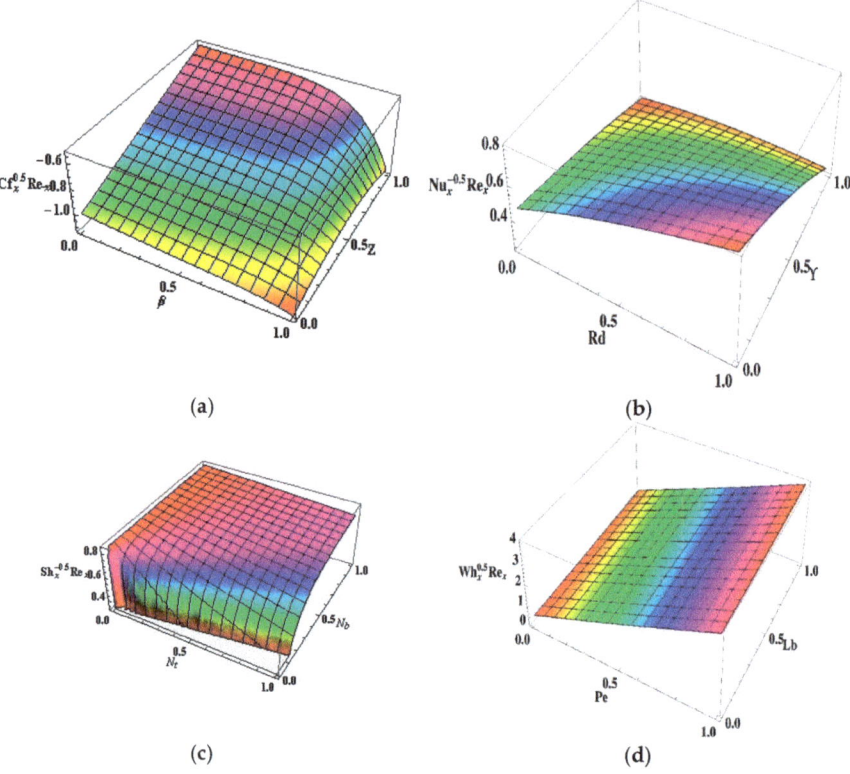

Figure 10. (**a**–**d**) Three-dimensional graphs; (**a**) Skin friction for β and Z; (**b**) Nusselt number for Rd and Υ; (**c**) Sherwood number for Nt and Nb; and (**d**) motile density for Pe and Lb.

5.8. Stream Line and Isotherm Line

Figure 11b shows the behaviour of the stream function for the current flow. The patterns depict that the streamlines are more obscured and split into two sections, pseudo-plastic $\beta < 0$ and dilatant $\beta > 0$; the shape is modest and fills the flow field. Figure 12a,b show the behaviour of the isotherm line for the present flow for both the cases.

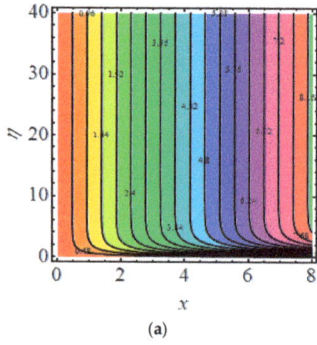

(**a**)

Figure 11. *Cont.*

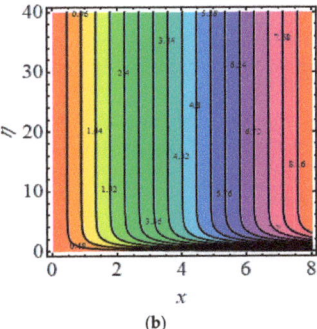

Figure 11. (a,b) Streamline for (a) $\beta = -2.5$ and (b) $\beta = 2.5$.

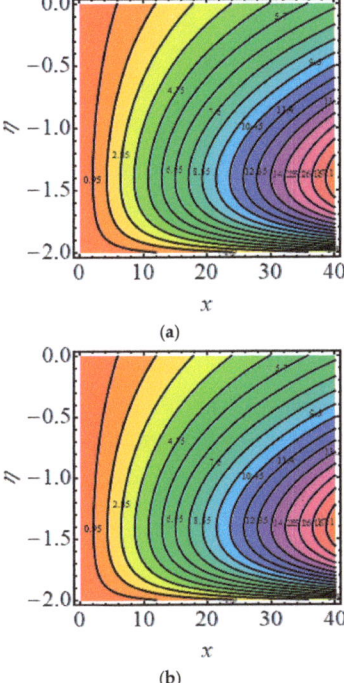

Figure 12. (a,b) Isotherm lines (a) $\beta = -2.5$ and (b) $\beta = -2.5$.

6. Major Outcomes

This investigation examined a Sutterby nanofluid with Cattaneo–Christov double diffusion theory over a Riga plate. Additionally, the bioconvection of the motile microorganisms and the chemical reaction was included. To obtain a non-linear system of ordinary differential problems, appropriate transformations were used. The non-linear systems were computed through the HAM technique. The main findings of the present study were as follows:

- The Deborah and Reynolds numbers produce the opposite behaviour in the flow field for the different cases of $\beta = -2.5$ and $\beta = 2.5$.
- The velocity shows the continuous improvement with increasing the Hartman number in both dilatant and pseudoplastic fluid cases.

- A larger chemical reaction reveals a decrement in the concentration, while the thermophoresis parameter Nt lead to the expansion in concentration.
- The microorganism field deteriorated for the higher values of Pe and microorganism difference parameter.
- The entropy generation number presented an increasing magnitude for large values of the Reynolds and Brinkman numbers, for the cases of pseudoplastic and dilatants fluid. Large values of entropy generation number appear in the area of the sheet due to the high viscous effects.
- Enhancing the value of the Deborah and Reynolds numbers results in the decrease in the Bejan profile in the case of the dilatant fluid, while the opposite effect is observed in the case of shear thinning.

Author Contributions: Conceptualization: M.F. and S.I.A.; Data curation: A.Z.; Formal analysis: M.F. and A.Z.; Investigation: F.A., K.L., A.Z. and S.I.A.; Methodology: K.L. and C.A.R.; Resources: M.F. and F.A.; Software: M.F. and K.L.; Supervision: S.I.A.; Validation: F.A. and S.I.A.; Visualization: C.A.R.; Writing—original draft: F.A., K.L. and M.F.; Writing—review and editing: C.A.R. and S.I.A. All authors have read and agreed to the published version of the manuscript.

Funding: This research received no external funding.

Data Availability Statement: Not applicable.

Acknowledgments: Sara I. Abdelsalam expresses her deep gratitude to Fundación Mujeres por África for supporting this work through the fellowship awarded to her in 2020.

Conflicts of Interest: The authors declare no conflict of interest.

Nomenclature

a	Stretching rate
f	Similarity function for velocity
T_∞	Ambient temperature
T	Fluid temperature
χ	Microorganism concentration
θ	Dimensionless temperature
C_∞	Ambient concentration
β	Power index number
δ	Deborah number
Re_γ	Local Reynolds number
Z	Modified Hartmann number
Rd	Thermal radiation
Υ	Heat source/sink parameter
Cr	Chemical reaction
λ_1	Thermal relaxation parameter
λ_2	Concentration relaxation parameter
Nt	Thermophoresis parameter
Nb	Brownian motion parameter
Bi	Biot number
Pr	Prandtl number
Sc	Schmidt number
Pe	Peclet number
Lb	Lewis number

ω	Microorganism concentration difference parameter
ρ	Fluid density
μ	Dynamic viscosity
∞	Ambient condition
C_f	Skin friction coefficient
Nu_x	Nusselt number
Sh_x	Sherwood number
Wh_x	Microorganism density number
τ	Ratio of the effective heat capacity
Br	Brinkman number
S_G	Local volumetric entropy generation rate
N_G	Entropy number
Be	Bejan number

References

1. Choi, S.U.; Eastman, J.A. Enhancing thermal conductivity of fluids with nanoparticles. in development and applications of non-Newtonian flow. *ASME* **1995**, *66*, 99–105.
2. Buongiorno, J. Convective transport in nanofluids. *J. Heat Transf.* **2006**, *128*, 240–250. [CrossRef]
3. Hussain, S.; Ahmad, S.; Mehmod, K.; Sagheer, M. Effects of inclination angle on mixed convetive nanofluid flow in a double lid-driven cavity with discrete heat sources. *Int. J. Heat Mass Transf.* **2017**, *106*, 847–860. [CrossRef]
4. Hussain, S.; Ahmed, S.E.; Saleem, F. Impact of periodic magnetic field on entropy generation and mixed convection. *J. Thermophys. Heat Transf.* **2018**, *32*, 999–1012. [CrossRef]
5. Haq, F.; Saleem, M.; Rahman, M.U. Investigation of natural bio-convective flow of cross nanofluid containing gyrotactic microorganisems subject to activation energy and magnetic field. *Phys. Scr.* **2020**, *95*, 105219. [CrossRef]
6. Prabakaran, R.; Eswaramoorthi, S.; Loganathan, K.; Sarris, I.E. Investigation on Thermally Radiative Mixed Convective Flow of Carbon Nanotubes/Al$_2$O$_3$ Nanofluid in Water Past a Stretching Plate with Joule Heating and Viscous Dissipation. *Micromachines* **2022**, *13*, 1424. [CrossRef]
7. Mjankwi, M.A.; Masanja, V.G.; Mureithi, E.W.; James, M.N. Unsteady MHD flow of nanofluid with variable properties over a stretching sheet in the presence of thermal radiation and chemical reaction. *Int. J. Math. Math. Sci.* **2019**, *2019*, 7392459.
8. Shahid, A. The effectiveness of mass transfer in the MHD upper-convected Maxwell fluid flow on a stretched porous sheet near stagnation point: A numerical invstigation. *Inventions* **2020**, *5*, 64. [CrossRef]
9. Rafique, K.; Alotaibi, H.; Ibrar, N.; Khan, I. Stratified flow of micropolar nanofluid over riga plate: Numerical analysis. *Energies* **2022**, *15*, 316.
10. Parvine, M.; Alam, M.M. Nanofluid flow along the riga plate with electromagnetic field in a rotating system. *AIP Conf. Proc.* **2019**, *2121*, 070003. [CrossRef]
11. Abbas, T.; Ayub, M.; Bhatti, M.M.; Rashidi, M.M.; Ali, M.E.S. Entropy generation on nanofluidflow through a horizontal riga plate. *Entropy* **2016**, *18*, 223. [CrossRef]
12. Sannad, M.; Hussein, A.K.; Abidi, A.; Homod, R.Z.; Biswal, U.; Ali, B.; Kolsi, L.; Younis, O. Numeical study of MHD natural convection inside a cubical cavity loaded with copper-water nanofluid by using a non-homogeneous dynamic mathematical model. *Mathematics* **2022**, *10*, 2072. [CrossRef]
13. Awan, A.U.; Ahammad, N.A.; Majeed, S.; Gamaoun, F.; Ali, B. Significance of hybrid nanoparticles, Lorentz and Coriolis forces on the dynamics of water-based flow. *Int. Commun. Heat Mass Transf.* **2022**, *135*, 106084. [CrossRef]
14. Elanchezhian, E.; Nirmalkumar, R.; Balamurugan, M.; Mohana, K.; Prabu, K.M.; Viloria, A. Heat and mass transmission of an Oldroyd-B nanofluid flow through a stratified medium with swimming of motile gyrotactic microorganisms and nanoparticles. *J. Therm. Anal. Calorim.* **2020**, *141*, 2613–2623. [CrossRef]
15. Loganathan, K.; Mohana, K.; Mohanraj, M.; Sakthivel, P.; Rajan, S. Impact of third-grade nanofluid flow across a convective surface in the presence of inclined Lorentz force: An approach to entropy optimization. *J. Therm. Anal. Calorim.* **2020**, *144*, 1935–1947. [CrossRef]
16. Ahmad, S.; Khan, M.I.; Hayat, T.; Khan, M.I.; Alsaedi, A. Entropy genertion optimization and unsteady squeezing flow of viscous fluid with five different shapes of nanoparticles. *Colloids Surf. A Physicochem. Eng. Asp.* **2018**, *554*, 197–210. [CrossRef]
17. Loganathan, K.; Rajan, S. An entropy approach of Williamson nanofluid flow with Joule heating and zero nanoparticle mass flux. *J. Therm. Anal. Calorim.* **2020**, *141*, 2599–2612. [CrossRef]
18. Waqas, H.; Farooq, U.; Muhammad, T.; Hussain, S.; Khan, I. Thermal effect on bioconvection flow of Sutterby fluid between two rotating diskswith motiole microorganisems. *Case Stud. Therm. Eng.* **2021**, *26*, 101136. [CrossRef]
19. Yahya, A.U.; Salamat, N.; Habib, D.; Ali, B.; Hussain, S.; Abdal, S. Implication of Bio-convection and Cattaneo-Christov heat flux on Williamson Sutterby nanofluid transportation caused by a stretching surface with convective boundary. *Chin. J. Phys.* **2021**, *73*, 706–718. [CrossRef]
20. Fayyadh, M.M.; Naganthran, K.; Basir, M.F.M.; Hashim, I.; Roslan, R. Raiative MHD Sutterby Nanofluid Flow Past a Moving Sheet: Scaling Group Analysis. *Mathemtics* **2020**, *8*, 1430.

21. Gowda, R.J.P.; Kumar, R.N.; Rauf, A.; Prasannakumara, B.C.; Shehzad, S.A. Magnetized flow of sutterby nanofluid through cattneo-christov theory of heat diffusion and stefan blowing condition. *Appl. Nanosci.* **2021**. [CrossRef]
22. Aldabesh, A.; Haredy, A.; Al-Khaled, K.; Khan, S.U.; Tlili, I. Darcy resistance flow of Sutterby nanofluid with microorganisms with applications of nano-biofuel cells. *Sci. Rep.* **2022**, *12*, 7514. [CrossRef] [PubMed]
23. Hayat, T.; Masood, F.; Qayyum, S.; Alsaedi, A. Sutterby fluid flow subject to homogeneous-heterogeneous reactions and nonlinear radiation. *Phys. A Stat. Mech. Appl.* **2019**, *2019*, 123439. [CrossRef]
24. Fujii, T.; Miyatake, O.; Fujii, M.; Tanaka, H.; Murakami, K. Natural convective heat transfer from a vertical isothermal surface to a non-Newtonian Sutterby fluid. *Int. J. Heat Mass Transf.* **1973**, *16*, 2177–2187.
25. Bilal, S.; Sohail, M.; Naz, R.; Malik, M.Y. Dynamical and optimal procedure to analyse the exhibition of physical attribute imparted by Sutterby magneto nano fluid in Darcy medium yield by axially stretched cylindr. *Can. J. Phys.* **2019**, *98*, 1–10. [CrossRef]
26. Khan, M.I.; Waqas, H.; Farooq, U.; Khan, S.U.; Chu, Y.M.; Kadry, S. Assessment of bioconvection in magentized Sutterby nanofluid configured by a rotating disk: A numerical approach. *Mod. Phys. Lett. B* **2021**, *35*, 2150202. [CrossRef]
27. Sohail, M.; Naz, R. Modified heat and mass transmission models in the magnetohydrodynamic flow of Sutterby fluid flow in stretching cylinder. *Phys. A Stat. Mech. Appl.* **2020**, *549*, 124088. [CrossRef]
28. Saif-ur-Rehman; Mir, N.A.; Alqarni, M.S.; Farooq, M.; Malik, M.Y. Analysis of heat generation/absorption in thermally stratified Sutterby fluid flow with Cattaneo-Christov theory. *Microsyst. Technol.* **2019**, *25*, 3365–3373. [CrossRef]
29. Usman; Lin, P.; Ghaffari, A. Heat and mass transfer in a steady flow of Sutterby nanofluid over the surface of a stretching wedge. *Phys. Scr.* **2021**, *96*, 065003. [CrossRef]
30. Ali, F.; Loganathan, K.; Prabu, E.; Eswaramoorthi, S.; Faizan, M.; Zaib, A.; Chaudhary, D.K. Entropy Minimization on Sutterby Nanofluid past a Stretching Surface with Swimming of Gyrotactic Microorganisms and Nanoparticles. *Math. Probl. Eng.* **2021**, 5759671. [CrossRef]
31. Khan, M.I.; Qayyum, S.; Hayat, T. Stratified flow of Sutterby fluid homogeneous-heterogeneous reaction and Cattaneo-Christov heat flux. *Int. J. Numer. Methods Heat Fluid Flow* **2019**, *29*, 2977–2992. [CrossRef]
32. Kuznestov, A.V.; Nield, D.A. Natural convective boundary layer flow of a nanofluid past a verticle plate. *Int. Therm. Sci.* **2010**, *49*, 243–247.
33. Kuznetsov, A.V. The onset of nanofluid bioconvection in a suspension containing both nanoparticles and gyrotactic microorganisems. *Int. Commun. Heat Mass Transf.* **2010**, *37*, 1421–1425. [CrossRef]
34. Kotha, G.; Kolipaula, V.R.; Rao, M.V.S.; Penki, S.; Chamkha, A.J. Internal heat generation on bioconvection of an MHD nanofluid flow due to gyrotactic microorganisms. *Eur. Phys. J. Plus* **2020**, *135*, 135–600. [CrossRef]
35. Siddiq, M.K.; Ashraf, M. Bioconvection of micropolar nanofluid with modified cattaneo-christov theories. *Adv. Mech. Eng.* **2020**, *12*, 1687814020925217. [CrossRef]
36. Bagh, A.; Sajjad, H.; Yufeng, N.; Liaqat, A.; Ul, H.S. Finite element simulation of bioconvection and cattaneo-Christov effects on micropolar based nanofluid flow over a vertically stretching sheet. *Chin. J. Phys.* **2020**, *68*, 654–670.
37. Azam, M.; Mahbood, F.; Khan, M. Bioconvection and activation energy dynamisms on radiative sutterby melting nanomaterial with gyrotactic microorganism. *Case Stud. Therm. Eng.* **2022**, *30*, 101749.
38. Khashi'ie, N.S.; Arifin, N.M.; Pop, I.; Nazar, R. Dual solutions of bioconvection hybrid nanofluid flow due to gyrotactic microorganisms towards a vertical plate. *Chin. J. Phys.* **2021**, *72*, 461–474. [CrossRef]
39. Azam, M. Bioconvection and nonlinear thermal extrusion in development of chemically reactive Sutterbynano-material due to gyrotactic microorganisms. *Int. Commun. Heat Mass Transf.* **2022**, *130*, 105820. [CrossRef]
40. Hayat, T.; Inayatullah, A.; Alsaedi, A. Development of bioconvection flow of nano-material with melting effects. *Chaos Solitons Fractals* **2021**, *148*, 111015. [CrossRef]
41. Reddy, C.S.; Ali, F.; Ahmed, M.F.A.F. Aspect on unsteady for MHD flow of cross nanofluid having gyrotactic motile microorganism due to convectively heated sheet. *Int. J. Ambient Energy* **2021**. [CrossRef]
42. Sarkar, S.; Kumar, T.; Ali, A.; Das, S. Themo-bioconvection of gyrotactic microorganisms in a polymer solution near a perforated Riga plate immersed in a DF medium involving heat radiation, and Arrhenius kinetics. *Chem. Phys. Lett.* **2022**, *797*, 139557. [CrossRef]
43. Ali, F.; Zaib, A. Unsteady flow of an Eyring-Powell nanofluid near stagnation point past a convectively heated stretching sheet. *Arab. J. Basic Appl. Sci.* **2019**, *26*, 215–224. [CrossRef]
44. Rana, S.; Nawaz, M. Investigation of enhancement of heat transfer in Sutterby nanofluid using Koo-Kleinstreuer and Li (KKL) correlations and Cattaneo-Christov heat flux model. *Phys. Scr.* **2019**, *94*, 115213. [CrossRef]
45. Mehmood, A.; Ali, A.; Shah, T. Heat transfer analysis of unsteady boundary layer flow by homotopy analysis method. *Commun. Nonlinear Sci. Numer. Simul.* **2008**, *13*, 902–912. [CrossRef]
46. Karthik, T.S.; Loganathan, K.; Shankar, A.N.; Carmichael, M.J.; Mohan, A.; Kaabar, M.K.; Kayikci, S. Zero and nonzero mass flux effects of bioconvective viscoelastic nanofluid over a 3D Riga surface with the swimming of gyrotactic microorganisms. *Adv. Math. Phys.* **2021**, *2021*, 9914134. [CrossRef]
47. Saeed, A.; Kumam, P.; Nasir, S.; Gul, T.; Kumam, W. Non-linear convective flow of the thin film nanofluid over an inclined stretching surface. *Sci. Rep.* **2021**, *11*, 18410. [CrossRef]

48. Loganathan, K.; Sivasankaran, S.; Bhuvaneswari, M.; Rajan, S. Second-order slip, cross-diffusion and chemical reaction effects on magneto-convection of Oldroyd-B liquid using Cattaneo-Christov heat flux with convective heating. *J. Therm. Anal. Calorim.* **2019**, *136*, 401–409. [CrossRef]
49. Eswaramoorthi, S.; Loganathan, K.; Jain, R.; Gyeltshen, S. Darcy-Forchheimer 3D Flow of Glycerin-Based Carbon Nanotubes on a Riga Plate with Nonlinear Thermal Radiation and Cattaneo-Christov Heat Flux. *J. Nanomater.* **2022**, *2022*, 5286921. [CrossRef]
50. Gul, T.; Rehman, M.; Anwar, S.; Khan, I.; Khan, A.; Nasir, S.; Bariq, A. Magnetohydrodynamic impact on Carreau thin film couple stress nanofluid flow over an unsteady stretching sheet. *Math. Probl. Eng.* **2021**, *2021*, 8003805. [CrossRef]
51. Loganathan, K.; Alessa, N.; Kayikci, S. Heat Transfer Analysis of 3-D Viscoelastic Nanofluid Flow Over a Convectively Heated Porous Riga Plate with Cattaneo-Christov Double Flux. *Front. Phys.* **2021**, *9*, 641645. [CrossRef]
52. Wang, C.Y. Free Convection on a Vertical Stretching Surface. *Z. Angew. Math. Mech.* **1989**, *69*, 418–420. [CrossRef]
53. Gorla, R.S.R.; Sidawi, I. Free convection on a vertical stretching surface with suction and blowing. *Appl. Sci. Res.* **1994**, *52*, 247–257. [CrossRef]
54. Khan, W.A.; Pop, I. Boundary-layer flow of a nanofluid past a stretching sheet. *Int. J. Heat Mass Transf.* **2010**, *53*, 2477–2483. [CrossRef]

Article

Lie Symmetry Classification and Qualitative Analysis for the Fourth-Order Schrödinger Equation

Andronikos Paliathanasis [1,2,*], **Genly Leon** [1,3] **and Peter G. L. Leach** [1]

[1] Institute of Systems Science, Durban University of Technology, P.O. Box 1334, Durban 4000, South Africa; genly.leon@ucn.cl (G.L.); leachp@ukzn.ac.za (P.G.L.L.)
[2] Instituto de Ciencias Físicas y Matemáticas, Universidad Austral de Chile, Valdivia 5090000, Chile
[3] Departamento de Matemáticas, Universidad Católica del Norte, Avda. Angamos 0610, Casilla 1280, Antofagasta 1240000, Chile
* Correspondence: anpaliat@phys.uoa.gr

Abstract: The Lie symmetry analysis for the study of a $1+n$ fourth-order Schrödinger equation inspired by the modification of the deformation algebra in the presence of a minimum length is applied. Specifically, we perform a detailed classification for the scalar field potential function where non-trivial Lie symmetries exist and simplify the Schrödinger equation. Then, a qualitative analysis allows for the reduced ordinary differential equation to be analysed to understand the asymptotic dynamics.

Keywords: Lie symmetries; invariants; fourth-order Schrödinger equation

MSC: 35B06; 35G20; 35C20

Citation: Paliathanasis, A.; Leon, G.; Leach, P.G.L. Lie Symmetry Classification and Qualitative Analysis for the Fourth-Order Schrödinger Equation. *Mathematics* **2022**, *10*, 3204. https://doi.org/10.3390/math10173204

Academic Editors: Maria Luminiţa Scutaru and Catalin I. Pruncu

Received: 8 August 2022
Accepted: 3 September 2022
Published: 5 September 2022

Publisher's Note: MDPI stays neutral with regard to jurisdictional claims in published maps and institutional affiliations.

Copyright: © 2022 by the authors. Licensee MDPI, Basel, Switzerland. This article is an open access article distributed under the terms and conditions of the Creative Commons Attribution (CC BY) license (https://creativecommons.org/licenses/by/4.0/).

1. Introduction

The Lie symmetry analysis is a systematic approach to the study of nonlinear differential equations [1,2]. The existence of a symmetry vector for a given differential equation indicates the existence of invariant functions, which are then used to simplify the differential equation and, when it is possible, determine exact or analytic solutions [3–13]. Moreover, symmetries can be used for the determination of conservation laws and also identify equivalent dynamical systems [14–17]. Finally, the Lie symmetry analysis covers a wide range of applications in all areas of applied mathematics. In this work, we are interested in the symmetry classification of a higher-order differential equation.

Consider the fourth-order partial differential equations, known as the Schrödinger equation

$$i\frac{\partial \Psi}{\partial t} + \alpha \Delta \Psi + \gamma \Delta^2 \Psi + V(\Psi) = 0, \qquad (1)$$

with $\gamma \neq 0$, Δ the Laplace operator $\Delta = \frac{1}{\sqrt{|g|}} \frac{\partial}{\partial x^\mu} \left(\sqrt{|g|} g^{\mu\nu} \right) \frac{\partial}{\partial x^\nu}$, $g_{\mu\nu}$ is the metric tensor, which describes the physical space. The fourth-order Schrödinger equation was introduced in [18,19] in order to investigate the effects of the presence of small fourth-order dispersion terms in the propagation of laser beams in a bulk medium with Kerr nonlinearity. For $V(\Psi) = |\Psi|^{2p}\Psi$, the stability of solitons was investigated by Karpman in [18]. It was found that when $g_{\mu\nu}$ is the Euclidian manifold, then for $p \dim(g) < 4$, the soliton solutions are stable. Since then, the fourth-order Schrödinger equation has been the subject of study in various articles in the literature (see, for instance, [20–27]). Indeed, the soliton instabilities of the equation for $V(\Psi) = |\Psi|^{2p}\Psi$ are related to nonlinear fibre optics and optical solutions in gyrotropic media [28]. Moreover, optical and other soliton solitons have been constructed with the use of Equation (1) to describe localised electromagnetic waves that spread in nonlinear dispersive media [29]. In [29], the Ricatti–Bernoulli sub-ODE method and the modified Tanh-Coth method are applied for the derivation of solitons for Equation (1) and $V(\Psi) = V_0\left(|\Psi|^{2p} + \varepsilon|\Psi|^{4p}\right)\Psi$. For more physical applications and the relation of the free parameters α, γ and p to physical phenomena, see reference [29]. Equation (1) has also been used for the description of bright and grey/dark soliton-like solutions in the context of Madelung's fluid [30]. The orbital stability of standing wave solution in the context of Hamiltonian systems was investigated in [31] by constructing a Lyapunov function. Finally, the Cauchy problem for an inhomogeneous equation constructed by (1) was studied in [32].

Last but not least, we recall that for $\gamma \to 0$, the usual Schrödinger equation of quantum mechanics is recovered.

However, Equation (1) also describes the modified Schrödinger equation for a particle in the context of the Generalised Uncertainty Principle (GUP). Indeed, GUP can be used for the construction and derivation of Equation (1).

GUP has its origin in the existence of a minimal length of the order of the Planck length (l_{PL}). The latter is a standard prediction of different quantum physics and gravity approaches, that is, from string theory, noncommutative geometry, and others [33–36]. Specifically, the minimal length in Heisenberg's Uncertainty Principle [37] is introduced. For a review on GUP, we refer the reader to [38].

In the simplest case of quadratic GUP, the modified Heisenberg's Uncertainty Principle reads

$$\Delta X_\mu \Delta P_\nu \geqslant \frac{\hbar}{2}[\delta_{ij}(1+\beta P^2) + 2\beta P_\mu P_\nu]. \tag{2}$$

Consequently, the deformed algebra follows [39,40],

$$[X_\mu, P_\nu] = i\hbar[\delta_{ij}(1-\beta P^2) - 2\beta P_\mu P_\nu], \tag{3}$$

where β is the parameter of deformation defined by $\beta = \beta_0/M_{Pl}^2 c^2 = \beta_0 \ell_{Pl}^2/2\hbar^2$, where M_{Pl} is the Planck mass, ℓ_{Pl} ($\approx 10^{-35}$ m) is the Planck length and $M_{Pl}c^2$ ($\approx 1.2 \times 10^{19}$ GeV) the Planck energy, such that $\beta^2 \to 0$. Thus, we can consider the coordinate representation of the modified momentum operator $P_\mu = p_\mu(1 - \beta p^2)$ [40], while keeping $X_\mu = x_\mu$ undeformed. Thus, the time-independent Schrödinger equation reads

$$\left(g^{\mu\nu} P_\mu P_\nu - (mc)^2\right)\Psi = 0. \tag{4}$$

That is,

$$-2\beta\hbar^2 \Delta^2 \Psi + \Delta \Psi + \left(\frac{mc}{\hbar}\right)^2 \Psi = 0, \tag{5}$$

assuming terms with $\beta^2 \to 0$. The fourth-order Equation (5) is the static version of (1) for $V(\Psi)$, which is a linear function. For some recent applications of GUP in physical theories, see [41–45] and references therein.

In the following, we perform a complete classification of function $V(\Psi)$ according to the admitted Lie point symmetries of Equation (1). Such a classification scheme was proposed in the previous century by Ovsiannikov, where the Lie point symmetries for the nonlinear equation $u_t = (f(u)u_x)_x$ were classified [46], leading to new interesting problems in applied mathematics and physics [47–52]. Apart from the analysis of symmetries, the concept of asymptotic solutions and boundary layers is essential in this context [53].

The plan of the paper is as follows. In Section 2, we present the basic properties and definitions for the theory of Lie symmetries of differential equations, and we introduce the concept of the boundary layer. In Section 3, we present our classification scheme for the Lie point symmetries of the fourth-order Schrödinger equation. We present some applications of the Lie point symmetries for the construction of similarity solutions in Section 4. Finally, in Section 5, we summarise our results.

2. Preliminaries

A differential equation may be considered as a function $H = H(x^i, u^A, u^A_{,i}, u^A_{,ij}, \ldots)$ in the space $B = B(x^i, u^A, u^A_{,i}, u^A_{,ij}, \ldots)$, where x^i are the independent variables, and u^A are the dependent variables. In our consideration for Equation (1) $x^i = (t, x^\mu)$ and $u^A(x^i) = \Phi(x^i)$.

2.1. Lie Symmetry Vector

Consider now the infinitesimal transformation

$$\bar{x}^i = x^i + \varepsilon \xi^i(x^k, u^B), \tag{6}$$

$$\bar{u}^A = \bar{u}^A + \varepsilon \eta^A(x^k, u^B), \tag{7}$$

with the generator of the vector field

$$\mathbf{X} = \xi^i(x^k, u^B)\partial_{x^i} + \eta^A(x^k, u^B)\partial_{u^A}. \tag{8}$$

The generator $\mathbf{X}$ of the infinitesimal transformation (6), (7) is a Lie point symmetry for the function H if there exists a function λ such that the following condition holds [1,2]

$$\mathbf{X}^{[N]}(H) = \lambda H, \quad \text{mod } H = 0, \tag{9}$$

where

$$\mathbf{X}^{[N]} = \mathbf{X} + \eta^A_{[i]}\partial_{u^A_i} + \eta^A_{[ij]}\partial_{u^A_{ij}} + \cdots + \eta^A_{[ij\ldots j_N]}\partial_{u^A_{ij\ldots j_N}} \tag{10}$$

is the nth prolongation vector

$$\eta^A_{[i]} = \eta^A_{,i} + u^B_{,i}\eta^A_{,B} - \xi^j_{,i}u^A_{,j} - u^A_{,j}u^B_{,i}\xi^j_{,B} \tag{11}$$

with

$$\eta^A_{[ij]} = \eta^A_{,ij} + 2\eta^A_{,B(i}u^B_{,j)} - \xi^k_{,ij}u^A_{,k} + \eta^A_{,BC}u^B_{,i}u^C_{,j} - 2\xi^k_{,(i|B|}u^B_{,j)}u^A_{,k}$$
$$- \xi^k_{,BC}u^B_{,i}u^C_{,j}u^A_{,k} + \eta^A_{,B}u^B_{,ij} - 2\xi^k_{,(j}u^A_{,i)k} - \xi^k_{,B}\left(u^A_{,k}u^B_{,ij} + 2u^B_{(,j}u^A_{,i)k}\right), \tag{12}$$

and in general

$$\eta^A_{[ij\ldots j_N]} = D_{j_n}\left(\eta^A_{ij\ldots j_{n-1}}\right) - u^A_{ij\ldots k}D_{j_N}\xi^k. \tag{13}$$

The existence of a Lie point symmetry in a given differential equation is essential for simplifying the differential equation through the similarity transformations. Indeed, from a specific Lie symmetry vector, one may define the following Lagrange system

$$\frac{dx^i}{\xi^i} = \frac{du^A}{\eta^A} = \frac{du^A_i}{\eta^A_{[i]}} = \frac{du^A_{ij}}{\eta^A_{[ij]}} = \cdots \tag{14}$$

whose solution provides the characteristic functions $W^{[0]}\left(x^k, u^A\right)$, $W^{[1]}\left(x^k, u^A, u^A_i\right)$, etc. These functions can be used to define the corresponding similarity transformation.

2.2. The Concept of a Boundary Layer

In the following, we briefly discuss the concept of boundary layers to investigate the asymptotic behaviour of nonlinear differential equations, following the notation presented in [53].

Assume the function $\psi_\varepsilon(\tau)$ is defined on a domain $D \subset \mathbb{R}^n$ where ε is a small parameter. Consider now that there exists a connected subset $S \subset D$ with dimensions less or equal to n, such that $\psi_\varepsilon(\tau)$ has no regular expansion in each subset $E \subset D$ with $E \cap S \neq \emptyset$. Then, a neighbourhood of S in D, with a size to be determined, is a boundary layer of the function

$\psi_\varepsilon(\tau)$ [53]. Suppose $n = 1$ and let $\tau_0 \in S$, and suppose that near τ_0 the boundary layer is characterised in size by the order function $\delta(\varepsilon)$. For the analysis of the behaviour of ψ_ε near the boundary layer, we consider the map $\psi_\varepsilon(\tau) = \psi_\varepsilon(\tau_0 + \delta(\varepsilon)\xi) = \phi^*_\varepsilon(\xi)$, where $\xi = \frac{\tau-\tau_0}{\delta(\varepsilon)}$. When $\delta(\varepsilon) = O(1)$, parameter ξ is called a local variable. Hence, the concept is based on the construction of the approximation of function $\phi^*_\varepsilon(\xi)$ as $\phi^*_\varepsilon(\xi) = \sum_n \delta^*_n(\varepsilon)\psi_n(\xi)$ with $\delta^*_n(\varepsilon)$, $n = 0, 1, 2, \ldots$ an asymptotic sequence.

For more details on the method and various applications, we refer the reader to [53].

3. Symmetry Classification for the Fourth-Order Schrödinger Equation

Before we proceed with the symmetry classification, we set without loss of generality $\gamma = 1$, and by a change in transformation on the variable t, we can remove the coefficient i. Hence, Equation (1) can be written in the equivalent form

$$\frac{\partial \Psi}{\partial t} + \alpha \Delta \Psi + \Delta^2 \Psi + V(\Psi) = 0. \tag{15}$$

Moreover, with the use of the new variable $\Phi = \Delta \Psi$, the fourth-order differential Equation (15) is written as the following Schrödinger–Poisson system

$$\frac{\partial \Psi}{\partial t} + \Delta \Phi + \alpha \Phi + V(\Psi) = 0, \tag{16}$$

$$\Phi - \Delta \Psi = 0. \tag{17}$$

Assume now the generic vector field

$$X = \xi^t(t, x^\mu, \Psi, \Phi)\partial_t + \xi^\mu(t, x^\mu, \Psi, \Phi)\partial_\mu + \eta^\Psi(t, x^\mu, \Psi, \Phi)\partial_\Psi + \eta^\Phi(t, x^\mu, \Psi, \Phi)\partial_\Phi, \tag{18}$$

where in order to be the generator of a one-parameter point transformation in the space of variables $\{x^\mu, \Psi\}$, it should be $\xi^t_{,\Phi} = 0$, $\xi^\mu_{,\Phi} = 0$ and $\eta^\Psi_{,\Phi} = 0$.

The 2nd prolongation vector reads

$$X^{[2]} = X + \eta^\Psi_{[t]}\partial_{\Psi_t} + \eta^\Psi_{[\mu]}\partial_{\Psi_\mu} + \eta^\Phi_{[t]}\partial_{\Phi_t} + \eta^\Phi_{[\mu]}\partial_{\Phi_\mu} + \eta^\Psi_{[\mu\nu]}\partial_{\Psi_{\mu\nu}} + \eta^\Phi_{[\mu\nu]}\partial_{\Phi_{\mu\nu}}. \tag{19}$$

Consequently, we apply the symmetry condition (9), and by using the geometric approach described in [54], we summarise the classification scheme in the following theorem.

Theorem 1. *The generic Lie point symmetry vector for the Schrödinger–Poisson system (16), (17) in an arbitrary background space $g_{\mu\nu}$, and for arbitrary function $V(\Psi)$ is*

$$X_G = a_1 \partial_t + a_\sigma \mathbf{K}(x^\kappa)\partial_\mu, \tag{20}$$

where $\mathbf{K}(x^\mu)$ is an isometry for the metric tensor $g_{\mu\nu}$, that is $[\mathbf{K}(x^\kappa), g_{\mu\nu}(x^\kappa)] = 0$.

However, for specific functional forms of the potential $V(\Psi)$, the classification scheme is described as follows.

Theorem 2. *Let the metric tensor $g_{\mu\nu}(x^\kappa)$ and $\mathbf{K}(x^\kappa)$ describe the isometries of $g_{\mu\nu}(x^\kappa)$, and $\mathbf{H}(x^\kappa)$ is a proper Homothetic vector of $g_{\mu\nu}(x^\kappa)$, i.e., $[\mathbf{H}(x^\kappa), g_{\mu\nu}(x^\kappa)] = 2g_{\mu\nu}(x^\kappa)$. Then, for special functional forms of $V(\Psi)$, the generic symmetry vector for the Schrödinger–Poisson system (16), (17) is:*

For $\alpha \neq 0$,

I: For $V(\Psi) = V_0 \Psi$, the symmetry vector is $X^I_G = a_1 \partial_t + a_\sigma \mathbf{K}(x^\kappa)\partial_\mu + a_2(\Psi \partial_\Psi + \Phi \partial_\Phi) + a_3(F(t, x^\kappa)\partial_U + F_{,\mu\nu}(t, x^\kappa)\partial_\Phi)$, where $F(t, x^\kappa)$ is a solution of the original system. The new coefficients in the vector field indicate the linearisation of the system.

For $\alpha = 0$,

II: For $V(\Psi) = 0$, the generic symmetry vector is $X_G^{II} = a_1\partial_t + a_\sigma \mathbf{K}(x^\kappa)\partial_\mu + a_2(\Psi\partial_\Psi + \Phi\partial_\Phi) + a_3\big(F(t,x^\kappa)\partial_U + F_{,\mu\nu}(t,x^\kappa)\partial_\Phi\big) + a_4\big(4t\partial_t + \mathbf{H}(x^\kappa)\partial_\mu - 2\Phi\partial_\Phi\big)$.

III: For $V(\Psi) = V_0\Psi$, the generic symmetry vector is $X_G^{III} = a_1\partial_t + a_\sigma \mathbf{K}(x^\kappa)\partial_\mu + a_2(\Psi\partial_\Psi + \Phi\partial_\Phi) + a_3\big(F(t,x^\kappa)\partial_U + F_{,\mu\nu}(t,x^\kappa)\partial_\Phi\big) + a_4\big(4t\partial_t + \mathbf{H}(x^\kappa)\partial_\mu - 2\Phi\partial_\Phi - 4V_0 t(\Psi\partial_\Psi + \Phi\partial_\Phi)\big)$.

IV: For $V(\Psi) = V_0\Psi^{P+1}$, $P \neq -1, 0$, the generic symmetry vector is $X_G^{IV} = a_1\partial_t + a_\sigma \mathbf{K}(x^\kappa)\partial_\mu + a_4\big(4t\partial_t + \mathbf{H}(x^\kappa)\partial_\mu - 2\Phi\partial_\Phi - \frac{4}{P}(\Psi\partial_\Psi + \Phi\partial_\Phi)\big)$.

V: For $V(\Psi) = V_0\exp(P\Psi)$, $P \neq 0$, the generic symmetry vector is $X_G^{IV} = a_1\partial_t + a_\sigma \mathbf{K}(x^\kappa)\partial_\mu + a_4\big(4t\partial_t + \mathbf{H}(x^\kappa)\partial_\mu - 2\Phi\partial_\Phi - \frac{4}{P}(\partial_\Psi)\big)$.

It is easy to observe that the collineations of the underlying geometry generate the symmetries for the dynamical system of our study. Indeed, the isometries and the homothetic vectors construct the Lie symmetries. If a background geometry has no isometries and homothetic vector, then the admitted Lie symmetries for the dynamical system are the trivial symmetries. That connection of the Lie symmetries with the elements of the background geometry has been observed before for various differential equations [55,56]. Indeed, for the second-order Schrödinger equation, the Lie symmetries are constructed by the elements of the homothetic algebra of the geometry [56]. Thus, a similar physical interpretation can be given. The Lie symmetries generated by the isometries are related to the construction of differential operators generated by the conservation law of momentum for the classical particle. In contrast, the Lie symmetry constructed by the homothetic vector field is related to the derivation of scaling solutions. For more details, we refer the reader to [56].

We proceed with our analysis by considering specific metric tensor $g_{\mu\nu}$.

4. Application

Consider now that the metric tensor $g_{\mu\nu}$ is maximally symmetric and admit a homothetic vector field. Hence, $g_{\mu\nu}$ is necessary for the flat space. For simplicity of our calculations, assume further that $\dim g_{\mu\nu} = 1$. The one-dimensional flat space with line element $ds^2 = dx^2$ admits the isometry ∂_x and the proper Homothetic field $x\partial_x$.

Therefore the Schrödinger–Poisson system reads

$$\frac{\partial\Psi}{\partial t} + \frac{\partial^2\Phi}{\partial x^2} + \alpha\Phi + V(\Psi) = 0, \tag{21}$$

$$\Phi - \frac{\partial^2\Psi}{\partial x^2} = 0. \tag{22}$$

In the case where $\alpha \neq 0$, the generic vector field is $X^I = a_1\partial_t + a_2\partial_x$, for arbitrary potential function $V(\Psi)$. From the elements of X^I, we can reduce the dynamical system into the static and the stationary cases. However, from the vector field $\partial_t + c\partial_x$ we reduce the dynamical system as follows

$$-c\frac{\partial\Psi}{\partial\xi} + \frac{\partial^2\Phi}{\partial\xi^2} + \alpha\Phi + V(\Psi) = 0, \tag{23}$$

$$\Phi - \frac{\partial^2\Psi}{\partial\xi^2} = 0, \tag{24}$$

where $\xi = x - ct$ is the new independent variable, and c describes the speed of the travelling wave. For a linear function $V(\Psi)$, the closed-form solution of the system (23), (24) can be expressed in terms of exponential functions.

However, for $V(\Psi) = V_0\Psi$, there exist the additional possible reduction $\partial_t + c\partial_x + \beta(\Psi\partial_\Psi + \Phi\partial_\Phi)$, which provides the similarity transformation $\Psi = e^{\beta t}\psi(\xi)$, $\Phi = e^{\beta t}\phi(\xi)$, $\xi = x - ct$ with a reduced system

$$-c\frac{\partial \psi}{\partial \xi} + \frac{\partial^2 \phi}{\partial \xi^2} + \alpha\phi + \beta\psi + V_0\psi = 0, \quad (25)$$

$$\phi - \frac{\partial^2 \psi}{\partial \xi^2} = 0. \quad (26)$$

Let us focus now on the case where $\alpha = 0$ and assume $V(\Psi) = V_0\Psi^{P+1}$ and $V(\Psi) = V_0\exp(P\Psi)$.

4.1. Power-Law Function $V(\Psi) = V_0\Psi^{P+1}$, $P \neq 0$

For the power-law potential function, from the vector field $\left(4t\partial_t + x\partial_x - 2\Phi\partial_\Phi - \frac{4}{P}(\Psi\partial_\Psi + \Phi\partial_\Phi)\right)$, we define the similarity transformation

$$\Psi(t,x) = \psi(\sigma)t^{-\frac{1}{P}}, \quad \Phi(t,x) = \phi(\sigma)t^{-\frac{2+P}{2P}}, \quad \sigma(t,x) = \frac{x}{t^{\frac{1}{4}}},$$

and if $P \neq 0$, with reduced system

$$\frac{\partial^2 \phi}{\partial \sigma^2} + V_0\psi^{P+1} - \frac{1}{4}\sigma\frac{\partial \psi}{\partial \sigma} - \frac{1}{P}\psi = 0, \quad (27)$$

$$\phi - \frac{\partial^2 \psi}{\partial \sigma^2} = 0. \quad (28)$$

If $\phi = 0$, we have

$$\psi = \psi_1\sigma + \psi_0. \quad (29)$$

Then, from compatibility conditions, the only possible solution is the constant solution $\psi = \psi_0$, such that

$$V_0\psi_0^{P+1} - \frac{\psi_0}{P} = 0 \implies \psi_0 = (PV_0)^{-1/P}. \quad (30)$$

Therefore, we assume the non-trivial case $\phi \neq 0$. Then, we have the fourth-order equation

$$\frac{\partial^4 \psi}{\partial \sigma^4} + V_0\psi^{P+1} - \frac{1}{4}\sigma\frac{\partial \psi}{\partial \sigma} - \frac{1}{P}\psi = 0. \quad (31)$$

We introduce the logarithmic independent variable

$$\tau = \ln(\sigma), \quad (32)$$

and redefine

$$\psi(\sigma) = \bar{\psi}(\ln(\sigma)). \quad (33)$$

That is, for any function $f(\sigma)$, define

$$\bar{f}(\tau) = f(e^\tau). \quad (34)$$

Then, using the chain rule and the relation $\sigma = e^\tau$, we obtain

$$\frac{\partial f}{\partial \sigma} = e^{-\tau} \tilde{f}'(\tau), \tag{35}$$

$$\frac{\partial^2 f}{\partial \sigma^2} = e^{-2\tau} \left(\tilde{f}''(\tau) - \tilde{f}'(\tau) \right), \tag{36}$$

$$\frac{\partial^3 \psi}{\partial \sigma^3} = e^{-3\tau} \left(\tilde{f}^{(3)}(\tau) - 3\tilde{f}''(\tau) + 2\tilde{f}'(\tau) \right), \tag{37}$$

$$\frac{\partial^4 \psi}{\partial \sigma^4} = e^{-4\tau} \left(u^{(4)}(\tau) - 6u^{(3)}(\tau) + 11u''(\tau) - 6u'(\tau) \right). \tag{38}$$

Then, (31) becomes

$$\frac{\tilde{\psi}(\tau)\left(PV_0 \tilde{\psi}(\tau)^P - 1\right)}{P} + \left(-6e^{-4\tau} - \frac{1}{4}\right)\tilde{\psi}'(\tau) + 11e^{-4\tau}\tilde{\psi}''(\tau) - 6e^{-4\tau}\tilde{\psi}^{(3)}(\tau) + e^{-4\tau}\tilde{\psi}^{(4)}(\tau) = 0. \tag{39}$$

Assuming that $\tilde{\psi}$ is bounded with bounded derivatives as $\tau \to +\infty$, we obtain the asymptotic equation

$$\frac{\tilde{\psi}_+(\tau)\left(PV_0 \tilde{\psi}_+(\tau)^P - 1\right)}{P} - \frac{1}{4}\tilde{\psi}'_+(\tau) = 0, \tag{40}$$

which admits the first integral

$$c_1 \frac{\tilde{\psi}_+(\tau)^P}{(1 - PV_0 \tilde{\psi}_+(\tau)^P)} = e^{-4\tau} \implies \tilde{\psi}_+(\tau) = \left(PV_0 + c_1 e^{4\tau}\right)^{-1/P}. \tag{41}$$

Defining

$$z_+(\tau) := \frac{\tilde{\psi}_+(\tau)^P}{(1 - PV_0 \tilde{\psi}_+(\tau)^P)}, \tag{42}$$

$z_+(\tau)$ is monotone decreasing as $\tau \to +\infty$ for $P > 0$ and monotone increasing as $\tau \to +\infty$ for $P < 0$. In other words, the asymptotic states of $\tilde{\psi}_+(\tau)$ are

$$\lim_{\tau \to +\infty} \tilde{\psi}_+(\tau) = 0 \text{ if } P > 0, V_0 > 0, \tag{43}$$

$$\lim_{\tau \to -\infty} \tilde{\psi}_+(\tau) = \psi_0 := (PV_0)^{-1/P} \text{ if } P > 0, V_0 > 0, \tag{44}$$

and

$$\lim_{\tau \to +\infty} \tilde{\psi}_+(\tau) = \psi_0 := (PV_0)^{-1/P} \text{ if } P < 0, V_0 < 0, \tag{45}$$

$$\lim_{\tau \to -\infty} \tilde{\psi}_+(\tau) = 0 \text{ if } P > 0, V_0 > 0. \tag{46}$$

The cases of interest are as $\tau \to +\infty$. That is, the monotonic function z_+ unveils the asymptotic behaviour as $\tau \to +\infty$.

Now, assuming that $\tilde{\psi}$ is bounded with bounded derivatives as $\tau \to -\infty$, we obtain the asymptotic equation

$$-6\tilde{\psi}'_-(\tau) + 11\tilde{\psi}''_-(\tau) - 6\tilde{\psi}^{(3)}_-(\tau) + \tilde{\psi}^{(4)}_-(\tau) = 0, \tag{47}$$

with solution

$$\tilde{\psi}_-(\tau) = c_2 e^\tau + \frac{1}{2}c_3 e^{2\tau} + \frac{1}{3}c_4 e^{3\tau} + c_5, \tag{48}$$

such that
$$\lim_{\tau \to -\infty} \bar{\psi}_-(\tau) = c_5. \tag{49}$$

Substituting $\psi(\tau) = \bar{\psi}_-(\tau)$ in (39) and taking limit $\tau \to -\infty$, we obtain the compatibility condition
$$c_5\left(-1 + PV_0 c_5^P\right) = 0. \tag{50}$$

That is, $c_5 \in \left\{0, (PV_0)^{-1/P}\right\}$. The choice $c_5 = (PV_0)^{-1/P}$ gives the proper matching condition
$$\lim_{\tau \to -\infty} \bar{\psi}_+(\tau) = \lim_{\tau \to -\infty} \bar{\psi}_-(\tau) = (PV_0)^{-1/P}. \tag{51}$$

In summary, integrating from $\tau \to -\infty$ to $\tau > 0$, we obtain that $\psi(\tau) \approx \bar{\psi}_-(\tau)$ for large τ close the boundary layer, whereas, integrating backwards from $\tau \to +\infty$ to $\tau < 0$, we obtain that $\psi(\tau) \approx \bar{\psi}_+(\tau)$ as $\tau \to -\infty$. These results are illustrated in Figure 1.

Let us define the new time variable $s = (1 + \tanh(\tau))/2$ that brings the interval $(-\infty, \infty)$ to $(0, 1)$. Then, the original layer problem becomes a two-point problem, with endpoints 0 and 1. The asymptotic solutions can be found as
$$\Phi_-(s) = \bar{\psi}_-(-\text{arctanh}(1 - 2s)), \tag{52}$$

that is,
$$\Phi_-(s) = (PV_0)^{-1/P} + \frac{c_3 s}{2 - 2s} + \left(c_2\left(\frac{1}{s} - 1\right) + \frac{c_4}{3}\right)e^{-3\text{arctanh}(1-2s)}. \tag{53}$$

As $s \to 0^+$, we have the asymptotic behaviour $\Phi_- \to (PV_0)^{-1/P}$.

Moreover,
$$\Phi_+(s) = \bar{\psi}_+(-\text{arctanh}(1 - 2s)), \tag{54}$$

becomes
$$\Phi_+(s) = \left(PV_0 + \frac{c_1 s^2}{(1-s)^2}\right)^{-1/P}, \tag{55}$$

such that
$$\lim_{s \to 1^-} \Phi_+(s) = 0 \text{ if } P > 0, V_0 > 0. \tag{56}$$

We have the matching condition
$$\lim_{s \to 0^+} \Phi_-(s) = \lim_{s \to 0^+} \Phi_+(s) = (PV_0)^{-1/P}. \tag{57}$$

The next step is to introduce the stretched variables $\kappa = s/\varepsilon$ and $\lambda = (1-s)/\varepsilon$, and write a solution
$$\Phi(s, \varepsilon) = \zeta(\kappa, \varepsilon) + \eta(\lambda, \varepsilon) \tag{58}$$

where
$$\zeta \to (PV_0)^{-1/P} \text{ as } \kappa = s/\varepsilon \to \infty \tag{59}$$

and
$$\eta \to 0 \text{ as } \lambda = (1-s)/\varepsilon \to \infty. \tag{60}$$

Near $s = 0$, η and its derivatives will be asymptotically negligible, so $d^j \Phi(s, \varepsilon)/ds^j \sim (1/\varepsilon^j)\left[d^j \zeta(\kappa, \varepsilon)/d\kappa^j\right]$. Take, for example,
$$\zeta_0(\kappa, \varepsilon) = (PV_0)^{-1/P} + \frac{c_3 \kappa \varepsilon}{2 - 2\kappa\varepsilon} + \left(c_2\left(\frac{1}{\kappa\varepsilon} - 1\right) + \frac{c_4}{3}\right)e^{-3\text{arctanh}(1-2\kappa\varepsilon)}. \tag{61}$$

Using the notation

$$\bar{\psi}(\tau, \varepsilon) = \Phi(\kappa, \varepsilon), \quad \kappa = \frac{\tanh(\tau) + 1}{2\varepsilon} \tag{62}$$

the approximated Equation (47) becomes

$$6\varepsilon(4\kappa\varepsilon(4\kappa\varepsilon - 3) + 1)\Phi'(\kappa, \varepsilon)$$
$$+ (\kappa\varepsilon - 1)\left[3(24\kappa\varepsilon(2\kappa\varepsilon - 1) + 1)\Phi''(\kappa, \varepsilon)\right.$$
$$\left. + 4\kappa(\kappa\varepsilon - 1)\left(\kappa\Phi^{(4)}(\kappa, \varepsilon)(\kappa\varepsilon - 1) + 3\Phi^{(3)}(\kappa, \varepsilon)(4\kappa\varepsilon - 1)\right)\right] = 0, \tag{63}$$

where primes mean derivatives with respect to κ, which admits the exact solution (61). Since we are taking ε as a small parameter, we see that the initial layer problem is of type

$$\left(-3\Phi''(\kappa) - 4\kappa\left(\kappa\Phi^{(4)}(\kappa) + 3\Phi^{(3)}(\kappa)\right)\right)$$
$$+ \varepsilon\left(6\Phi'(\kappa) + 3\kappa\left(25\Phi''(\kappa) + 4\kappa\left(\kappa\Phi^{(4)}(\kappa) + 6\Phi^{(3)}(\kappa)\right)\right)\right) + O\left(\varepsilon^2\right) = 0. \tag{64}$$

Taking the expansion

$$\Phi(\kappa) = \Phi_0(\kappa) + \varepsilon\Phi_1(\kappa) + \dots \tag{65}$$

we obtain at first-order

$$-3\Phi_0''(\kappa) - 4\kappa\left(\kappa\Phi_0^{(4)}(\kappa) + 3\Phi_0^{(3)}(\kappa)\right) = 0. \tag{66}$$

Hence,

$$\Phi_0(\kappa) = \frac{4}{3}\sqrt{\kappa}(d_2\kappa - 3d_1) + d_4\kappa + d_3. \tag{67}$$

At second-order, we have

$$60d_2\sqrt{\kappa} + 6d_4 - 4\kappa^2\Phi_1^{(4)}(\kappa) - 12\kappa\Phi_1^{(3)}(\kappa) - 3\Phi_1''(\kappa) = 0. \tag{68}$$

Hence,

$$\Phi_1(\kappa) = 2d_2\kappa^{5/2} + \frac{4}{3}d_6\kappa^{3/2} + d_4\kappa^2 + d_8\kappa - 4d_5\sqrt{\kappa} + d_7, \tag{69}$$

and so on. Finally, we replace the leading order and second-order terms (67) and (69), respectively, in (65) with the replacement (62).

Near $s = 1$, ζ and its derivatives will be asymptotically negligible, so $d^j\Phi(s,\varepsilon)/ds^j \sim (1/\varepsilon^j)[d^j\eta(\lambda,\varepsilon)/d\lambda^j]$. Take, for example,

$$\eta_0(\lambda, \varepsilon) = \left(PV_0 + c_1 e^{4\operatorname{arctanh}(1-2\lambda\varepsilon)}\right)^{-1/P}. \tag{70}$$

Using the notation

$$\bar{\psi}(\tau, \varepsilon) = \Phi(\lambda), \quad \lambda = \frac{1 - \tanh(\tau)}{2\varepsilon}, \tag{71}$$

the approximated Equation (40), becomes

$$2V_0\Phi(\lambda)^{P+1} + \lambda(1 - \lambda\varepsilon)\Phi'(\lambda) = \frac{2\Phi(\lambda)}{P}, \tag{72}$$

which admits the solution (70).

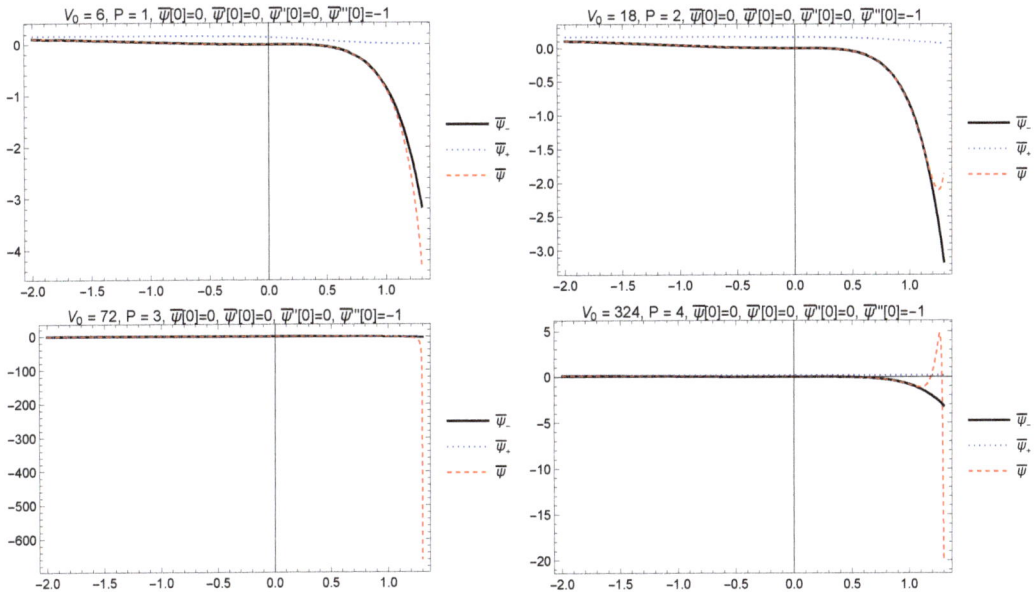

Figure 1. Comparison of exact solution $\bar{\psi}$ of (39) with initial conditions $\bar{\psi}(0) = 0, \bar{\psi}'(0) = 0, \bar{\psi}''(0) = 0, \bar{\psi}^{(3)}(0) = -1$ and the asymptotic solutions $\bar{\psi}_{\pm}$ for $V_0 = 6^P/P, P > 0$.

Figure 1 shows the exact solution $\bar{\psi}$ of (39) with initial conditions $\bar{\psi}(0) = 0, \bar{\psi}'(0) = 0, \bar{\psi}''(0) = 0, \bar{\psi}^{(3)}(0) = -1$ and the asymptotic solutions $\bar{\psi}_- = \frac{1}{6} - \frac{e^{\tau}}{2} + \frac{e^{2\tau}}{2} - \frac{e^{3\tau}}{6}$ and $\bar{\psi}_+ = (6^P + e^{4\tau})^{-1/P}$ for $V_0 = 6^P/P, P > 0$. This plot illustrates the accuracy of our analysis by selecting $\bar{\psi}_-$ as the inner solution for $\tau < \tau_0$, closing the boundary layer.

4.2. Exponential Function $V(\Psi) = V_0 \exp(P\Psi), P \neq 0$

On the other hand, for the exponential potential $V(\Psi) = V_0 \exp(P\Psi), P \neq 0$, the similarity transformation, which corresponds to the vector field $\left(4t\partial_t + x\partial_x - 2\Phi\partial_\Phi - \frac{4}{P}(\partial_\Psi)\right)$, is

$$\Psi(t,x) = \frac{\ln t}{P} + \psi(\sigma), \quad \Phi = t^{-\frac{1}{2}}\phi(\sigma), \quad \sigma(t,x) = \frac{x}{t^{\frac{1}{4}}},$$

where the reduced system is

$$\frac{\partial^2 \phi}{\partial \sigma^2} + V_0 e^{P\psi} - \frac{1}{P} - \frac{1}{4}\sigma\frac{\partial \psi}{\partial \sigma} = 0, \tag{73}$$

$$\phi - \frac{\partial^2 \psi}{\partial \sigma^2} = 0. \tag{74}$$

We introduce the logarithmic independent variable (32) and define $\psi(\sigma)$ by (33). Then, using the chain rule and the relation $\sigma = e^{\tau}$, we obtain

$$V_0 e^{P\bar{\psi}(\tau)} + \left(-6e^{-4\tau} - \frac{1}{4}\right)\bar{\psi}'(\tau) + 11e^{-4\tau}\bar{\psi}''(\tau) - 6e^{-4\tau}\bar{\psi}^{(3)}(\tau) + e^{-4\tau}\bar{\psi}^{(4)}(\tau) - \frac{1}{P} = 0. \tag{75}$$

Assuming that $\bar{\psi}$ is bounded with bounded derivatives as $\tau \to +\infty$, we obtain the asymptotic equation

$$V_0 e^{P\bar{\psi}_+(\tau)} - \frac{1}{P} - \frac{1}{4}\bar{\psi}'_+(\tau) = 0, \tag{76}$$

with solution
$$\bar{\psi}_+(\tau) = \ln\left(\left(PV_0 + e^{4\tau + c_1 P}\right)^{-1/P}\right). \tag{77}$$

Assuming that $\bar{\psi}$ and $V_0 e^{P\bar{\psi}(\tau)}$ are bounded with bounded derivatives as $\tau \to -\infty$, we obtain, as in Section 4.1, the asymptotic Equation (47), with solution (48). Substituting $\psi(\tau) = \bar{\psi}_-(\tau)$ in (75), and taking limit $\tau \to -\infty$, we obtain

$$-\frac{1}{P} + V_0 e^{c_5 P} = 0 \implies c_5 = \ln\left[(PV_0)^{-1/P}\right]. \tag{78}$$

That is, we have the matching condition

$$\lim_{\tau \to -\infty} \bar{\psi}_+(\tau) = \lim_{\tau \to -\infty} \bar{\psi}_-(\tau) = \ln\left[(PV_0)^{-1/P}\right]. \tag{79}$$

As in Section 4.1, integrating from $\tau \to -\infty$ to $\tau > 0$, we obtain that $\psi(\tau) \approx \bar{\psi}_-(\tau)$ for large τ, whereas, integrating backwards from $\tau \to +\infty$ to $\tau < 0$, we obtain that $\psi(\tau) \approx \bar{\psi}_+(\tau)$ as $\tau \to -\infty$. These results are illustrated in Figures 2 and 3. Nevertheless, when the term $V_0 e^{P\bar{\psi}(\tau)}$ in (75) is not negligible, the approximation of $\bar{\psi}$ by the solution of the asymptotic Equation (47) is not accurate as $\tau \to +\infty$. Then, the asymptotic Equation (47) is replaced by

$$V_0 e^{P\psi(\tau) + 4\tau} + \psi^{(4)}(\tau) - 6\psi^{(3)}(\tau) + 11\psi''(\tau) - 6\psi'(\tau) = 0, \tag{80}$$

which cannot be solved analytically.

Using the same method, we define the new time variable $s = (1 + \tanh(\tau))/2$ that brings the interval $(-\infty, \infty)$ to $(0, 1)$. Then, the original layer problem becomes a two-point problem, with endpoints 0 and 1. The asymptotic solutions can be found as

$$\Phi_-(s) = \ln\left[(PV_0)^{-1/P}\right] + \frac{c_3 s}{2 - 2s} + \left(c_2\left(\frac{1}{s} - 1\right) + \frac{c_4}{3}\right) e^{-3\operatorname{arctanh}(1-2s)}. \tag{81}$$

As $s \to 0^+$, we have the asymptotic behaviour $e^{\Phi_-} \to (PV_0)^{-1/P}$.
Similarly, we have

$$e^{\Phi_+(s)} = \left(PV_0 + \frac{c_1 s^2}{(1-s)^2}\right)^{-1/P}, \tag{82}$$

such that

$$\lim_{s \to 1^-} e^{\Phi_+(s)} = 0 \text{ if } P > 0, V_0 > 0. \tag{83}$$

Finally, by introducing the stretched variables $\kappa = s/\varepsilon$ and $\lambda = (1-s)/\varepsilon$, we write a solution

$$\Phi(s, \varepsilon) = \zeta(\kappa, \varepsilon) + \eta(\lambda, \varepsilon), \tag{84}$$

where

$$\zeta \to \ln\left[(PV_0)^{-1/P}\right] \text{ as } \kappa = s/\varepsilon \to \infty, \tag{85}$$

and

$$\eta \to 0 \text{ as } \lambda = (1-s)/\varepsilon \to \infty. \tag{86}$$

Then, the layer problem becomes a two-point problem, with endpoints 0 and 1, and we obtain the asymptotic solutions following similar approaches as in Section 4.1.

Figure 2 shows the exact solution $\bar{\psi}$ of (75) with initial conditions $\bar{\psi}(0) = 0$, $\bar{\psi}'(0) = 0$, $\bar{\psi}''(0) = 0$, $\bar{\psi}^{(3)}(0) = 1$ and the asymptotic solutions $\bar{\psi}_- = \frac{e^\tau}{2} - \frac{e^{2\tau}}{2} + \frac{e^{3\tau}}{6} - \frac{1}{6}$

and $\bar{\psi}_+ = -\dfrac{\ln(e^{P+4\tau}+e^{P/6})}{P}$ for $V_0 = \dfrac{e^{P/6}}{P}, P < 0$. In this example, the approximations are accurate.

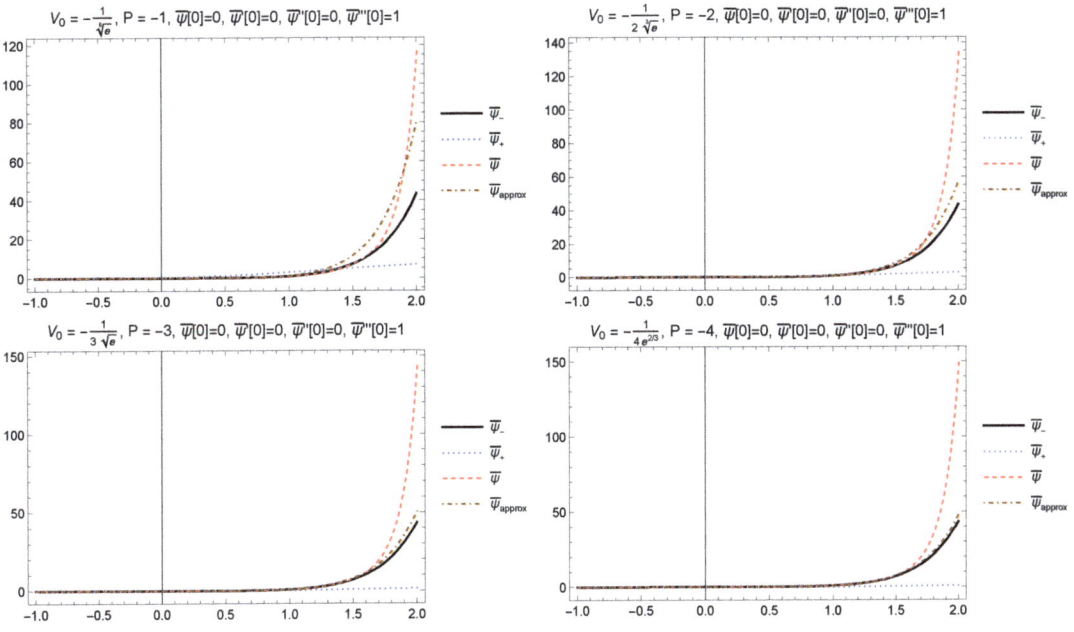

Figure 2. Comparison of exact solution $\bar{\psi}$ of (75) with initial conditions $\bar{\psi}(0) = 0, \bar{\psi}'(0) = 0$, $\bar{\psi}''(0) = 0, \bar{\psi}^{(3)}(0) = 1$ and the asymptotic solutions $\bar{\psi}_\pm$ for $V_0 = \dfrac{e^{P/6}}{P}, P < 0$.

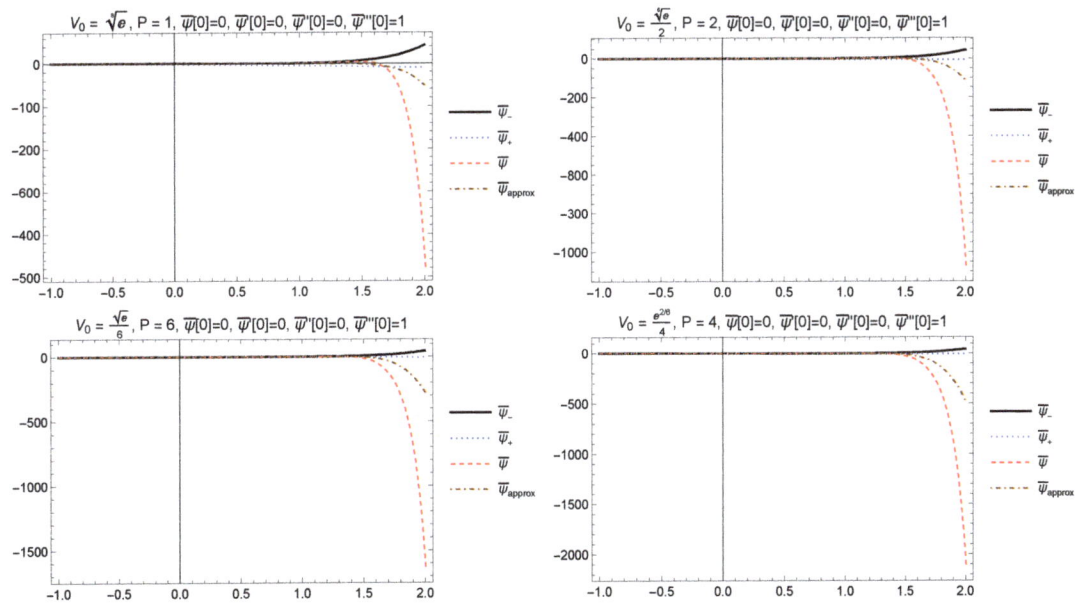

Figure 3. Comparison of exact solution $\bar{\psi}$ of (39) with initial conditions $\bar{\psi}(0) = 0, \bar{\psi}'(0) = 0$, $\bar{\psi}''(0) = 0, \bar{\psi}^{(3)}(0) = 1$ and the asymptotic solutions $\bar{\psi}_\pm$ for $V_0 = \dfrac{e^{P/6}}{P}, P > 0$.

Figure 3 shows the exact solution $\bar{\psi}$ of (75) with the same initial conditions, and the asymptotic solutions $\bar{\psi}_\pm$ for $V_0 = \frac{e^{P/6}}{P}, P > 0$. The approximation of $\bar{\psi}$ by the solution of the asymptotic Equation (47) is not accurate as $\tau \to +\infty$. Then, the asymptotic Equation (47) is replaced by (80). The numerical solution $\bar{\psi}_{approx}$ of (80) is represented by a dot-dashed line in Figures 2 and 3.

5. Conclusions

Lie symmetry analysis is a powerful method for analysing nonlinear differential equations. In this study, the Lie symmetry analysis was applied to solve the group classification problem for a $1 + n$-dimensional nonlinear higher-order Schrödinger equation inspired by GUP. The partial differential equation of our analysis admits an arbitrary potential function, which was a constraint according to the admitted Lie point symmetries. For an arbitrary potential function, we found that the admitted Lie symmetries are the Killing vectors of the n-dimensional space in addition to the vector field ∂_t. However, a new symmetry vector presented in Theorems 1 and 2 can be found for specific function forms of the potential function. To demonstrate the application of the Lie symmetry vectors, we used the corresponding Lie invariants to define similarity transformations and reduce the partial-differential equation into an ordinary differential equation. Because of the nonlinearity of the reduced equation, we studied the asymptotic dynamics and evolution.

Concerning asymptotic analysis, we have obtained asymptotic solutions

$$\bar{\psi}_-(\tau) = c_2 e^\tau + \frac{1}{2} c_3 e^{2\tau} + \frac{1}{3} c_4 e^{3\tau} + \begin{cases} (PV_0)^{-1/P} & \text{power-law function} \\ \ln\left[(PV_0)^{-1/P}\right] & \text{exponential function} \end{cases},$$

$$\bar{\psi}_+(\tau) = \begin{cases} (PV_0 + c_1 e^{4\tau})^{-1/P} & \text{power-law function} \\ \ln\left((PV_0 + e^{4\tau + c_1 P})^{-1/P}\right) & \text{exponential function} \end{cases},$$

with the proper matching condition

$$\lim_{\tau \to -\infty} \bar{\psi}_+(\tau) = \lim_{\tau \to -\infty} \bar{\psi}_-(\tau) = \begin{cases} (PV_0)^{-1/P} & \text{power-law function} \\ \ln\left[(PV_0)^{-1/P}\right] & \text{exponential function} \end{cases}.$$

For the power-law potential, it is confirmed numerically that as $\tau \to -\infty$, $\psi(\tau) \approx \bar{\psi}_+(\tau)$, whereas, for large τ, $\psi(\tau) \approx \bar{\psi}_-(\tau)$. However, in the exponential case, when the term $V_0 e^{P\bar{\psi}(\tau)}$ is not negligible, the approximation by $\bar{\psi}_-(\tau)$ is not accurate as the boundary layer is approached and has to be replaced by $\bar{\psi}_{approx}(\tau)$.

Finally, the layer problem becomes a two-point problem, with endpoints 0 and 1 by introducing the stretched variables $\kappa = s/\varepsilon$ and $\lambda = (1-s)/\varepsilon$, and writing a formal solution

$$\Phi(s, \varepsilon) = \zeta(\kappa, \varepsilon) + \eta(\lambda, \varepsilon), \tag{87}$$

where

$$\zeta \to \begin{cases} (PV_0)^{-1/P} & \text{power-law function} \\ \ln\left[(PV_0)^{-1/P}\right] & \text{exponential function} \end{cases}, \text{ as } \kappa = s/\varepsilon \to \infty, \tag{88}$$

and

$$\eta \to 0 \text{ as } \lambda = (1-s)/\varepsilon \to \infty. \tag{89}$$

Then, it is interesting to analyse possible asymptotic solutions for different initial/boundary conditions, but this numerical treatment is out of the scope of the present research. In general, when solving the problem of approximating a function $\psi_\varepsilon(\tau)$ depending on a small parameter ε in a domain D, the algorithm presented in [53] can be applied.

This work contributes to the subject of the application of Lie point symmetries on nonlinear differential equations. In this study, we considered a Schrödinger equation constructed by the deformation algebra of the quadratic GUP. However, that is not the unique proposed GUP, and other deformations algebras exist. Therefore, in future work, we plan to perform a detailed classification of the higher-order Schrödinger equations for different models of GUP. Finally, we will present formal expansions, representing valid asymptotic approximations of the function $\psi_\varepsilon(\tau)$ for other initial conditions that we set out to study by singular perturbation methods, boundary layers, and multiple time scales.

Author Contributions: A.P. organised the project and performed the symmetry analysis. G.L. was involved in the asymptotic solutions. P.G.L.L. wrote the final version of the paper. All authors have read and agreed to the published version of the manuscript.

Funding: G.L. was funded by Vicerrectoría de Investigación y Desarrollo Tecnológico (Vridt) at Universidad Católica del Norte through Concurso De Pasantías De Investigación Año 2022, Resolución Vridt No. 040/2022 and through Resolución Vridt No. 054/2022.

Institutional Review Board Statement: Not applicable.

Informed Consent Statement: Not applicable.

Data Availability Statement: The study did not report any data.

Conflicts of Interest: The authors declare no conflict of interest.

References

1. Stephani, H. *Differential Equations: Their Solutions Using Symmetry*; Cambridge University Press: New York, NY, USA, 1989.
2. Bluman, G.W.; Kumei, S. *Symmetries of Differential Equations*; Springer: New York, NY, USA, 1989.
3. Leach, P.G.L.; Gorringe, V.M. A conserved Laplace-Runge-Lenz-like vector for a class of three-dimensional motions. *Phys. Lett. A* **1988**, *133*, 289. [CrossRef]
4. Gazinov, R.K.; Ibragimov, N.H. Lie Symmetry Analysis of Differential Equations in Finance. *Nonlinear Dyn.* **1998**, *17*, 387. [CrossRef]
5. Ibragimov, N.H. On the group classification of second order differential equations. *(Russ.) Dokl. Akad. Nauk SSSR* **1968**, *183*, 274,
6. Azad, H.; Mustafa, M.T. Symmetry analysis of wave equation on sphere. *J. Math. Anal. Appl.* **2007**, *333*, 1180. [CrossRef]
7. Tsamparlis, M.; Paliathanasis, A. Two-dimensional dynamical systems which admit Lie and Noether symmetries. *J. Phys. A Math.Theor.* **2011**, *44*, 175202. [CrossRef]
8. Mahomed, F.M. Symmetry group classification of ordinary differential equations: Survey of some results. *Math. Methods Appl. Sci.* **2007**, *30*, 1995. [CrossRef]
9. Jamal, S.; Kara, A.H.; Bokhari, À.H. Symmetries, conservation laws, reductions, and exact solutions for the Klein–Gordon equation in de Sitter space–times. *Can. J. Phys.* **2012**, *90*, 667. [CrossRef]
10. Halder, A.K.; Paliathanasis, A.; Rangasamy, S.; Leach, P.G.L. Similarity solutions for the complex Burgers' hierarchy. *Z. Naturforschung A* **2019**, *74*, 597. [CrossRef]
11. Jamal, S.; Kara, A.H. New higher-order conservation laws of some classes of wave and Gordon-type equations. *Nonlinear Dyn.* **2012**, *67*, 97. [CrossRef]
12. Chesnokov, A.A. Symmetries and exact solutions of the rotating shallow-water equations. *J. Appl. Mech. Techn. Phys.* **2008**, *49*, 737. [CrossRef]
13. Jamal, S. Solutions of quasi-geostrophic turbulence in multi-layered configurations. *Quaest. Math.* **2018**, *41*, 409. [CrossRef]
14. Halder, A.K.; Paliathanasis, A.; Leach, P.G.L. Noether's Theorem and Symmetry. *Symmetry* **2018**, *10*, 744. [CrossRef]
15. Schwarz, F. Solving second order ordinary differential equations with maximal symmetry group. *Computing* **1999**, *62*, 1. [CrossRef]
16. Reid, G.J.; Wittkopf, A.D. Determination of maximal symmetry groups of classes of differential equations. In *ISSAC '00: Proceedings of the 2000 International Symposium on Symbolic and Algebraic Computation*; Association for Computing Machinery: New York, NY, USA, 2000; pp. 272–280.
17. Ali, S.; Safdar, M.; Qadir, A. Linearization from complex Lie point transformations. *J. Appl. Math.* **2014**, *2014*, 793247. [CrossRef]
18. Karpman, V.I. Lyapunov approach to the soliton stability in highly dispersive systems. I. Fourth order nonlinear Schrödinger equations. *Phys. Lett. A* **1996**, *215*, 254. [CrossRef]
19. Karpman, V.I.; Shagalov, A.G. Stability of solitons described by nonlinear Schrödinger-type equations with higher-order dispersion. *Phys. D* **2000**, *144*, 194. [CrossRef]
20. Segata, J. Factorization technique for the fourth-order nonlinear Schrödinger equation. *Math. Methods Appl. Sci.* **2006**, *26*, 1785. [CrossRef]
21. Pausader, B. The cubic fourth-order Schrödinger equation. *J. Funct. Anal.* **2009**, *256*, 2473. [CrossRef]
22. Pausader, B.; Shao, S. The mass-critical fourth-order Schrödinger equation in high dimensions. *J. Hyperbolic Differ.* **2010**, *7*, 651 [CrossRef]
23. Baquet, C.; Villamizar-Roa, E.J. On the management fourth-order Schrodinger-Hartree equation. *Evol. Equ. Control* **2020**, *9*, 865.
24. Liu, X.; Zhang, T. The Cauchy problem for the fourth-order Schrödinger equation in Hs. *J. Math. Phys.* **2021**, *62*, 071501. [CrossRef]

25. Erdogan, B.; Green, W.R.; Torpak, E. On the fourth order Schrödinger equation in three dimensions: Dispersive estimates and zero energy resonances. *J. Differ. Equ.* **2021**, *271*, 152. [CrossRef]
26. Fibich, G.; Ilan, B.; Papanicolaou, G. Self-focusing with fourth-order dispersion. *SIAM J. Appl. Math.* **2002**, *62*, 1437.
27. Fibich, G.; Ilan, B.; Schochet, S. Critical exponents and collapse of nonlinear Schrödinger equations with anisotropic fourth-order dispersion. *Nonlinearity* **2003**, *16*, 1809. [CrossRef]
28. Karpman, V.I. Envelope solitons in gyrotropic media. *Phys. Rev. Lett.* **1995**, *74*, 2455. [CrossRef]
29. Quarshi, M.M.A.; Yusuf, A.; Aliyu, A.I.; Inc, M. Optical and other solitons for the fourth-order dispersive nonlinear Schrödinger equation with dual-power law nonlinearity. *Superlattices Microstruct.* **2017**, *105*, 183. [CrossRef]
30. Fedele, R.; Schamel, H.; Shukla, P.K. Solitons in the Madelung's Fluid. *Phys. Scr.* **2002**, *2002*, 18. [CrossRef]
31. Natali, F.; Pastor, A. The Fourth-Order Dispersive Nonlinear Schrödinger Equation: Orbital Stability of a Standing Wave. *SIAM J. Appl. Dyn. Syst.* **2015**, *14*, 1326–1347. [CrossRef]
32. Hayaski, N.; Naumkin, P.I. On the inhomogeneous fourth-order nonlinear Schrödinger equation. *J. Math. Phys.* **2015**, *56*, 093502. [CrossRef]
33. Konishi, K.; Paffuti, G.; Provero, P. Minimum physical length and the generalized uncertainty principle in string theory. *Phys. Lett. B* **1990**, *234*, 276. [CrossRef]
34. Camelia, A. Relativity in spacetimes with short-distance structure governed by an observer-independent (Planckian) length scale. *Int.J. Mod. Phys. D* **2002**, *11*, 35. [CrossRef]
35. Martinetti, P.; Mercati, F.; Tomassini, L. Minimal length in quantum space and integrations of the line element in noncommutative geometry. *Rev. Math. Phys.* **2012**, *24*, 1250010. [CrossRef]
36. Ashtekar, A.; Lewandowski, J. Background independent quantum gravity: A status report. *Class. Quantum Grav.* 2004, 21, R53. [CrossRef]
37. Maggiore, M. A generalized uncertainty principle in quantum gravity. *Phys. Lett. B* **1993**, *304*, 65. [CrossRef]
38. Hossenfelder, S. Minimal length scale scenarios for quantum gravity. *Living Rev. Relativ.* **2013**, *16*, 2. [CrossRef]
39. Das, S.; Vagenas, E.C. Universality of quantum gravity corrections. *Phys. Rev. Lett.* **2008**, *101*, 221301. [CrossRef]
40. Moayedi, S.K.; Setare, M.R.; Moayeri, H. Quantum gravitational corrections to the real klein-gordon field in the presence of a minimal length. *Int. J. Theor. Phys.* **2010**, *49*, 2080. [CrossRef]
41. Hamil, B.; Merad, M.; Birkandan, T. Applications of the extended uncertainty principle in AdS and dS spaces. *Eur Phys. J. Plus* **2019**, *134*, 278. [CrossRef]
42. Dabrowski, M.P.; Wagner, F. Asymptotic generalized extended uncertainty principle. *EPJC* **2020**, *80*, 676. [CrossRef]
43. Nenmeli, V.; Shankaranarayanan, S.; Todorinov, V.; Das, S. Maximal momentum GUP leads to quadratic gravity. *Phys. Lett. B* **2021**, *821*, 136621. [CrossRef]
44. Das, A.; Das, S.; Vagenas, E.C. Discreteness of space from GUP in strong gravitational fields. *Phys. Lett. B* **2020**, *809*, 135772. [CrossRef]
45. Aghababaei, S.; Mordpour, H.; Vagenas, E.C. Hubble tension bounds the GUP and EUP parameters. *Eur. Phys. J. Plus* **2021**, *136*, 997. [CrossRef]
46. Ovsiannikov, L.V. *Group Analysis of Differential Equations*; Academic Press: New York, NY, USA, 1982.
47. Zhang, Z.-Y.; Li, G.-F. Lie symmetry analysis and exact solutions of the time-fractional biological population model. *Phys. A* **2020**, *540*, 123134. [CrossRef]
48. Jamal, S.; Kara, A.H.; Narain, R. Wave equations in Bianchi Space-times. *J. App. Math.* **2012**, *2012*, 765361. [CrossRef]
49. Lahno, V.; Zhdanov, R.; Magda, O. Group classification and exact solutions of nonlinear wave equations. *Acta Appl. Math.* **2006**, *91*, 253. [CrossRef]
50. Baikov, V.A.; Gladkov, A.V.; Wiltshire, R.J. Lie symmetry classification analysis for nonlinear coupled diffusion. *J. Phys. A Math. Gen.* **1998**, *31*, 7483. [CrossRef]
51. Huang, D.; Ivanova, N.M. Group analysis and exact solutions of a class of variable coefficient nonlinear telegraph equations. *J. Math. Phys.* **2007**, *48*, 073507. [CrossRef]
52. Cherniha, R.; Serov, M.; Prystavka, Y. A complete Lie symmetry classification of a class of (1+2)-dimensional reaction-diffusion-convection equations. *Commun. Nonlinear Sci. Numer. Simul.* **2021**, *92*, 105466. [CrossRef]
53. Verhulst, F. *Methods and Applications of Singular Perturbations: Boundary Layers and Multiple Timescale Dynamics, Texts in Applied Mathematics*; Springer: New York, NY, USA, 2005. [CrossRef]
54. Paliathanasis, A.; Tsamparlis, M. Lie and Noether point symmetries of a class of quasilinear systems of second-order differential equations. *J. Geom. Phys.* **2016**, *107*, 45. [CrossRef]
55. Karpathopoulos, L.; Paliathanasis, A.; Tsamparlis, M. Lie and Noether point symmetries for a class of nonautonomous dynamical systems. *J. Math. Phys.* **2017**, *58*, 082301. [CrossRef]
56. Paliathanasis, A.; Tsamparlis, M. The geometric origin of Lie point symmetries of the Schrödinger and the Klein–Gordon equations. *Int. J. Geom. Meth. Mod. Phys.* **2014**, *11*, 1450037. [CrossRef]

Article

Numerical Simulation for Brinkman System with Varied Permeability Tensor [†]

Lahcen El Ouadefli [1], Abdeslam El Akkad [1,2], Omar El Moutea [3], Hassan Moustabchir [4], Ahmed Elkhalfi [1], Maria Luminița Scutaru [5,*] and Radu Muntean [6]

[1] Mechanical Engineering Laboratory, Faculty of Science and Technology, B.P. 30000 Route Imouzzer, Fez 30000, Morocco
[2] Department of Mathematics Regional Centre for Professions of Education and Training (CREMF Fès-Meknès), Rue Koweit, B.P: 49 Commune Agudal, Ville Nouvelle, Fez 30050, Morocco
[3] Laboratory of Mathematics and Applications, ENS, Hassan II University Casablanca, Casablanca 20000, Morocco
[4] Laboratory of Systems Engineering and Applications (LISA), National School of Applied Sciences of Fez, Sidi Mohamed Ben Abdellah University, Fez 30000, Morocco
[5] Faculty of Mechanical Engineering, Transilvania University of Brasov, 500036 Brasov, Romania
[6] Faculty of Civil Engineering, Transilvania University of Brasov, 500036 Brasov, Romania
* Correspondence: lscutaru@unitbv.ro
[†] This paper is an extended version of our paper: Numerical computation of the Brinkman system in a heterogeneous porous medium by mini-element P1–Bubble/P1, published in *2021 Fifth International Conference on Intelligent Computing in Data Sciences (ICDS)*; 20–22 October 2021, pp. 1–5; IEEE. https://ieeexplore.ieee.org/document/9626767 (accessed on 1 December 2021).

Abstract: The aim of this paper is to study a stationary Brinkman problem in an anisotropic porous medium by using a mini-element method with a general boundary condition. One of the important aspects of the $P1 - Bubble/P1$ method is satisfying the inf-sup condition, which allows us the existence and the uniqueness of the weak solution to our problem. To go further in this theoretical study, an a priori error estimate is established. To see the importance of this method in reality, we applied this method to a real problem. The numerical simulation studies support our results and demonstrate the effectiveness of this method.

Keywords: anisotropic porous media; ADINA system; a priori estimate error; Brinkman equation; mini-element; stability

MSC: 65N30; 65N15; 65G99; 76D07; 76D99

1. Introduction

The purpose of this paper is to approach the Brinkman system using a finite-element method. The Brinkman system involves modifying the usual Darcy law by the addition of a standard viscosity term; this system was first defined by H.C. Brinkman [1]. In reality, many applications use this equation; for example, in a porous media it used to model fluid flow in a complex domain [2–4] and in a fictitious domain [5]. Shahnazari and al. worked on the nonlinear cases and products of the nonlinear Brinkman equation where the viscosity is nonlinear [6–8]. The Brinkman equations have very important practical applications in the field of anisotropic porous media [9–11], as well as in several other real domains such as nanofluids [12–20].

One important method for the resolution of differential equations is the mixed finite-element method (MFEM) [21–23]. This method has been used by several researchers to solve incompressible fluid flow problems [24–27]. Many research papers [24,28] are interested in solving the Brinkman equation using the mixed finite-element method, therefore the a priori and a posteriori error estimates for the Brinkman system are studied [28].

In this paper, we study the discretization, and we will establish the stability and a priori error estimate of the Brinkman problem with the permeability as a matrix by the finite-element method (mini-element); this method was introduced by Arnold, Brezzi and Fortin [29]. The method $P1/P1$ is not stable, so to overcome this obstacle we propose to use the $P1 - Bubble/P1$. The basic idea for $P1 - Bubble/P1$ is that the construction of the mini-element starts with standard finite-element spaces for velocity and pressure and then enriches the velocity space such that the discrete inf-sup condition is satisfied. This method leads to a relatively low number of degrees of freedom with a good approximate solution [29–31].

The numerical study of this linear problem is obtained in the matrix form of large size; indeed, we propose an efficient (preconditioned) Uzawa conjugate gradient method to accelerate the convergence of the numerical solution derived from the one used with $P2/P1$ (or $P1 - iso - P2/P1$) [32,33]. To simulate the Brinkman equation in a heterogeneous reservoir, we modified the code suggested by J. Koko for the generalized Stokes problem [34], such that our model is based on the permeability as a matrix.

This paper is organized as follows: The governing equations and assumptions to conserve the existence and uniqueness of the solution are described in Section 2; Then a presentation of the mini-element method and the notations used in the approximation of our problem is performed in Section 3; The important theoretical results—the stability and a priori estimation—are proved in Section 4; Finally, to see the importance of this method, we propose several numerical experiments in Section 5 to prove that the convergence of our method is validated for an exact solution example.

2. Governing Equations

Let $\Omega \subset \mathbb{R}^d$, $(d = 2,3)$ be a bounded open set with a Lipschitz boundary Γ. The Brinkman system is represented by the following equations

$$\begin{cases} -\nabla \cdot (\tilde{\mu}\nabla u) + \nabla p + \mu K^{-1}u = f & \text{in } \Omega, \\ \nabla \cdot u = 0 & \text{in } \Omega. \end{cases} \quad (1)$$

The system in Equation (1) is completed by the boundary conditions on Γ given by

$$A^{-1}u + B(\tilde{\mu}\nabla u - pI)\cdot n = g \quad \text{on } \Gamma. \quad (2)$$

where u and p represent, respectively, the velocity field and the pressure, with the pressure equation belonging in the space $L^2(\Omega)$ and satisfying $\int p\, dx = 0$ there by enforcing a null mean value of the pressure field over the entire domain Ω, restoring uniqueness. Moreover, f is the external volumetric force acting on the fluid ($f \in \left[L^2(\Omega)\right]^d$), and in the boundary condition we assume that $g \in \left[L^2(\Gamma)\right]^d$ and the functions $\tilde{\mu}$, μ are continuous bounded functions that represent, respectively, the Newtonian viscosity and dynamic viscosity of a fluid. The matrix K defines the permeability of the reservoir such that two constants $k_1, k_2 \succ 0$ exist:

$$k_1 \psi^t \psi \leq \psi^t K^{-1} \psi \leq k_2 \psi^t \psi, \quad \forall \psi \in \mathbb{R}^d. \quad (3)$$

The matrix B is invertible and is a bounded matrix function belonging to $L^\infty(\Gamma)$, i.e., there exist two constants $b_1, b_2 \succ 0$ such that

$$b_1 \psi^t \psi \leq \psi^t B^{-1} \psi \leq b_2 \psi^t \psi, \quad \forall \psi \in \mathbb{R}^d. \quad (4)$$

The matrix A is invertible and is a bounded matrix function belonging to $L^\infty(\Gamma)$, i.e., there exist two constants $a_1, a_2 > 0$ such that

$$a_1 \psi^t \psi \leq \psi^t A^{-1} \psi \leq a_2 \psi^t \psi, \quad \forall \psi \in \mathbb{R}^d. \quad (5)$$

Remark: Under the notation $|||A||| = max|a_{i,j}|$, $(i,j = 1,2,3)$, we can observe that

- If $|||B||| \ll |||A^{-1}|||$ then the boundary conditions are the Dirichlet condition.
- If $|||A^{-1}||| \ll |||B|||$ then the boundary conditions are the Neumann condition.

We denote by $H^1(\Omega)$ the standard Sobolev space of order 1, and by $H_0^1(\Omega)$ its subspace made of all functions equal to 0 on the boundary Γ. We introduce the spaces

$$V = [H^1(\Omega)]^d, \tag{6}$$

for the velocity field and

$$Q = \left\{ q \in L^2(\Omega), \int_\Omega q dx = 0 \right\}, \tag{7}$$

for the pressure.

The Brinkman problem (1) and (2) has a unique solution $(u,p) \in V \times Q$ [5]. In order to analyze the numerical solution of this problem using the finite-element method $P1 - Bubble/P1$, we must first describe the weak formulation of the Brinkman system.

The weak formulation of the system (1) and (2) is to find $(u,p) \in V \times Q$ such that

$$\begin{cases} a(u,v) + b(v,p) = F(v) & \forall v \in V, \\ b(q,u) = 0 & \forall q \in Q, \end{cases} \tag{8}$$

where $a : V \times V \to \mathbb{R}$ is a bilinear form defined by

$$a(u,v) = \int_\Omega \tilde{\mu} \nabla u \cdot \nabla v dx + \int_\Omega K^{-1} \mu u \cdot v dx + \int_\Gamma B^{-1} A^{-1} u \cdot v d\sigma, \tag{9}$$

$b : V \times Q \to \mathbb{R}$ is a bilinear form given by

$$b(v,p) = -\int_\Omega p \nabla \cdot v \, dx, \tag{10}$$

and $F : V \to \mathbb{R}$ is a linear continuous function given by

$$F(v) = \int_\Omega f \cdot v dx + \int_\Gamma B^{-1} g \cdot v d\sigma. \tag{11}$$

We define the norms for the spaces Q, $H^1(\Omega)$, V and $V \times Q$ by

$$\| v \|_{0,\Omega} := \| v \|_Q = \| v \|_{L^2(\Omega)} = \left(\int_\Omega |v|^2 dx \right)^{\frac{1}{2}} \forall v \in L^2(\Omega), \tag{12}$$

$$\| v \|_1^2 = \| \nabla v \|_{0,\Omega}^2 + \| v \|_{0,\Omega}^2, \tag{13}$$

$$\| v \|_V = a(v,v)^{\frac{1}{2}}, \tag{14}$$

and

$$\| (v,q) \|_{V \times Q} = \| v \|_V + \| q \|_Q. \tag{15}$$

In what follows, we will show the existence and uniqueness of the weak solution of the system (1) and (2), for which we use these theorems.

Theorem 1. *There exist two strictly positive constants c_1 and c_2 such that*

$$c_1 \| u \|_1 \leq \| u \|_V \leq c_2 \| u \|_1, \forall u \in H^1(\Omega). \tag{16}$$

Proof of Theorem 1. The mapping

$$\gamma : H^1 \to L^2(\Gamma) \ u \mapsto \gamma(u) = u_\Gamma$$

is continuous, so a strictly positive constant c_3 exists such that

$$\| u \|_{0,\Gamma} \leq c_3 \| u \|_1 \tag{17}$$

from (4) and (5), we obtain

$$\| u \|_V \leq c_2 \| u \|_1, \quad \forall u \in H^1(\Omega). \tag{18}$$

On the other hand, there exists a strictly positive constant α such that

$$\| u \|_{0,\Omega}^2 \leq \alpha (\| u \|_{0,\Gamma}^2 + \| \nabla u \|_{0,\Omega}^2), \tag{19}$$

by using the assumptions (3)–(5), a constant c_1 exists such that

$$c_1 \| u \|_1 \leq \| u \|_V, \quad \forall u \in H^1(\Omega). \tag{20}$$

Finally, based on the inequalities (18)–(20), the norms $\| . \|_1$ and $\| . \|_V$ are equivalents. □

Corollary 1. *The space V that includes the norm $\| . \|_V$ is a Helbert space.*

Theorem 2. *The bilinear continuous form $b(\cdot,\cdot)$ satisfies the inf-sup condition defined by the fact that there exists a constant $\beta \succ 0$ such that*

$$\inf_{q \in Q} \sup_{v \in V} \frac{b(q,v)}{\|v\|_V \|q\|_Q} \geq \beta, \tag{21}$$

Proof of Theorem 2. See Section 2 in [29]. □

It is well known that, under these Assumptions $(3) - (5)$, the bilinear form $a(\cdot,\cdot)$ is a continuous coercive function. The bilinear form $b(\cdot,\cdot)$ is a continuous function that satisfies the $inf - sup$ condition defined by (21). Under the Assumption (4), $F(\cdot)$ is a linear continuous function. Therefore, the Problem (8) is well-posed and has only one solution [24].

3. Mini-Element Method Approximation

Our goal here is to approximate the stationary Brinkman equations with general boundary conditions in a d-dimensional domain ($d = 2,3$) by using the mini-element method $P1 - Bubble/P1$.

The mini-element method was first created by Arnold, Brezzi and Fortin [29]. The basic idea of the mini-element method is to add local functions called bubbles to correctly enrich the discrete velocity space in order to stabilize the unstable method $P1/P1$. Figures 1 and 2 present the reference element of the mini-element $P1 - Bubble/P1$ in two dimensions below and in three dimensions above.

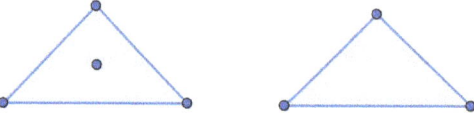

Figure 1. Mini-element $P1 - Bubble/P1$ in 2D.

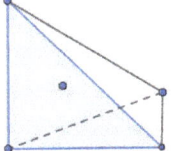 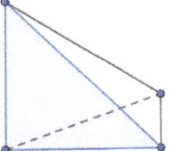

Figure 2. Mini-element $P1 - Bubble/P1$ in 3D.

Let T_h be a triangulation of Ω; we consider the function $b \in H^1(T)$, which takes the value 1 at the barycenter and zero at the boundary ∂T of the reference triangle T and verifies $0 \leq b \leq 1$. Such a function is known as a bubble function. The space associated with the bubble is defined by

$$B_h = \left\{ v_h \in C(\overline{\Omega}); v_h^T = xb^T, \forall T \in T_h \right\}, \tag{22}$$

where x is a real number.

We define the discrete function spaces

$$V_{ih} = \left\{ v_h \in C(\overline{\Omega}) : v_h^T \in P_1(T); , \forall T \in T_h \right\}, i = 1, \ldots, d. \tag{23}$$

$$Q_h = \{q_h \in C(\overline{\Omega}) : q_h^T \in P_1(T); , \forall T \in T_h, \int_\Omega q_h dx = 0\}, \tag{24}$$

where $P_1(T)$ is the set of all 1-order polynomials on triangle T.

And we set

$$X_{ih} = V_{ih} \oplus B_h, \tag{25}$$

$$X_h = X_{1h} \times X_{2h} \times \ldots \times X_{dh}. \tag{26}$$

As a result, $X_h \subset V$, the $P1 - Bubble/P1$ finite-element approximation of problem (8), will find $(u_h, p_h) \in X_h \times Q_h$ such that

$$\begin{cases} a(u_h, v_h) + b(v_h, p_h) = F(v_h) & \forall v_h \in X_h, \\ b(q_h, u_h) = 0 & \forall q_h \in Q_h. \end{cases} \tag{27}$$

The velocity field u_h and the pressure p_h for a given triangle T are approximated by linear combinations of the basis functions $(\phi_i)_{i=1,\ldots,d+1}$ in the form

$$u_h^T = \sum_{i=1}^{d+1} u_i \phi_i(x) + u_b \phi_b(x), \quad p_h^T = \sum_{i=1}^{d+1} p_i \phi_i(x), \quad d = 2, 3 \tag{28}$$

where u_i and p_i are nodal values of u_h and p_h, while u_b is the bubble value. The basis functions are defined by

$$\phi_1(x,y) = 1 - x - y, \quad \phi_2(x,y) = x, \quad \phi_3(x,y) = y, \quad \phi_b(x,y) = 27\phi_1(x,y)\phi_2(x,y)\phi_3(x,y)$$

if $d = 2$ and

$$\phi_1(x,y) = 1 - x - y - z, \quad \phi_2(x,y) = x, \quad \phi_3(x,y) = y, \quad \phi_4(x,y) = z,$$
$$\phi_b(x,y) = 256\phi_1(x,y)\phi_2(x,y)\phi_3(x,y)\phi_4(x,y)$$

if $d = 3$.

We can rephrase system (27) as a (large) square matrix problem with the vectors U and P as the unknowns. By consequence, we obtain the following algebraic form:

$$\begin{bmatrix} A & B^t \\ B & 0 \end{bmatrix} \begin{bmatrix} U \\ P \end{bmatrix} = \begin{bmatrix} F \\ 0 \end{bmatrix}, \tag{29}$$

where the matrices A, B, and the vector F are defined by

$$A = (A_{ij}), A_{ij} = \int_\Omega \tilde{\mu} \nabla \phi_i \nabla \phi_j dx + \int_\Omega K^{-1} \mu \phi_i \phi_j, dx + \int_{\partial \Omega} B^{-1} A^{-1} \phi_i \phi_j d\sigma,$$
$$i, j = 1, \ldots, n_u.$$
$$B = (B_{kj}), B_{kj} = -\int_\Omega \partial_1 \phi_k \phi_j, dx - \int_\Omega \partial_2 \phi_k \phi_j, dx, k = 1, \ldots, n_p \text{ and}$$
$$j = 1, \ldots, n_u.$$
$$F = (F_i), F_i = \int_\Omega f \phi_i, dx + \int_{\partial \Omega} B^{-1} g \phi_i, d\sigma, i = 1, \ldots, n_u.$$

To solve the large system we can be use the Uzawa conjugate gradient algorithm [32–34].

4. Stability and a Priori Error Estimates

In this section, we will establish the stability and a priori estimate for the pressure and the velocity of our problem.

Lemma 1. *There is a constant $c_4 \succ 0$ independent from the mesh parameter h such that*

$$\sup_{v_h \in X_h} \frac{b(v_h, q_h)}{\|v_h\|_V} \geq C_4 \|q_h\|_{0,\Omega}, \forall q_h \in Q_h. \tag{30}$$

Proof of Lemma 1. This Lemma can be established by the same proof of Lemma 2 in [35]. □

Theorem 3. *For any $(w_h, s_h) \in X_h \times Q_h$ there is a constant $c_5 \succ 0$ independent from the mesh parameter h such that*

$$\sup_{(v_h, q_h) \in X_h \times Q_h} \frac{a(w_h, v_h) + d(s_h, q_h)}{\|v_h\|_V + \|q_h\|_{0,\Omega}} \geq C_5 (\|w_h\|_V + \|s_h\|_{0,\Omega}), \tag{31}$$

where $d(s_h, q_h) = \int_\Omega s_h q_h, dx, \forall (q_h, s_h) \in Q_h^2$.

Proof of Theorem 3. For any (w_h, s_h) in $X_h \times Q_h$ we have:
Firstly,

$$\sup_{(v_h, q_h) \in X_h \times Q_h} \frac{a(w_h, v_h) + d(s_h, q_h)}{\|v_h\|_V + \|q_h\|_{0,\Omega}} \geq \frac{a(w_h, w_h) + d(s_h, 0)}{\|w_h\|_V + \|0\|_{0,\Omega}} \geq \|w_h\|_V, \tag{32}$$

On the other hand,

$$\sup_{(v_h, q_h) \in X_h \times Q_h} \frac{a(w_h, v_h) + d(s_h, q_h)}{\|v_h\|_V + \|q_h\|_{0,\Omega}} \geq \frac{a(w_h, 0) + d(s_h, s_h)}{\|0\|_V + \|s_h\|_{0,\Omega}} \geq \|s_h\|_{0,\Omega}, \tag{33}$$

by combining these inequalities in Equations (32)–(33), we obtain the result Equation (31), of which the constant is $C_5 = \frac{1}{2}$. □

Now, we will introduce and demonstrate the a priori estimate error.

Theorem 4. *Let (u, p) be the solution of (1)–(2), and (u_h, p_h) be the solution of (27). Then the following error estimate holds*

$$\|u - u_h\|_V + \|p - p_h\|_{0,\Omega} \leq C \left\{ \inf_{v \in X_h} \|u - v\|_V + \inf_{q \in Q_h} \|p - q\|_{0,\Omega} \right\}, \tag{34}$$

where C is a constant independent of the mesh size h.

Proof of Theorem 4. Using the triangle inequality, we have

$$\| u - u_h \|_V + \| p - p_h \|_{0,\Omega} \leq \| u - v \|_V + \| p - q \|_{0,\Omega} + \| u_h - v \|_V + \| p_h - q \|_{0,\Omega}, \quad (35)$$

from Equation (31) there exists $(w, q) \in X_h \times Q_h$ with

$$\| w \|_{X_h} + \| q \|_{0,\Omega} \leq \gamma_1, \quad (36)$$

such that

$$\| u_h - v \|_V + \| p_h - q \|_{0,\Omega} \leq a(u_h - v, w) + b(w, p_h - q). \quad (37)$$

Since

$$a(u - v, w) + b(w, p - q) = a(u_h - v, w) + b(w, p_h - q), \quad (38)$$

and by using the Schwartz inequality we obtain

$$\begin{aligned}
a(u - v, w) + b(w, p - q) &= \int_\Omega \tilde{\mu} \nabla(u - v) \nabla w\, dx + \int_\Omega K^{-1} \mu (u - v) \cdot w\, dx \\
&\quad + \int_\Gamma B^{-1} A^{-1} (u - v) \cdot w\, d\sigma + \int_\Omega (p - q) \nabla \cdot w\, dx \\
&\leq \tilde{\mu}_0 \| \nabla(u - v) \|_{0,\Omega} \| \nabla w \|_{0,\Omega} + k_2 \mu_0 \| u - v \|_{0,\Omega} \| w \|_{0,\Omega} \\
&\quad + b_2 a_2 \| u - v \|_{0,\Gamma} \| w \|_{0,\Gamma} + \| p - q \|_{0,\Omega} \| \nabla w \|_{0,\Omega} \\
&\leq C_6 \| u - v \|_V \| w \|_V + C_7 \| p - q \|_{0,\Omega} \| w \|_V \\
&\leq C(\| u - v \|_V + \| p - q \|_{0,\Omega})
\end{aligned}$$

by the consistency, we have the result Equation (34). □

5. Numerical Simulation

In this section, some numerical results were obtained by programming the mini-element method in MATLAB and we compare these obtained results with those constructed from the ADINA system. Using our solver, we ran two test problems regarding the flow around a cylinder; our tests were focused on the change in the value of the diagonal coefficients of the permeability matrix. For both of the tests, the domain considered in the simulation experiment is the one studied by Schäfer et al. in [36] for two dimensions.

Example 1. *In this test, we performed simulations for the flow around a cylinder (Figure 3) by the change in the values of the coefficients α_1 and α_2 of the matrix K^{-1} defined as $K^{-1} = \begin{pmatrix} \alpha_1 & 0 \\ 0 & \alpha_2 \end{pmatrix}$, where α_1 and α_2 are two positive real numbers.*

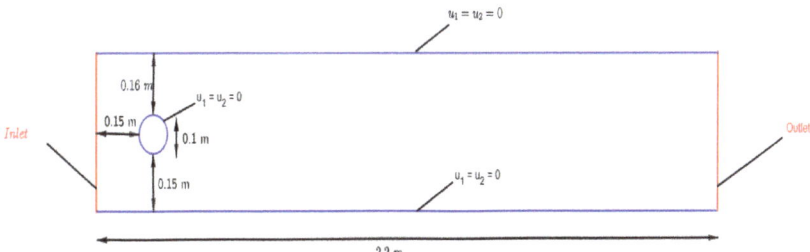

Figure 3. The simulated geometry of the cylinder and notations for the boundary conditions of the 2D test case.

The Figure 3 presents the domain geometry of the cylinder. The channel height is $H = 0.41$ m and the diameter is $D = 0.1$ m.

Next, we present the simulation made with the MATLAB software with the validation tests performed by the ADINA system. We used the Newtonian viscosity and dynamic viscosity, $\mu = \tilde{\mu} = 1$.

For the boundary conditions, we considered the boundary defined in [36], for which we considered the matrix A^{-1} and B defined by

$$A^{-1} = \begin{pmatrix} 1 & 0 \\ 0 & 1 \end{pmatrix}, B = \begin{pmatrix} 10^{-6} & 0 \\ 0 & 10^{-6} \end{pmatrix}. \tag{39}$$

The Figure 4 shows the ADINA created domain mesh upon which the various tests are based.

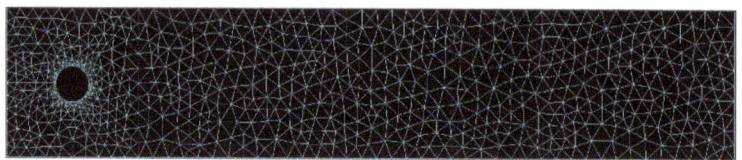

Figure 4. Mesh sample of domain created by the ADINA system.

Firstly, we present in Figures 5 and 6 the velocity field of our problem (1) and (2) in the following different cases $\alpha_1 = \alpha_2 = 10^{-6}$ and $\alpha_1 = 10^{-4}$, $\alpha_2 = 1$.

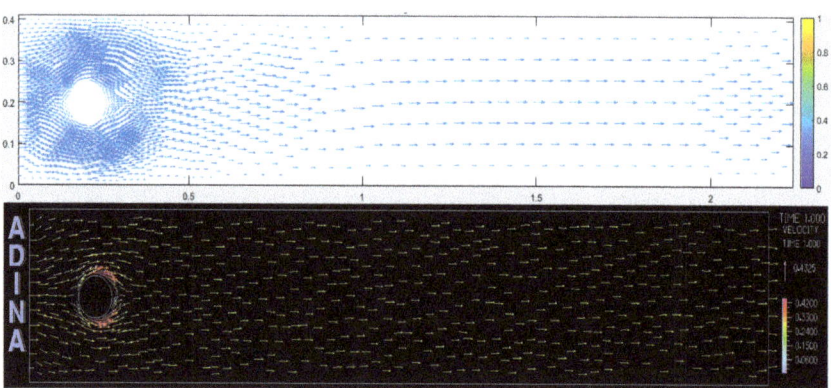

Figure 5. Velocity vector solution by $P1 - Bubble/P1$ (**above**) and velocity vector solution computed by the ADINA system (**below**) with $\alpha_1 = \alpha_2 = 10^{-6}$.

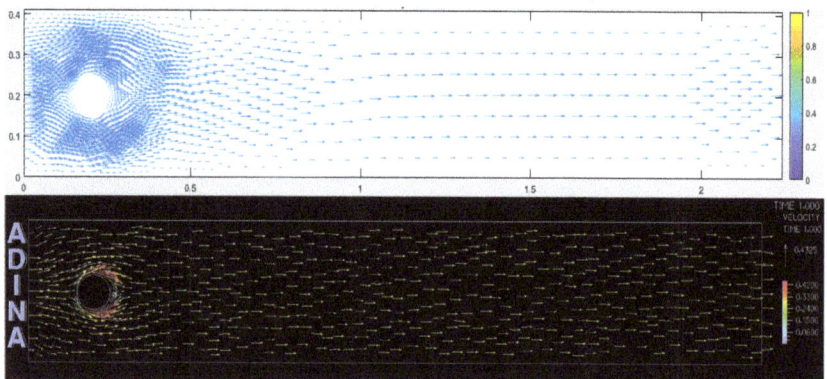

Figure 6. Velocity vector solution by $P1 - Bubble/P1$ (**above**) and velocity vector solution computed by the ADINA system (**below**) with $\alpha_1 = 10^{-4}$, $\alpha_2 = 1$.

The streamlines were derived from the velocity solution by numerically solving the Poisson equation with a zero Dirichlet boundary condition. Figures 7 and 8 present the streamlines in the following different cases: $\alpha_1 = \alpha_2 = 10^{-6}$ and $\alpha_1 = 10^{-4}$, $\alpha_2 = 1$.

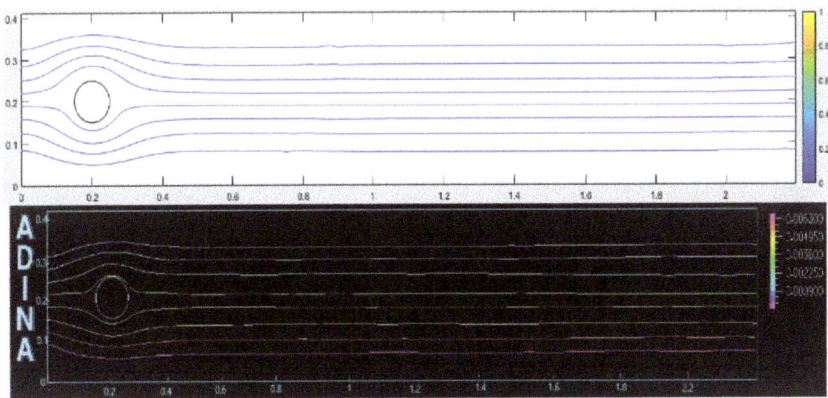

Figure 7. Solution computed with MATLAB (**above**) and with the ADINA system (**below**). The plots show the streamlines associated with a $\alpha_1 = \alpha_2 = 10^{-6}$.

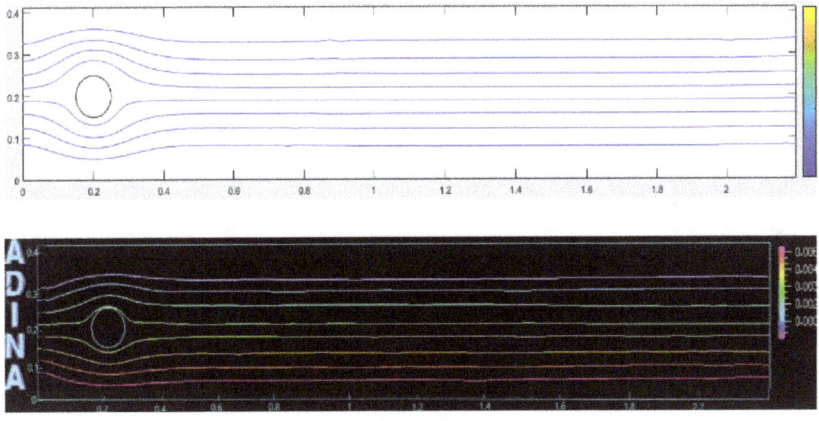

Figure 8. Solution computed with MATLAB (**above**) and with the ADINA system (**below**). The plots show the streamlines associated with a $\alpha_1 = 10^{-4}$, $\alpha_2 = 1$.

Isobar lines: Figures 9 and 10 present the isobar lines in the following different cases $\alpha_1 = \alpha_2 = 10^{-6}$ and $\alpha_1 = 10^{-4}$, $\alpha_2 = 1$.

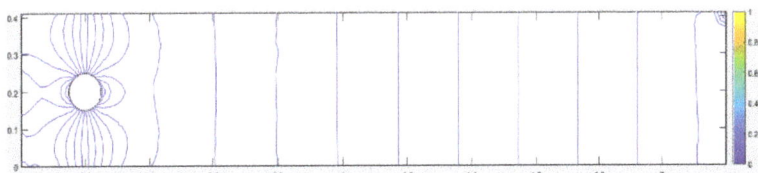

Figure 9. Isobar lines, $\alpha_1 = \alpha_2 = 10^{-6}$.

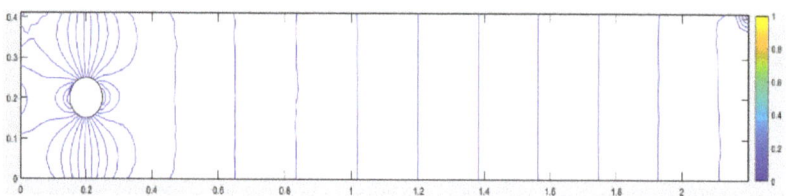

Figure 10. Isobar lines, $\alpha_1 = 10^{-4}$, $\alpha_2 = 1$.

In the previous example, the two-dimensional flow past a circular cylinder was simulated for varied permeability tensor K^{-1}. The objective of the present simulation was to investigate the solution of Brinkman's equations by using the mini-elements method $P1 - Bubble/P1$. Our simulation focused on two tests with deferent values for K^{-1} such that the first was $\alpha_1 = \alpha_2 = 10^{-6}$ and the second was $\alpha_1 = 10^{-4}$, $\alpha_2 = 1$. The computations with MATLAB and the ADINA system led to very similar results.

Example 2. We consider the stationary Brinkman problem (1) in $\Omega = [0;1] \times [0;1]$, with $\mu = 1$ and $\tilde{\mu} = 1$, the function f on the right-hand side in (1) is adjusted so that the exact solution is

$$u_1(x,y) = x^2(\frac{x}{3} - \frac{1}{2}), u_2(x,y) = xy(1-x), \tag{40}$$

for the velocity, and we take the pressure to be

$$p(x,y) = x^2 - \frac{1}{3}, \tag{41}$$

with the boundary conditions $\begin{bmatrix} 1 & 0 \\ 0 & 1 \end{bmatrix} \begin{bmatrix} u_1 \\ u_2 \end{bmatrix} + \begin{bmatrix} 10^{-6} & 0 \\ 0 & 10^{-6} \end{bmatrix} (\nabla u - pI).n = 0 \text{ on } \Gamma.$

The domain Ω is first discretized by a uniform mesh of size $h = 1/16$ (289 nodes and 512 triangles in the fine mesh). This initial mesh is successively refined to produce meshes with sizes $2^{-5}, 2^{-6}, 2^{-7}, 2^{-8}, 2^{-9}$ and 2^{-10}. We report in Table 1 the convergence rates and the distances $\|u - u_h\|_{H^1}$ and $\|u - u_h\|_{L^2}$ between the exact solution (40) and (41) and approximate solution. For this test, we took two values of K^{-1}, and we noticed that these norms were converging to zero.

Table 1. Numerical error and convergence rates for example 2.

Permeability	Mesh Size	$\|u-u_h\|_{L^2}$	Rate	$\|u-u_h\|_{H^1}$	Rate
$K^{-1} = \begin{pmatrix} 1 & 0 \\ 0 & 1 \end{pmatrix}$	2^{-5}	$2.58490367 \times 10^{-3}$		$7.30459072 \times 10^{-2}$	
	2^{-6}	$7.29374932 \times 10^{-4}$	1.23	$3.65242949 \times 10^{-2}$	1.26
	2^{-7}	$2.00944198 \times 10^{-4}$	1.12	$1.82662182 \times 10^{-2}$	1.20
	2^{-8}	$5.45035935 \times 10^{-5}$	1.20	$9.13565045 \times 10^{-3}$	1.17
	2^{-9}	$1.46182239 \times 10^{-5}$	1.13	$4.56876194 \times 10^{-3}$	1.14
	2^{-10}	$6.34523145 \times 10^{-6}$	1.07	8.5232210×10^{-4}	1.31
$K^{-1} = \begin{pmatrix} 10^4 & 0 \\ 0 & 10^4 \end{pmatrix}$	2^{-5}	$9.79901277 \times 10^{-2}$		1.71655622×10^{0}	
	2^{-6}	$5.71231633 \times 10^{-2}$	1.23	1.13006936×10^{0}	1.30
	2^{-7}	$2.10804196 \times 10^{-2}$	1.34	$4.88759130 \times 10^{-1}$	1.29
	2^{-8}	$5.96212978 \times 10^{-3}$	1.32	$1.82645760 \times 10^{-1}$	1.30
	2^{-9}	$1.54001284 \times 10^{-3}$	1.26	$6.50585157 \times 10^{-2}$	1.27
	2^{-10}	$3.88183415 \times 10^{-4}$	1.21	$2.29466805 \times 10^{-2}$	1.31

Since the assembly process is essentially based on the number of elements, we expect that the time to assemble the matrices will increase by approximately the same factor. We can see that Table 2 shows an almost linear optimal time-scaling for our implementation.

Table 2. CPU time in seconds for example 2 with $K^{-1} = \begin{pmatrix} 1 & 0 \\ 0 & 1 \end{pmatrix}$.

Mesh Size	2^{-5}	2^{-6}	2^{-7}	2^{-8}	2^{-9}	2^{-10}
CPU Time (s)	0.4521	0.1894	0.5811	2.4645	14.1669	26.20

6. Conclusions

We were interested in this work on the numeric solution of this equation in a heterogeneous porous media with a permeability tensor. In this study, we used the discretization of the mini-element method $P1 - Bubble/P1$. We established the stability and a priori error estimate for this approximation. The numerical and bidimensional simulations are presented and show the accuracy and efficiency of the proposed finite-element method.

Author Contributions: Conceptualization, L.E.O. and A.E.A.; methodology, L.E.O., O.E.M. and A.E.A.; software, L.E.O., A.E. and O.E.M.; validation, A.E. and A.E.A.; formal analysis, L.E.O.; investigation, A.E. and A.E.A.; resources, L.E.O.; data curation, L.E.O. and O.E.M.; writing—original draft preparation, L.E.O.; writing—review and editing, M.L.S., H.M. and R.M.; supervision, A.E. and A.E.A. All authors have read and agreed to the published version of the manuscript.

Funding: This research received no external funding.

Institutional Review Board Statement: Not applicable.

Informed Consent Statement: Not applicable.

Data Availability Statement: Data associated with this research is available at request.

Acknowledgments: The authors would like to express their sincere thanks for the referee for his/her helpful suggestions.

Conflicts of Interest: The authors declare no conflict of interest.

References

1. Brinkman, H.C. On the Permeability of Media Consisting of Closely Packed Porous Particles. *Flow Turbul. Combust.* **1949**, *1*, 81–86. [CrossRef]
2. Iliev, O.; Lazarov, R.; Willems, J. Variational Multiscale Finite Element Method for Flows in Highly Porous Media. *Multiscale Modeling Simul.* **2011**, *9*, 1350–1372. [CrossRef]
3. Kanschat, G.; Lazarov, R.; Mao, Y. Geometric Multigrid for Darcy and Brinkman Models of Flows in Highly Heterogeneous Porous Media: A Numerical Study. *J. Comput. Appl. Math.* **2017**, *310*, 174–185. [CrossRef]
4. Koplik, J.; Levine, H.; Zee, A. Viscosity Renormalization in the Brinkman Equation. *Phys. Fluids* **1983**, *26*, 2864–2870. [CrossRef]
5. Angot, P. Analysis of Singular Perturbations on the Brinkman Problem for Fictitious Domain Models of Viscous Flows. *Math. Methods Appl. Sci.* **1999**, *22*, 1395–1412. [CrossRef]
6. Shahnazari, M.R.; Moosavi, M.H. Investigation of Nonlinear Fluid Flow Equation in a Porous Media and Evaluation of Convection Heat Transfer Coefficient, By Taking the Forchheimer Term into Account. *Int. J. Theor. Appl. Mech.* **2022**, *7*, 12–17. [CrossRef]
7. Shahnazari, M.R.; Hagh, M.Z.B. Theoretical and Experimental Investigation of the Channeling Effect in Fluid Flow through Porous Media. *J. Porous Media* **2005**, *8*, 115–124. [CrossRef]
8. Shahnazari, M.R.; Ahmadi, Z.; Masooleh, L.S. Perturbation Analysis of Heat Transfer and a Novel Method for Changing the Third Kind Boundary Condition into the First Kind. *J. Porous Media* **2017**, *20*, 449–460. [CrossRef]
9. Iasiello, M.; Bianco, N.; Chiu, W.K.; Naso, V. Anisotropic Convective Heat Transfer in Open-Cell Metal Foams: Assessment and Correlations. *Int. J. Heat Mass Transf.* **2020**, *154*, 119682. [CrossRef]
10. Iasiello, M.; Bianco, N.; Chiu, W.K.S.; Naso, V. Anisotropy Effects on Convective Heat Transfer and Pressure Drop in Kelvin's Open-Cell Foams. *J. Phys. Conf. Ser.* **2017**, *923*, 012035. [CrossRef]
11. Amani, Y.; Takahashi, A.; Chantrenne, P.; Maruyama, S.; Dancette, S.; Maire, E. Thermal Conductivity of Highly Porous Metal Foams: Experimental and Image Based Finite Element Analysis. *Int. J. Heat Mass Transf.* **2018**, *122*, 1–10. [CrossRef]
12. Shah, N.A.; Wakif, A.; El-Zahar, E.R.; Ahmad, S.; Yook, S.-J. Numerical Simulation of a Thermally Enhanced EMHD Flow of a Heterogeneous Micropolar Mixture Comprising (60%)-Ethylene Glycol (EG),(40%)-Water (W), and Copper Oxide Nanomaterials (CuO). *Case Stud. Therm. Eng.* **2022**, *35*, 102046. [CrossRef]
13. Wakif, A.; Chamkha, A.; Animasaun, I.L.; Zaydan, M.; Waqas, H.; Sehaqui, R. Novel Physical Insights into the Thermodynamic Irreversibilities within Dissipative EMHD Fluid Flows Past over a Moving Horizontal Riga Plate in the Coexistence of Wall Suction and Joule Heating Effects: A Comprehensive Numerical Investigation. *Arab. J. Sci. Eng.* **2020**, *45*, 9423–9438. [CrossRef]

14. Nayak, M.K.; Wakif, A.; Animasaun, I.L.; Alaoui, M. Numerical Differential Quadrature Examination of Steady Mixed Convection Nanofluid Flows over an Isothermal Thin Needle Conveying Metallic and Metallic Oxide Nanomaterials: A Comparative Investigation. *Arab. J. Sci. Eng.* **2020**, *45*, 5331–5346. [CrossRef]
15. Wakif, A. A Novel Numerical Procedure for Simulating Steady MHD Convective Flows of Radiative Casson Fluids over a Horizontal Stretching Sheet with Irregular Geometry under the Combined Influence of Temperature-Dependent Viscosity and Thermal Conductivity. *Math. Probl. Eng.* **2020**, *2020*, 1675350. [CrossRef]
16. Ashraf, M.U.; Qasim, M.; Wakif, A.; Afridi, M.I.; Animasaun, I.L. A Generalized Differential Quadrature Algorithm for Simulating Magnetohydrodynamic Peristaltic Flow of Blood-Based Nanofluid Containing Magnetite Nanoparticles: A Physiological Application. *Numer. Methods Partial. Differ. Equ.* **2022**, *38*, 666–692. [CrossRef]
17. Wakif, A.; Zaydan, M.; Alshomrani, A.S.; Muhammad, T.; Sehaqui, R. New Insights into the Dynamics of Alumina-(60% Ethylene Glycol+ 40% Water) over an Isothermal Stretching Sheet Using a Renovated Buongiorno's Approach: A Numerical GDQLLM Analysis. *Int. Commun. Heat Mass Transf.* **2022**, *133*, 105937. [CrossRef]
18. Xiong, Q.; Hajjar, A.; Alshuraiaan, B.; Izadi, M.; Altnji, S.; Shehzad, S.A. State-of-the-Art Review of Nanofluids in Solar Collectors: A Review Based on the Type of the Dispersed Nanoparticles. *J. Clean. Prod.* **2021**, *310*, 127528. [CrossRef]
19. Ramesh, G.K.; Shehzad, S.A.; Izadi, M. Thermal Transport of Hybrid Liquid over Thin Needle with Heat Sink/Source and Darcy–Forchheimer Porous Medium Aspects. *Arab. J. Sci. Eng.* **2020**, *45*, 9569–9578. [CrossRef]
20. Huu-Quan, D.; Mohammad Rostami, A.; Shokri Rad, M.; Izadi, M.; Hajjar, A.; Xiong, Q. 3D Numerical Investigation of Turbulent Forced Convection in a Double-Pipe Heat Exchanger with Flat Inner Pipe. *Appl. Therm. Eng.* **2021**, *182*, 116106. [CrossRef]
21. Ern, A. *Aide-Mémoire Des Éléments Finis*; Dunod: Malakoff, France, 2005.
22. Raviart, P.-A. *Introduction à L'Analyse Numérique Des Équations Aux Dérivées Partielles*; Dunod: Malakoff, France, 1983.
23. Boffi, D.; Brezzi, F.; Fortin, M. *Mixed Finite Element Methods and Applications*; Springer: Berlin/Heidelberg, Germany, 2013; Volume 44.
24. El Moutea, O.; El Amri, H.; El Akkad, A. Mixed Finite Element Method for Flow of Fluid in Complex Porous Media with a New Boundary Condition. *Comput. Sci.* **2020**, *15*, 413–431.
25. John, V. *Finite Element Methods for Incompressible Flow Problems*; Springer: Berlin/Heidelberg, Germany, 2016; Volume 51.
26. Elakkad, A.; Elkhalfi, A.; Guessous, N. An a Posteriori Error Estimate for Mixed Finite Element Approximations of the Navier-Stokes Equations. *J. Korean Math. Soc.* **2011**, *48*, 529–550. [CrossRef]
27. Tinsley Oden, J.; Wu, W.; Ainsworth, M. An a Posteriori Error Estimate for Finite Element Approximations of the Navier-Stokes Equations. *Comput. Methods Appl. Mech. Eng.* **1994**, *111*, 185–202. [CrossRef]
28. Hannukainen, A.; Juntunen, M.; Stenberg, R. Computations with Finite Element Methods for the Brinkman Problem. *Comput. Geosci.* **2011**, *15*, 155–166. [CrossRef]
29. Arnold, D.N.; Brezzi, F.; Fortin, M. A Stable Finite Element for the Stokes Equations. *Calcolo* **1984**, *21*, 337–344. [CrossRef]
30. Brezzi, F.; Fortin, M. *Mixed and Hybrid Finite Element Methods*; Springer Science & Business Media: Berlin/Heidelberg, Germany, 2012; Volume 15.
31. Koubaiti, O.; Elkhalfi, A.; El-Mekkaoui, J.; Mastorakis, N. Solving the Problem of Constraints Due to Dirichlet Boundary Conditions in the Context of the Mini Element Method. *Int. J. Mech.* **2020**, *14*, 12–21.
32. Bramble, J.H.; Pasciak, J.E.; Vassilev, A.T. Analysis of the Inexact Uzawa Algorithm for Saddle Point Problems. *SIAM J. Numer. Anal.* **1997**, *34*, 1072–1092. [CrossRef]
33. Hackbusch, W. *Iterative Solution of Large Sparse Systems of Equations*; Springer: Berlin/Heidelberg, Germany, 1994; Volume 95.
34. Koko, J. Efficient MATLAB Codes for the 2D/3D Stokes Equation with the Mini-Element. *Informatica* **2019**, *30*, 243–268. [CrossRef]
35. Juntunen, M.; Stenberg, R. Analysis of Finite Element Methods for the Brinkman Problem. *Calcolo* **2010**, *47*, 129–147. [CrossRef]
36. Schäfer, M.; Turek, S.; Durst, F.; Krause, E.; Rannacher, R. Benchmark Computations of Laminar Flow around a Cylinder. In *Flow Simulation with High-Performance Computers II*; Springer: Berlin/Heidelberg, Germany, 1996; pp. 547–566.

Article

Study on Vibration Friction Reducing Mechanism of Materials

Yunnan Teng *, Quan Wen, Liyang Xie and Bangchun Wen

Department of Mechanical Engineering and Automation, Northeastern University, Shenyang 110819, China
* Correspondence: ynteng@me.neu.edu.cn

Abstract: Friction has a vital role in studying materials' and systems' behavior. The friction between two objects and the inner friction of materials under the condition of vibration usually can present different characteristics. These characteristics are different from the conventional conditions. It is shown in practice that vibration can reduce the friction coefficient and friction force between two objects. Vibration can lighten abrasion of objects and reduce energy consumption. All of these can give great efficiency, but, until now, the vibration friction-reducing mechanism has not been fully revealed. In this manuscript, the friction-reducing mechanism of materials under arbitrary vibration forces is investigated. The results show that the effective friction coefficient of materials under arbitrary vibration forces is always the minimum. The relationship between the effective friction coefficient and the negative gradient is investigated in this research. When the vibration force direction projects are in the first and the third quadrants, the negative gradient of the effective friction coefficient gets larger slowly, and then it becomes stable. When the vibration force direction projects are in the second and the fourth quadrants, the negative gradient of the effective friction coefficient decays to zero at the initial stage and then increases rapidly.

Keywords: vibration; friction; effective friction coefficient; negative gradient

MSC: 74H45

1. Introduction

Vibration is common in engineering practice and daily life, and it is the main content in the study of vibration friction mechanics. We are always in a vibration environment, such as the vibration of houses and bridges, the vibration of machine tools, the vibration of engines, and the vibration of road rollers and sinking and pulling machines. In the progress of science and engineering, a lot of mechanical equipment are moving towards high speed, high precision, and miniaturization [1,2]. Research on vibration is becoming more and more important. It is necessary to master vibration law and the transmission path of the interface so as to reasonably use or suppress vibration. One of the most important problems with vibration is the friction between interfaces. It is the key to improving the reliability and life of machinery and equipment, and its economic significance is very clear. In industry, generally in this case, the main reason leading to the failure of machines is not damage of the components of the machine itself but the wear of the contact interface of various parts under the action of fretting or sliding friction [3–8]. As one of the most fundamental physical phenomena, friction is the most common phenomenon, and vibration friction usually happens in mechanical systems [9–12]. Many researchers have focused on the relationships between vibration and friction. On the basis of oil film dynamic pressure lubrication and an elastic contact model of the asperities, Bao et al. set up a kinematic coupling model of the rotation-axial engagement process according to friction elements and gave the engagement characteristics of the multi-disc wet friction clutch [13]. Marques et al. studied several friction force models dealing with different friction phenomena in the research of multibody system dynamics [14]. To study the random stick-slip vibration of duffing systems of dry friction, a numerical approximate solution was performed by Jin et al. [15].

Some researchers performed experimental validation and investigations of vibration friction systems [16–18]. Sun et al. analyzed the friction coefficient based on the recurrence plots and proposed a new method to identify the running-in state of the friction pair [19,20]. Many nonlinear phenomena were presented in engineering of the discontinuities introduced by friction in the governing equations [21–23]. In engineering practice, friction between the contact bodies can cause lots of undesirable effects on the system, such as frictional chatter [24], wear in friction-induced vibrations [25,26], and reduction characteristics of silicon [27]. The natural frequencies and damped forced vibrations were investigated by Safaei for an improved and lightweight sandwich plate of a periodic load in a limited time [28]. Doan et al. analyzed the free vibration and static bucking of flexoelectric variable thickness nanoplates. To emphasize the affection of flexoelectricity in free vibration and static buckling of the nanoplates, a variety of parameter studies was conducted [29]. A nonlinear static bending study of microplates resting on imperfect Pasternak elastic foundations was carried out by Thai Dung et al. By the improved couple stress theory and finite element methods, the nonlinear finite element formulations were performed [30]. For illustration as a stationary process with white noise, the vibration response of beams in the condition of random load was studied by Nguyen et al. To predict the fundamental frequencies of the structures, the artificial neural network (ANN) model was presented [31]. The dynamic problem for the moment theory of elasticity related to the finite length crack in normal stress conditions on the banks was demoted to a series of displacement and rotation integral equations in [32], which were performed mathematically. Moreover, in [33], the dynamic problems related to micro-polar elastic bodies were carried out by an eigenvalues technique. Lai Thanh Tuan et al. devised and performed numerical and analytical solutions for problems in two dimensions, including the spreading of unsteady axisymmetric boundary disturbances of a "non-classical" elastic medium of spherical boundaries [34]. Recently, based on a serious of methodologies, many researchers have performed numerous studies on the computation of plate and shell structures. Many beneficial discoveries were made [35–39].

However, several problems for vibration friction in the case of arbitrary vibration working environments have not yet been sufficiently studied, including the effective coefficient of dynamic friction and the friction mechanism in arbitrary vibration of materials and the negative gradient of friction.

The purpose of this paper is to present the friction-reducing mechanism of materials under arbitrary vibration forces. Due to limitations associated with the negative gradient of the effective friction coefficient and the effective friction coefficient in arbitrary vibration working environments, the vibration friction characteristics of materials have not been thoroughly explained. Based on the effective coefficient of dynamic friction and the friction mechanism in arbitrary vibration of materials, the effective friction coefficient was deduced in this research, and the negative gradient of friction was also discussed.

The main body of this paper is split into four sections. The material model is presented in Section 2. The effective coefficient of friction is studied in Section 3. The negative gradient of the effective friction coefficient is given in Section 4. In Section 5, important conclusions are summarized.

2. Model of Material

It is a very common phenomenon that materials always vibrate under the vibration condition in engineering. In the last century, some researchers proposed the concept of effective friction coefficient from the perspective of breaking static conditions by using pure mechanical methods [14,17]. In this paper, the concept of effective friction coefficient is used to study the friction reduction effect of vibration under three conditions: that the vibration direction is parallel to the force, the vibration direction is parallel to the normal pressure, and the vibration direction is perpendicular to the force and the normal pressure. Then, on the basis of these three conditions, the effective friction coefficient formula of vibration in an arbitrary direction is further derived. It is proved that vibration can reduce friction. The influence and control of vibration parameters on friction reduction are explained by the change in effective friction coefficient reduction rate in this paper.

Firstly, the model is established in a Cartesian coordinate system. This is shown in Figure 1. The effective friction coefficient is f^*; f_1 is the coefficient of the maximum static friction between the material and the surface; N is the normal compression force (opposite paralleled axis Z); Q is the tension force (paralleled axis X); F_0 is the amplitude of the force $F(t)$; $F(t) = F_0 \sin(\omega t + \phi)$; Q_{min} is the minimum force to move the material. P is the gravity force, $P = mg$.

$$Q_{min} = (N + mg)f_1 - F_0 = f_1(N + mg)\left(1 - \frac{F_0}{f_1(N + mg)}\right), \quad (1)$$

$$f^* = \frac{Q_{min}}{N + mg} = f_1\left(1 - \frac{F_0}{f_1(N + mg)}\right). \quad (2)$$

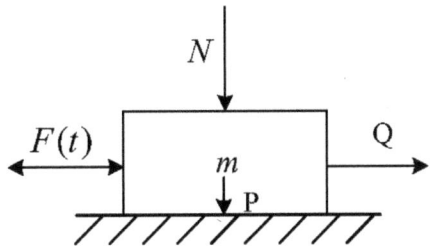

Figure 1. The vibration model of parallel force.

This is the effective friction coefficient formula under the condition that the vibration and the force direction are parallel. Since $\frac{F_0}{f_1(N+mg)} > 0$, the effective friction coefficient under vibration is less than the coefficient of the max static friction f_1; thus, the effective friction under vibration is reduced.

When the vibration direction is parallel to the normal pressure, the material model is shown in Figure 2.

$$Q_{min} = (N + mg - F_0)f_1 = f_1(N + mg)\left(1 - \frac{F_0}{N + mg}\right), \quad (3)$$

$$f^* = \frac{Q_{min}}{N + mg} = f_1\left(1 - \frac{F_0}{N + mg}\right). \quad (4)$$

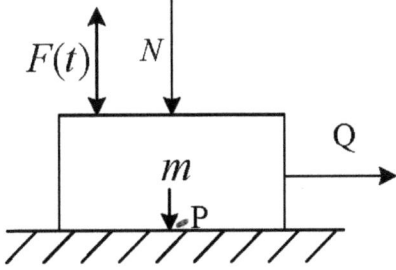

Figure 2. The vibration model of vertical force.

When the vibration direction is perpendicular to the force and the normal pressure, the material model is shown in Figure 3.

$$Q_{min} = \sqrt{(f_1(N+mg))^2 - F_0^2} = f_1(N+mg)\sqrt{1 - \left(\frac{F_0}{f_1(N+mg)}\right)^2}, \quad (5)$$

$$f^* = \frac{Q_{min}}{N+mg} = f_1\sqrt{1 - \left(\frac{F_0}{f_1 A}\right)^2}. \quad (6)$$

where $A = N + mg$, and P is the gravity force; $P = mg$.

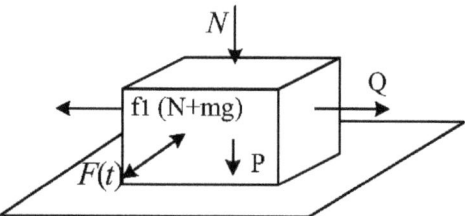

Figure 3. The model of vibration vertical to the friction and the normal pressure.

Similarly, the effective friction under vibration is reduced in these conditions. Then, on the basis of these three conditions, the effective friction coefficient formula of vibration in an arbitrary direction is further derived. Arbitrary vibration force can be seen as three components, and the effective friction coefficient under the arbitrary time-varying external forces is one of the critical characters to show the nonlinear dynamic characteristics of the system. Herein, it is studied in different conditions, respectively.

Firstly, the model is established in a Cartesian coordinate system, as shown in Figure 4. Next, m is the mass; f_1 is the coefficient of the maximum static friction between the material and the surface; N is the normal compression force (opposite paralleled axis Z); Q is the tension force (paralleled axis X); F_0 is the amplitude of the force $F(t)$; $F(t) = F_0 \sin(\omega t + \phi)$ is the arbitrary time-varying external forces, and its vectors are α, β, γ. P is the gravity force, $P = mg$. Then, the arbitrary time-varying external forces in different conditions are discussed separately.

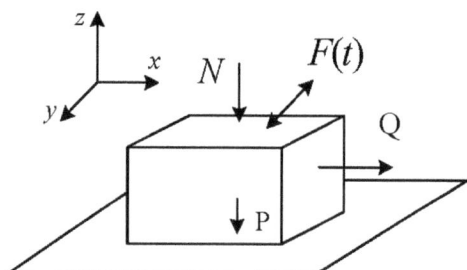

Figure 4. Model of the vibratory material under arbitrary vibration.

3. Effective Coefficient of Friction f^*

When the arbitrary time-varying external force projects are in the first and the third quadrants of the xz plane (including the limit boundary: projection in the axis z), the maximum synthetic tension and the minimum compression are obtained, as shown in Figure 5. Herein, the force Q comes to Q_{min} and yields

$$(Q_{min} + F_0 \cos \alpha)^2 + (F_0 \cos \beta)^2 = (f_1(N + mg - F_0 \cos \gamma))^2, \qquad (7)$$

where Q_{min} is the minimum force to move the material.

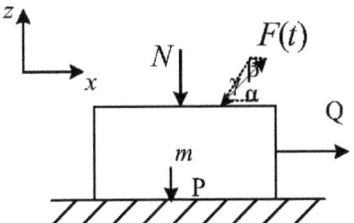

Figure 5. Vibration force projects in the first and the third quadrants.

Then, there is

$$f^* = f_1 \left(\sqrt{\left(1 - \frac{F_0 \cos \gamma}{N + mg}\right)^2 - \left(\frac{F_0 \cos \beta}{f_1(N + mg)}\right)^2} - \frac{F_0 \cos \alpha}{f_1(N + mg)} \right), \qquad (8)$$

where f^* is the effective coefficient of friction.

Here, supposing $f^* \geq f_1$, there is

$$\sqrt{\left(1 - \frac{F_0 \cos \gamma}{N + mg}\right)^2 - \left(\frac{F_0 \cos \beta}{f_1(N + mg)}\right)^2} - \frac{F_0 \cos \alpha}{f_1 N + mg} \geq 1. \qquad (9)$$

$A = N + mg$, then there is

$$\left(1 - \frac{F_0 \cos \gamma}{A}\right)^2 - \left(\frac{F_0 \cos \beta}{f_1 A}\right)^2 \geq \left(1 + \frac{F_0 \cos \alpha}{f_1 A}\right)^2, \qquad (10)$$

there is $\left(1 - \frac{F_0 \cos \gamma}{A}\right)^2 - \left(\frac{F_0 \cos \beta}{f_1 A}\right)^2 \geq \left(1 + \frac{F_0 \cos \alpha}{f_1 A}\right)^2 \geq 1$.

For the above equation, when $\cos \beta = 0$, $\cos \gamma = 0$, and $\cos \alpha = 0$ at the same time, then the left could be equal to the right. However, $\cos \alpha^2 + \cos \beta^2 + \cos \gamma^2 = 1$, and so $\cos \alpha$, $\cos \beta$, and $\cos \gamma$ cannot be all zero simultaneously. Hence, the supposition is not tenable. Therefore, there is $f^* < f_1$.

When the vibration force projects are in the second and the fourth quadrants of the xz plane, the model is shown in Figure 6.

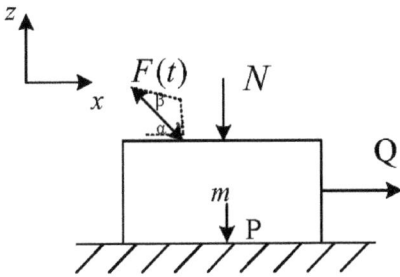

Figure 6. Vibration force projects in the second and the fourth quadrants.

Assume $|\cos \alpha| = i$, $|\cos \beta| = j$, $|\cos \gamma| = k$ and $i > 0$, $j \geq 0$, $k > 0$, there is,

$$(Q_{min} - F_0 i)^2 + (F_0 j)^2 = (f_1(N + mg - F_0 k))^2. \tag{11}$$

Substituting $N + mg = A$ into the above equation, there is

$$f_1^* = f_1 \left(\sqrt{\left(1 - \frac{F_0 k}{A}\right)^2 - \left(\frac{F_0 j}{f_1 A}\right)^2} + \frac{F_0 i}{f_1 A} \right), \tag{12}$$

where f_1^* is the effective coefficient of the friction when the vibration force project is in the second quadrant. Meanwhile, when the vibration force project is in the fourth quadrant, there is

$$(Q_{min} + F_0 i)^2 + (F_0 j)^2 = (f_1(N + mg + F_0 k))^2, \tag{13}$$

where Q_{min} is the minimum force to move the material.

Simplifying the above expression yields

$$f_2^* = f_1 \left(\sqrt{\left(1 + \frac{F_0 k}{A}\right)^2 - \left(\frac{F_0 j}{f_1 A}\right)^2} - \frac{F_0 i}{f_1 A} \right), \tag{14}$$

where f_2^* is the effective coefficient of friction when the vibration force project is in the fourth quadrant.

Hence, the effective friction coefficient f^* should be the minimum of the above, that is, $f^* = \min(f_1^*, f_2^*)$.

Suppose $\frac{i}{k} < f_1$, $\frac{F_0 i}{f_1 A} < \frac{F_0 k}{A}$, $\left(1 - \frac{F_0 i}{f_1 A}\right)^2 > \left(1 - \frac{F_0 k}{A}\right)^2 \geq \left(1 - \frac{F_0 k}{A}\right)^2 - \left(\frac{F_0 j}{f_1 A}\right)^2$, there is

$$f_1^* = f_1 \left(\sqrt{\left(1 - \frac{F_0 k}{A}\right)^2 - \left(\frac{F_0 j}{f_1 A}\right)^2} + \frac{F_0 i}{f_1 A} \right) < f_1. \tag{15}$$

Suppose $\frac{i}{k} > f_1$, $\frac{F_0 i}{f_1 A} > \frac{F_0 k}{A}$, $\left(1 + \frac{F_0 i}{f_1 A}\right)^2 > \left(1 + \frac{F_0 k}{A}\right)^2 \geq \left(1 + \frac{F_0 k}{A}\right)^2 - \left(\frac{F_0 j}{f_1 A}\right)^2$, there is

$$f_1^* = f_1 \left(\sqrt{\left(1 + \frac{F_0 k}{A}\right)^2 - \left(\frac{F_0 j}{f_1 A}\right)^2} - \frac{F_0 i}{f_1 A} \right) < f_1. \tag{16}$$

When $\frac{i}{k} = f_1$ and $j \neq 0$, there is $f_1^* < f_1$, $f_2^* < f_1$; when $\frac{i}{k} = f_1$ and $j = 0$, there is $f_1^* = f_2^* = f_1$.

To sum up, the results show that when $\frac{i}{k} = f_1$ and $j = 0$, there is $f^* = \min(f_1^*, f_2^*) = f_1$. Otherwise, there is $f^* < f_1$ always.

4. Negative Gradient of the Effective Friction Coefficient

In addition, the negative gradient η of the effective friction coefficient is discussed in this paper. The negative gradient has a critical effect on the ratio of the effective friction coefficient to the friction coefficient. Suppose $|\cos \alpha| = i$, $|\cos \beta| = j$, $|\cos \gamma| = k$, $\rho = \frac{F_0}{A}$. When $i \geq 0, j > 0, k > 0$ (in the first coordination), there is $1 - \rho k > 0$.

$$\eta = 1 - \frac{f^*}{f_1} = 1 - (|1 - \rho k| - \frac{\rho i}{f_1}) = \rho \sqrt{1 - i^2} + \frac{\rho i}{f_1} \tag{17}$$

and $i = \frac{1}{\sqrt{1+f_1^2}}$, $\eta'|_i = 0$; η obtains the max value.

By deriving Equation (17), there is

$$\eta'|_i = -\rho(\frac{i}{\sqrt{1-i^2}} - \frac{1}{f_1}) \tag{18}$$

According to the values shown in Figure 7, there is no negative gradient at the $f_1 = 0$ stage. The curve is absolutely smooth, and the negative gradient η is always zero in this stage. When $f_1 = 0.1$, η is increased with ρ immediately, and the curve is much steeper. With the increase in f_1, η will be stable gradually. When $f_1 = 1$, η will be flat.

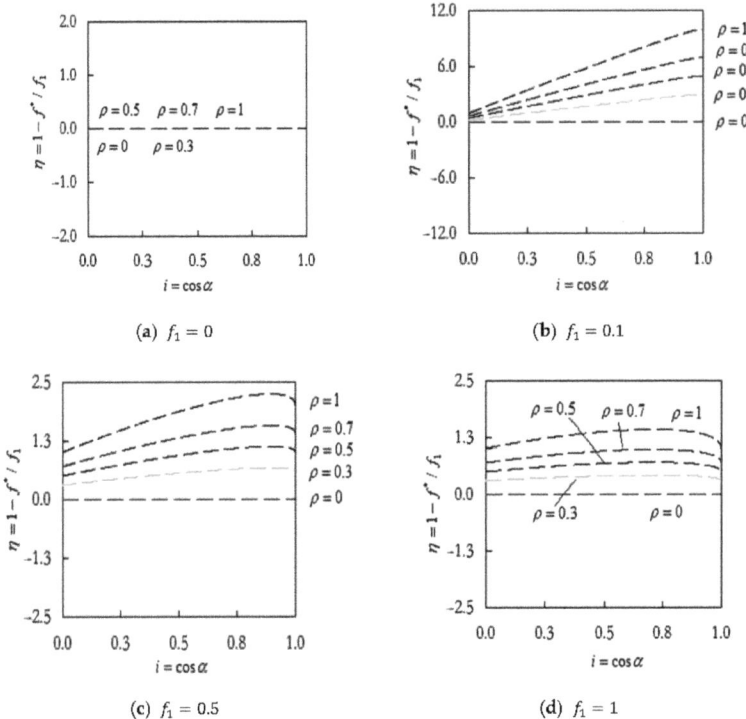

Figure 7. The negative gradient of the effective friction coefficient η.

According to $\begin{cases} i^2 + k^2 = 1 \\ i/k = f_1 \\ j = 0 \end{cases}$, there is

$$\begin{cases} i = \frac{f_1}{\sqrt{1+f_1^2}} \\ k = \frac{1}{\sqrt{1+f_1^2}} \\ j = 0 \end{cases} \tag{19}$$

Then, there is

$$\eta = 1 - \frac{f^*}{f_1} = \begin{cases} 1 - \left(|1 - \rho k| + \frac{\rho i}{f_1}\right), i/k < f_1 \\ 1 - \left(|1 + \rho k| - \frac{\rho i}{f_1}\right), i/k \geq f_1 \end{cases} = \left|\rho\sqrt{1-i^2} - \frac{\rho i}{f_1}\right|. \tag{20}$$

$$\eta'|_i = \begin{cases} -\rho\left(\frac{i}{\sqrt{1-i^2}} + \frac{1}{f_1}\right), 0 \leq i < \frac{f_1}{\sqrt{1+f_1^2}} \\ \rho\left(\frac{i}{\sqrt{1-i^2}} + \frac{1}{f_1}\right), i = \frac{f_1}{\sqrt{1+f_1^2}} \end{cases}. \tag{21}$$

To sum up, according to the values shown in Figure 8, there is no negative gradient in the stage of $f_1 = 0$. Obviously, there is no friction in this stage; η is always zero with increasing ρ. When $f_1 = 0.1$, η increases with ρ obviously, and then the curve will be steeper. When $f_1 = 0.5$, η decreases with ρ and decays to zero first, but then η increases with ρ gradually. In conclusion, the negative gradient of effective friction has a critical effect on friction. It was shown that the changes in the negative gradient of the effective friction coefficient changed the effective friction coefficient under the arbitrary time-varying external forces, which consequently reduced the friction. From a tribological perspective, the negative gradient of the effective friction coefficient plays a great role in the course of vibration affection on the friction. The rules concerning the negative gradient of the effective friction coefficient resulted in an effective friction coefficient, especially under the arbitrary time-varying external forces.

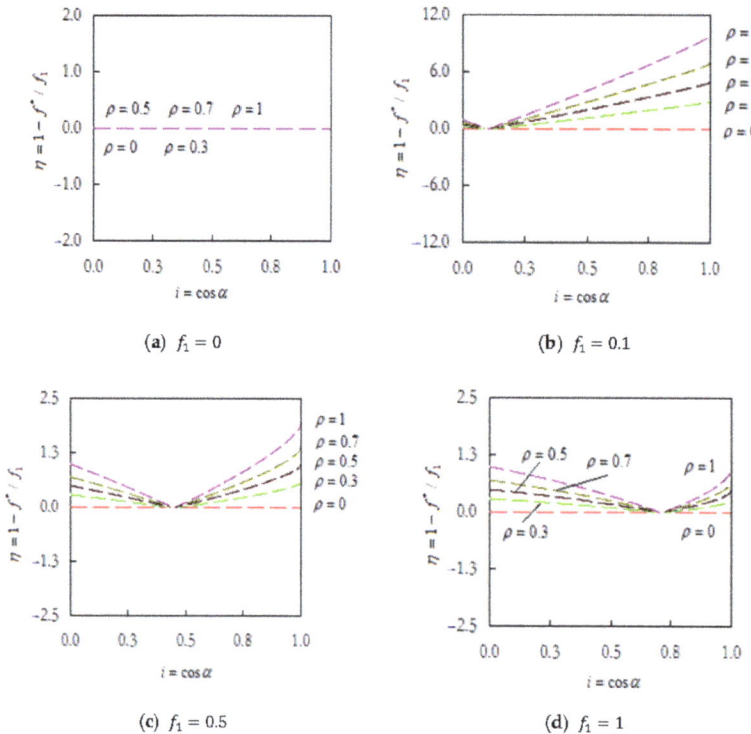

Figure 8. The negative gradient of effective friction coefficient η.

5. Conclusions

In conclusion, this paper investigated the effective coefficient of friction under arbitrary time-varying external forces. The results show the relationship of the effective friction coefficient and the negative gradient of friction.

(1) When the vibration force direction projects are in the first and the third quadrants, the negative gradient η increases first, and then η will be stable gradually. When the vibration force direction projects are in the second and the fourth quadrants, η decreases but then increases gradually.

(2) From a tribological perspective, the negative gradient of the effective friction coefficient plays a great role in the course of vibration affection on the friction. The changes in the negative gradient of the effective friction coefficient resulted in an effective friction coefficient, especially under the arbitrary time-varying external forces. The effective friction coefficient was closely related to vibration properties and the influence and control on vibration systems with friction.

(3) It is shown that the numerical and analytical results of the rules concerning the negative gradient of the effective friction coefficient change the effective friction coefficient under the arbitrary time-varying external forces, which consequently reduce the friction in vibration.

Author Contributions: Q.W.: software, writing the original draft, investigation. Y.T.: formulation, approach, review and editing, supervision, formal analysis. L.X.: validation. B.W.: validation. All authors have read and agreed to the published version of the manuscript.

Funding: This research has been supported by the National Natural Science Foundation of China NNSFC (Grant, No. 51305069).

Data Availability Statement: Some data, models, or code generated or used during the study are available from the corresponding author by request.

Conflicts of Interest: The authors declare no conflict of interest.

References

1. Pérez-Aracil, J.; Camacho-Gómez, C.; Pereira, E.; Vaziri, V.; Aphale, S.S.; Salcedo-Sanz, S. Eliminating Stick-Slip Vibrations in Drill-Strings witha Dual-Loop Control Strategy Optimised by the CRO-SL Algorithm. *Mathmatics* **2021**, *9*, 1526. [CrossRef]
2. Sun, X.Q.; Wang, T.; Zhang, R.L.; Gu, F.S.; Ball, A.D. Numerical Modelling of Vibration Responses of Helical Gears under Progressive Tooth Wear for Condition Monitoring. *Mathematics* **2021**, *9*, 213. [CrossRef]
3. Wu, J.T.; Yang, Y.; Yang, X.K.; Cheng, J.S. Fault feature analysis of cracked gear based on LOD and analytical-FE method. *Mech. Syst. Signal Pr.* **2018**, *98*, 951–967. [CrossRef]
4. Sugiura, J.; Jones, S. Real-time stick-slip and vibration detection for 8 1/2"-hole-size rotary steerable tools in deeper wells and more aggressive drilling. In Proceedings of the AADE National Technical Conference, Houston, TX, USA, 10–12 April 2007.
5. Robnett, E.; Hood, J.; Heisig, G.; Macpherson, J. Analysis of the stick-slip phenomenon using downhole drill string rotation data. In Proceedings of the SPE/IADC Drilling Conference, Amsterdam, The Netherlands, 9–11 March 1999.
6. Baradaran-Nia, M.; Afizadeh, G.; Khanmohammadi, S.; Azar, B.F. Optimal sliding mode control of single degree-of-freedom hysteretic structural system. *Commun. Nonlinear Sci. Numer. Simul.* **2012**, *17*, 4455–4466. [CrossRef]
7. Fu, X.; Ai, H.; Li, C. Repetitive Learning Sliding Mode Stabilization Control for a Flexible-Base, Flexible-Link and Flexible-Joint Space Robot Capturing a Satellite. *Appl. Sci.* **2021**, *11*, 8077. [CrossRef]
8. Kumar, V.C.; Hutchings, I.M. Reduction of the sliding friction of metals by the application of longitudinal or transverse ultrasonic vibration. *Tribol. Int.* **2004**, *37*, 833–840. [CrossRef]
9. Adachi, K.; Kato, K.; Sasatani, Y. The micro-mechanism of friction drive with ultrasonic wave. *Wear* **1996**, *194*, 137–142. [CrossRef]
10. Tucker, W.; Wang, C. On the effective control of torsional vibrations in drilling systems. *J. Sound Vib.* **1999**, *224*, 101–122. [CrossRef]
11. Carducci, G.; Giannoccaro, N.I.; Messina, A.; Rollo, G. Identification of viscous friction coefficients for a pneumatic system model using optimization methods. *Math. Comput. Simul.* **2006**, *71*, 385–394. [CrossRef]
12. Tsai, C.C.; Tseng, C.H. The effect of friction reduction in the presence of in-plane vibrations. *Arch. Appl. Mech.* **2006**, *75*, 164–176. [CrossRef]
13. Bao, H.; Huang, W.; Lu, F. Investigation of engagement characteristics of a multi-disc wet friction clutch. *Tribol. Int.* **2021**, *159*, 106940.
14. Jia, S.H. The effective friction coefficient under the vibration. *J. Tsinghua Univ.* **1959**, *5*, 165–170.
15. Jin, X.; Xu, H.; Wang, Y.; Huang, Z. Approximately analytical procedure to evaluate random stick-slip vibration of Duffing system including dry friction. *J. Sound Vib.* **2019**, *443*, 520–536. [CrossRef]
16. Marino, L.; Cicirello, A. Experimental investigation of a single-degree-of-freedom system with Coulomb friction. *Nonlinear Dyn.* **2020**, *99*, 1781–1799. [CrossRef]
17. Wang, D.W.; Mo, J.L.; Wang, Z.G.; Chen, G.X.; Ouyang, H.; Zhou, Z.R. Numerical study of friction-induced vibration and noise on groove-textured surface. *Tribol. Int.* **2013**, *64*, 1–7. [CrossRef]
18. Wang, X.C.; Huang, B.; Wang, R.L.; Mo, J.L.; Ouyang, H. Friction-induced stick-slip vibration and its experimental validation. *Mech. Syst. Signal Process.* **2020**, *142*, 106705. [CrossRef]
19. Sun, G.D.; Zhu, H.; Ding, C. Using Recurrence Plots for Stability Analysis of Ring-on-Disc Tribopairs. *Ind. Lubr. Tribol.* **2019**, *71*, 532–539. [CrossRef]

20. Sun, G.D.; Zhu, H.; Ding, C.; Jiang, Y.; Wei, C.L. On the Boundedness of Running-In Attractors Based on Recurrence Plot and Recurrence Qualification Analysis. *Friction* **2019**, *7*, 432–443. [CrossRef]
21. Liu, Y.; Pavlovskaia, E.; Hendry, D.; Wiercigroch, M. Vibro-impact responses of capsule system with various friction models. *Int. J. Mech. Sci.* **2013**, *72*, 39–54. [CrossRef]
22. Marques, F.; Flores, P.; Pimenta Claro, J.C.; Lankarani, H.M. A survey and comparison of several friction force models for dynamic analysis of multibody mechanical systems. *Nonlinear Dyn.* **2016**, *86*, 1407–1443. [CrossRef]
23. Mostaghel, N. A non-standard analysis approach to systems involving friction. *J. Sound Vib.* **2005**, *284*, 583–595. [CrossRef]
24. Rusinek, R.; Wiercigroch, M.; Wahi, P. Modelling of frictional chatter in metal cutting. *Int. J. Mech. Sci.* **2014**, *89*, 167–176. [CrossRef]
25. Saha, A.; Wiercigroch, M.; Jankowski, K.; Wahi, P.; Stefański, A. Investigation of two different friction models from the perspective of friction-induced vibrations. *Tribol. Int.* **2015**, *90*, 185–197. [CrossRef]
26. Yan, Y.; Liu, G.; Wiercigroch, M.; Xu, J. Safety estimation for a new model of regenerative and frictional cutting dynamics. *Int. J. Mech. Sci.* **2021**, *201*, 106468. [CrossRef]
27. Yoo, S.S.; Kim, D.E. Effects of vibration frequency and amplitude on friction reduction and wear characteristics of silicon. *Tribol. Int.* **2016**, *16*, 198–206. [CrossRef]
28. Safaei, B. Frequency-dependent damped vibrations of multifunctional foam plates sandwiched and integrated by composite faces. *Eur. Phys. J. Plus* **2021**, *136*, 646. [CrossRef]
29. Duc, D.H.; Thom, D.V.; Cong, P.H.; Minh, P.V.; Nguyen, N.X. Vibration and static buckling behavior of variable thickness flexoelectric nanoplates. *Mech. Based Des. Struct. Mach.* **2022**, *8*, 1–29. [CrossRef]
30. Dung, N.T.; Van Ke, T.; Huyen, T.T.H.; Van Minh, P. Nonlinear static bending analysis of microplates resting on imperfect two-parameter elastic foundations using modified couple stress theory. *Comptes Rendus Mec.* **2022**, *350*, 121–141. [CrossRef]
31. Tho, N.C.; Ta, N.T.; Thom, D.V. New Numerical Results from Simulations of Beams and Space Frame Systems with a Tuned Mass Damper. *Materials* **2019**, *12*, 1329. [CrossRef] [PubMed]
32. Han, S.Y.; Narasimhan, M.N.L.; Kennedy, T.C. Finite crack propagation in a micropolar elastic solid. *KSME J.* **1989**, *3*, 103. [CrossRef]
33. Kumar, R.; Singh, R.; Chadha, T.K. Eigen value approach to second dynamic problem of micropolar elastic solid. *Indian J. Pure Appl. Math.* **2003**, *34*, 743–754.
34. Tuan, L.T.; Dung, N.T.; Van Thom, D.; Van Minh, P.; Zenkour, A.M. Propagation of non-stationary kinematic disturbances from a spherical cavity in the pseudo-elastic cosserat medium. *Eur. Phys. J. Plus* **2021**, *136*, 1199. [CrossRef]
35. Tran, T.T.; Tran, V.K.; Le, P.B.; Phung, V.M.; Do, V.T.; Nguyen, H.N. Forced vibration analysis of laminated composite shells reinforced with graphene nanoplatelets using finite element method. *Adv. Civ. Eng.* **2020**, *2020*, 1471037. [CrossRef]
36. Nam, V.H.; Nam, N.H.; Vinh, P.V.; Khoa, D.N.; Thom, D.V.; Minh, P.V. A new efficient modified first-order shear model for static bending and vibration behaviors of two-layer composite plate. *Adv. Civ. Eng.* **2019**, *2019*, 6814367. [CrossRef]
37. van Thom, D.; Duc, D.H.; van Minh, P.; Tung, N.S. Finite element modelling for free vibration response of cracked stiffened fgm plates. *Vietnam J. Sci. Technol.* **2020**, *58*, 119. [CrossRef]
38. Tho, N.C.; Thanh, N.T.; Tho, T.D.; van Minh, P.; Hoa, L.K. Modelling of the flexoelectric effect on rotating nanobeams with geometrical imperfection. *J. Braz. Soc. Mech. Sci. Eng.* **2021**, *43*, 510. [CrossRef]
39. Dung, N.T.; van Minh, P.; Hung, H.M.; Tien, D.M. The third-order shear deformation theory for modelling the static bending and dynamic responses of piezoelectric bidirectional functionally graded plates. *Adv. Mater. Sci. Eng.* **2021**, *2021*, 5520240. [CrossRef]

Article

CFD Model Studies of Dust Dispersion in Driven Dog Headings

Magdalena Tutak [1], Jarosław Brodny [2], Antoni John [3], Janos Száva [4,*], Sorin Vlase [4,5] and Maria Luminita Scutaru [4,*]

1. Faculty of Mining, Safety Engineering and Industrial Automation, Silesian University of Technology, 41-800 Zabrze, Poland
2. Faculty of Organization and Management, Silesian University of Technology, Roosevelta 26-28, 41-800 Zabrze, Poland
3. Faculty of Mechanical Engineering, Silesian University of Technology, Konarskiego 18A, 44-100 Gliwice, Poland
4. Department of Mechanical Engineering, Transilvania University of Brasov, B-dul Eroilor, 29, 500036 Brasov, Romania
5. Romanian Academy of Technical Sciences, 010071 Bucharest, Romania
* Correspondence: eet@unitbv.ro (J.S.); lscutaru@unitbv.ro (M.L.S.)

Citation: Tutak, M.; Brodny, J.; John, A.; Száva, J.; Vlase, S.; Scutaru, M.L. CFD Model Studies of Dust Dispersion in Driven Dog Headings. *Mathematics* **2022**, *10*, 3798. https://doi.org/10.3390/math10203798

Academic Editor: Elena Benvenuti

Received: 8 September 2022
Accepted: 12 October 2022
Published: 14 October 2022

Publisher's Note: MDPI stays neutral with regard to jurisdictional claims in published maps and institutional affiliations.

Copyright: © 2022 by the authors. Licensee MDPI, Basel, Switzerland. This article is an open access article distributed under the terms and conditions of the Creative Commons Attribution (CC BY) license (https://creativecommons.org/licenses/by/4.0/).

Abstract: Dust is one of the most burdensome hazards found in the environment. It is composed of crushed solids that pose a threat to the health and life of people, machines and machine components. At high concentration levels, it can reduce visibility. All of these negative phenomena occur during the process of underground mining, where dust hazards are common. The negative impact of dust on the efficacy of the mining process prompts research in this area. The following study presents a method developed for model studies of dust dispersion in driven dog headings. This issue is immensely important due to the fact that these dog headings belong to a group of unidirectional excavations (including tunnelling). This paper presents the results of model studies on dust dispersion in driven dog headings. The main focus is on the analysis of the distribution of dust concentration along a dog heading during the mining process. In order to achieve this goal, a model test method based on the finite volume method, which is included in the group of CFD methods, was developed. Analyses were carried out for two different values of dust emission from the face of the excavation for the transient state. The results made it possible to determine areas with the highest potential for dust concentration. The size and location of these areas are mainly dependent on the amount of dust emissions during the mining process. The results can support the process of managing dust prevention and protection of workers during the mining excavation process.

Keywords: dust dispersion; driven dog heading; CFD model; underground mining

MSC: 76B15

1. Introduction

One of the most commonly reported threats associated with the extraction of solid minerals in underground mines, including hard coal, is dust. In hard coal mines, this hazard results from the common occurrence of coal and hard dust in mining excavations (including a mixture of silica, aluminosilicates and other components, such as trace metals). The dust is produced in the process of mining and transporting the mine output [1–3]. The main reason for the formation of large amounts of dust in this process is current machining-based technology used for mining the rock mass. During this process, the rock is crushed and ground, which causes the formation of large amounts of rock and coal dust. In the case of mining operations, quantities of dust are directly proportional to the amount of the mine output.

In addition, large amounts of dust are generated during horizontal and vertical transport and repeated pouring of the mine output. The dust generated in the mining process is very dangerous for both employees and machines [4]. It floats in the mine atmosphere and can reach most mining excavation sites through a ventilation system, even those far from its place of origin. This causes the dust hazard to occur in virtually all mining excavations. However, the largest amount of dust can be found in excavations with unmined coal (coal body), including driven dog headings.

Dog headings (tunnels) driven in coal and rock belong to a group of the so-called "blind" or unidirectional excavations (Figure 1). This means that they only have one connection to the central (general) ventilation system. This, in turn, means that both fresh and exhaust air is transported through the same excavation. As a result, fresh air must be delivered to the face zone, where the rock mass is mined, in such a way that it does not impede the outflow of exhaust air and gases that are emitted into this dog heading from the rock mass.

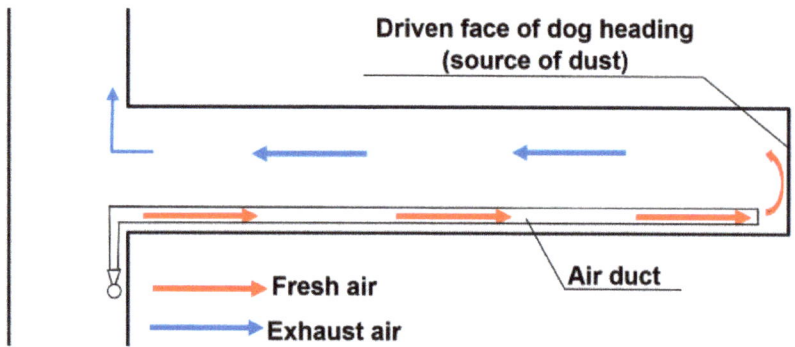

Figure 1. Ventilation diagram for a driven dog heading.

The face of such excavations is also characterized as having the greatest amount of dustiness [5]. In addition to profound harmfulness to employees' health, this dustiness also reduces visibility, leading to total darkness. This significantly hinders operations. Dust is also considered to have an immensely negative effect on the operation of machines and their individual elements. According to statistics, dust generated in the mining process accounts for 60–80% of the dust generated in the entire mine [5]. The presence of dust in mine workings poses a great threat to the health of workers, both physical and psychological, as well as to the environment. Additionally, high concentrations of dust are the cause of very dangerous dust explosions [5–8]. Thus, it can be assumed that dustiness, which cannot be eliminated in the mining production process, is a very unfavorable phenomenon both to the health and life of the crew and the efficiency of the mining process.

Due to the very unfavorable effects of dust in mine workings, this topic has been addressed by many researchers. For example, probability experiments, direct field measurements and numerical simulations have been used to study dust in mine workings. Experimental studies have been conducted on scaled simulation models, among other aspects. Tan et al. designed an experimental model for a fully mechanized face at the Tongxin coal mine. They conducted a study of the distribution of dust concentrations of different moisture contents generated during coal mining, casing shifting, collapse and coal transport [9]. In turn, Shi et al. developed an experimental model to analyze the variation of dust concentrations during coal mining at different ventilation air velocities [10]. The simplifications they introduced to the structure and environmental conditions resulted in large deviations from the actual measurement results.

In terms of direct measurements, it is worth mentioning a study [11] that measured the distribution of PM2.5 dust concentrations in a coal face. Liu et al. carried out measurements of changes in dust concentrations along a driven dog heading during coal mining in a fully mechanized coal face [12]. It should be noted that field studies also show a number of shortcomings, including issues related to measurement uncertainty and the influence of very harsh environmental conditions on the quality of these measurements. Oftentimes, however, the results of these measurements are used to validate the accuracy of analytical experiments and the numerical simulations carried out.

In the case of model studies (numerical simulations), measurements in real conditions are crucial for mapping the studied region and the air flow field and diffusion behavior of dust emitted from various sources. Therefore, it is clear that model studies using structural models are now becoming an alternative to studies under real conditions. They also provide extensive opportunities for multivariate analysis of different states of the phenomenon under study. Therefore, their application in underground mining is becoming increasingly widespread.

Due to these aspects, it is crucial to conduct research in the field in order to expand knowledge of dust dispersion in mining processes. In this regard, both on-site and real-life studies are conducted. Model studies are increasingly used to analyse phenomena that would be hard to examine in real conditions.

Nevertheless, the use of model studies to examine the phenomenon of dustiness requires analysing two media, namely a gas medium (Euler) and a solid medium (Lagrange). Therefore, the analysis of dust dispersion in mining excavations requires a combination of gas and solid media.

The main objective was to determine a method of dust dispersion in driven dog headings and its concentration levels along these dog headings during the mining process. In order to achieve this goal, a model study method based on the finite volume method was developed. The study was performed for the actual driven dog heading, and the ventilation parameters adopted as boundary conditions were obtained based on direct studies. The analyses covered two different values of dust emissions from the face of the driven dog heading and were carried out for the transient state. In addition to the emission of dust into driven dog headings, the study also looked at the release of methane from the excavated coal seam, which makes it possible to reflect the actual ventilation processes in underground mine workings.

An important problem when modeling dust issues, including those in mine workings, is the issue of particle size distribution. This problem is extremely complex and depends on the type of seam being excavated and its geological properties, as well as the condition of the knives of the excavating machine organ and the process of sprinkling the seam. The analysis presented here adopts the distribution of dust particles according to the Rosin–Ramler model, often used in studies of dusting processes. This distribution is used to describe the diameter distribution of dust particles (materials) from processes such as grinding, milling, mincing and crushing, as well as for the diameter distribution of particles formed in other processes [13–17].

Adopting this model for the distribution of dust particles, taking into account the release of methane and analyzing the pumping system represent a new approach to the problem under study.

The ANSYS Fluent software was utilized for the analysis, which enabled the authors to determine the parameters of the mine gas and dust mixture at individual points of the studied dog heading (in a spatial arrangement).

2. Materials and Methods

The analysis of the impact of dust mass expenditure (quantity) on the dustiness of the driven dog heading was conducted using the computational fluid mechanics (CFD) in the Ansys Fluent software. In order to model a biphasic system, i.e., gas and solid, the Eulerian–Lagrangian approach was used. This approach assumes that the gas phase is regarded as a continuum by solving the Navier–Stokes equation, while the dispersed (dust) phase is solved by tracking the movement of a large number of particles in the calculated continuous phase field.

In accordance with the principles of fluid mechanics, the flow of air stream (gas) through the studied driven dog heading was adopted as a continuous phase, and dust was adopted as a discrete phase.

2.1. Mathematical Model of the Gas Flow through a Dog Heading

The mathematical model of airflow consists of conservation equations of turbulent mass, momentum, species and energy, as well as the scalar transport equations for the turbulence model [18,19]:

$$\nabla \cdot \rho U = 0 \tag{1}$$

$$\nabla \cdot \rho U U = \nabla \cdot \sigma + \rho g \tag{2}$$

where:

$$\sigma = -pI + \left[(\mu + \mu_t)\left(\nabla U + (\nabla U)^T\right)\right] - \frac{2}{3}(((\mu + \mu)(\nabla \cdot U)I)\rho k I) \tag{3}$$

$$\nabla \cdot (\rho c_p U T) = \nabla \cdot \left(k_{eff} + \frac{c_p \mu_t}{Pr_t}\right)\nabla T \tag{4}$$

$$\nabla \cdot (\rho w_i U) = \nabla \cdot \left(\rho D_{i,eff} + \frac{\mu_t}{Sc_i}\right)\nabla w_i \tag{5}$$

where: ρ is gas density (kg/m^3); U is air velocity (m/s); p is pressure (Pa); g is gravity acceleration (m·s^{-2}); w_i is mass fraction of species i; μ/μ_t are dynamic viscosity, Pa·s^{-1}; T is temperature, K; Sci is the Schmidt number; Pr_t is Prandtl number; k_{eff} is effective thermal conductivity, W·m^{-1}·K^{-1}; and $D_{i,eff}$ is effective diffusivity of species i, m·s^{-2}.

The stream of the air flowing through driven dog headings is turbulent in nature. In order to model the turbulent flow, the k-ε model was used. This model is based on solving Navier–Stokes equations averaged over time (the so-called RANS equation—Reynolds-Averaged Navier–Stokes). These equations are incomplete; hence, it is necessary to solve the variables k—the so-called kinetic turbulence energy and ε—energy dissipation, which were introduced to close the equations. The equation of kinetic turbulent energy and the equation of kinetic turbulent energy dissipation can be expressed as follows [20]:

$$\partial\frac{\partial k}{\partial t} + \frac{\partial}{\partial x_i}(\rho k u_i) = \frac{\partial}{\partial x_j}\left[(\mu + \frac{\mu_t}{\sigma_k})\frac{\partial k}{\partial x_j}\right] + G_k + G_b - \rho\varepsilon - Y_M + S_k \tag{6}$$

$$\partial\frac{\partial \varepsilon}{\partial t} + \frac{\partial}{\partial xi}(\rho \varepsilon u_i) = \frac{\partial}{\partial x_j}\left[(\mu + \frac{\mu_t}{\sigma_\varepsilon})\frac{\partial \varepsilon}{\partial x_j}\right] + C_{1\varepsilon}\frac{\varepsilon}{k}(G_k + C_{3\varepsilon}G_b) - C_{2\varepsilon}\rho\frac{\varepsilon^2}{k} + S_\varepsilon \tag{7}$$

where: $C_{1\varepsilon}$, $C_{2\varepsilon}$, $C_{3\varepsilon}$ are constants; σ_k, σ_ε are turbulent Prandtl numbers for k and ε; G_b is the generation of turbulence kinetic energy due to buoyancy; G_k is the generation of turbulence kinetic energy due to the mean velocity gradients; Y_M is a contribution of the fluctuating dilatation in compressible turbulence to the overall dissipation rate; and S_k, S_ε are user-defined source terms.

2.2. Mathematical Model of the Coal Dust Flow through a Dog Heading

The Lagrange method is used to track the trajectory of DPM particles. In this method, the motion of particles takes place according to Newton's second law. The movement of dust particles is influenced by many forces, which makes their interactions extremely complex. These forces mainly include gravity, adhesive force, drag force, buoyancy force, Magnus force, Saffman force, Basset force and False mass force [21]. However, since many of these interactions are small, most of them are ignored, with resistance force, gravity and pressure gradient force predominantly taken into account. According to Newton's second law, the force acting on a single dust particle can be determined based on the following relationship [22–26]:

$$m_p \frac{dv_p}{dt} = F_{drag} + F_g \tag{8}$$

where: m_p is the mass of dust particles (kg); v_p is the velocity of dust particles (m/s); F_{drag} is the drag force on the particles, (N); and F_g is gravity (N).

Therefore, F_{drag} is expressed as:

$$F_{drag} = \frac{\frac{1}{8}C_d \rho \pi d_p^2 |v - uv_p|}{v - v_p} \tag{9}$$

where: d_p is the particle diameter (m); u is the air velocity (m/s); v_p is the particle velocity (m/s); and C_d is the drag coefficient.

Therefore, C_d is given as:

$$C_d = \begin{cases} \frac{24}{Re \cdot C_c} \text{ for } Re \leq 1 \\ \frac{24(1+0.15Re^{0.687})}{Re} \text{ for } 1 < Re \leq 1000, \\ 0.44 \text{ for } Re > 1000 \end{cases} \tag{10}$$

where: C_c is the Cunningham slip correction factor, which is expressed by:

$$C_c = 1 + \frac{\lambda}{d_p}\left(2.514 + 0.8e^{\frac{-0.55d_p}{\lambda}}\right), \tag{11}$$

where: λ is the mean free path of gas molecules.

Velocity of dust particles with different sizes can be calculated by the following equation:

$$v_p = \sqrt{\frac{4(\rho_p - \rho_g)gd_p}{3\rho_g C_d}}, \tag{12}$$

3. Problem Statement and Boundary Conditions

The basis for the numerical analysis was the dog heading model with its real geometry, ventilation parameters (measured in real conditions) and equipment. The geometrical parameters along with the location of the auxiliary air duct line are shown in Figure 2. The diameter of the air duct line was 0.6 m. The air outlet of the air duct line was located 5.0 m from the mined coal body. The air duct line was built at a height of 2.5 m, and 0.65 m from the side wall of the dog heading (Figure 2). The source of dust was located on the surface of the mined coal body (as in reality).

The study was conducted for a forced (air-duct) ventilation system through pressing. This system is characterized by more intensive removal of noxious gases from the face than in the case of suction or combined ventilation, lower air losses and more favorable climatic conditions in the excavation. The disadvantage of this system is that used air flows through the entire length of the excavation, which causes difficulties in removing methane gas emitted from the excavated face, which tends to accumulate under the roof. With suction ventilation, the dilution of gases is faster, and the conditions in the entire excavation are more favorable because the gases do not flow out through the excavation, but through the air-duct ventilation. Combined ventilation, on the other hand, combines the advantages of suction and press ventilation. It is implemented by changing the direction of rotation of the axial fans' impeller, using a reversible device or two fans and bolts.

As previously mentioned, a pumping (pressing) system was used in this study. After developing a geometric model and defining boundary conditions (Figure 2), discretization of the developed model was carried out. This consisted of generating a polyhedral mesh consisting of a finite number of control volumes (Figure 3).

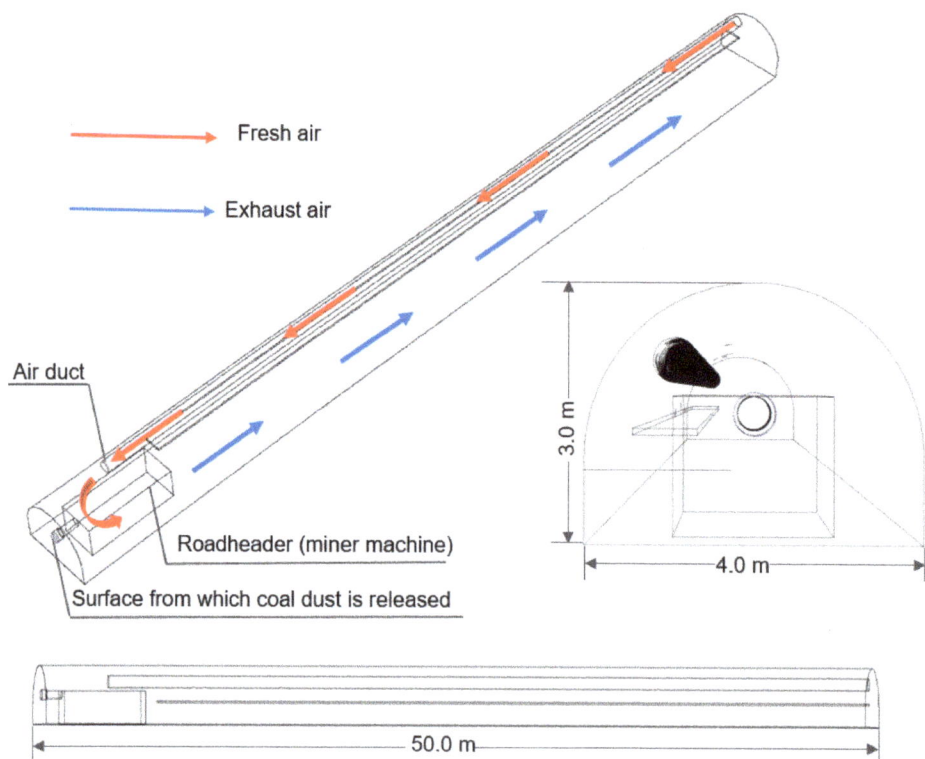

Figure 2. Geometric model of the studied dog heading with marked air flow directions.

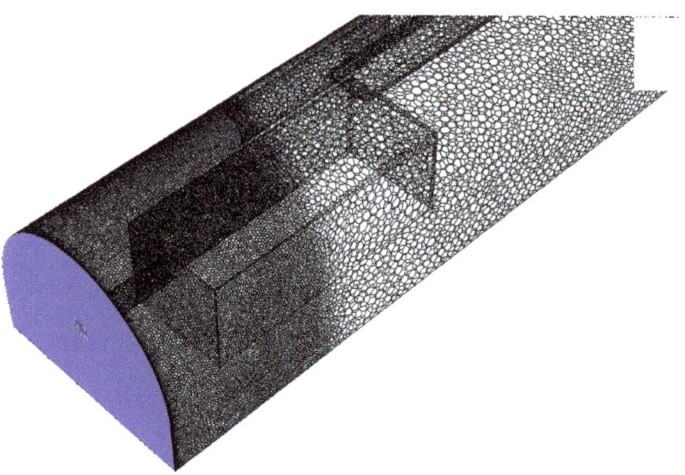

Figure 3. Fragment of the discrete model of the studied dog heading.

The boundary conditions were then adopted, including the physical model, which was used for numerical calculations. The basic parameters of the calculation model are shown in Table 1.

Table 1. The major parameter setting.

Name	Parametr Setting
Solver Type	Pressure-Based
Viscous Model	k-epsilon
Diameter Distribution	Rosin-Rammler
Total Flow Rate, kg/s	0.00125/0.00075
Material	Coal-hv
Max Diameter, m	0.001
Min Diameter, m	0.000001
Mean Diameter, m	0.0005
Density of dust, kg/m^3	1200

Calculations were made for the transient state. The analysis time was 180 s. Two variants of the emission volume of dust produced during the driving of the dog heading were analysed: 0.00125 and 0.00075 kg/s.

For each of the studied variants, the air flow delivered to the driven dog heading by means of the air duct line was the same and amounted to 376.8 m^3/min.

The research focused on the analysis of dust dispersion in the face zone from the commencement of mining the coal body. It was assumed that dust was released into the dog heading from the fragment of mined forehead. The dust grain composition was described according to the Rosin–Rammler distribution.

Numerical studies were conducted using Ansys Fluent 19.2 software (Canonsburg, PA, USA).

4. Results and Discussions

Research on the impact of the mass expenditure (quantity) of dust released into the dog heading during mining was carried out for the model, in which the biphasic medium created from the continuous air phase and the discrete phase in the form of dust particles was taken into account. The analysis involved the interaction between these phases.

A number of interesting results were obtained regarding both the ventilation parameters of the air stream and the distribution of dust particles itself.

In the first stage, ventilation parameters were determined for the system without dust. The air flow trajectories (without dust) through the driven dog heading are shown in Figure 4.

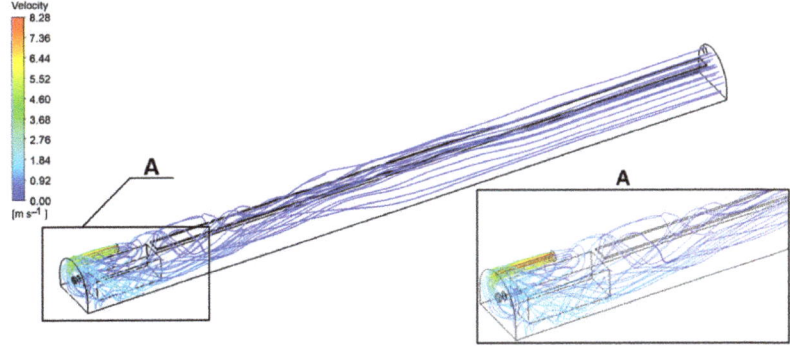

Figure 4. Trajectories of air flowing through the driven dog heading (without dust).

Based on the results, the highest air velocity was reported to occur in the face zone of the driven dog heading, in the area of the air stream outlet from the air duct line. It was also found that there was an area of significant air recirculation in this zone, where the air flow was most turbulent. This is due to the fact that in this area, the air flowing out of the air duct line hits the mined coal body and is bounced off, thereby changing its return flow. At the same time, having bounced off the air duct line, the air stream encounters an obstacle in the form of a road header.

In the second stage, the study looked at the impact of mass expenditure (quantity) of dust released into the dog heading during mining on the level of dustiness.

Here, the focus was placed on the increase of dustiness in the face zone during mining. During the analysis, dust dispersion in the studied dog heading was determined, with its emission intensity being 0.00125 and 0.00075 kg/s, respectively. Dustiness in subsequent phases of the analysis with consideration of the size of dust particles is presented in Figures 5 and 6.

The results of the calculations help to trace changes in the level of dustiness in the studied dog heading with the passage of time for both studied emissions. It is also possible to trace how the dust spreads along with the moving air stream. The results also allow for the determination of the location of individual dust grains for the selected timeframe. It is clear that the greater the distance from the face of the dog heading, the smaller the dust particles that move with the air stream will be. In turn, the larger dust particles fall on the footwall of the dog heading, which is caused by the force of inertia. This phenomenon is dangerous to the health of the workers, because these pathogenic particles of the smallest diameter are transferred over considerable distances and are inhaled.

Dust concentration levels in vertical cross-sections of the dog heading for both emissions are presented in Figures 7 and 8. They are shown in cross-sections of the dog heading located every 5.0 m from the exposed surface of the mining area (for 10 cross-sections).

Based on the results, the authors were able to determine changes in dust concentration levels along the measurement line located in the central plane of the dog heading at a height of 1.75 m (average height of the human mouth and nose) from its base. Distributions were determined after the total analysis time (180 s) for both studied emissions at 10 points located on this line (Figure 9).

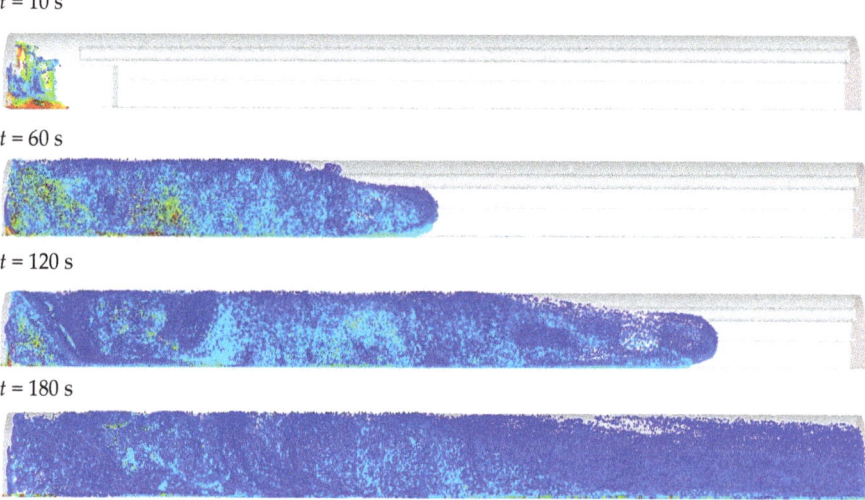

Figure 5. Distribution of different-sized dust particles in the dog heading at various time points for total dust rate = 0.00125 kg/s.

Figure 6. Distribution of different-sized dust particles in the dog heading at various times for total dust rate = 0.00075 kg/s.

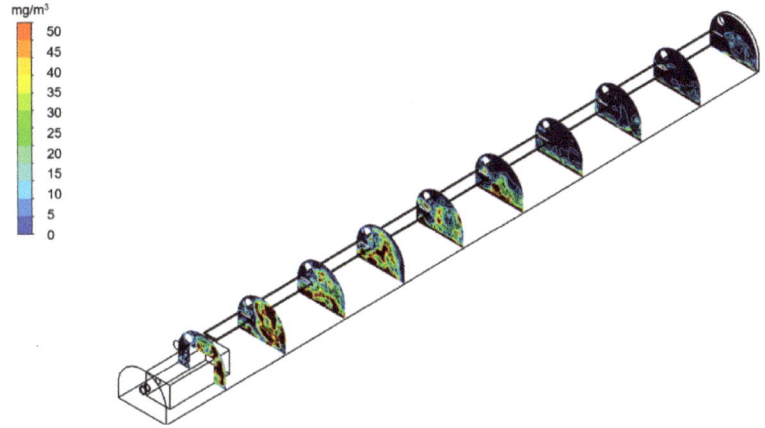

Figure 7. Mass dust concentration in the dog heading for time analysis t = 180 s for total dust rate = 0.00125 kg/s.

The presented methodology of the research procedure and the results obtained complement the previous level of knowledge in the field of modeling the flow of air with dust through driven dog headings. Previous research in this area has focused on modeling the air flow and determining the trajectories of the overflow for various ventilation systems and the release of methane into them from the mined coal seam. These studies were carried out for steady-state flow. On the other hand, the analyses presented in this paper represent the first stage of research on dust dispersion in mine workings for conditions in underground coal mines. The undoubted advantage is the inclusion of transients in the analysis, which has not been used for this type of condition. Thus, there are no methods analyzing the presented condition. By contrast, similar analyses have been carried out for the combustion process and for turbulent flows with a dispersive phase [27–31].

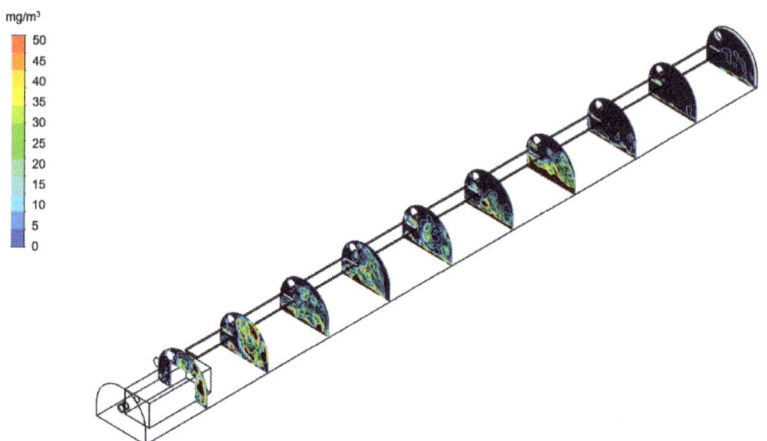

Figure 8. Mass dust concentration in the dog heading for time analysis $t = 180$ s for total dust rate = 0.00075 kg/s.

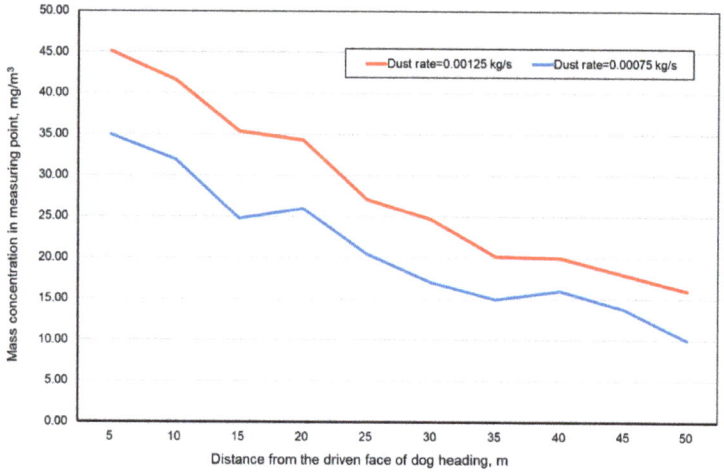

Figure 9. Distribution of dust concentration along the adopted measurement lines for studied variants.

5. Conclusions

Dust emissions from both mining and tunnel excavations constitute a major technical, organizational and health problem. Unfortunately, this dust has immensely harmful effects on the mining process. In order to reduce these effects, it is necessary to take measures to reduce dust emissions and movement in excavations. For this reason, it is important to know how dust disperses and distributes over time for various ventilation parameters. The method developed and presented in this paper allowed the authors to conduct such studies. However, it required an analysis of a biphasic medium with interaction. This approach makes it possible to trace the movement of dust particles in a gaseous medium for various ventilation parameters and the intensity of such emissions.

The method presented in this paper enables the determination of many interesting parameters of the gas–dust mixture. Undoubtedly, it creates opportunities for a much broader analysis of the phenomenon of dustiness in various areas and during various processes.

The results clearly indicate that the main reason for dust dispersion in mining excavations is an active ventilation system that transports dust particles over considerable distances from the place of their formation. The analysis of the distribution of this dust and trajectories of individual grains shows that its concentration is very uneven. This distribution largely depends on dust grain composition, the volume of emissions and ventilation parameters.

Based on the findings, it can be concluded that:

(1) The highest concentrations of dust during the mining of the coal seam were reported at the face of the driven dog heading. Due to the ventilation system used for such a heading (press–air-duct ventilation), the diffusion of dust with high concentrations along the length of this excavation was significant.

(2) The lowest dust concentrations, regardless of the size of dust emissions during the mining process, was reported on the side of the heading without a built-in air-duct ventilation system. This is because this side is where the air flows through the entire heading.

(3) A significant decrease in dust concentrations was reported at a distance of about 40 m from the seam being mined in the heading.

These conclusions should be widely used by the services responsible for mine safety.

The presented methodology, based on numerical simulations, makes it possible to conduct a multivariate analysis of the state of dustiness, taking into account various parameters of the studied phenomenon. The universality of this methodology also allows its application for the analysis of dustiness, including dust reduction agents.

Author Contributions: Conceptualization, M.T., J.B. and A.J.; methodology, M.T. and J.B.; software, M.T. and J.B.; validation, M.T. and J.B.; formal analysis, M.T. and J.B.; investigation, M.T., J.B., A.J. and J.S.; resources, M.T. and J.B.; data curation, M.T., J.B. and A.J.; writing—original draft preparation, M.T., J.B., A.J. and M.L.S.; writing—review and editing, M.T. and J.B.; visualization, M.T. and J.B.; supervision, M.T. and J.B.; project administration, M.T., J.B. and J.S.; funding acquisition, J.S., M.L.S. and S.V. All authors have read and agreed to the published version of the manuscript.

Funding: This research received no external funding. The APC was funded by Transilvania University of Brasov.

Data Availability Statement: Not applicable.

Conflicts of Interest: The authors declare no conflict of interest.

References

1. Brodny, J.; Tutak, M. Exposure to Harmful Dusts on Fully Powered Longwall Coal Mines in Poland. *Int. J. Environ. Res. Public Health* **2018**, *15*, 1846. [CrossRef] [PubMed]
2. Lebecki, K.; Małachowski, M.; Sołtysiak, T. Continuous dust monitoring in headings in underground coal mines. *J. Sustain. Min.* **2016**, *15*, 125–132. [CrossRef]
3. Ren, T.; Wang, Z.; Zhang, J. Improved dust management at a longwall top coal caving (LTCC) face—A CFD modelling approach. *Adv. Powder Technol.* **2018**, *29*, 2368–2379. [CrossRef]
4. Lilic, N.; Cvjetic, A.; Knezevic, D.; Milisavljevic, V.; Pantelic, U. Dust and Noise Environmental Impact Assessment and Control in Serbian Mining Practice. *Minerals* **2018**, *8*, 34. [CrossRef]
5. Wang, Z.; Li, S.; Ren, T.; Wu, J.; Lin, H.; Shaung, H. Respirable dust pollution characteristics within an underground heading face driven with continuous miner—A CFD modelling approach. *J. Clean. Prod.* **2019**, *217*, 267–283. [CrossRef]
6. Zhang, G.; Sun, B.; Song, S.; Wang, H.; Zhou, G. CFD comparative analysis on the pollution characteristics of coal dust under turbulent airflow from coal cutting in the fully mechanized mining face. *Process Saf. Environ. Prot.* **2021**, *146*, 515–530. [CrossRef]
7. Cai, P.; Nie, W.; Hua, Y.; Wei, W.; Jin, H. Diffusion and pollution of multi-source dusts in a fully mechanized coal face. *Process Saf. Environ. Prot.* **2018**, *118*, 93–105. [CrossRef]
8. Zhou, G.; Zhang, Q.; Bai, R.; Fan, T.; Wang, G. The diffusion behavior law of respirable dust at fully mechanized caving face in coal mine: CFD numerical simulation and engineering application. *Process Saf. Environ. Prot.* **2017**, *106*, 117–128. [CrossRef]
9. Tan, C.; Jiang, Z.-A.; Chen, J.-S.; Wang, P. Numerical simulation of influencing factors on dust movement during coal cutting at fully mechanized working faces. *Beijing Keji Daxue Xuebao/J. Univ. Sci. Technol. Beijing* **2014**, *36*, 716–721.
10. Shi, X.-X.; Jiang, Z.-A.; Zhou, S.-Y.; Cai, W. Experimental study on dust distribution regularity of fully mechanized mining face. *Meitan Xuebao/J. China Coal Soc.* **2008**, *33*, 1117–1121.

11. Nie, B.-S.; Li, X.-C.; Yang, T.; Hu, W.-X.; Guo, J.-H. Distribution of PM2.5 dust during mining operation in coal workface. *Meitan Xuebao/J. China Coal Soc.* **2013**, *38*, 33–37.
12. Liu, Y.; Jiang, Z.A.; Cai, W. Site measurement and digital smiulation of dust density distribution in fully mechanized longwall coal mining face. *J. Coal Sci. Technol.* **2006**, *34*, 80–82.
13. Colorado-Arango, L.; Menéndez-Aguado, J.M.; Osorio-Correa, A. Particle Size Distribution Models for Metallurgical Coke Grinding Products. *Metals* **2021**, *11*, 1288. [CrossRef]
14. Hossein, A.; Gholamreza, S. Investigating the shape and size distribution of dust in mechanized longwall method in Tabas coal mine. *Hum. Ecol. Risk Assess. Int. J.* **2017**, *23*, 28–39.
15. Coello-Velázquez, A.L.; Quijano Arteaga, V.; Menéndez-Aguado, J.M.; Pole, F.M.; Llorente, L. Use of the Swebrec Function to Model Particle Size Distribution in an Industrial-Scale Ni-Co Ore Grinding Circuit. *Metals* **2019**, *9*, 882. [CrossRef]
16. Papáček, Š.; Petera, K.; Císař, P.; Stejskal, V.; Saberioon, M. Experimental & Computational Fluid Dynamics Study of the Suitability of Different Solid Feed Pellets for Aquaculture Systems. *Appl. Sci.* **2020**, *10*, 6954.
17. Li, B.; Zeng, M.; Wang, Q. Numerical Simulation of Erosion Wear for Continuous Elbows in Different Directions. *Energies* **2022**, *15*, 1901. [CrossRef]
18. Kurnia, J.C.; Sasmito, A.P.; Mujumdar, A.S. CFD simulation of methane disperse, on and innovative methane management in underground mining faces. *Appl. Math. Model.* **2014**, *38*, 3467–3484. [CrossRef]
19. Sasmito, A.P.; Birgersson, E.; Ly, H.C.; Mujumdar, A.S. Some approaches to improve ventilation system in underground coalmines environment—A computational fluid dynamic study. *Tunn. Undergr. Space Technol.* **2013**, *34*, 82–95. [CrossRef]
20. Ansys Fluent 12.0 Theory Guide. Available online: https://www.afs.enea.it/project/neptunius/docs/fluent/html/th/main_pre.htm (accessed on 11 October 2022).
21. Hu, S.; Liao, Q.; Feng, G.; Huang, Y.; Shao, H.; Gao, Y.; Hu, F. Influences of ventilation velocity on dust dispersion in coal roadways. *Powder Technol.* **2020**, *360*, 683–694. [CrossRef]
22. Geng, F.; Gui, C.G.; Wang, Y.; Zhou, F.B.; Hu, S.Y.; Luo, G. Dust distribution and control in a coal roadway driven by an air curtain system: A numerical study. *Process Saf. Environ. Prot.* **2019**, *121*, 32–42. [CrossRef]
23. Geng, F.; Gang, L.; Wang, Y.C.; Li, Y.M.; Yuan, Z.L. Numerical investigation on particle mixing in a ball mill. *Powder Technol.* **2016**, *292*, 64–73. [CrossRef]
24. Lu, H.; Lu, L. CFD investigation on particle deposition in aligned and staggered ribbed duct air flows. *Appl. Therm. Eng.* **2016**, *93*, 697–706. [CrossRef]
25. Yao, G.X. Coarse Particle Settling Properties Study Based on Particle Analysis. Master's Thesis, Jiangxi University of Science and Technology, Ganzhou, China, 2012.
26. Cardu, M.; Clerici, C.; Morandini, A.; Ocella, E. An experimental research on the comminution law and work index in jaw. In Proceedings of the XVIII International Mineral Processing Congress, Sydney, NSW, Australia, 23–28 May 1993.
27. Lu, Y.; Akthar, S.; Sasmito, A.; Kurnia, J. Prediction of air flow, methane, and coal dust dispersion in a room and pillar mining face. *Int. J. Min. Sci. Technol.* **2017**, *27*, 657–662.
28. Eaton, J.K.; Fessler, J.R. Preferential concentration of particles by turbulence. *Int. J. Multiph. Flows* **1994**, *20*, 169–209. [CrossRef]
29. Eaton, J.K. Two-way coupled turbulence simulations of gas-particle flows using point-particle tracking. *Int. J. Multiph. Flow* **2009**, *35*, 792–800. [CrossRef]
30. Varaksin, A.Y. Fluid dynamics and thermal physics of two-phase flows: Problems and achievements. *High Temp.* **2013**, *51*, 377–407. [CrossRef]
31. Greifzu, F.; Kratzsch, C.; Forgber, T.; Lindner, F.; Schwarze, R. Assessment of parti-cle-tracking models for dispersed particle-laden flows implemented in OpenFOAM and ANSYS FLUENT. *Eng. Appl. Comput. Fluid Mech.* **2016**, *10*, 30–43.

Article

Dynamic Absorption of Vibration in a Multi Degree of Freedom Elastic System

Maria Luminita Scutaru [1,*], Marin Marin [2] and Sorin Vlase [1,3]

1. Department of Mechanical Engineering, Transilvania University of Brasov, 500036 Brasov, Romania
2. Department of Mathematics and Computer Science, Transilvania University of Brasov, 500036 Brasov, Romania
3. Romanian Academy of Technical Sciences, 700506 Bucharest, Romania
* Correspondence: lscutaru@unitbv.ro; Tel.: +40-723-242-735

Abstract: The paper aims to identify the situations in which a complex elastic system, which is subject to mechanical vibrations, can act as a dynamic absorber of vibrations for certain frequencies. The conditions that the system must fulfill in order to achieve this goal are determined and then a calculation example is presented. The method is interesting because it allows to avoid attaching an absorber specially built for this, a situation that complicates the project and increases manufacturing costs.

Keywords: dynamic absorber; multi degree of freedom; vibration; mechanical system

MSC: 70J30; 70J35

Citation: Scutaru, M.L.; Marin, M.; Vlase, S. Dynamic Absorption of Vibration in a Multi Degree of Freedom Elastic System. *Mathematics* **2022**, *10*, 4045. https://doi.org/10.3390/math10214045

Academic Editor: Eva H. Dulf

Received: 1 October 2022
Accepted: 27 October 2022
Published: 31 October 2022

Publisher's Note: MDPI stays neutral with regard to jurisdictional claims in published maps and institutional affiliations.

Copyright: © 2022 by the authors. Licensee MDPI, Basel, Switzerland. This article is an open access article distributed under the terms and conditions of the Creative Commons Attribution (CC BY) license (https://creativecommons.org/licenses/by/4.0/).

1. Introduction

Dynamic absorbers represent an ingenious and relatively cheap solution to reduce vibrations, with numerous applications in engineering, from civil engineering, mechanical engineering, vehicles, aeronautics, naval engineering and the examples can go on. The first dynamic absorber was patented by Frahm [1] in 1909. The theoretical foundations are laid by the work of Ormondroyd and Den Hartog [2] in 1928. Taking into account the performance of this vibration reduction system and the low manufacturing price, numerous studies followed in this field. The aim was to increase the effectiveness of the designed absorbers and to optimize the various constructive parameters. Numerous improvements have also been proposed and numerous types of unconventional absorbers, active or passive, have been created. At the moment, the dynamic absorber is still finding new applications, in new fields, requiring a continuous study of the subject.

For example, a dynamic absorber that attenuates the vibrations of three resonance frequencies simultaneously is studied and proposed in [3]. It is known to suppress a disturbing frequency it is sufficient to install a single damper whose natural frequency is adjusted to the excitation frequency. Obviously, to suppress more frequencies, more absorbers can be mounted, but this approach leads to additional costs and a more complicated device. The paper presents a system that allows, by adjusting the geometric dimensions, the precise adjustment of the natural frequency of the absorber according to the value of the frequency to be absorbed. Numerical examples prove the validity of the proposed solution. In [4], a nonlinear dynamic vibration absorber (DVA) with variable frequency and damping is analyzed. Numerical simulation for this vibration absorber for a coupled system with two degrees of freedom shows that the proposed absorber can adapt to different conditions that may occur in operation. For the seismic impact protection of a building, in [5] a DVA with several frequencies is proposed in the form of an elastic continuum. This material has several natural frequencies in the frequency range of seismic effects. When the absorber has several natural frequencies close to the resonant frequency of the protected building, part of the building's oscillation energy is transferred to the absorber's oscillations and the peak level of the frequency response function is reduced. A specific problem is presented in [6] where a DVA is designed to help prevent the overturning of a rigid block. For this, a pendulum shock absorber is used. Variable parameters are considered geometric characteristics. The results prove that the existence of DVA leads to a general improvement of the dynamic response of the system. The experimental results confirm the validity of the analytical model and validate the effectiveness of the pendulum mass damper.

DVA are mainly used for the damping of forced vibrations with harmonic excitation. One or more harmful frequencies are usually eliminated. Interesting research that uses magnetic force to achieve dynamic absorption is presented in [7]. Vibration control in rotating systems is studied. Two Jeffcott rotor vibration absorption systems are proposed. For the first version, the shock absorber is located between the absorber mass and the disc, and in the second, it is located between the absorber mass and the ground. The optimal parameters of the absorption system are obtained analytically using the classical theory. To evaluate and validate the obtained results, the experimental data of the proposed dynamic absorbers were compared with the simulation results. The effectiveness of the proposed solution was thus verified.

Devices operating at supercritical speeds need to go through all speeds, including the critical ones, during start-up. Passing through the resonance zone can lead to machine failures, if the amplitude level when passing through the resonance is too high. This raises the problem of designing some DVA that will act during the passage of the car through the critical speeds. For this, in [8] a rotating dynamic absorber with a viscoelastic element is proposed. A finite element modeling is used in the dimensioning step. A significant reduction of the amplitudes and requests that occur when passing through the critical zone is obtained. Thus, the rotating system can reach a super-critical speed through a smooth run-up.

New methods as use of the magneto-rheological elastomer (a smart materials with elastic property variable in the external magnetic field) were developed in the last period to absorb the vibration energy [9,10]. In the paper [11], two versions of a possible semi-active suspension of a work machine seat are presented. The first version uses a magneto-rheological damper and the second a combination of magneto-rheological damper and passive dynamic absorber. The optimum of the passive parameters of the seat suspension and the dynamic absorber was obtained using genetic algorithms according to the defined minimization function. In [12,13] various aspects of the design of DVA were studied. More results are presented in [14–20].

Although most works deal with the introduction of special elements to achieve dynamic absorption, the calculation methods involved can be very useful in the development of our work. We present some such works that helped us in the development of the proposed ideas below.

In the case of boring processes, it is necessary to reduce the excessive vibrations caused by the low rigidity of the material of the tools used [21]. Vibration reduction is achieved using a DVA, located on the edge of the boring bar. The dynamic absorber is represented by a thin steel tube inside which there is natural rubber. Tuning the DVA to the vibration that is desired to be absorbed is achieved by varying the number of inserted rubber sleeves. Thus a customized design of the drill rod with DVA can remain stable at higher forces.

In [22], a new e-DVA module is proposed that signals the synergy that exists between vehicle driving and vibration attenuation. This allows the design of a mechanism that ensures the tuning of the absorber in relation to the excitation of the road. An analysis of the vertical dynamics in the frequency and time domain demonstrates the increase in comfort while driving and the stability of handling. This synergy represented a suggestion regarding the use of a judicious design in order to use the mechanical system as a mechanical absorber.

In the paper [23], a new method is proposed to allow the optimal configuration of the DVA attached to a non-damped/damped primary structure. Based on the Lyapunov equation, the performance indices are expressed by quadratic matrix forms. Using this method, the classical solutions can be obtained in the case of an external force or an excitation by acceleration of the base. More interesting method to calculate the vibration absorbtion of a mechanical system are presented in [24–27].

In the current work, it is studied to what extent a judicious dimensioning of a system allows it to function as a dynamic absorber, for one or more exciting frequencies. In this way, a reduction of vibrations on certain frequency ranges can be ensured, without mounting an additional absorber. In this way, the design of the elastic system is simplified and, obviously, the manufacturing costs decrease. The complexity of the system and the large number of parameters involved allow that by changing some of these parameters, a dynamic absorption can be obtained for the mass that is of interest to the user, without adding a dedicated absorber.

2. Model and Method

For simplicity, let's consider a vibrating system, without damping, with degrees of freedom. It is also assume that the system is subject to a harmonic excitation with pulsation ω. The equations of motion for this system are given by the system of differential equations [28–31]:

$$[M]\{\ddot{X}\} + [K]\{X\} = \{F\}\cos\omega t, \tag{1}$$

where $[M]$ represents the mass matrix, $[K]$ represents the stifness matyrix and $\{F\}$ the excitation forces vector. Let's also assume that the excitation acts on a single element of the system, let's say on the element n. It is desired that the system as a whole act as a dynamic shock absorber, that is, p masses not to move if the excitation acts. Let's assume that these are the last p masses in the system (this can be achieved, regardless of the masses we focus on, by renumbering the masses). We propose to determine the condition that the masses and rigidities of the system must fulfill for this to happen. Let's partition the system of equations as follows:

$$\begin{bmatrix}[M_{11}] & [M_{12}]\\ \{M_{21}\} & [M_{22}]\end{bmatrix}\left\{\begin{matrix}\{\ddot{X}_1\}\\ \{\ddot{X}_2\}\end{matrix}\right\} + \begin{bmatrix}[K_{11}] & [K_{12}]\\ [K_{21}] & [K_{22}]\end{bmatrix}\left\{\begin{matrix}\{X_1\}\\ \{X_2\}\end{matrix}\right\} = \left\{\begin{matrix}\{F_1\}\\ \{F_2\}\end{matrix}\right\}\cos\omega t, \tag{2}$$

where the vector $\{X_1\} = \begin{bmatrix}x_1 & x_2 & \ldots & x_{n-p}\end{bmatrix}$ contains the first n-p masses of the system (has dimension $(n-p) \times 1$ and $\{X_2\} = \begin{bmatrix}x_{n-p+1} & \ldots & x_n\end{bmatrix}$ the next p masses (has dimension $(p \times 1)$. The matrices $[M_{11}]$, $[K_{11}]$ have dimension $((n-p) \times (n-p)$, matrices matricele $[M_{12}]$, $[K_{12}]$ have dimension $(n-p) \times p$, the matrices $[M_{21}]$, $[K_{21}]$ have the dimension $p \times (n-p)$, and also $[M_{22}]$, $[K_{22}]$ the dimension $p \times p$. The solution is chosen in the form:

$$\left\{\begin{matrix}\{X_1\}\\ \{X_2\}\end{matrix}\right\} = \left\{\begin{matrix}\{\Phi\}_1\\ \{\Phi_2\}\end{matrix}\right\}\cos\omega t, \tag{3}$$

One obtain:

$$\left\{\begin{matrix}\{\ddot{X}_1\}\\ \{\ddot{X}_2\}\end{matrix}\right\} = -\omega^2\left\{\begin{matrix}\{\Phi_1\}\\ \{\Phi_2\}\end{matrix}\right\}\cos\omega t, \tag{4}$$

Putting the condition that the solution (3) verifies Equation (2), it obtains:

$$\begin{bmatrix}[K_{11}]-\omega^2[M_{11}] & [K_{12}]-\omega^2[M_{12}]\\ [K_{21}]-\omega^2[M_{21}] & [K_{22}]-\omega^2[M_{22}]\end{bmatrix}\left\{\begin{matrix}\{X_1\}\\ \{X_2\}\end{matrix}\right\} = \left\{\begin{matrix}\{F_1\}\\ \{F_2\}\end{matrix}\right\}, \tag{5}$$

or:

$$\begin{matrix}([K_{11}]-\omega^2[M_{11}])\{X_1\} + ([K_{12}]-\omega^2[M_{12}])\{X_2\} = \{F_1\}\\ ([K_{21}]-\omega^2[M_{21}])\{X_1\} + ([K_{22}]-\omega^2[M_{22}])\{X_2\} = \{F_2\}\end{matrix} \tag{6}$$

In the conditions in which $\{F_1\} = 0$ (there is no excitation on the first part of the system) it is impose that $\{X_2\} = 0$. Let's look for the conditions for this to happen. By entering the conditions in Equation (6), we get:

$$\left([K_{11}] - \omega^2[M_{11}]\right)\{X_1\} = \{0\}, \tag{7}$$

$$\left([K_{21}] - \omega^2[M_{21}]\right)\{X_1\} = \{F_2\}, \tag{8}$$

It is denoted:

$$[C_{11}] = [K_{11}] - \omega^2[M_{11}] \tag{9}$$

In order for the first system to admit a non-zero solution, it must have the condition:

$$P(\omega) = \det\left([K_{11}] - \omega^2[M_{11}]\right) = \{0\}, \tag{10}$$

which represents a first condition.

Suppose that we have determined a normalized solution of system (7), denote it by $\{Y\}$ Then any vector $\{X\} = \lambda\{Y\}$ is a solution of system (7) and system (8) can be written:

$$\left([K_{21}] - \omega^2[M_{21}]\right)\lambda\{Y_1\} = \{F_2\}, \tag{11}$$

Equation (11) represents a system of p conditions that must be respected in order to have rest of the p bodies. λ can be eliminated if is multiplied Equation (11) by $\{Y_1\}^T$.

$$\lambda\{Y_1\}^T\left([K_{21}] - \omega^2[M_{21}]\right)\{Y_1\} = \{Y_1\}^T\{F_2\}, \tag{12}$$

It results λ:

$$\lambda = \frac{\{Y_1\}^T\{F_2\}}{\{Y_1\}^T([K_{21}] - \omega^2[M_{21}])\{Y_1\}}, \tag{13}$$

Introducing into Equation (12) it obtains:

$$\left([K_{21}] - \omega^2[M_{21}]\right)\frac{\{Y_1\}^T\{F_2\}}{\{Y_1\}^T([K_{21}] - \omega^2[M_{21}])\{Y_1\}}\{Y_1\} = \{F_2\}. \tag{14}$$

From this set (Equation (14)) of p conditions only $p - 1$ are now independent. Now there are $1 + p - 1 = p$ conditions that must be respected by the parameters of the system, so p masses (in our case the last p numebered) remain in rest.

Let's now deal with the most common case in practice, namely the one where we have a work machine that, powered by a motor (usually electric) that rotates at a speed ω, and it desired it to work without vibrating. So we want to dynamically isolate a single mass m_n and then $p = 1$. The matrix $[K_{11}]$ has size $(n - 1)x(n - 1)$, the vector $\{F_2\}$ has only one element F, the condition that the geometric, mass and elastic quantities must fulfill are given by $\det([K_{11}] - \omega^2[M_{11}]) = \{0\}$ (to have zero displacement of mass n at frequency ω). So: $\{X_2\} = x_n$,

$$\begin{bmatrix} [K_{11}] - \omega^2[M_{11}] & [K_{12}] - \omega^2[M_{12}] \\ [K_{21}] - \omega^2[M_{21}] & k_n - \omega^2 m_n \end{bmatrix}\begin{Bmatrix} \{X_1\} \\ x_n \end{Bmatrix} = \begin{Bmatrix} 0 \\ F_n \end{Bmatrix}, \tag{15}$$

$$\left([K_{11}] - \omega^2[M_{11}]\right)\{X_1\} = \{0\}, \tag{16}$$

$$\left([K_{21}] - \omega^2[M_{21}]\right)\{X_1\} = F_n, \tag{17}$$

In order for the first system to admit a non-zero solution, it must to have condition (10), which in this case is the only condition that must be fulfilled.

It is assumed that it was determined a normalized solution of system (16), denote it by $\{Y_1\}$. Then any vector $\{X_1\} = \lambda\{Y_1\}$ is a solution of system (16) and system (17) can be written:

$$\left([K_{21}] - \omega^2[M_{21}]\right)\lambda\{Y_1\} = F_n, \tag{18}$$

which provides λ, therefore also provides the amplitudes of the forced oscillations of the other $n - 1$ flywheels.

The cases in which there is not damping do not exist in practice. In any engineering system there are frictions and processes through which the energy of the system is dissipated. Let's then analyze a system in which it is considered that there is a viscous damping. From the point of view of the obtained results, all the previous considerations remain valid from a qualitative point of view. The difference lies in the fact that the phases of the oscillations of the different masses are different. Also, the number of parameters involved is higher, additional damping properties appear, but from the point of view of the proposed purpose, this represents an advantage, the number of parameters that can be varied increases, so the possibilities of tuning the system to reduce unwanted frequencies increase.

System (1) becomes in this case:

$$[M]\{\ddot{X}\} + [C]\{\dot{X}\} + [K]\{X\} = \{F\}\cos\omega t, \tag{19}$$

There are different forms for the matrix $[C]$, but in what follows this is not important. The harmonic solution that must check the system (19) is:

$$\begin{Bmatrix}\{X_1\}\\\{X_2\}\end{Bmatrix} = \begin{Bmatrix}\{A_1\}\\\{A_2\}\end{Bmatrix}\cos\omega t + \begin{Bmatrix}\{B_1\}\\\{B_2\}\end{Bmatrix}\sin\omega t. \tag{20}$$

It obtains, successively:

$$\begin{Bmatrix}\{\dot{X}_1\}\\\{\dot{X}_2\}\end{Bmatrix} = -\omega\begin{Bmatrix}\{A_1\}\\\{A_2\}\end{Bmatrix}\sin\omega t + \omega\begin{Bmatrix}\{B_1\}\\\{B_2\}\end{Bmatrix}\cos\omega t. \tag{21}$$

$$\begin{Bmatrix}\ddot{X}_1\\\ddot{X}_2\end{Bmatrix} = -\omega^2\begin{Bmatrix}A_1\\A_2\end{Bmatrix}\cos\omega t - \omega^2\begin{Bmatrix}B_1\\B_2\end{Bmatrix}\sin\omega t. \tag{22}$$

By partitioning the matrices, in accordance with the previous considerations, it obtains:

$$\begin{bmatrix}[M_{11}] & [M_{12}]\\\{M_{21}\} & [M_{22}]\end{bmatrix}\begin{Bmatrix}\{\ddot{X}_1\}\\\{\ddot{X}_2\}\end{Bmatrix} + \begin{bmatrix}[C_{11}] & [C_{12}]\\\{C_{21}\} & [C_{22}]\end{bmatrix}\begin{Bmatrix}\{\dot{X}_1\}\\\{\dot{X}_2\}\end{Bmatrix} + \begin{bmatrix}[K_{11}] & [K_{12}]\\[K_{21}] & [K_{22}]\end{bmatrix}\begin{Bmatrix}\{X_1\}\\\{X_2\}\end{Bmatrix} = \begin{Bmatrix}\{F_1\}\\\{F_2\}\end{Bmatrix}\cos\omega t. \tag{23}$$

By introducing this solution into system (19), it obtains:

$$\begin{bmatrix}[M_{11}] & [M_{12}]\\\{M_{21}\} & [M_{22}]\end{bmatrix}\left(-\omega^2\begin{Bmatrix}\{A_1\}\\\{A_2\}\end{Bmatrix}\cos\omega t - \omega^2\begin{Bmatrix}\{B_1\}\\\{B_2\}\end{Bmatrix}\sin\omega t\right) + \begin{bmatrix}[C_{11}] & [C_{12}]\\\{C_{21}\} & [C_{22}]\end{bmatrix}\left(-\omega\begin{Bmatrix}\{A_1\}\\\{A_2\}\end{Bmatrix}\sin\omega t + \omega\begin{Bmatrix}\{B_1\}\\\{B_2\}\end{Bmatrix}\cos\omega t\right) + \begin{bmatrix}[K_{11}] & [K_{12}]\\[K_{21}] & [K_{22}]\end{bmatrix}\left(\begin{Bmatrix}\{A_1\}\\\{A_2\}\end{Bmatrix}\cos\omega t + \begin{Bmatrix}\{B_1\}\\\{B_2\}\end{Bmatrix}\sin\omega t\right) = \begin{Bmatrix}\{F_1\}\\\{F_2\}\end{Bmatrix}\cos\omega t \tag{24}$$

or:

$$
\begin{aligned}
&\left(-\omega^2\begin{bmatrix}[M_{11}]&[M_{12}]\\[M_{21}]&[M_{22}]\end{bmatrix}\begin{Bmatrix}\{A_1\}\\\{A_2\}\end{Bmatrix}+\omega\begin{bmatrix}[C_{11}]&[C_{12}]\\[C_{21}]&[C_{22}]\end{bmatrix}\begin{Bmatrix}\{B_1\}\\\{B_2\}\end{Bmatrix}+\begin{bmatrix}[K_{11}]&[K_{12}]\\[K_{21}]&[K_{22}]\end{bmatrix}\begin{Bmatrix}\{A_1\}\\\{A_2\}\end{Bmatrix}-\begin{Bmatrix}\{F_1\}\\\{F_2\}\end{Bmatrix}\right)\cos\omega t+\\
&+\left(-\omega^2\begin{bmatrix}[M_{11}]&[M_{12}]\\[M_{21}]&[M_{22}]\end{bmatrix}\begin{Bmatrix}\{B_1\}\\\{B_2\}\end{Bmatrix}-\begin{bmatrix}[C_{11}]&[C_{12}]\\[C_{21}]&[C_{22}]\end{bmatrix}\begin{Bmatrix}\{A_1\}\\\{A_2\}\end{Bmatrix}+\begin{bmatrix}[K_{11}]&[K_{12}]\\[K_{21}]&[K_{22}]\end{bmatrix}\begin{Bmatrix}\{B_1\}\\\{B_2\}\end{Bmatrix}\right)\sin\omega t=0
\end{aligned}
\quad(25)
$$

Since Equation (24) must be valid at any time, this equation is equivalent to the following two systems:

$$
\left(\begin{bmatrix}[K_{11}]&[K_{12}]\\[K_{21}]&[K_{22}]\end{bmatrix}-\omega^2\begin{bmatrix}[M_{11}]&[M_{12}]\\[M_{21}]&[M_{22}]\end{bmatrix}\right)\begin{Bmatrix}\{A_1\}\\\{A_2\}\end{Bmatrix}+\omega\begin{bmatrix}[C_{11}]&[C_{12}]\\[C_{21}]&[C_{22}]\end{bmatrix}\begin{Bmatrix}\{B_1\}\\\{B_2\}\end{Bmatrix}=\begin{Bmatrix}\{F_1\}\\\{F_2\}\end{Bmatrix}. \quad(26)
$$

$$
-\begin{bmatrix}[C_{11}]&[C_{12}]\\\{C_{21}\}&[C_{22}]\end{bmatrix}\begin{Bmatrix}A_1\\A_2\end{Bmatrix}+\left(\begin{bmatrix}[K_{11}]&[K_{12}]\\[K_{21}]&[K_{22}]\end{bmatrix}-\omega^2\begin{bmatrix}[M_{11}]&[M_{12}]\\[M_{21}]&[M_{22}]\end{bmatrix}\right)\begin{Bmatrix}B_1\\B_2\end{Bmatrix}=0. \quad(27)
$$

or:

$$
\begin{bmatrix}\begin{bmatrix}[K_{11}]&[K_{12}]\\[K_{21}]&[K_{22}]\end{bmatrix}-\omega^2\begin{bmatrix}[M_{11}]&[M_{12}]\\[M_{21}]&[M_{22}]\end{bmatrix} & \omega\begin{bmatrix}[C_{11}]&[C_{12}]\\\{C_{21}\}&[C_{22}]\end{bmatrix}\\ -\omega\begin{bmatrix}[C_{11}]&[C_{12}]\\\{C_{21}\}&[C_{22}]\end{bmatrix} & \begin{bmatrix}[K_{11}]&[K_{12}]\\[K_{21}]&[K_{22}]\end{bmatrix}-\omega^2\begin{bmatrix}[M_{11}]&[M_{12}]\\[M_{21}]&[M_{22}]\end{bmatrix}\end{bmatrix}\begin{Bmatrix}\{A_1\}\\\{A_2\}\\\{B_1\}\\\{B_2\}\end{Bmatrix}=\begin{Bmatrix}\langle0\rangle\\\langle0\rangle\\\{F_1\}\\\{F_2\}\end{Bmatrix} \quad(28)
$$

It can obtain $\{A_1\}, \{B_1\}, \{A_2\}, \{B_2\}$ and the harmonic solution:

$$
\begin{Bmatrix}\{X_1\}\\\{X_2\}\end{Bmatrix}=\begin{Bmatrix}\{A_1\}\\\{A_2\}\end{Bmatrix}\cos\omega t+\begin{Bmatrix}\{B_1\}\\\{B_2\}\end{Bmatrix}\sin\omega t=\begin{Bmatrix}a_1\cos(\omega t+\varphi_1)\\a_2\cos(\omega t+\varphi_2)\\\vdots\\a_{n-p}\cos(\omega t+\varphi_{n-p})\\a_{n-p+1}\cos(\omega t+\varphi_{n-p+1})\\a_{n-p+2}\cos(\omega t+\varphi_{n-p+2})\\\vdots\\a_n\cos(\omega t+\varphi_n)\end{Bmatrix}. \quad(29)
$$

The notation:

$$
\begin{Bmatrix}\{A_1\}\\\{A_2\}\end{Bmatrix}=\begin{Bmatrix}A_1\\A_2\\\vdots\\A_{n-p}\\A_{n-p+1}\\A_{n-p+2}\\\vdots\\A_n\end{Bmatrix};\quad \begin{Bmatrix}\{B_1\}\\\{B_2\}\end{Bmatrix}=\begin{Bmatrix}B_1\\B_2\\\vdots\\B_{n-p}\\B_{n-p+1}\\B_{n-p+2}\\\vdots\\B_n\end{Bmatrix}. \quad(30)
$$

is made. Solution (29) can also be written:

$$
\begin{Bmatrix}\{X_1\}\\\{X_2\}\end{Bmatrix}=[\backslash d\backslash]\{a\}. \quad(31)
$$

$$
\{a\}=\lfloor a_1\ a_2\ \cdots\ a_{n-p}\ a_{n-p+1}\ a_{n-p+2}\ \cdots\ a_n\rfloor. \quad(32)
$$

where:

$$
\varphi_j=\operatorname{atan}\left(\frac{B_j}{A_j}\right);\ a_j=\sqrt{A_j^2+B_j^2};\ i=1,2;\ j=\overline{1,n}.\ \text{where}: \quad(33)
$$

$$
[\backslash d \backslash] = \begin{bmatrix} \cos(\omega t + \varphi_1) & & & & 0 \\ & \cos(\omega t + \varphi_2) & & & \\ & & \ddots & & \\ & & & 0 & \\ 0 & & & & \ddots \\ & & & & & \cos(\omega t + \varphi_n) \end{bmatrix}. \quad (34)
$$

Imposing the conditions $\{F_1\} = 0$ (there is no excitation on the first part of the system) and the solution $\{X_2\} = 0$. it obtain:

$$
\begin{aligned}
([K_{11}] - \omega^2[M_{11}])\{A_1\} + \omega[C_{11}]\{B_1\} &= \{0\} \\
([K_{21}] - \omega^2[M_{21}])\{A_1\} + \omega[C_{21}]\{B_1\} &= \{0\} \\
-\omega[C_{11}]\{A_1\} + ([K_{11}] - \omega^2[M_{11}])\{B_1\} &= \{0\} \\
-\omega[C_{21}]\{A_1\} + ([K_{21}] - \omega^2[M_{21}])\{B_1\} &= \{F_2\}
\end{aligned} \quad (35)
$$

which represent the conditions that must be met to obtain a maximum absorption of vibrations for the masses $n - p + 1, n - p + 2, \ldots, n$.

3. Results and Discussion

Through a careful dimensioning of the system, it can also play the role of a dynamic shock absorber, without the need to add an additional element.

A simple example will illustrate this. Consider an elastic system presented in Figure 1 made up of 6 flywheels, linked together with elastic elements having known stiffness. Flywheels can have rotational movement. An exciting moment acts on the last flywheel. It results the problem of determining the conditions for which, under the action of this excitation, flywheel 4 stays in place, without vibrating. The number of DOF for this system is six.

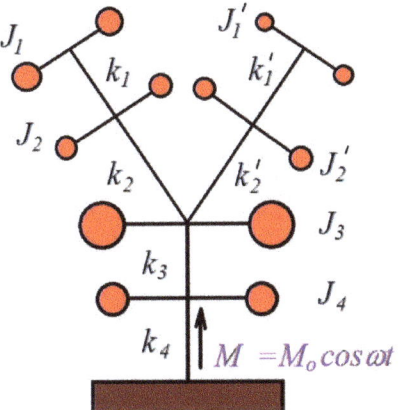

Figure 1. Elastic system with wheels.

The equations of motion for this system are:

$$
\begin{bmatrix} J_1 & 0 & 0 & 0 & 0 & 0 \\ 0 & J_2 & 0 & 0 & 0 & 0 \\ 0 & 0 & J_1' & 0 & 0 & 0 \\ 0 & 0 & 0 & J_2' & 0 & 0 \\ 0 & 0 & 0 & 0 & J_3 & 0 \\ 0 & 0 & 0 & 0 & 0 & J_4 \end{bmatrix} \begin{Bmatrix} \ddot{\varphi}_1 \\ \ddot{\varphi}_2 \\ \ddot{\varphi}_1' \\ \ddot{\varphi}_2' \\ \ddot{\varphi}_3 \\ \ddot{\varphi}_4 \end{Bmatrix} + \begin{bmatrix} k_1 & -k_1 & 0 & 0 & 0 & 0 \\ -k_1 & k_1+k_2 & 0 & 0 & -k_2 & 0 \\ 0 & 0 & k_1' & -k_1' & 0 & 0 \\ 0 & 0 & -k_1' & k_1'+k_2' & -k_2' & 0 \\ 0 & -k_2 & 0 & -k_2' & k_2+k_2'+k_3 & -k_3 \\ 0 & 0 & 0 & 0 & -k_3 & k_3+k_4 \end{bmatrix} \begin{Bmatrix} \varphi_1 \\ \varphi_2 \\ \varphi_1' \\ \varphi_2' \\ \varphi_3 \\ \varphi_4 \end{Bmatrix} = \begin{Bmatrix} 0 \\ 0 \\ 0 \\ 0 \\ 0 \\ M_o \cos \omega t \end{Bmatrix}
$$

It is noted:

$$[J] = \begin{bmatrix} J_1 & 0 & 0 & 0 & 0 & 0 \\ 0 & J_2 & 0 & 0 & 0 & 0 \\ 0 & 0 & J_1' & 0 & 0 & 0 \\ 0 & 0 & 0 & J_2' & 0 & 0 \\ 0 & 0 & 0 & 0 & J_3 & 0 \\ 0 & 0 & 0 & 0 & 0 & J_4 \end{bmatrix};$$

$$[K] = \begin{bmatrix} k_1 & -k_1 & 0 & 0 & 0 & 0 \\ -k_1 & k_1+k_2 & 0 & 0 & -k_2 & 0 \\ 0 & 0 & k_1' & -k_1' & 0 & 0 \\ 0 & 0 & -k_1' & k_1'+k_2' & -k_2' & 0 \\ 0 & -k_2 & 0 & -k_2' & k_2+k_2'+k_3 & -k_3 \\ 0 & 0 & 0 & 0 & -k_3 & k_3+k_4 \end{bmatrix}; \{M\} = \begin{Bmatrix} 0 \\ 0 \\ 0 \\ 0 \\ 0 \\ M_o \cos \omega t \end{Bmatrix}.$$

If it is considered a harmonic solution and put the condition that this solution verifies the system of differential equations, it obtains:

$$\left(\begin{bmatrix} k_1 & -k_1 & 0 & 0 & 0 & 0 \\ -k_1 & k_1+k_2 & 0 & 0 & -k_2 & 0 \\ 0 & 0 & k_1' & -k_1' & 0 & 0 \\ 0 & 0 & -k_1' & k_1'+k_2' & -k_2' & 0 \\ 0 & -k_2 & 0 & -k_2' & k_2+k_2'+k_3 & -k_3 \\ 0 & 0 & 0 & 0 & -k_3 & k_3+k_4 \end{bmatrix} - \omega^2 \begin{bmatrix} J_1 & 0 & 0 & 0 & 0 & 0 \\ 0 & J_2 & 0 & 0 & 0 & 0 \\ 0 & 0 & J_1' & 0 & 0 & 0 \\ 0 & 0 & 0 & J_2' & 0 & 0 \\ 0 & 0 & 0 & 0 & J_3 & 0 \\ 0 & 0 & 0 & 0 & 0 & J_4 \end{bmatrix} \right) \begin{Bmatrix} e_1 \\ e_2 \\ e_1' \\ e_2' \\ e_3 \\ e_4 \end{Bmatrix} = \begin{Bmatrix} 0 \\ 0 \\ 0 \\ 0 \\ 0 \\ M_o \end{Bmatrix}$$

where the amplitude of the harmonic oscillations is found in the vector: $\{X\} = \begin{bmatrix} e_1 & e_2 & e_1' & e_2' & e_3 & e_4 \end{bmatrix}^T$. It must to find the condition for which: $e_4 = 0$. The determinant of the system is:

$$[C] = \begin{bmatrix} k_1-\omega^2 J_1 & -k_1 & 0 & 0 & 0 & 0 \\ -k_1 & k_1+k_2-\omega^2 J_2 & 0 & 0 & -k_2 & 0 \\ 0 & 0 & k_1'-\omega^2 J_1' & -k_1' & 0 & 0 \\ 0 & 0 & -k_1' & k_1'+k_2'-\omega^2 J_2' & -k_2' & 0 \\ 0 & -k_2 & 0 & -k_2' & k_2+k_2'+k_3-\omega^2 J_3 & -k_3 \\ 0 & 0 & 0 & 0 & -k_3 & k_3+k_4-\omega^2 J_4 \end{bmatrix}$$

$$[C_{11}] = \begin{bmatrix} k_1-\omega^2 J_1 & -k_1 & 0 & 0 & 0 \\ -k_1 & k_1+k_2-\omega^2 J_2 & 0 & 0 & -k_2 \\ 0 & 0 & k_1'-\omega^2 J_1' & -k_1' & 0 \\ 0 & 0 & -k_1' & k_1'+k_2'-\omega^2 J_2' & -k_2' \\ 0 & -k_2 & 0 & -k_2' & k_2+k_2'+k_3-\omega^2 J_3 \end{bmatrix}$$

The values considered in the applications are:
$J_1 = 1.0$ kgm^2; $J_2 = 3.0$ kgm^2; $J_1' = 1.0$ kgm^2; $J_2' = 6.0$ kgm^2; $J_3 = 2.0$ kgm^2; $J_4 = 6.0$ kgm^2; $k_1 = k_1' = 1,000,000$ N·m/rad; $k_2 = k_2' = 3,000,000$ N·m/rad; $k_3 = 2,000,000$ N·m/rad; $k_4 = 1,000,000$ N·m/rad and the excitation moment $M = 10,1000$ N·m.

The condition $P(\omega) = \det(K_{11} - \omega^2 M_{11}) = \{0\}$ leads to the pulsation:

A graph of the function from condition (9) where it can follow the ω values where this condition is fulfilled is represented in Figure 2. The values obtained in Table 1 can be seen.

The five values obtained for the considered data represent frequencies for which, upon excitation with a harmonic moment with an amplitude of 100 Nm acting on flywheel 6, a total vibration absorption is obtained at this flywheel (in the case of zero damping). If there is damping, the absorption is very high around these determined values. So we note that for a complex system, there are several eigenpulsations at which vibration absorption can be done. If the system has many components, then the number of excitation frequencies that can be absorbed increase. In Figure 3 it can be seen the amplitude of the forced vibrations at different excitation frequencies.

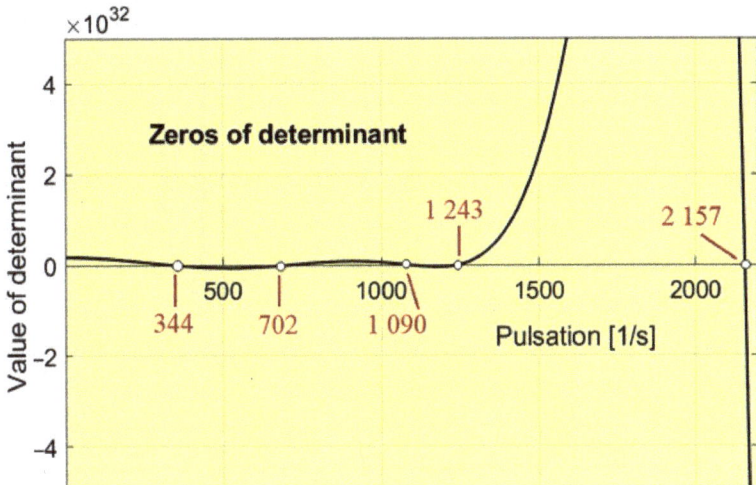

Figure 2. The representation of the function $P(\omega)$.

Table 1. The frequencies at which absorption occurs to flywheel 6.

Frequency	ω_1	ω_2	ω_3	ω_4	ω_5
[Hz]	344	702	1089	1243	2157

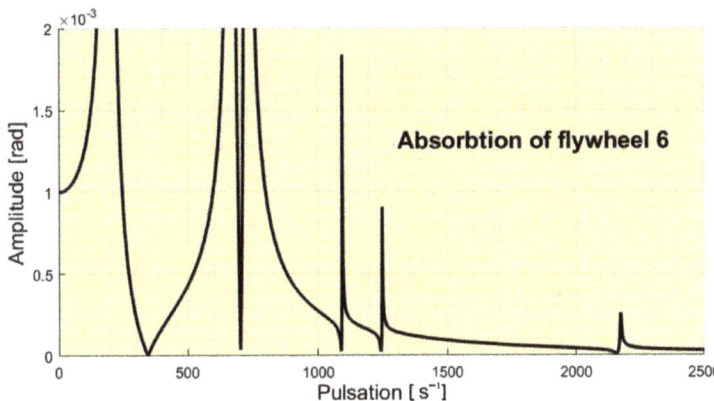

Figure 3. The absorbtion of the flywheel 6.

If one refer to flywheel 5, then the condition that it absorbs vibrations gives us the five frequencies that will be absorbed, presented in the Table 2.

Table 2. The frequencies at which absorption occurs to flywheel 5.

Frequency	ω_1	ω_2	ω_3	ω_4	ω_5
[Hz]	626	707	752	1128	1329

In Figure 4 it can be seen the amplitude of the forced vibrations at different pulsations/excitation frequencies of the flywheel 5.

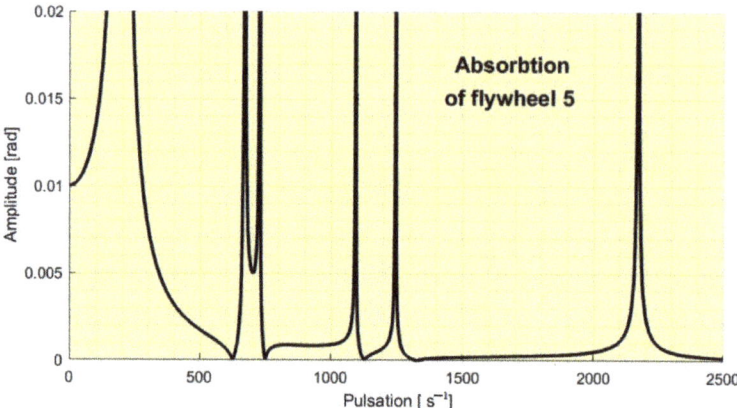

Figure 4. The absorbtion of the flywheel 5.

In a similar way the Figures 5–8 presents us the absorbtion of the flywheel 4, 3, 2 and 1.

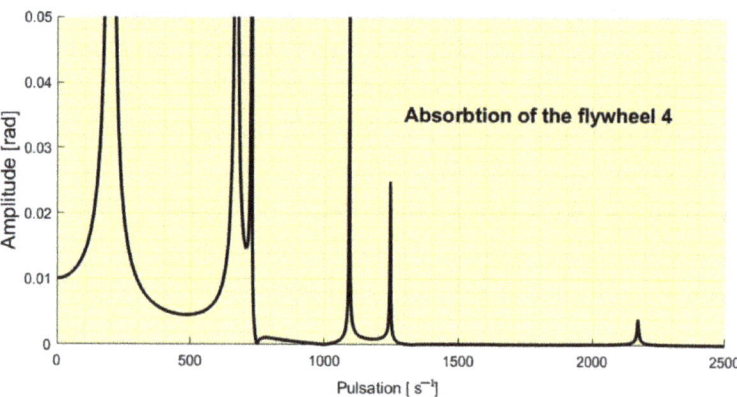

Figure 5. The absorbtion of the flywheel 4.

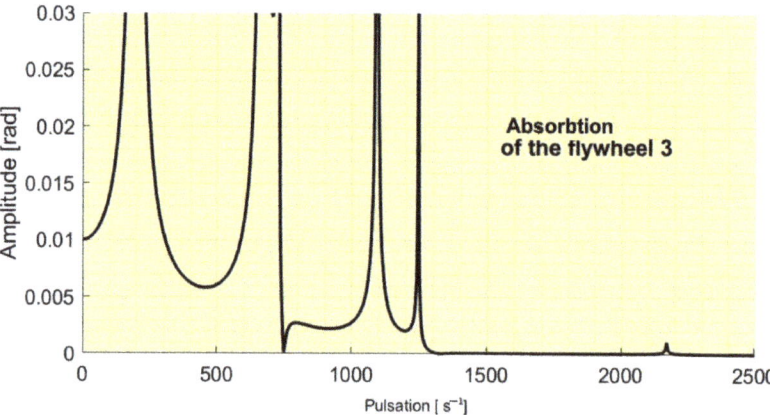

Figure 6. The absorbtion of the flywheel 3.

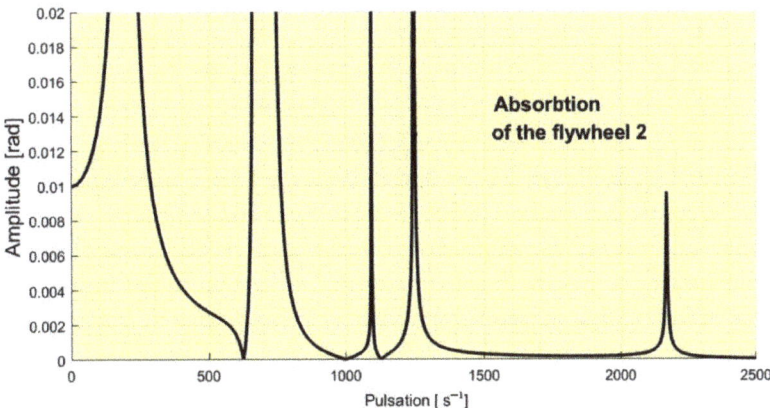

Figure 7. The absorbtion of the flywheel 2.

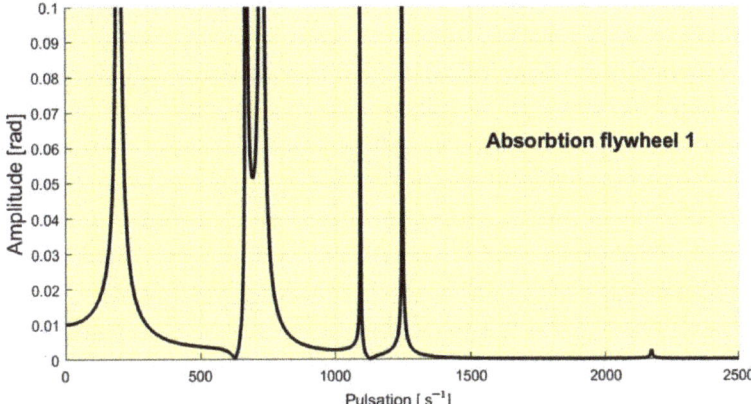

Figure 8. The absorbtion of the flywheel 1.

The eigenpulsations of the system are presented in the Table 3.
In Figure 9 are presented the amplitude of the all six flywheel overlapped.

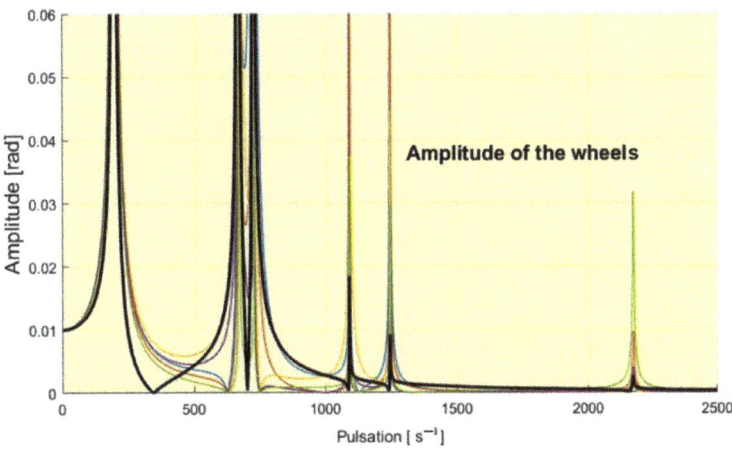

Figure 9. The amplitudes of the flywheels overlapped. With black is the graph for the flywheel 6.

Table 3. The eigenpulsations of the system.

Frequency [Hz]	p_1	p_2	p_3	p_4	p_5	p_6
	198.5	671.2	729.7	1094	1248	2172

Figure 10 shows the interval of pulsations that ensure the rest of the flywheel six. For each value of the moment of inertia for flywheel two, five pulsations are obtained for which the total vibration absorption of this flywheel takes place.

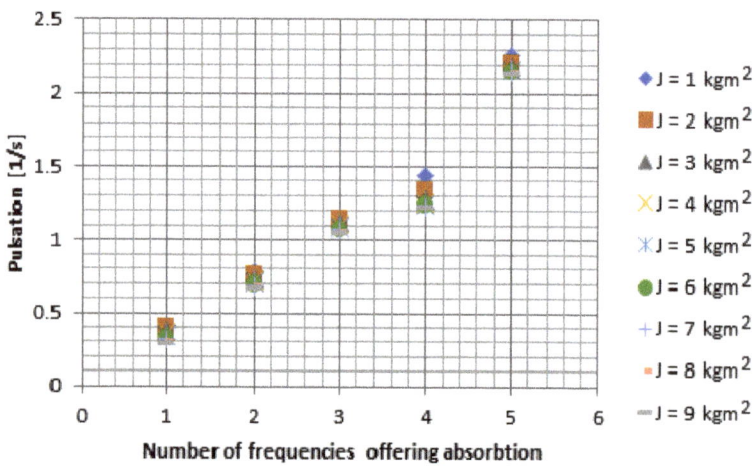

Figure 10. The intervals of pulsations that ensure the rest of the flywheel 6 for different moment of inertia of the flywheel 2.

A comparison with a system with a simplified system having four flywheels (Figure 11) is presented in Figure 12. In Figure 13 are presented the behavior of all flywheels. The number of the DOF in this case is four.

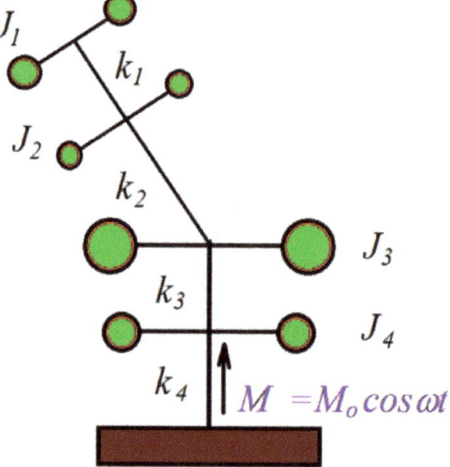

Figure 11. Elastic system with four wheels.

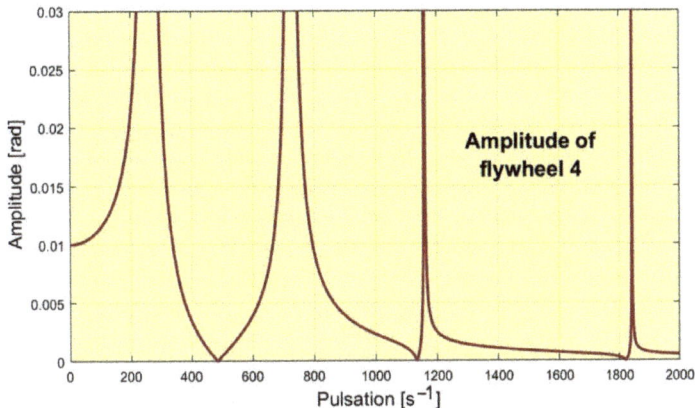

Figure 12. The absorbtion of the flywheel 4 for the simplified system.

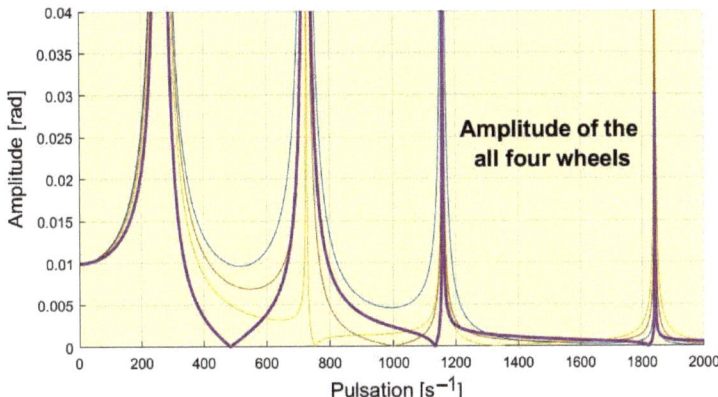

Figure 13. The amplitudes of the flywheels for the simplified system overlapped.

Consider now a damping introduce in the system in the form: $[C] = \alpha[K]$. In Figure 14 are presented the amplitude of forced vibration considering different damping coefficient.

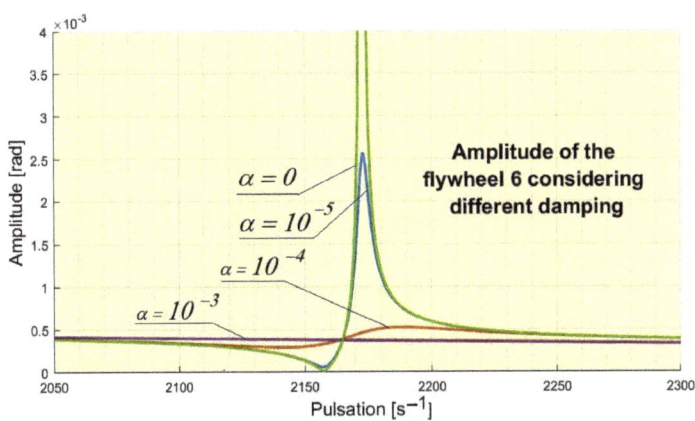

Figure 14. Effect of damping on the amplitude of the flywheel 6.

4. Conclusions

Dynamic absorbers represent one of the most spectacular methods of reducing vibrations. The main advantage is its simplicity and the low price with which vibration absorption can be ensured. In the work, the authors wanted to show that, in the case of complex elastic systems, with several vibrating masses, dynamic absorption can be ensured without introducing additional systems, by properly designing the system, so that certain parts of it are dynamic absorbers for other parties. The more complex the system, the more possibilities for dynamic absorption there are. Moreover, for complex systems, the number of exciting frequencies for which dynamic absorption can be achieved is more numerous. So for a judiciously dimensioned system, dynamic absorption can be achieved, so without major expenses, for frequency intervals, useful in practice.

In other words, a judicious design of an elastic system allows managing the problem of resonance frequencies without using special devices, such as DVA, an operation that requires a redesign and the attachment of an expensive device. In this way, the price of realizing a dynamic absorption drops a lot. Also, the installation of an absorber in the system leads to the modification, which in certain cases can become important, of the vibration response of the entire system. By the method described in the paper, the modification of the system's behavior is avoided due to the addition of some DVA.

An example shows these properties that complex dynamic systems can provide. A possibility of development of the subject is the construction of algorithms that offer the optimal solution for different practical applications.

Author Contributions: Conceptualization, M.L.S. and M.M.; methodology, M.L.S. and M.M.; software, M.L.S., M.M. and S.V.; validation, M.L.S., M.M. and S.V.; formal analysis, M.L.S., M.M. and S.V.; investigation, M.L.S., M.M. and S.V.; resources, M.L.S., M.M. and S.V.; data curation, M.L.S., M.M. and S.V.; writing—original draft preparation, M.L.S.; writing—review and editing, M.L.S., M.M. and S.V.; visualization, M.L.S., M.M. and S.V.; supervision, M.M. and S.V.; project administration, M.L.S., M.M. and S.V.; funding acquisition, M.L.S., M.M. and S.V. All authors have read and agreed to the published version of the manuscript.

Funding: This research received no external funding. The APC was funded by Transilvania University of Brasov.

Institutional Review Board Statement: Not applicable.

Informed Consent Statement: Not applicable.

Data Availability Statement: Not applicable.

Conflicts of Interest: The authors declare no conflict of interest.

References

1. Frahm, H. Device for Damping Vibrations of Bodies. U.S. Patent US989958A, 30 October 1909.
2. Ormondroyd, J.; Den Hartog, J.P. Theory of the dynamic vibration absorber. *Trans. ASME* **1928**, *50*, 9–22.
3. Yoon, G.H.; Choi, H.; So, H.Y. Development and optimization of a resonance-based mechanical dynamic absorber structure for multiple frequencies. *J. Low Freq. Noise Vib. Act. Control* **2021**, *40*, 880–897. [CrossRef]
4. Wang, T.; Tian, R.L.; Yang, X.W.; Zhang, Z.W. A Novel Dynamic Absorber with Variable Frequency and Damping. *Shock Vib.* **2021**, *2021*, 8833089. [CrossRef]
5. Makarov, S.B.; Pankova, N.V. On the Possibility of Applying a Multi-frequency Dynamic Absorber (MDA) to Seismic Protection Tasks. *Adv. Intell. Syst. Comput.* **2020**, *1127*, 395–403. [CrossRef]
6. Di Egidio, A.; Alaggio, R.; Aloisio, A.; de Leo, A.M.; Contento, A.; Tursini, M. Analytical and experimental investigation into the effectiveness of a pendulum dynamic absorber to protect rigid blocks from overturning. *Int. J. Non-Linear Mech.* **2019**, *115*, 1–10. [CrossRef]
7. Heidari, H.; Monjezi, B. Vibration control of imbalanced Jeffcott rotor by virtual passive dynamic absorber with optimal parameter values. *Proc. Inst. Mech. Eng. Part C J. Mech. Eng. Sci.* **2018**, *232*, 4278–4288. [CrossRef]
8. Fontes, Y.C.; Nicoletti, R. Rotating dynamic absorber with viscoelastic element. *J. Braz. Soc. Mech. Sci. Eng.* **2016**, *38*, 377–383. [CrossRef]

9. Komatsuzaki, T.; Inoue, T.; Terashima, O. A broadband frequency-tunable dynamic absorber for the vibration control of structures. In Proceedings of the 13th International Conference on Motion and Vibration Control (MOVIC), Southampton, UK, 3–6 July 2016; Volume 744, p. 012167. [CrossRef]
10. Komatsuzaki, T.; Inoue, T.; Iwata, Y. MRE-based adaptive-tuned dynamic absorber with self-sensing function for vibration control of structures. In Proceedings of the 7th Annual ASME Conference on Smart Materials, Adaptive Structures and Intelligent Systems (SMASIS), Newport, RI, USA, 8–10 September 2014; Volume 1, p. V001T03A011.
11. Orecny, M.; Segl'a, S.; Hunady, R.; Ferkova, Z. Application of a magneto-rheological damper and a dynamic absorber for a suspension of a working machine seat. *Procedia Eng.* **2014**, *96*, 338–344. [CrossRef]
12. Nicoara, D.D. The Damped Dynamic Vibration Absorber—A Numerical Optimization Method. In Proceedings of the International Conference COMAT 2018, Brasov, Romania, 25–26 October 2018.
13. Pennestri, E. An application of Chebyshev's min-max criterion to the optimum design of a damped dynamic vibration absorber. *J. Sound Vib.* **1998**, *217*, 757–765. [CrossRef]
14. Diveyev, B.; Horbay, O.; Kernytskyy, I.; Cherchyk, H.; Burtak, V. 52 DVA for the MEMS Devices. In *Proceedings of the International Conference on Perspective Technologies and Methods in MEMS Design (MEMSTECH), Polyana, Ukraine, 22–26 May 2019*; IEEE Book Series; IEEE: Piscataway, NJ, USA, 2019; pp. 52–55.
15. Song, J.; Si, P.; Hua, H.; Li, Z. A DVA-Beam Element for Dynamic Simulation of DVA-Beam System: Modeling, Validation and Application. *Symmetry* **2022**, *14*, 1608. [CrossRef]
16. Byrnes, P.W.G.; Lacy, G. Modal vibration testing of the DVA-1 radio telescope. In *Ground-Based and Airborne Telescopes VI, Proceedings of the SPIE Astronomical Telescopes + Instrumentation, Edinburgh, UK, 26 June–1 July 2016*; Book Series; SPIE: Paris, France, 2016; Volume 9906, Part 1, p. 99063P. [CrossRef]
17. Sharma, S.K.; Sharma, R.C.; Lee, J.; Jang, H.L. Numerical and Experimental Analysis of DVA on the Flexible-Rigid Rail Veicle Carbody Resonant Vibration. *Sensors* **2022**, *22*, 1922. [CrossRef]
18. De Oliveira, D.B.P.; Coelho, J.P.; Sanches, L.; Michon, G. Dynamics of Helicopters with DVA Under Structural Uncertainties. In *Proceedings of the DINAME 2017, São Sebastião, Brazil, 5–10 March 2017*; Book Series, Lecture Notes in Mechanical Engineering; Springer: Berlin, Germany, 2019; pp. 111–123. [CrossRef]
19. Dong, G.; Xiaojie, C.; Jing, L.; Peiben, W.; Zhengwei, Y.; Xingjian, J. Theoretical modeling and optimal matching on the damping property of mechatronic shock absorber with low speed and heavy load capacity. *J. Sound Vib.* **2022**, *535*, 117113. [CrossRef]
20. Dong, G.; Xingjian, J.; Hui, S.; Li, J.; Junjie, G. Test and simulation the failure characteristics of twin tube shock absorber. *Mech. Syst. Signal Process.* **2019**, *122*, 707–719.
21. Hendrowati, W.; Merdekawan, N. Modeling and analysis of boring bar vibration response in internal turning due to variation of the amount of DVA rubber in finish boring cut. *J. Mech. Sci. Technol.* **2021**, *35*, 4353–4362. [CrossRef]
22. Gu, C.; Zhu, J.; Chen, X. A Novel E-DVA Module Synthesis Featuring of Synergy between Driving and Vibration Attenuation. *Shock Vib.* **2016**, *2016*, 8464317. [CrossRef]
23. Du, D. Analytical solutions for DVA optimization based on the lyapunov equation. *J. Vib. Acoust. Trans. ASME* **2008**, *130*, 054501. [CrossRef]
24. Abouelregal, A.E.; Marin, M. Thesize-dependent thermoelastic vibrations of nanobeams subjected to harmonic excitation and rectified sine wave heating. *Mathematics* **2020**, *8*, 1128. [CrossRef]
25. Mocanu, S.; Rece, L.; Burlacu, A.; Florescu, V.; Rontescu, C.; Modrea, A. Novel Procedures for Sustainable Design in Structural Rehabilitation on Oversized Metal Structures. *Metals* **2022**, *12*, 1107. [CrossRef]
26. Diveyev, B.; Dorosh, I.; Cherchyk, H.; Burtak, V.; Ostashuk, M.; Hlobchak, M.; Kotiv, M. DVA for the High-Rise Object. In Proceedings of the 16th Intenational Conference on Experience of Designing and Application of CAD Systems in Microelectronics—CADSM, Lviv, Ukraine, 22–26 February 2021. [CrossRef]
27. Vlase, S.; Marin, M.; Scutaru, M.L.; Munteanu, R. New analytical method based on dynamic response of planar mechanical elastic systems. *AIP Adv.* **2017**, *7*, 1–15.
28. Vlase, S.; Nastac, C.; Marin, M.; Mihalcica, M. A Method for the Study of the Vibration of Mechanical Bars Systems with Symmetries. *Acta Tech. Napoc. Ser. Appl. Math. Mech. Eng.* **2017**, *60*, 539–544.
29. Vlase, S.; Marin, M.; Iuliu, N. Finite Element Method-Based Elastic Analysis of Multibody Systems: A Review. *Mathematics* **2022**, *10*, 257. [CrossRef]
30. Bencze, A.; Scutaru, M.L.; Marin, M.; Vlase, S.; Toderiță, A. Adder Box Used in the Heavy Trucks Transmission Noise Reduction. *Symmetry* **2021**, *13*, 2165. [CrossRef]
31. Scutaru, M.L.; Vlase, S.; Marin, M.; Modrea, A. New analytical method based on dynamic response of planar mechanical elastic systems. *Bound. Value Probl.* **2020**, *2020*, 104. [CrossRef]

Article

Steady-State Solutions for MHD Motions of Burgers' Fluids through Porous Media with Differential Expressions of Shear on Boundary and Applications

Constantin Fetecau [1,*], Abdul Rauf [2], Tahir Mushtaq Qureshi [3] and Dumitru Vieru [4]

[1] Section of Mathematics, Academy of Romanian Scientists, 050094 Bucharest, Romania
[2] Department of Computer Science and Engineering, Air University Islamabad, Islamabad 44000, Pakistan
[3] Department of Mathematics, COMSATS University Islamabad, Vehari Campus, Vehari 61100, Pakistan
[4] Department of Theoretical Mechanics, Technical University of Iasi, 700050 Iasi, Romania
* Correspondence: fetecau@math.tuiasi.ro or c_fetecau@yahoo.com

Abstract: Steady-state solutions for two mixed initial-boundary value problems are provided. They describe isothermal MHD steady-state motions of incompressible Burgers' fluids over an infinite flat plate embedded in a porous medium when differential expressions of shear stress are given on a part of the boundary. The fluid is electrically conductive under the influence of a uniform transverse magnetic field. For the validation of the results, the expressions of the obtained solutions are presented in different forms and their equivalence is graphically proved. All of the obtained results could easily be particularized to give exact solutions for the incompressible Oldroyd-B, Maxwell, second-grade, and Newtonian fluids that were performing similar motions. For illustration, the solutions corresponding to Newtonian fluids are provided. In addition, as an application, the velocity fields were used to determine the time required to reach the steady or permanent state for distinct values of magnetic and porous parameters. We found that this time declined with increasing values of the magnetic or porous parameters. Consequently, the steady state for such motions of Burgers' fluids was earlier reached in the presence of a magnetic field or porous medium.

Keywords: Burgers' fluids; isothermal MHD motions; porous medium; steady-state solutions; steady or permanent state

MSC: 76A05

1. Introduction

The isothermal motions of incompressible Newtonian or non-Newtonian fluids over an infinite plate have been extensively studied in the past. They are some of the most important motion problems near moving bodies and have multiple industrial applications including the processing of polymers, food products, pharmaceuticals, clay suspensions, and many others. Generally, in practice, an infinite plate cannot be used. However, its dimensions can be large enough so that the solutions corresponding to motions over such a plate can be sufficiently approximated by solutions for motions over an infinite plate. In the existing literature, there are many studies on the motion problems of fluids over an infinite plate or between two infinite parallel plates. The most recent results regarding oscillatory motions of incompressible Burgers' fluids over an infinite plate seem to be those of Akram et al. [1]. The MHD motions of these fluids also have different applications in hydrology, horticulture, and engineering structures. The exact solutions for the MHD second Stokes flow of the same fluids can be obtained from the work of Khan et al. [2]. In addition, the study of different motions through porous media has a distinguished importance in different fields, including those in the natural sciences and technology. Hydrodynamic studies of the Maxwell fluid flow through a porous medium were recently provided by Ullah et al. [3] and Fetecau et al. [4]. Exact solutions for MHD unsteady motions of incompressible non-Newtonian fluids over an infinite flat plate embedded in a porous medium were previously established; for instance, by Hayat et al. [5] and Ali et al. [6] for second-grade fluids, Khan et al. [7] for Oldroyd-B fluids, and Alghatani and Khan [8] and Hussain et al. [9] for Burgers' fluids. General solutions for isothermal MHD motions of incompressible Newtonian fluids over an infinite plate embedded in a porous medium were obtained by Fetecau et al. [10]. The combined effects of free convection MHD flow past a vertical plate embedded in a porous medium were recently investigated by Vijayalakshmi et al. [11].

Many exact solutions for MHD unsteady motions of the incompressible non-Newtonian fluids over an infinite plate embedded in a porous medium were determined previously by different authors. However, Khan et al. [2] seemed to be the first authors who established exact solutions for such motions of incompressible Burgers' fluids. The one-dimensional form of the constitutive equation of incompressible Burgers' fluids was proposed by Burgers [12]; his model is often used to describe the behavior of different viscoelastic materials such as polymeric liquids, cheese, soil, and asphalt [13,14]. A good agreement between the prediction of this model and the behavior of asphalt and sand-asphalt was found by Lee and Markwick [15]. The extension of the one-dimensional Burgers' model to a frame-indifferent three-dimensional form was provided by Krishnan and Rajagopal [16], while the first exact steady solutions for motions of such fluids seem to be those of Ravindran et al. [17] for a fluid flow in an orthogonal rheometer. Other interesting solutions for oscillatory motions of incompressible Burgers' fluids were established by Hayat et al. [18], Khan et al. [19,20], and recently Safdar et al. [21]. Exact steady-state solutions for isothermal motions of same fluids when a differential expression of shear stress was given on a part of the boundary were recently obtained by Fetecau et al. [22]. In order to study similar flows of the same fluids in bounded domains, which are useful in industrial applications, readers can use the recent works by Çolak et al. [23] and Abderrahmane et al. [24].

Earlier, Renardy [25,26] showed that boundary conditions containing differential expressions of stresses must be imposed in order to formulate well-posed boundary value problems for motions of rate-type fluids. The main purpose of this work was to provide the first exact steady-state solutions for motions of incompressible Burgers' fluids, which are rate-type fluids, when differential expressions of the shear stress were given on a part of the boundary and the magnetic and porous effects were taken into consideration. These solutions, which are presented in simple forms, could easily be particularized to give exact solutions for incompressible Oldroyd-B, Maxwell, second-grade and Newtonian fluids that were performing similar motions. For illustration, the adequate solutions for the Newtonian fluids are brought to light. In addition, for the validation of the results, all of the solutions are presented in different forms and their equivalence is graphically proved. Finally, as an application, the required time to reach the steady or permanent state was graphically determined for distinct values of the magnetic and porous parameters.

2. Statement of the Problem

Consider an incompressible, electrically conducting Burgers' fluid (IECBF) at rest over an infinite horizontal flat plate embedded in a porous medium. Its constitutive equations, as presented by Ravindran et al. [15], are given by the relations:

$$T = -pI + S, \ S + \alpha \frac{DS}{Dt} + \beta \frac{D^2 S}{Dt^2} = \mu\left(A + \gamma \frac{DA}{Dt}\right), \tag{1}$$

where T is the Cauchy stress tensor; S is the extra-stress tensor; I is the unit tensor; $A = L + L^T$ is the first Rivlin–Ericksen tensor (L being the gradient of the velocity vector v); p is the hydrostatic pressure; μ is the fluid viscosity; α, β, and γ ($\leq \alpha$) are material constants; and D/Dt denotes the well-known upper-convected derivative. Since the incompressible fluids undergo isochoric motions only, the following continuity equation must be satisfied:

$$\text{div} v = 0 \text{ or equivalent tr } A = 0. \tag{2}$$

We also most consider the fact that the fluids characterized by the constitutive Equation (1) contain the incompressible Oldroyd-B, Maxwell, and Newtonian fluids as special cases if $\beta = 0$, $\beta = \gamma = 0$, or $\alpha = \beta = \gamma = 0$, respectively. For the motions to be considered here, the governing equations corresponding to the incompressible second-grade fluids can also be obtained as particular cases of the present equations.

In the following, and based on Khan et al. [2], we shall consider isothermal MHD unsteady motions of an IECBF over an infinite flat plate embedded in a porous medium for which

$$v = v(y,t) = u(y,t)\mathbf{e}_x, \quad S = S(y,t), \tag{3}$$

where $\mathbf{e}_x$ is the unit vector along the x-direction of a convenient Cartesian coordinate system of x, y, and z with the y-axis perpendicular to the plate. For such motions, the continuity equation is identically satisfied. Substituting $v(y,t)$ and $S(y,t)$ from Equation (3) in the second equality from the relations in (1) and bearing in mind the fact that the fluid has been at rest up to the initial moment $t = 0$, one can prove that the components S_{yy}, S_{yz}, S_{zz} and S_{zx} of S are zero. On the other hand, the non-trivial shear stress $\tau(y,t) = S_{xy}(y,t)$ must satisfy the next partial differential equation [18].

$$\left(1 + \alpha\frac{\partial}{\partial t} + \beta\frac{\partial^2}{\partial t^2}\right)\tau(y,t) = \mu\left(1 + \gamma\frac{\partial}{\partial t}\right)\frac{\partial u(y,t)}{\partial y}; \quad y > 0, \; t > 0. \tag{4}$$

The balance of linear momentum in the presence of conservative body forces and of a transverse magnetic field of the magnitude B but in the absence of a pressure gradient in the flow direction reduces to the following partial differential equation [2]:

$$\rho\frac{\partial u(y,t)}{\partial t} = \frac{\partial \tau(y,t)}{\partial y} - \sigma B^2 u(y,t) + R(y,t); \quad y > 0, \; t > 0, \tag{5}$$

where ρ is the constant density of the fluid, σ is its electrical conductivity, and the Darcy's resistance $R(y,t)$ satisfies the relation [2].

$$\left(1 + \alpha\frac{\partial}{\partial t} + \beta\frac{\partial^2}{\partial t^2}\right)R(y,t) = -\frac{\mu\varphi}{k}\left(1 + \gamma\frac{\partial}{\partial t}\right)u(y,t); \quad y > 0, \; t > 0. \tag{6}$$

In the above relation, φ and k are the porosity and the permeability, respectively, of the porous medium.

The appropriate initial conditions of:

$$u(y,0) = \left.\frac{\partial u(y,t)}{\partial t}\right|_{t=0} = \left.\frac{\partial^2 u(y,t)}{\partial t^2}\right|_{t=0} = 0; \; \tau(y,0) = \left.\frac{\partial \tau(y,t)}{\partial t}\right|_{t=0} = 0; \; y \geq 0, \tag{7}$$

have been already used to show that some of the components of the extra-stress S are zero. The boundary conditions to be here used are given by the following relations:

$$\left(1 + \alpha\frac{\partial}{\partial t} + \beta\frac{\partial^2}{\partial t^2}\right)\tau(0,t) = \mu\left(1 + \gamma\frac{\partial}{\partial t}\right)\left.\frac{\partial u(y,t)}{\partial y}\right|_{y=0} = S\cos(\omega t), \; \lim_{y\to\infty} u(y,t) = 0; \; t > 0, \tag{8}$$

or

$$\left(1 + \alpha\frac{\partial}{\partial t} + \beta\frac{\partial^2}{\partial t^2}\right)\tau(0,t) = \mu\left(1 + \gamma\frac{\partial}{\partial t}\right)\left.\frac{\partial u(y,t)}{\partial y}\right|_{y=0} = S\sin(\omega t), \; \lim_{y\to\infty} u(y,t) = 0; \; t > 0. \tag{9}$$

In the above relations, S is a constant shear stress and ω is the frequency of the oscillations. The second condition from the relations (8) and (9) assures us that the fluid is quiescently far away from the plate. We also assume that there is no shear in the free stream; i.e.,:

$$\lim_{y\to\infty} \tau(y,t) = 0. \tag{10}$$

For convenience, we also assume that the fluid is finitely conducting so that the Joule heating due to the presence of external magnetic field is negligible. In addition, the magnetic Reynolds number is small enough so that the induced magnetic field can be neglected and the electromagnetic energy does not penetrate the boundary for computing the Umov–Poynting vector [27]. Moreover, there is no surplus electric charge distribution present in the fluid and the Hall effects can be ignored due to moderate values of the Hartman number.

In order to provide exact solutions that are independent of the flow geometry, let us introduce the next dimensionless functions, variables and parameters:

$$u^* = u\sqrt{\tfrac{\rho}{S}}, \quad \tau^* = \tfrac{\tau}{S}, \quad R^* = \tfrac{\nu\sqrt{\rho}}{S\sqrt{S}}R, \quad y^* = y\sqrt{\tfrac{S}{\mu\nu}}, \quad t^* = \tfrac{S}{\mu}t,$$
$$\alpha^* = \tfrac{S}{\mu}\alpha, \quad \beta^* = \tfrac{S^2}{\mu^2}\beta, \quad \gamma^* = \tfrac{S}{\mu}\gamma, \quad \omega^* = \tfrac{\mu}{S}\omega. \tag{11}$$

Using the non-dimensional entities from the relations in (11) in the equalities (4)–(6) and abandoning the star notation for writing simplicity, one obtains the non-dimensional forms of these equations:

$$\left(1 + \alpha \frac{\partial}{\partial t} + \beta \frac{\partial^2}{\partial t^2}\right)\tau(y,t) = \left(1 + \gamma \frac{\partial}{\partial t}\right)\frac{\partial u(y,t)}{\partial y}; \quad y > 0, \quad t > 0, \tag{12}$$

$$\frac{\partial u(y,t)}{\partial t} = \frac{\partial \tau(y,t)}{\partial y} - Mu(y,t) + R(y,t); \quad y > 0, \quad t > 0, \tag{13}$$

$$\left(1 + \alpha \frac{\partial}{\partial t} + \beta \frac{\partial^2}{\partial t^2}\right)R(y,t) = -K\left(1 + \gamma \frac{\partial}{\partial t}\right)u(y,t); \quad y > 0, \quad t > 0, \tag{14}$$

where the constants M and K are the magnetic and porous parameters, respectively, which are defined by the following relations:

$$M = \frac{\sigma B^2}{\rho}\frac{\mu}{S} = \frac{\nu}{S}\sigma B^2, \quad K = \frac{\mu\nu\varphi}{kS} = \frac{\mu\varphi}{k}\frac{\nu}{S}. \tag{15}$$

When eliminating $\tau(y,t)$ between Equations (12) and (13) and bearing in mind Equation (14), one obtains for the dimensionless velocity field $u(y,t)$ the following partial differential equation:

$$\left(1 + \alpha \frac{\partial}{\partial t} + \beta \frac{\partial^2}{\partial t^2}\right)\frac{\partial u(y,t)}{\partial t} = \left(1 + \gamma \frac{\partial}{\partial t}\right)\frac{\partial^2 u(y,t)}{\partial y^2}$$
$$-M\left(1 + \alpha \frac{\partial}{\partial t} + \beta \frac{\partial^2}{\partial t^2}\right)u(y,t) - K\left(1 + \gamma \frac{\partial}{\partial t}\right)u(y,t); \quad y > 0, \quad t > 0. \tag{16}$$

The corresponding boundary conditions are given by the next equalities:

$$\left(1 + \alpha \frac{\partial}{\partial t} + \beta \frac{\partial^2}{\partial t^2}\right)\tau(0,t) = \left(1 + \gamma \frac{\partial}{\partial t}\right)\frac{\partial u(y,t)}{\partial y}\bigg|_{y=0} = \cos(\omega t), \quad \lim_{y \to \infty} u(y,t) = 0; \quad t > 0, \tag{17}$$

or

$$\left(1 + \alpha \frac{\partial}{\partial t} + \beta \frac{\partial^2}{\partial t^2}\right)\tau(0,t) = \left(1 + \gamma \frac{\partial}{\partial t}\right)\frac{\partial u(y,t)}{\partial y}\bigg|_{y=0} = \sin(\omega t), \quad \lim_{y \to \infty} u(y,t) = 0; \quad t > 0. \tag{18}$$

The adequate initial conditions have the same forms as in Equation (7) but they will not be used in the following because only steady-state (permanent or long-term) solutions will be provided. The non-dimensional shear stress $\tau(y,t)$ also must satisfy the following condition:

$$\lim_{y \to \infty} \tau(y,t) = 0. \tag{19}$$

The form of the boundary conditions in (17) and (18), as well as the fact that the fluid was at rest at the moment $t = 0$, suggests that the two motions become steady in time. For such motions, a very important problem for experimental researchers is to know the time needed to reach the steady or permanent state. This is the time after which the fluid moves according to the steady-state solutions. In the following, in order to avoid a possible confusion, we denote by $u_c(y,t)$, $\tau_c(y,t)$, $R_c(y,t)$ and $u_s(y,t)$, $\tau_s(y,t)$, $R_s(y,t)$ the starting solutions corresponding to the two fluid motions whose boundary conditions are given by the relations in (17) and (18), respectively. These solutions, which characterize the fluid motion some time after its initiation, can be written as sum of their respective steady-state and transient components; i.e.,:

$$u_c(y,t) = u_{cp}(y,t) + u_{ct}(y,t), \quad \tau_c(y,t) = \tau_{cp}(y,t) + \tau_{ct}(y,t), \quad R_c(y,t) = R_{cp}(y,t) + R_{ct}(y,t), \tag{20}$$

and

$$u_s(y,t) = u_{sp}(y,t) + u_{st}(y,t), \quad \tau_s(y,t) = \tau_{sp}(y,t) + \tau_{st}(y,t), \quad R_s(y,t) = R_{sp}(y,t) + R_{st}(y,t). \tag{21}$$

After this time, when the transients disappear or can be negligible, the fluid behavior is described by the steady-state or permanent solutions $u_{cp}(y,t)$, $\tau_{cp}(y,t)$, $R_{cp}(y,t)$ or $u_{sp}(y,t)$, $\tau_{sp}(y,t)$, $R_{sp}(y,t)$. In order to determine this time for a given motion, at least the steady-state or transient solutions have to be known. Since, for the transient solutions of the motions, we do not know a modality to verify their correctness, in the following we shall provide closed-form expressions for the steady-state solutions of the two above-mentioned motion problems. These steady-state solutions, which are independent of the initial conditions, satisfy the boundary conditions and governing equations.

3. Dimensionless Steady-State Solutions

In this section, we provide closed-form expressions for the dimensionless steady-state velocity and shear stress fields $u_{cp}(y,t)$, $u_{sp}(y,t)$ and $\tau_{cp}(y,t)$, $\tau_{sp}(y,t)$, respectively, and the corresponding Darcy's resistances $R_{cp}(y,t)$, $R_{sp}(y,t)$. For a check of the obtained results, these expressions are presented in different forms and their equivalence is graphically proved.

3.1. Calculation of the Steady-State Velocities $u_{cp}(y,t)$ and $u_{sp}(y,t)$

To determine the dimensionless velocity fields $u_{cp}(y,t)$ and $u_{sp}(y,t)$ that satisfy the governing Equation (16) and the respective boundary conditions (17) and (18), we follow two different methods. Firstly, while bearing in mind the linearity of the governing Equation (16) and the form of the boundary conditions (17) and (18), we define the steady-state complex velocity:

$$u_p(y,t) = u_{cp}(y,t) + i u_{sp}(y,t); \quad y > 0, \quad t \in R, \tag{22}$$

where i is the imaginary unit and is searching for a solution of the form:

$$u_p(y,t) = U(y)e^{i\omega t}; \quad y > 0, \quad t \in R, \tag{23}$$

where $U(\cdot)$ is a complex function. Of course, the dimensionless complex velocity $u_p(y,t)$ must satisfy the governing Equation (16) and the boundary conditions.

$$\left(1 + \gamma \frac{\partial}{\partial t}\right) \frac{\partial u_p(y,t)}{\partial y}\bigg|_{y=0} = e^{i\omega t}, \quad \lim_{y \to \infty} u_p(y,t) = 0; \quad t \in R. \tag{24}$$

Direct computations show that $u_p(y,t)$ can be presented in the following form:

$$u_p(y,t) = -\frac{1}{(1+i\omega\gamma)\delta} e^{-\delta y + i\omega t}; \quad y > 0, \quad t \in R, \tag{25}$$

while the dimensionless steady-state velocity fields $u_{cp}(y,t)$ and $u_{sp}(y,t)$ are given by the following relations:

$$u_{cp}(y,t) = -\text{Re}\left\{\frac{1}{(1+i\omega\gamma)\delta}e^{-\delta y+i\omega t}\right\}, \quad u_{sp}(y,t) = -\text{Im}\left\{\frac{1}{(1+i\omega\gamma)\delta}e^{-\delta y+i\omega t}\right\}, \quad (26)$$

where Re and Im denote the real and imaginary parts, respectively, of that which follows, and:

$$\delta = \sqrt{\frac{(1-\beta\omega^2+i\omega\alpha)(M+i\omega)+K(1+i\omega\gamma)}{1+i\omega\gamma}}. \quad (27)$$

Secondly, in order to determine the equivalent forms for the dimensionless steady-state solutions given by Equation (26), we use the dimensionless steady-state solutions:

$$u_{Scp}(y,t) = e^{-my}\cos(\omega t - ny), \quad u_{Ssp}(y,t) = e^{-my}\sin(\omega t - ny), \quad (28)$$

of the second problem of Stokes for incompressible Burgers' fluids. It is the fluid motion over an infinite flat plate that oscillates in its plane with the dimensionless velocity $\cos(\omega t)$ or $\sin(\omega t)$. In these solutions, which were determined by direct computations, the constants m and n are given by the following relations:

$$m = \sqrt{\frac{\omega}{2}}\sqrt{\frac{a\omega+\sqrt{(a\omega)^2+b^2}}{1+(\gamma\omega)^2}}, \quad n = \sqrt{\frac{\omega}{2}}\sqrt{\frac{-a\omega+\sqrt{(a\omega)^2+b^2}}{1+(\gamma\omega)^2}}, \quad (29)$$

which satisfy the algebraic system of equations:

$$m^2 - n^2 = \frac{a\omega^2}{1+(\gamma\omega)^2}, \quad mn = \frac{b\omega}{2[1+(\gamma\omega)^2]}, \quad (30)$$

where a and b are defined by following equalities:

$$a = \gamma(1-\beta\omega^2) - \alpha, \quad b = 1 - \beta\omega^2 + \alpha\gamma\omega^2. \quad (31)$$

More precisely, we are looking for the present dimensionless steady-state velocity fields $u_{cp}(y,t)$ and $u_{sp}(y,t)$ under the following forms:

$$u_{cp}(y,t) = p_1 u_{Scp}(y,t) + q_1 u_{Ssp}(y,t), \quad u_{sp}(y,t) = p_2 u_{Scp}(y,t) + q_2 u_{Ssp}(y,t). \quad (32)$$

They must satisfy the respective boundary conditions in (17) and (18). Lengthy but straightforward computations show that $u_{cp}(y,t)$ and $u_{sp}(y,t)$ can be presented in the following simple forms:

$$\begin{aligned} u_{cp}(y,t) &= -\sqrt{p^2+q^2}\,e^{-\tilde{m}y}\cos(\omega t - \tilde{n}y + \varphi), \\ u_{sp}(y,t) &= -\sqrt{p^2+q^2}\,e^{-\tilde{m}y}\sin(\omega t - \tilde{n}y + \varphi). \end{aligned} \quad (33)$$

In the last two relations, the angle $\varphi = \text{arctg}(q/p)$ while the constants $\tilde{m}, \tilde{n}, p$, and q have the following expressions:

$$\tilde{m} = \sqrt{\frac{\omega}{2}}\sqrt{\frac{c\omega+\sqrt{(c\omega)^2+d^2}}{1+(\gamma\omega)^2}}, \quad \tilde{n} = \sqrt{\frac{\omega}{2}}\sqrt{\frac{-c\omega+\sqrt{(c\omega)^2+d^2}}{1+(\gamma\omega)^2}}, \quad (34)$$

$$p = \frac{\tilde{n}\omega\gamma - \tilde{m}}{(\tilde{m}\omega\gamma+\tilde{n})^2+(\tilde{n}\omega\gamma-\tilde{m})^2}, \quad q = \frac{\tilde{m}\omega\gamma+\tilde{n}}{(\tilde{m}\omega\gamma+\tilde{n})^2+(\tilde{n}\omega\gamma-\tilde{m})^2}, \quad (35)$$

in which c and d are given by the following relations:

$$c = \gamma(1-\beta\omega^2) - \alpha + \frac{(1-\beta\omega^2+\alpha\gamma\omega^2)M+[1+(\gamma\omega)^2]K}{\omega^2},$$
$$d = 1 - \beta\omega^2 + \alpha\gamma\omega^2 + [\alpha - \gamma(1-\beta\omega^2)]M. \tag{36}$$

The equivalence of the dimensionless steady-state solutions given by the equalities in (26) and (33) is graphically proved in Figure 1a,b.

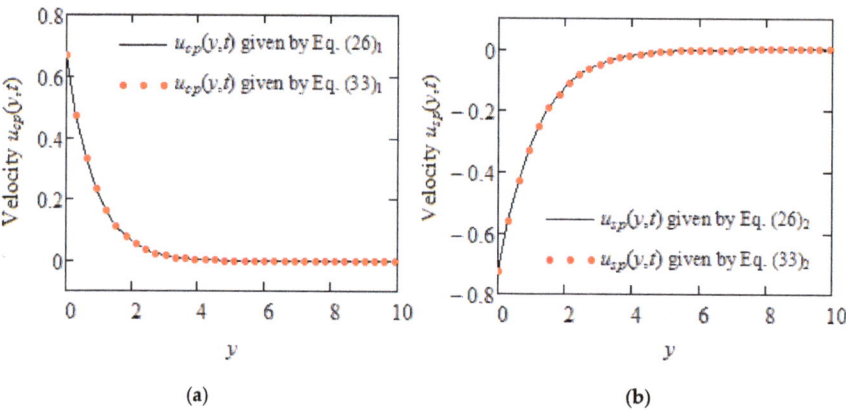

Figure 1. Equivalence of velocity fields $u_{cp}(y,t)$ and $u_{sp}(y,t)$ given by Equations (26) and (33) for $\alpha = 0.8$, $\beta = 0.7$, $\gamma = 0.6$, $\omega = \pi/12$, $M = 0.6$, $K = 0.4$, $K_{eff} = 1$, and $t = 10$.

The dimensionless steady-state velocity fields $u_{cp}(y,t)$ and $u_{sp}(y,t)$ corresponding to isothermal motions of the same fluids in the absence of magnetic or porous effects can immediately be obtained by taking $M = 0$, respectively $K = 0$ in Equations (26) and (33), respectively. In the absence of both effects, when $M = K = 0$, the present solutions reduce to those obtained by Fetecau et al. [22] (Equations (19) and (20)). Moreover, the dimensionless steady-state solutions corresponding to incompressible Oldroyd-B, Maxwell, and Newtonian fluids that are performing similar motions are immediately obtained by taking $\beta = 0$, $\beta = \gamma = 0$ or $\alpha = \beta = \gamma = 0$, respectively, in the previous relations. The dimensionless steady-state velocity fields corresponding to motions of the incompressible Newtonian fluids over an infinite flat plate that apply an oscillatory shear stress $S\cos(\omega t)$ or $S\sin(\omega t)$ to the fluid, for instance, have the following simple forms:

$$u_{Ncp}(y,t) = -\text{Re}\left\{\frac{1}{\sqrt{K_{eff}+i\omega}}e^{-y\sqrt{K_{eff}+i\omega}+i\omega t}\right\},$$
$$u_{Nsp}(y,t) = -\text{Im}\left\{\frac{1}{\sqrt{K_{eff}+i\omega}}e^{-y\sqrt{K_{eff}+i\omega}+i\omega t}\right\}, \tag{37}$$

or the equivalent

$$u_{Ncp}(y,t) = -\frac{1}{\sqrt[4]{K_{eff}^2+\omega^2}}e^{-fy}\cos(\omega t - gy + \psi),$$
$$u_{Nsp}(y,t) = -\frac{1}{\sqrt[4]{K_{eff}^2+\omega^2}}e^{-fy}\sin(\omega t - gy + \psi), \tag{38}$$

where

$$f = \sqrt{\frac{K_{eff}+\sqrt{K_{eff}^2+\omega^2}}{2}}, \quad g = \sqrt{\frac{-K_{eff}+\sqrt{K_{eff}^2+\omega^2}}{2}}, \quad \psi = \text{arctg}\left(\frac{K_{eff}-\sqrt{K_{eff}^2+\omega^2}}{\omega}\right) \tag{39}$$

and $K_{eff} = M + K$ is the effective permeability [10]. The equivalence of the solutions in (37) and (38) is graphically proved in Figure 2a,b.

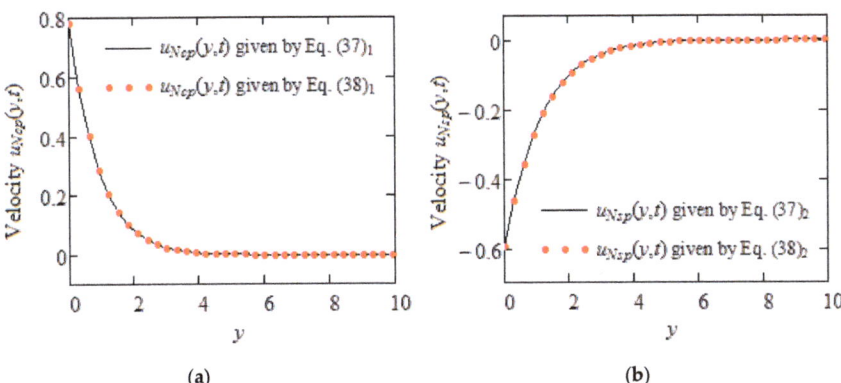

Figure 2. Equivalence of velocity fields $u_{Ncp}(y,t)$ and $u_{Nsp}(y,t)$ given by Equations (37) and (38) for $\omega = \pi/12$, $K_{eff} = 1$, and $t = 10$.

3.2. Exact Expressions for $\tau_{cp}(y,t), \tau_{sp}(y,t)$ and $R_{cp}(y,t), R_{sp}(y,t)$

In order to determine the dimensionless steady-state shear stresses $\tau_{cp}(y,t), \tau_{sp}(y,t)$ and the Darcy's resistances $R_{cp}(y,t), R_{sp}(y,t)$ corresponding to the two unsteady motions of the IECBF when magnetic and porous effects are taken into account, we firstly use the complex shear stress and Darcy's resistance:

$$\tau_p(y,t) = \tau_{cp}(y,t) + i\tau_{sp}(y,t), \quad R_p(y,t) = R_{cp}(y,t) + iR_{sp}(y,t) \tag{40}$$

and follow the same method as for the steady-state velocities. The obtained results when using for $u_{cp}(y,t)$ and $u_{sp}(y,t)$ the expressions from the equalities in (26) are given by the following respective relations:

$$\tau_{cp}(y,t) = \text{Re}\left\{\frac{1}{1-\beta\omega^2+i\omega\alpha}e^{-\delta y+i\omega t}\right\}, \quad \tau_{sp}(y,t) = \text{Im}\left\{\frac{1}{1-\beta\omega^2+i\omega\alpha}e^{-\delta y+i\omega t}\right\}, \tag{41}$$

and

$$R_{cp}(y,t) = K\text{Re}\left\{\frac{1}{(1-\beta\omega^2+i\omega\alpha)\delta}e^{-\delta y+i\omega t}\right\},$$
$$R_{sp}(y,t) = K\text{Im}\left\{\frac{1}{(1-\beta\omega^2+i\omega\alpha)\delta}e^{-\delta y+i\omega t}\right\}. \tag{42}$$

Direct computations clearly show that the dimensionless steady-state velocity, shear stress, and Darcy's resistance fields $u_{cp}(y,t)$, $\tau_{cp}(y,t)$, $R_{cp}(y,t)$ and $u_{sp}(y,t)$, $\tau_{sp}(y,t)$, $R_{sp}(y,t)$ given by the relations in (26), (41), and (42) satisfy the governing Equations (12)–(14) and the respective boundary conditions in (17) and (18).

Equivalent expressions for $\tau_{cp}(y,t)$, $\tau_{sp}(y,t)$ and $R_{cp}(y,t)$, $R_{sp}(y,t)$, namely:

$$\tau_{cp}(y,t) = \sqrt{p_1^2+q_1^2}\, e^{-\tilde{m}y}\cos(\omega t - \tilde{n}y + \varphi - \chi),$$
$$\tau_{sp}(y,t) = \sqrt{p_1^2+q_1^2}\, e^{-\tilde{m}y}\sin(\omega t - \tilde{n}y + \varphi - \chi), \tag{43}$$

and

$$R_{cp}(y,t) = \sqrt{p_2^2+q_2^2}\, e^{-\tilde{m}y}\cos(\omega t - \tilde{n}y + \varphi - \theta),$$
$$R_{sp}(y,t) = \sqrt{p_2^2+q_2^2}\, e^{-\tilde{m}y}\sin(\omega t - \tilde{n}y + \varphi - \theta), \tag{44}$$

were obtained by using the corresponding velocity fields $u_{cp}(y,t)$ and $u_{sp}(y,t)$ from the equalities in (33). In these relations:

$$p_1 = \frac{(1-\beta\omega^2)(\tilde{m}-\tilde{n}\omega\gamma)+\alpha\omega(\tilde{n}+\tilde{m}\omega\gamma)}{(1-\beta\omega^2)^2+(\alpha\omega)^2}\sqrt{p^2+q^2},$$
$$q_1 = \frac{\alpha\omega(\tilde{m}-\tilde{n}\omega\gamma)-(1-\beta\omega^2)(\tilde{n}+\tilde{m}\omega\gamma)}{(1-\beta\omega^2)^2+(\alpha\omega)^2}\sqrt{p^2+q^2},$$
(45)

$$p_2 = K\frac{1-\beta\omega^2+\alpha\gamma\omega^2}{(1-\beta\omega^2)^2+(\alpha\omega)^2}\sqrt{p^2+q^2}, \quad q_2 = \omega K\frac{\alpha-\gamma(1-\beta\omega^2)}{(1-\beta\omega^2)^2+(\alpha\omega)^2}\sqrt{p^2+q^2},$$
(46)

where $\chi = \arctan(q_1/p_1)$ and $\theta = \arctan(q_2/p_2)$. The equivalence of the dimensionless shear stresses $\tau_{cp}(y,t)$, $\tau_{sp}(y,t)$ and of the Darcy's resistances $R_{cp}(y,t)$, $R_{sp}(y,t)$ given by Equation (41) and (42), respectively, to those from the relations in (43) and (44) is proved in Figures 3 and 4.

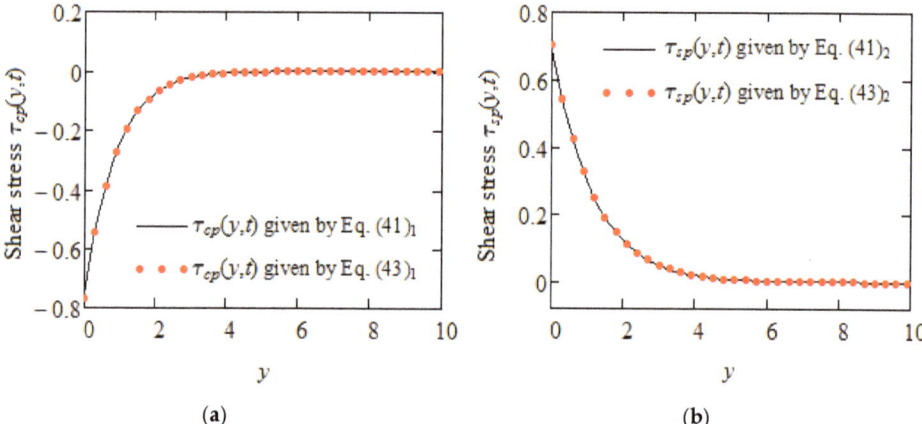

Figure 3. Equivalence of shear stresses $\tau_{cp}(y,t)$ and $\tau_{sp}(y,t)$ given by Equations (41) and (43) for $\alpha = 0.8$, $\beta = 0.7$, $\gamma = 0.6$, $\omega = \pi/12$, $M = 0.6$, $K = 0.4$, $K_{eff} = 1$, and $t = 10$.

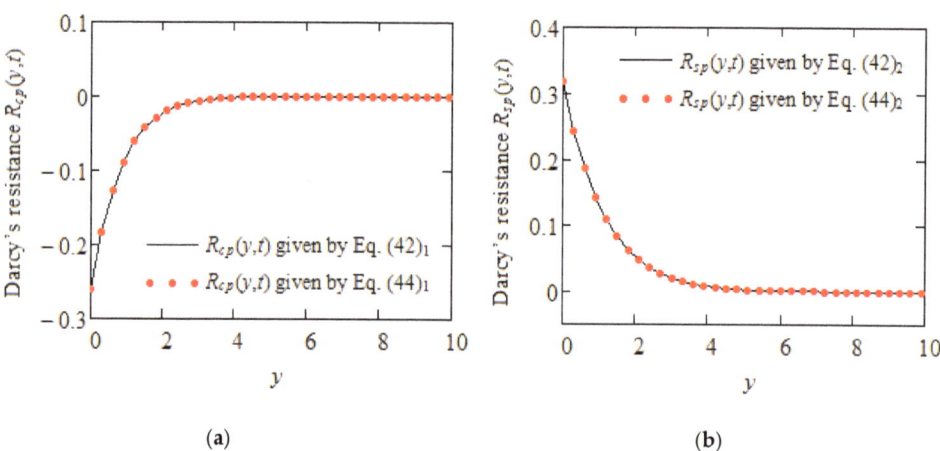

Figure 4. Equivalence of Darcy's resistances $R_{cp}(y,t)$ and $R_{sp}(y,t)$ given by Equations (42) and (44), for $\alpha = 0.8$, $\omega = \pi/12$, $M = 0.6$, $K = 0.4$, and $t = 10$.

The dimensionless steady-state shear stresses and Darcy's resistances corresponding to the velocity fields $u_{Ncp}(y,t)$ and $u_{Nsp}(y,t)$ of incompressible Newtonian fluids given by the relations in (37) and (38) have the following simple forms:

$$\tau_{Ncp}(y,t) = \text{Re}\left\{e^{-y\sqrt{K_{eff}+i\omega}+i\omega t}\right\}, \quad \tau_{Nsp}(y,t) = \text{Im}\left\{e^{-y\sqrt{K_{eff}+i\omega}+i\omega t}\right\}, \quad (47)$$

$$R_{Ncp}(y,t) = K\text{Re}\left\{\frac{1}{\sqrt{K_{eff}+i\omega}}e^{-y\sqrt{K_{eff}+i\omega}+i\omega t}\right\},$$
$$R_{Nsp}(y,t) = K\text{Im}\left\{\frac{1}{\sqrt{K_{eff}+i\omega}}e^{-y\sqrt{K_{eff}+i\omega}+i\omega t}\right\}, \quad (48)$$

or the equivalent:

$$\tau_{Ncp}(y,t) = e^{-fy}\cos(\omega t - gy), \quad \tau_{Nsp}(y,t) = e^{-fy}\sin(\omega t - gy), \quad (49)$$

$$R_{Ncp}(y,t) = \frac{K}{\sqrt[4]{K_{eff}^2+\omega^2}}e^{-fy}\cos(\omega t - gy + \psi),$$
$$R_{Nsp}(y,t) = \frac{K}{\sqrt[4]{K_{eff}^2+\omega^2}}e^{-fy}\sin(\omega t - gy + \psi). \quad (50)$$

4. Some Numerical Results and Applications

Closed-form expressions for the dimensionless steady-state solutions $u_{cp}(y,t)$, $\tau_{cp}(y,t)$, $R_{cp}(y,t)$ and $u_{sp}(y,t)$, $\tau_{sp}(y,t)$, $R_{sp}(y,t)$ corresponding to two isothermal MHD motions of an IECBF over an infinite flat plate embedded in a porous medium were presented in simple forms in the previous section. They are the first exact solutions for MHD motions of an IECBF with differential expressions of shear stress on the boundary. For validation, all solutions are presented in double forms and their equivalence was graphically proved. These solutions can easily be particularized to give corresponding solutions for incompressible Oldroyd-B, Maxwell, and Newtonian fluids that are performing similar motions.

As an application, some of the obtained results were used to determine the required time to reach the steady or permanent state. From a mathematical point of view, this was the time after which the diagrams of the starting velocities $u_c(y,t)$ and $u_s(y,t)$ (numerical solutions) were almost identical to those of their steady-state components $u_{cp}(y,t)$ and $u_{sp}(y,t)$, respectively. The convergence of the two starting velocities to their steady-state components was proved in Figures 5–8 for increasing values of the time t at distinct values of M and K and fixed values of the other parameters. Based on these figures, it was clear that the required time to reach the steady state diminished with increasing values of the magnetic or porous parameters (M and K, respectively). Consequently, the steady state for isothermal motions of the IECBF was earlier reached in the presence of a magnetic field or porous medium. In addition, as expected, in all cases the fluid velocity tended to zero with increasing values of the spatial variable y.

For comparison, as well as to bring to light some characteristic features of the two motions, the spatial distributions of the dimensionless starting velocity fields $u_c(y,t)$ and $u_s(y,t)$ (numerical solutions) are presented together in Figure 9a,b, respectively, for the same values of the physical parameters. The oscillatory behavior of the two motions, as well as the phase difference between them, can be easily observed. In addition, the initial and boundary conditions were clearly satisfied. Blue and yellow colors were used in the current figure to designate the minimum and maximum values of the two solutions, respectively. The intermediate values between the maximum and minimum are denoted by the gradient of the colors between yellow and blue.

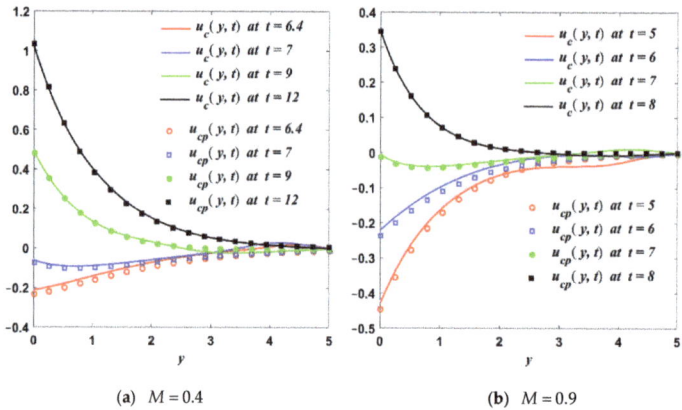

Figure 5. Convergence of starting velocity $u_c(y,t)$ (numerical solution) to its steady-state component $u_{cp}(y,t)$ for $\alpha = 0.8$, $\beta = 0.7$, $\gamma = 0.6$, $\omega = \pi/12$, $K = 0.4$, and two values of M.

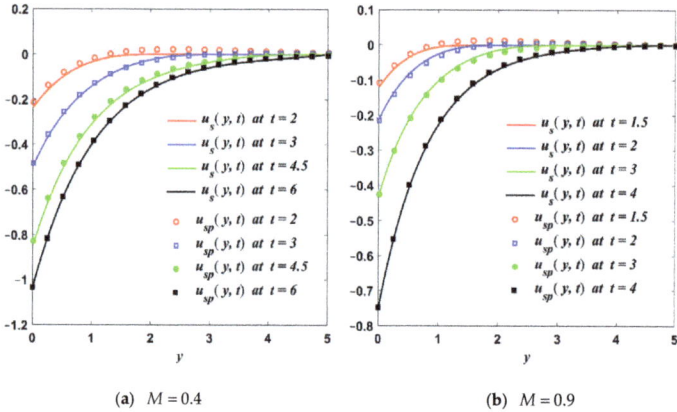

Figure 6. Convergence of starting velocity $u_s(y,t)$ (numerical solution) to its steady-state component $u_{sp}(y,t)$ for $\alpha = 0.8$, $\beta = 0.7$, $\gamma = 0.6$, $\omega = \pi/12$, $K = 0.4$, and two values of M.

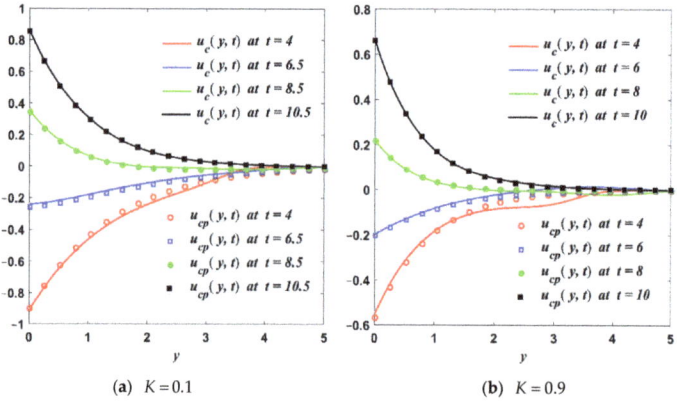

Figure 7. Convergence of starting velocity $u_c(y,t)$ (numerical solution) to its steady-state component $u_{cp}(y,t)$ for $\alpha = 0.8$, $\beta = 0.7$, $\gamma = 0.6$, $\omega = \pi/12$, $M = 0.6$, and two values of K.

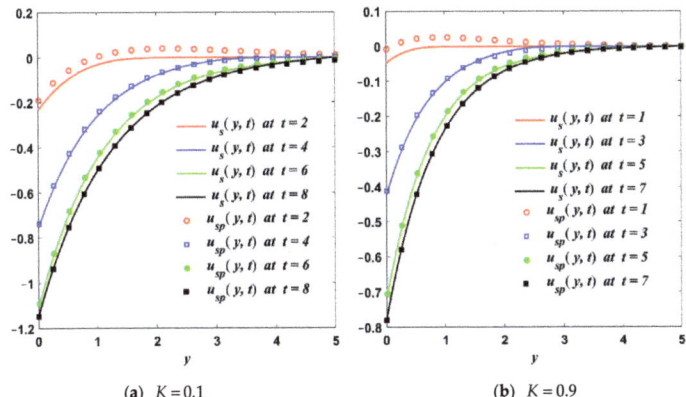

Figure 8. Convergence of starting velocity $u_s(y,t)$ (numerical solution) to its steady-state component $u_{sp}(y,t)$ for $\alpha = 0.8$, $\beta = 0.7$, $\gamma = 0.6$, $\omega = \pi/12$, $M = 0.6$, and two values of K.

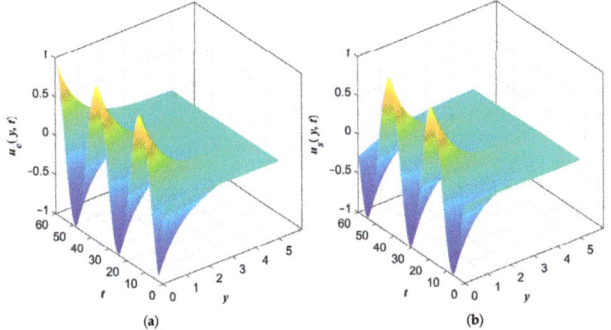

Figure 9. Spatial distributions of the dimensionless starting solutions $u_c(y,t)$ (numerical solutions) for $\alpha = 0.8$, $\beta = 0.7$, $\gamma = 0.6$, $\omega = \pi/12$, $M = 0.6$, and $K = 0.4$.

The three-dimensional distributions of the same non-dimensional starting velocities $u_c(y,t)$ and $u_s(y,t)$ are also visualized by means of the two-dimensional contour graphs (see, for example, the paper of Fullard and Wake [28]) in Figure 10a,b, respectively, for $\alpha = 0.8$, $\beta = 0.7$, $\gamma = 0.6$, $\omega = \pi/12$, $M = 0.6$, and $K = 0.4$.

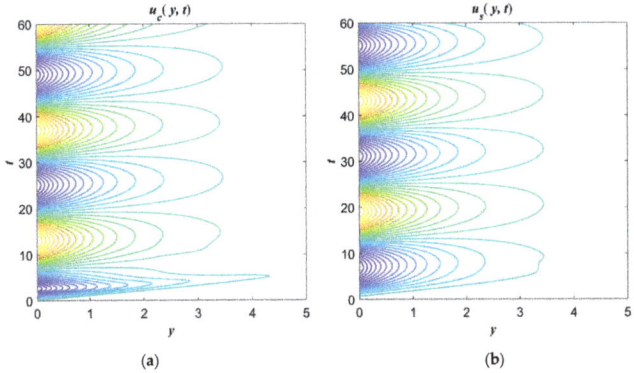

Figure 10. Contours profiles of the dimensionless starting solutions $u_c(y,t)$ and $u_s(y,t)$ (numerical solutions) for $\alpha = 0.8$, $\beta = 0.7$, $\gamma = 0.6$, $\omega = \pi/12$, $M = 0.6$, and $K = 0.4$. The trajectory paths with

the minimum value are denoted in blue colors while those with the maximum value are marked in yellow colors. The trajectory paths with intermediate values are represented by the gradient of blue and yellow colors. The oscillatory behavior of the fluid motions is represented by an alternation of two distinct sets of almost-closed trajectories along the time t with blue and yellow colors.

5. Conclusions

Some unsteady motions of incompressible fluids become steady or permanent in time if the fluid is at rest at the initial moment. Of course, this also depends on the boundary conditions. For such motions, in practice, a very important problem is to know the time required to reach the steady or permanent state. This is the time after which the fluid moves according to the steady-state solutions. In order to determine this time for a given motion, it is sufficient to know the corresponding steady-state solutions. This is the reason why we established closed-form expressions for the dimensionless steady-state solutions corresponding to two isothermal MHD unidirectional motions of an IECBF over an infinite flat plate embedded in a porous medium. The boundary conditions that were used, contrary to what is usually found in the existing literature, contained differential expressions of the non-trivial shear stress on a part of the boundary. For a check of results that were obtained here, all solutions have been presented in different forms and their equivalence was graphically proved.

It is worth pointing out the fact that all of the obtained solutions could easily be particularized to give dimensionless steady-state solutions for the incompressible Oldroyd-B, Maxwell, second-grade and Newtonian fluids that were performing similar motions. By taking $\alpha = \beta = \gamma = 0$, for instance, dimensionless steady-state solutions corresponding to motions of an incompressible Newtonian fluid induced by the flat plate that applied a shear stress $S\cos(\omega t)$ or $S\sin(\omega t)$ to the fluid were brought to light. In addition, the solutions for motions of Burgers' fluids were used to determine the required time to reach the steady state. This time, which in practice is very important for experimental researchers, was graphically determined by showing the convergence of the starting solutions to the corresponding steady-state solutions. The oscillatory behavior of the two motions, as well as the phase difference between them, was graphically underlined. The main outcomes that were here obtained are:

- The first exact solutions for MHD motions of Burgers' fluids through a porous medium were determined when differential expressions of shear stress were given on the boundary.
- The solutions corresponding to Oldroyd-B, Maxwell, and Newtonian fluids that were performing similar motions were immediately obtained as limiting cases of the present results.
- The convergence of the dimensionless starting velocities $u_c(y,t)$ and $u_s(y,t)$ to their respective steady-state components $u_{cp}(y,t)$ and $u_{sp}(y,t)$ was graphically proved. In addition, all of the obtained solutions were presented in different forms and their equivalence was proved.
- The steady state for isothermal motions of incompressible Burgers fluids' was earlier reached in the presence of a magnetic field or porous medium.

Author Contributions: Conceptualization, C.F., D.V. and A.R.; Methodology, C.F., D.V. and A.R.; Software, T.M.Q. and A.R.; Validation, C.F., D.V., A.R. and T.M.Q.; Writing—review and editing, C.F., D.V., A.R. and T.M.Q. All authors have read and agreed to the published version of the manuscript.

Funding: This research received no external funding.

Acknowledgments: The authors would like to express their gratitude to the Editor and reviewers for their careful assessments, kind appreciations, and fruitful suggestions regarding the first version of the manuscript.

Conflicts of Interest: The authors declare no conflict of interest.

Nomenclature

T	Cauchy stress tensor	S	Extra-stress tensor
A	First Rivlin–Ericksen tensor	L	Velocity gradient
u	Fluid velocity	S	Constant shear stress
p	Hydrostatic pressure	x, y, Z	Cartesian coordinates
$R(y, t)$	Darcy's resistance	k	Permeability of porous medium
M	Magnetic parameter	K	Porous parameter
B	Magnitude of magnetic field	$S_{yy}, S_{yz}, S_{zz}, S_{zx}$	Components of S
Greek Symbols			
τ	Non-trivial shear stress	ρ	Fluid density
μ	Dynamic viscosity	ν	Kinematic viscosity
v	Velocity vector	σ	Electrical conductivity
α, β, γ	Material constants	φ	Porosity
ω	Frequency of oscillations		

References

1. Akram, S.; Anjum, A.; Khan, M.; Hussain, A. On Stokes' second problem for Burgers' fluid over a plane wall. *J. Appl. Comput. Mech.* **2021**, *7*, 1514–1526.
2. Khan, M.; Malik, R.; Anjum, A. Exact solutions of MHD second Stokes flow of generalized Burgers fluid. *Appl. Math. Mech.–Engl.* **2015**, *36*, 211–224. [CrossRef]
3. Ullah, H.; Lu, D.; Siddiqui, A.M.; Haroon, T.; Maqbool, K. Hydrodynamical study of creeping Maxwell fluid flow through a porous slit with uniform reabsorption and wall slip. *Mathematics* **2020**, *8*, 1852. [CrossRef]
4. Fetecau, C.; Ellahi, R.; Sait, S.M. Mathematical analysis of Maxwell fluid flow through a porous plate channel induced by a constantly accelerating or oscillating wall. *Mathematics* **2021**, *9*, 90. [CrossRef]
5. Hayat, T.; Khan, I.; Ellahi, R.; Fetecau, C. Some MHD flows of a second grade fluid through the porous medium. *J. Porous Media* **2008**, *11*, 389–400. [CrossRef]
6. Ali, F.; Norzieha, M.; Sharidan, S.; Khan, I.; Hayat, T. New exact solutions of Stokes' second problem for an MHD second grade fluid in a porous space. *Int. J. Non-Linear Mech.* **2012**, *47*, 521–525. [CrossRef]
7. Khan, M.; Khan, S.B.; Hayat, T. Exact solution for the magnetohydrodynamic flows of an Oldroyd-B fluid through porous medium. *J. Porous Media* **2007**, *10*, 391–399. [CrossRef]
8. Alqahtami, A.M.; Khan, I. Time-dependent MHD flow of non-Newtonian generalized Burgers' fluid over a suddenly moved plate with generalized Darcy' law. *Front. Phys.* **2020**, *7*, 214. [CrossRef]
9. Hussain, M.; Qayyum, M.; Afzal, S. Modeling and analysis of MHD oscillatory flows of generalized Burgers' fluid in a porous medium using Fourier transform. *J. Math.* **2022**, 2373084. [CrossRef]
10. Fetecau, C.; Ellahi, R.; Khan, M.; Shah, N.A. Combined porous and magnetic effects on some fundamental motions of Newtonian fluids over an infinite plate. *J. Porous Media* **2018**, *21*, 589–605. [CrossRef]
11. Vijayalakshmi, E.A.; Santra, S.S.; Botmart, T.; Alotaibi, H.; Loganathan, G.B.; Kannan, M.; Visuvasam, J.; Govindan, V. Analysis of the magnetohydrodynamic flow in a porous medium. *AIMS Math.* **2022**, *7*, 15182–15194. [CrossRef]
12. Burgers, J.M. *Mechanical considerations-model system-phenomenological theories of relaxation and of viscosity. First Report on Viscosity and Plasticity*; Burgers, J.M., Ed.; Nordemann Publishing Company: New York, NY, USA, 1939.
13. Tovar, C.A.; Cerdeirina, C.A.; Romani, L.; Prieto, B.; Carballo, J. Viscoelastic behavior of Arzua-Ulloa cheese. *J. Texture Stud.* **2003**, *34*, 115–129. [CrossRef]
14. Krishnan, J.M.; Rajagopal, K.R. Review of the uses and modeling of bitumen from ancient to modern times. *Appl. Mech. Rev.* **2003**, *56*, 149–214. [CrossRef]
15. Lee, A.R.; Markwick, A.H.D. The mechanical properties of bituminous surfacing materials under constant stress. *J. Soc. Chem. Ind.* **1937**, *56*, 146–156.
16. Krishnan, J.M.; Rajagopal, K.R. Thermodynamic frame work for the constitutive modeling of asphalt concrete: Theory and applications. *J. Mater. Civil Eng.* **2004**, *16*, 155–166. [CrossRef]
17. Ravindran, P.; Krishnan, J.M.; Rajagopal, K.R. A note on the flow of a Burgers' fluid in an orthogonal rheometer. *Int. J. Eng. Sci.* **2004**, *42*, 1973–1985. [CrossRef]
18. Hayat, T.; Fetecau, C.; Asghar, S. Some simple flows of a Burgers' fluid. *Int. J. Eng. Sci.* **2006**, *44*, 1423–1431. [CrossRef]
19. Khan, M.; Anjum, A.; Fetecau, C. On exact solutions of Stokes second problem for a Burgers'fluid. I. The case $\gamma < \lambda^2/4$. *Z. Angew. Math. Phys.* **2010**, *61*, 697–720. [CrossRef]
20. Khan, M.; Anjum, A.; Fetecau, C. On exact solutions of Stokes second problem for a Burgers' fluid. II. The cases $\gamma < \lambda^2/4$ and $\gamma < \lambda^2/4$. *Z. Angew. Math. Phys.* **2011**, *62*, 749–759. [CrossRef]
21. Safdar, R.; Imran, M.; Tahir, M.; Sadiq, N.; Imran, M.A. MHD flow of Burgers' fluid under the effect of pressure gradient through a porous material pipe. *Punjab Univ. J. Math.* **2018**, *50*, 73–90.

22. Fetecau, C.; Ahammad, N.A.; Shah, N.A.; Vieru, D. Steady-state solutions for two mixed initial-boundary value problems which describe motions of Burgers fluids. *Application. Mathematics* **2022**, *10*, 3681. [CrossRef]
23. Çolak, E.; Öztop, H.F.; Ekici, Ö. MHD mixed convection in a chamfered lid-driven cavity with partial heating. *Int. J. Heat Mass Transf.* **2020**, *156*, 119901. [CrossRef]
24. Abderrahmane, A.; Younis, O.; Al-Khaleel, M.; Laidoudi, H.; Akkurt, N.; Guedri, K.; Marzouki, R. 2D MHD Mixed Convection in a Zigzag Trapezoidal Thermal Energy Storage System Using NEPCM. *Nanomaterials* **2022**, *12*, 3270. [CrossRef] [PubMed]
25. Renardy, M. Inflow boundary conditions for steady flow of viscoelastic fluids with differential constitutive laws. *Rocky Mt. J. Math.* **1988**, *18*, 445–453. [CrossRef]
26. Renardy, M. An alternative approach to inflow boundary conditions for Maxwell fluids in three space dimensions. *J. Non-Newtonian Fluid Mech.* **1990**, *36*, 419–425. [CrossRef]
27. Scofield, D.F.; Huq, P. Fluid dynamical Lorentz force law and Poynting theorem-derivation and implications. *Fluid Dyn. Res.* **2014**, *46*, 055514. [CrossRef]
28. Fullard, L.A.; Wake, G.C. An analytical series solution to the steady laminar flow of a Newtonian fluid in a partially filled pipe, including the velocity distribution and the dip phenomenon. *IMA J. Appl. Math.* **2015**, *80*, 1890–1901. [CrossRef]

Article

Phase-Space Modeling and Control of Robots in the Screw Theory Framework Using Geometric Algebra

Jesús Alfonso Medrano-Hermosillo [†], Ricardo Lozoya-Ponce [*,†], Abraham Efraím Rodriguez-Mata [†] and Rogelio Baray-Arana [†]

Instituto Tecnológico de Chihuahua (ITCH), Chihuahua 31310, Mexico
* Correspondence: ricardo.lp@chihuahua.tecnm.mx
† This author contributed equally to this work.

Abstract: The following paper talks about the dynamic modeling and control of robot manipulators using Hamilton's equations in the screw theory framework. The difference between the proposed work with diverse methods in the literature is the ease of obtaining the laws of control directly with screws and co-screws, which is considered modern robotics by diverse authors. In addition, geometric algebra (GA) is introduced as a simple and iterative tool to obtain screws and co-screws. On the other hand, such as the controllers, the Hamiltonian equations of motion (in the phase space) are developed using co-screws and screws, which is a novel approach to compute the dynamic equations for robots. Regarding the controllers, two laws of control are designed to ensure the error's convergence to zero. The controllers are computed using the traditional feedback linearization and the sliding mode control theory. The first one is easy to program and the second theory provides robustness for matched disturbances. On the other hand, to prove the stability of the closed loop system, different Lyapunov functions are computed with co-screws and screws to guarantee its convergence to zero. Finally, diverse simulations are illustrated to show a comparison of the designed controllers with the most famous approaches.

Keywords: screw theory; geometric algebra; Hamilton's equations; sliding mode control; Lyapunov theory

MSC: 70e60; 70b15

1. Introduction

In the Lagrangian approach, the two fundamental variables, written as position (θ) and velocity ($\dot{\theta}$), are mutually dependent. However, in the Hamiltonian formalism, the fundamental variables, computed as position (θ) and momentum (p), provide more abstract and profound formulations mechanics [1]. For example, Hamiltonian formalism is very important in the study of the energy changes that are possible in molecules and atoms. In addition, it is crucial if it is interested in quantizing a dynamical system or in quantum theory. Thus, this field should be taken into account [1,2].

The Lagrangian formalism (traditionally used in robots) is based on the kinetic and potential energies of the robot. This function is used to construct the body dynamics and then the control of the system [3]. Therefore, the resulting dynamic model and its controller will be represented by positions and velocities. However, in robotics, it is possible to compute controllers using Hamiltonian formalism, because the momenta, in theory, change very quickly (in rate 1/10) [4]. In addition, in practice, it is easier to measure these forces with sensors. Hence, there are motivations to implement controllers using the Hamiltonian approach. Some relevant works about Hamiltonian controllers are mentioned below.

In [5], the authors present a proportional-derivative control with gravity compensation (PD+G) using Hamilton's equations for robot manipulators with multiple degrees of

freedom, demonstrating and proving the analysis using a simulation for a planar robot. In [6], the authors propose a hybrid controller for a SCARA robot. The work is based on a port-controlled Hamiltonian system to reduce the position tracking error. In [7], using Hamilton's equations, the work describes a formalism to control electromechanical systems. On the other hand, there are other advanced works formulating Hamiltonian mechanics using a geometric framework. In [8], the work proposes Hamiltonian mechanics in terms of Geometric Calculus, where the author mentioned that their Hamiltonian formalism would be highly important for application with robots. On the other hand, other works are using GA to reduce the computational cost, as mentioned in [9]. In [10], geometric algebra is utilized to compute Hamiltonian mechanics and the Poisson bracket, where this work could be used in robotics. The authors in [11] illustrate the importance of Hamiltonians in robotics. The technique computes the dynamic equations using Newton–Euler and describes the local Hamiltonians in each joint to implement its law of control. Based on the above, the Hamiltonian equations can be used to control electromechanical systems. However, the previous works have been developed using the traditional Euler–Lagrange or Newton–Euler equations, where in some robots, the computational cost is high due to the considerable multiplications between the diverse components. In addition, the development is tedious for some robots. Hence, the new proposed method expands the Hamiltonian control approach using screw theory, where this powerful mathematical tool has been used in recent years for the analysis of spatial mechanisms and some works have expressed it as "the forgotten tool in multibody dynamics" [12,13].

Screw theory is a mathematical tool for the analysis of spatial mechanics, the main element of this theory is the screw [14]. The screw is constructed by two three-dimensional vectors, where these vectors are angular velocity and linear velocity [15,16]. Therefore, it is possible to study rigid bodies using this technique. The screw theory has gained importance because it is an elegant mathematical tool and can reduce the number of multiplications between the Lie group $SE(3)$ (as is common in traditional techniques) [17]. Moreover, some authors describe the analysis of the kinematics and dynamics of rigid bodies using screw theory as modern robotics [18]. In robotics, several works using screw theory have gained prominence in recent years. For example, diverse authors propose the screw theory approach in the process of inverse and/or forward kinematics [19–22]. Other relevant techniques are described below. In [23], the paper describes an analysis of error sources of industrial robots, where they proposed a pose error model of industrial robots with screw theory. In [24], the authors propose a mathematical model using Kane's dynamic equations in the framework of screw theory. In [25], they study the rigid-body dynamics of serial robots subject to time-invariant holonomic constraints on their end-effectors. The paper proposes a technique to compute the dynamic model of robots in the framework of screw theory. On the other hand, other interesting approaches for the dynamic models are mentioned in [26,27]. Alternatively, in [28], the method suggests a motion control approach with a focus on robotic manipulators based on screw theory and dual quaternions, where they add a stability analysis to propose a law of control for a desired trajectory. However, the drawback is that, while previous works consider kinematics and dynamics in rigid bodies, controllers are not directly proposed using screw theory. Therefore, it is an interesting motivation to compute controllers using the screw theory and the Hamiltonian approach. In addition, GA is proposed to compute the screws of the controllers and dynamics of the system; this novel approach reduces the number of operations and is intuitive for new researchers in the robotics field (due to previous knowledge of vector calculus not being required).

Taking into account the previous literature, it is possible to see that the Hamilton's equations can be used as a methodology to compute controllers for robots, where our work extends these equations for robots in the screw theory framework and iteratively. In addition, GA is proposed for computing the diverse screws and co-screws, which is an advantage for new users interested in robotics. Regarding the controllers, the equations of the robot are designed with co-screws and screws using the approach in [17]. Later, to prove convergence, functions with screws and co-screws are computed to satisfy the Lyapunov theory and thus obtain the law of control. The main advantages of our approach are:

- Due to the use of GA, vector calculus knowledge is not required [29,30].
- Using the screw theory, the Denavit–rtenberg (D–H) representation and the homogeneous matrices are avoided. It is well known that with the traditional method, it is possible to have multiple results (this is due to the D–H technique). The above could be a risk of confusion by different designers [20].
- As the proposed technique is iterative, it is possible to be implemented in serial robots with any degrees of freedom. In addition, the Euler–Lagrange and Newton–Euler methods are avoided. Therefore, robot dynamics and control can be computed easily.
- Due to the laws of control being computed directly using screw theory, they are intuitive and can be programmed easily.
- Using sliding mode control, the robustness of the system under matched perturbations is obtained [31].

The document is organized as follows: In Section 2, we illustrate the theoretical bases of geometric algebra. In Section 3, the mathematical development necessary to construct the controllers is presented. In Section 4, we show the laws of control and their stability. In Section 5, we present a numerical example with a simulation to prove the designed located controllers. Finally, in Section 6, we illustrate the conclusions.

2. Geometric Algebra

In mathematics, geometric algebra is a term applied to Clifford's theory of algebras [29,32]. The GA of an n-dimensional space is denoted by $\mathbb{G}_{p,q,r}$, where p, q and r represent the orthonormal basis vectors that square to $1, -1$ and 0, respectively. On the other hand, in additional to scalar multiplication and vector addition, GA is endowed with a noncommutative product, this product is the Clifford product (or geometric product). For example, the Clifford product for two vectors a, b are:

$$ab = a \cdot b + a \wedge b \qquad (1)$$

In Equation (1), the right side illustrates two elements: the first one is the inner product or dot product (symmetric part); the second one is the wedge product or exterior product (antisymmetric part), where the wedge product is a distributive, associative, and anticommutative operator. The elements computed by the exterior product of k independent vectors span the k-th exterior power. In this space, each element is called a $k-vector$. The diverse multi-vectors are entities computed by the sum of elements of the set of $\mathbb{G}_n$, written as:

$$A = \langle A \rangle_1 + \langle A \rangle_2 + \cdots + \langle A \rangle_n \qquad (2)$$

In addition to Equation (2), contemplate two homogeneous multi-vectors A and B of grade r and s, respectively. The Clifford product can be shown as:

$$AB = \langle AB \rangle_{r+s} + \langle AB \rangle_{r+s-2} + \cdots + \langle AB \rangle_{|r-s|} \qquad (3)$$

where $\langle AB \rangle_t$, indicate the t-grade part of the multi-vector AB. Suppose a n-dimensional space with diverse orthonormal basis vectors $\{e_i\}, i = 1, \ldots, n$, such that $e_i \cdot e_j = \delta_{i,j}$, where $\delta_{i,j} = 1 \mid i = j$ and $\delta_{i,j} = 0 \mid i \neq j$. The basis vectors for the entire GA are:

$$\{1; e_i; e_i \wedge e_j; e_i \wedge e_j \wedge e_k; \cdots ; I = e_1 \wedge \cdots \wedge e_n\} \qquad (4)$$

where I is called the pseudoscalar. Below, we include some important definitions that are useful in geometric algebra, for details consult [8,29,32,33].

Definition 1. *Let a multi-vector A of grade r. After, the reverse of A, written as $\widetilde{A}$, is defined by:*

$$\widetilde{A} = \sum_{i=0}^{r}(-1)^{\frac{i(i-1)}{2}}\langle A\rangle_i \tag{5}$$

Definition 2. *Let a multi-vector A of grade r. After, the Clifford conjugate of A, written as $\bar{A}$, is defined by:*

$$\bar{A} = \sum_{i=0}^{r}(-1)^{\frac{i(i+1)}{2}}\langle A\rangle_i \tag{6}$$

Definition 3. *Let $a \in \mathbb{G}_3$. The rotation of a, written as a', is defined by the following versor product:*

$$a' = R_\theta a \widetilde{R_\theta} = e^{-\frac{\theta}{2}L} a e^{\frac{\theta}{2}L} \tag{7}$$

where R_θ is the rotor operator, θ is the rotation angle, and L is the Lie algebra generator. The 2-vector L is the operator of rotation used in quaternions; in a different way, just consider $e_2 e_3 \to i$, $e_3 e_1 \to j$ and $e_1 e_2 \to k$.

Definition 4. *Let $I \in \mathbb{G}_n$. After, the inverse of I, written as I^{-1}, is defined by:*

$$I^{-1} = \frac{\widetilde{I}}{I\widetilde{I}} \tag{8}$$

Definition 5. *Let a multi-vector A of grade r. After, the dual of A, written as A^*, is defined by:*

$$A^* = \sum_{i=0}^{r}\langle A\rangle_i I^{-1} \tag{9}$$

Definition 6. *Consider two homogeneous multi-vectors A and B. After, the commutator product between A and B is defined by:*

$$A \underline{\times} B = \frac{1}{2}(AB - BA) \tag{10}$$

Definition 7. *Consider two homogeneous multi-vectors A and B. After, the anti-commutator product between A and B is defined by:*

$$A \overline{\times} B = \frac{1}{2}(AB + BA) \tag{11}$$

3. Mathematical Development
3.1. Screws

Suppose the following Lie group:

$$SE(3) := \left\{ \begin{pmatrix} R & x \\ 0 & 1 \end{pmatrix} : R \in SO(3), x \in \mathbb{R}^3 \right\} \tag{12}$$

The Lie algebra of $SE(3)$ is:

$$se(3) := \left\{ \begin{pmatrix} w & vs. \\ 0 & 0 \end{pmatrix} : w \in so(3), vs. \in \mathbb{R}^3 \right\} \tag{13}$$

where $se(3)$, w and v represent the Lie algebra of the Lie group $SE(3)$, the angular velocity, and the linear velocity, respectively [18]. On the other hand, the Lie algebra elements are often illustrated as follows:

$$s = \begin{pmatrix} w \\ vs. \end{pmatrix} \qquad (14)$$

where s is constructed by two three-dimensional vectors called screws.

Lie Algebra Elements

Consider a path through the identity (e) in a group (G):

$$\gamma : \mathbb{R} \to G \qquad (15)$$

where $\gamma(0) = e$. The Lie algebra element is calculated by following a path $\gamma(t)$ starting at the identity element of $SE(3)$ and evaluating $\frac{d}{dt}|_{t=0}\gamma(t)$ [14,17]. Therefore, suppose the following path:

$$\mathbf{t} = x - R_\theta \, x \, \widetilde{R_\theta} \qquad (16)$$

where $\mathbf{t}$ is the translation vector. After, computing the Lie algebra element:

$$v = -\left(\frac{d}{dt}(R_\theta) \, x \, \widetilde{R_\theta} + R_\theta \, x \, \frac{d}{dt}\left(\widetilde{R_\theta} \right) \right) \qquad (17)$$

Considering $\frac{d}{dt}(R_\theta) = -\frac{\dot\theta}{2} L R_\theta$ and $\frac{d}{dt}\left(\widetilde{R_\theta} \right) = \frac{\dot\theta}{2} L \widetilde{R_\theta}$:

$$v = -\left(\left(-\frac{\dot\theta}{2} L R_\theta \right) x \, \widetilde{R_\theta} + R_\theta \, x \, \left(\frac{\dot\theta}{2} L \widetilde{R_\theta} \right) \right) \qquad (18)$$

Now, evaluating around the entity, where $R_\theta(0) = \widetilde{R_\theta}(0) = 1$:

$$v(0) = -\frac{1}{2}(xL - Lx)\dot\theta \qquad (19)$$

Finally, using Definition 6:

$$v(0) = (L \underline{\times} x)\dot\theta \qquad (20)$$

Therefore, the linear velocity is the commutator between the Lie algebra generator of the rotor and the point x. On the other hand, the angular velocity is solved using the same methodology. The path through the identity is $\gamma(t) = R_\theta$, where $R_\theta(0) = 1$ and $R_\theta \widetilde{R_\theta} = 1$. Differentiating the last relation:

$$\frac{d}{dt}(R_\theta)\widetilde{R_\theta} + R_\theta \frac{d}{dt}\left(\widetilde{R_\theta} \right) = 0 \qquad (21)$$

Now, evaluating around the entity:

$$L\dot\theta - L\dot\theta = 0 \qquad (22)$$

Hence, the Lie algebra element consists of a $2 - vector$ L. In consequence, the angular velocity is expressed by the Lie algebra generator of the rotor. However, traditionally, the angular velocity is written as a unit vector [34–36]. Thus, this notation can be used by Definition 5. Therefore, the angular velocity is:

$$w(0) = L^*\dot\theta \qquad (23)$$

Finally, with our approach, the screw described above can be written as:

$$s(0) = \begin{pmatrix} L^* \\ L \underline{\times} x \end{pmatrix} \dot\theta \qquad (24)$$

137

It is possible to see that each screw can be computed easily with the previous equation. In each DoF, it is only necessary to record the Lie algebra element and its Cartesian position.

3.2. Velocity Kinematics

In robotics, the screws express the velocities of the diverse joints, where the velocity for a robot with n degrees of freedom (DoF) can be illustrated by:

$$V_n(0) = \sum_{j=1}^{n} s_j(0)\dot{\theta}_j \tag{25}$$

where the previous velocity is only valid in the identity or in the home position. To find the velocity in the current position of the robot, it is necessary to compute the current screw (s). To write the current screw, it is indispensable to use the following notation:

$$s_j = e^{\theta_i ad(s_i)} s_j(0)\dot{\theta} \tag{26}$$

Here, we use the adjoint representation and the exponential mapping to compute the current screw [37]. Therefore, the velocity of a serial robot with n DoF, in any position, is:

$$V_n = \sum_{j=1}^{n} s_j \dot{\theta}_j \tag{27}$$

From Equation (27), you can see that the different screws are the columns of the Jacobian matrix in robotics.

3.3. Co-Screws

Properly speaking, co-screws are linear functional on the velocities, satisfying the following:

$$\mathcal{F} : se(3) \to \mathbb{R} \text{ where } \mathcal{F}(as_1 + bs_2) = a\mathcal{F}(s_1) + b\mathcal{F}(s_2) \tag{28}$$

Here, $a, b \in \mathbb{R}$, and $\mathcal{F}(s)$ are often called the evaluation map. The co-screws are constructed using two three-dimensional vectors, but, contrary to screws, these elements are computed by the dual Lie algebra $se^*(3)$. Thus, in robotics, the momentum co-screw $(\mathcal{P})$ can be written as follows:

$$\mathcal{P} = \begin{pmatrix} j \\ p \end{pmatrix} \tag{29}$$

where j and p represent the angular and linear momentum, respectively, [17]. Furthermore, the evaluation map is illustrated as:

$$\mathcal{P}(V) = \mathcal{P}^T V \tag{30}$$

Another choice to construct the momentum co-screw is using the inertia operator, where the inertia provides an isomorphism as:

$$N : se(3) \to se^*(3) \tag{31}$$

and it is computed by:

$$N = e^{-\theta_i ad^T(s_i)} N(0) e^{-\theta_i ad(s_i)} \text{ and } N(0) = \begin{pmatrix} \mathcal{I} & mC \\ mC^T & mI_3 \end{pmatrix} \tag{32}$$

Here $\mathcal{I}$ represents the inertia tensor, m the mass of the link, C the adjoint representation of the center of mass and I_3 the identity matrix in $\mathbb{R}^3$. Hence, the momentum co-screw can be written as [17]:

$$\mathcal{P} = NV \tag{33}$$

3.4. Lagrangian Formulation of Dynamics Using Screw Theory

The kinetic energy can be described, in the context of the screw theory, as a combination of the momentum co-screw and the screw:

$$E_k(\theta, \dot{\theta}) = \sum_{j=1}^{n} \frac{1}{2}(j_j \cdot w_j + p_j \cdot v_j) = \sum_{j=1}^{n} \frac{1}{2} \mathcal{P}_j(V_j) = \sum_{j=1}^{n} \frac{1}{2} N_j V_j(V_j) \quad (34)$$

Using the evaluation map, Equation (34) changes to:

$$E_k(\theta, \dot{\theta}) = \sum_{j=1}^{n} \frac{1}{2} V_j^T N_j V_j \quad (35)$$

On the other hand, the potential energy is written by:

$$E_p(\theta) = \sum_{j=1}^{n} \tilde{g}^T \tilde{c}_j \quad (36)$$

where:

$$\tilde{g} = \begin{pmatrix} -ge_2 \\ 0 \end{pmatrix} \quad \tilde{c}_j = \begin{pmatrix} m_j c_j \\ m_j \end{pmatrix} \quad (37)$$

Here, g is the gravitational force, m_j is the mass of each link and c_j is the position of the center of mass. Then, using the Euler–Lagrange equation, it is computed the dynamic equations of the robotic system (for details see the Appendix A). Therefore:

$$\tau_i = \frac{d}{dt}\left(\frac{\partial \mathcal{L}(\theta, \dot{\theta}, t)}{\partial \dot{\theta}_i}\right) - \frac{\partial \mathcal{L}(\theta, \dot{\theta}, t)}{\partial \theta_i} \quad (38)$$

where:

$$\frac{d}{dt}\left(\frac{\partial \mathcal{L}(\theta, \dot{\theta}, t)}{\partial \dot{\theta}_i}\right) = \sum_{j=i}^{n} s_i^T N_j \dot{V}_j + V_j^T N_j [s_i, V_j] + V_j^T N_j [V_i, s_i] \quad (39)$$

$$\frac{\partial \mathcal{L}(\theta, \dot{\theta}, t)}{\partial \theta_i} = \sum_{j=i}^{n} \mathcal{G}_j^T s_i - V_j^T N_j [s_i, V_i] \quad (40)$$

Therefore, the robot dynamics are described by:

$$\tau_i = \sum_{j=i}^{n} \dot{V}_j^T N_j s_i + V_j^T N_j [s_i, V_j] - \mathcal{G}_j^T s_i \quad (41)$$

where $\mathcal{G}$ is the co-screw of the gravitational forces and $[s_i, V_j]$ is the Lie bracket [17,25].

3.5. Hamilton's Equations

Hamilton's equations can be computed using the Legendre transformation [1]:

$$\mathcal{H}(\theta, p, t) = \sum_{i=1}^{n} p_i \dot{\theta}_i - \mathcal{L}(\theta, \dot{\theta}, t) \quad (42)$$

where the partial derivation with respect to p_i provides:

$$\frac{\partial \mathcal{H}(\theta, p, t)}{\partial p_i} = \dot{\theta}_i \quad (43)$$

The previous equation is one of Hamilton's equations. To compute the second equation is necessary to use the partial derivation of Equation (42) with respect to θ_i:

$$\frac{\partial \mathcal{H}(\theta, p, t)}{\partial \theta_i} = -\frac{\partial \mathcal{L}(\theta, \dot\theta, t)}{\partial \theta_i} \tag{44}$$

Finally, the third Hamilton's equation is computed using Equation (38) with Equation (44) and $p_i = \frac{\partial \mathcal{L}(\theta,\dot\theta,t)}{\partial \dot\theta_i}$:

$$\dot p_i = \tau_i - \frac{\partial \mathcal{H}(\theta, p, t)}{\partial \theta_i} \tag{45}$$

4. Hamilton Control Using Screw Theory

With our approach using screw theory, Hamilton's equations can be written as (for details see Appendix A):

$$\frac{\partial \mathcal{H}(\theta, p, t)}{\partial p_i} = \dot\theta_i \tag{46}$$

$$\frac{\partial \mathcal{H}(\theta, p, t)}{\partial \theta_i} = \sum_{j=i}^{n} \mathcal{P}_j^T \left[s_i, N_i^{-1} \mathcal{P}_i \right] - \mathcal{G}_j^T s_i \tag{47}$$

$$\dot p_i = \tau_i + \sum_{j=i}^{n} \mathcal{G}_j^T s_i - \mathcal{P}_j^T \left[s_i, N_i^{-1} \mathcal{P}_i \right] \tag{48}$$

The previous equations could be used to compute the dynamic equations of robots in the phase space. After, to ensure that the robot reaches the desired position using the Hamiltonian approach, it is necessary to consult the following theorems.

Theorem 1. *A serial robot system reaches a desired position using the following control law:*

$$\tau_i = K_i \text{sign}(\mathcal{S}_i) + K_{\mathcal{S}_i} \mathcal{S}_i - \frac{\partial \mathcal{H}(\theta, p, t)}{\partial p_i} - \sum_{j=i}^{n} \mathcal{P}_j^T \left[N_i^{-1} \mathcal{P}_i, s_i \right] - \mathcal{G}_j^T s_i \tag{49}$$

where $\mathcal{S}_i = \tilde p_i + \tilde\theta_i$ is the sliding surface, $\tilde p_i = p_{di} - p_i$ is the error between the desired and measured momentum, $\tilde\theta_i = \theta_{di} - \theta_i$ is the error between the desired and the measured joint position, and $K_i, K_{\mathcal{S}_i} \in \mathbb{R}^+$.

Proof. In sliding mode control, the convergence of the surface needs to be satisfied [38]. Hence, the following Lyapunov function is proposed:

$$\mathcal{V}(\mathcal{S}_i) = \frac{1}{2} \mathcal{S}_i \overline\times \mathcal{S}_i \tag{50}$$

Now, use Definition 7 and differentiate the Lyapunov function in terms of time:

$$\mathcal{V}(\dot{\mathcal{S}}_i) = \mathcal{S}_i \overline\times \dot{\mathcal{S}}_i = \mathcal{S}_i \overline\times \frac{d}{dt}\left(\tilde p_i + \tilde\theta_i\right) \tag{51}$$

Using $\dot{\tilde\theta}_i = -\dot\theta_i$, Equations (46) and (48):

$$\mathcal{V}(\dot{\mathcal{S}}_i) = \mathcal{S}_i \overline\times \left(-\tau_i - \sum_{j=i}^{n} \mathcal{P}_j^T \left[N_i^{-1} \mathcal{P}_i, s_i \right] - \mathcal{G}_j^T s_i - \frac{\partial \mathcal{H}(\theta, p, t)}{\partial p_i} \right) \tag{52}$$

Applying the controller in Equation (49):

$$\mathcal{V}(\dot{\mathcal{S}}_i) = -K_i |\mathcal{S}_i| - K_{\mathcal{S}_i} \mathcal{S}_i \overline\times \mathcal{S}_i \tag{53}$$

Thus, as the derivative of the Lyapunov function is negative definite, the convergence of the sliding surface is satisfied. Then, $\mathcal{S}_i = 0 \to \tilde{\theta}_i = 0$. Hence, the serial robot with the proposed controller will reach the desired position [38]. On the other hand, the closed-loop system can be computed applying Equation (49) into Equation (48):

$$\dot{\tilde{p}}_i = \frac{\partial \mathcal{H}(\theta, p, t)}{\partial p_i} - K_i \text{sign}(\mathcal{S}_i) - K_{\mathcal{S}_i} \mathcal{S}_i \tag{54}$$

□

Theorem 2. *A serial robotic arm will track a desired smooth function by applying the following law of control:*

$$\tau_i = K_{p_i}\tilde{\theta}_i + K_{vi}\tilde{p}_i + \dot{p}_{di} - \sum_{j=i}^{n} \mathcal{P}_j^T \left[N_i^{-1} \mathcal{P}_i, s_i \right] - \mathcal{G}_j^T s_i \tag{55}$$

where $\mathcal{S}_i = \tilde{p}_i + \tilde{\theta}_i$ *is the sliding surface,* $\tilde{p}_i = p_{di} - p_i$ *is the error between the desired and measured momentum,* $\tilde{\theta}_i = \theta_{di} - \theta_i$ *is the error between the desired and the measured joint position, and* $K_{p_i}, K_{vi} \in \mathbb{R}^+$.

Proof. The proof of this theorem is easily solved. If one converts the law of control in Equation (55) into Equation (48), it provides:

$$K_{p_i}\tilde{\theta}_i + K_{vi}\tilde{p}_i + \dot{\tilde{p}}_i = 0 \tag{56}$$

The previous equation is linear and the closed-loop system is globally asymptotically stable, if and only if, $K_{p_i}, K_{vi} \in \mathbb{R}^+$[39]. This law of control is similar to the traditional PD-CTC (computed-torque control with a proportional-derivative action), but the proposed controller is in the phase space [35]. On the other hand, the closed-loop system can be represented as follows:

$$\dot{\tilde{p}}_i = -K_{p_i}\tilde{\theta}_i - K_{vi}\tilde{p}_i \tag{57}$$

□

5. Examples

5.1. Single Degree-of-Freedom Robot

Consider the manipulator in Figure 1. After, using Equation (48), the dynamic equation of the robot in the phase space is:

$$\dot{p}_1 = \tau_1 + \mathcal{G}_1^T s_1 - \mathcal{P}_1^T \left[s_1, N_1^{-1} \mathcal{P}_1 \right] = \tau_1 + \mathcal{G}_1^T s_1 \tag{58}$$

The screw can be computed as $s_1(0) = \begin{pmatrix} L* \\ L \times x \end{pmatrix} = \begin{pmatrix} e_1 e_2 * \\ e_1 e_2 \times 0 \end{pmatrix} = \begin{pmatrix} e_3 \\ 0 \end{pmatrix}$ and the wrench of gravitational forces as $\mathcal{G}_1 = \begin{pmatrix} -mgc(0) \times e_2 \\ -mg\, e_2 \end{pmatrix}$. Therefore:

$$\dot{p}_1 = \tau_1 + \begin{pmatrix} -mgc(0) \times e_2 \\ -mg\, e_2 \end{pmatrix}^T \begin{pmatrix} e_3 \\ 0 \end{pmatrix} \tag{59}$$

$$\dot{p}_1 = \tau_1 - mg\, e_1 \cdot c(0) \tag{60}$$

The previous equation is in the initial position, to transform to the actual position is necessary to change the initial position of the center of mass to the actual. Hence, as the center of mass is concentrated at the end of the link, the dynamic equations of the system are:

$$\dot{p}_1 = \tau_1 - mg\, e_1 \cdot l(cos(\theta_1)\, e_1 + sin(\theta_1)\, e_2) = \tau_1 - mgl cos(\theta_1) \quad (61)$$

The above result is the dynamic equation of the robot in the phase space, demonstrating the ease of computing the motion equation. Remember that if we use another approach, it is necessary to develop the Euler–Lagrange equation and then use the Legendre transform, the traditional process is tedious instead of the proposed technique. Now, to illustrate the behavior of the previous system with Theorem 1, it is necessary to apply Equation (49) in Equation (61). Therefore, the system can be written as:

$$\dot{p}_1 = K_1 sign(S_1) + K_{S_1} S_1 - \frac{\partial \mathcal{H}(\theta, p, t)}{\partial p_1} = K_1 sign(S_1) + K_{S_1} S_1 - \frac{p}{ml^2} \quad (62)$$

where:

$$S_1 = \tilde{\theta}_1 + \tilde{p}_1 \quad (63)$$

Based on the above, it is possible to conclude that the behavior of the system will be determined by the constant values. However, it is easy to check that the previous second-order differential equation is stable if and only if the constant values are positive and then the desired position will be reached. On the other hand, the behavior of Equation (61) with Theorem 2 can be written as:

$$\dot{p}_1 = K_{p_1} \tilde{\theta}_1 + K_{v_1} \tilde{p}_1 + \dot{p}_{d_1} \quad (64)$$

Similar as Equation (62), the previous second-order differential equation is stable if and only if the constant values are positive.

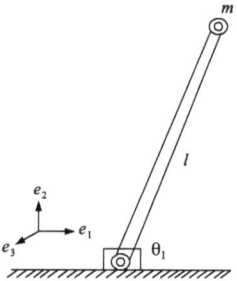

Figure 1. Single degree-of-freedom robot.

Comparison with Other Techniques

In the above section, the dynamic equations of the example were computed. It was seen the advantages of the proposed work instead of the traditional method. However, in this section, the diverse proposed laws of control are compared with other traditional techniques. To simulate the results of the example, it is necessary to implement the parameters in Table 1, where these elements are the proposed components for the robot. The laws of control to be compared are shown in Table 2, where it is possible to see the most famous controllers in the industry (PD and PID). The diverse gains for the controllers were calculated according to [40].

Table 1. Parameters of the robot.

Parameter	Value	Unit
m	0.25	kg
l	0.5	m
g	9.81	$\frac{m}{s^2}$

Table 2. Feedback controllers for the single degree-of-freedom robot.

Law of Control	Law of Control	Gains
Theorem 1	See Equation (49)	$K_1 = 1, K_{S1} = 10$
Theorem 2	See Equation (55)	$K_{p_1} = 25, K_{v1} = 25$
PD	$\tau = K_p\, e(t) + K_v \frac{de(t)}{dt}$	$K_p = 25, K_v = 25$
PID	$\tau = K_p\, e(t) + K_I \int e(t)dt + K_v \frac{de(t)}{dt}$	$K_p = 25, K_I = 15, K_v = 25$

The simulations were conducted using the Euler integration method, with a step size of 0.001 s. The initial conditions were selected as $\theta_1(0) = p_1(0) = 0$ and the desired value as $\theta_{d1} = 45°$. Thus, the behavior of the error, with diverse controllers, can be seen in Figure 2.

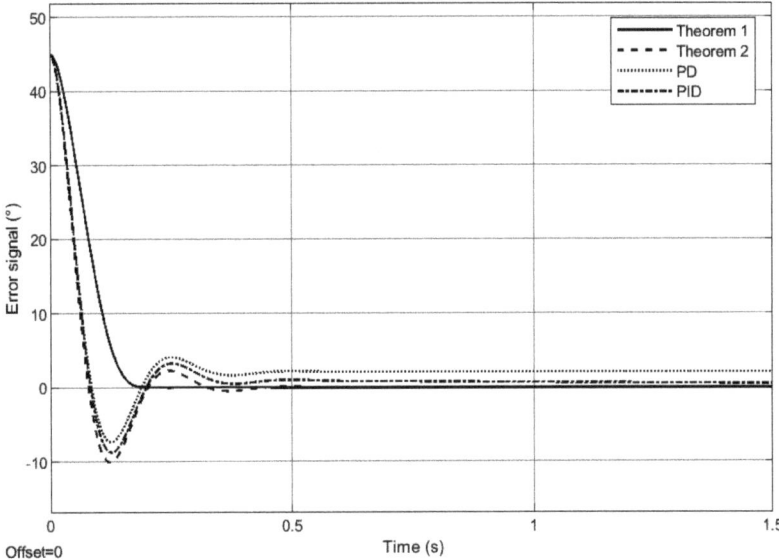

Figure 2. Error signals with diverse controllers in θ_1 for a single degree of freedom robot arm.

In Figure 2, the performances of the robot with different controllers are shown, where the two proposed laws of control reach convergence to zero. In addition, our approaches are faster than traditional techniques. Thus, the methodology proposed can be used to compute the dynamic equations of the robot in a simple manner and the controllers are efficient to be implemented physically.

5.2. Two Degrees-of-Freedom Robot

Suppose the two-link manipulator with pivot joints of Figure 3. The link lengths of the manipulator are l_1 and l_2 and the link masses are m_1 and m_2, with these masses concentrated at the end of each link.

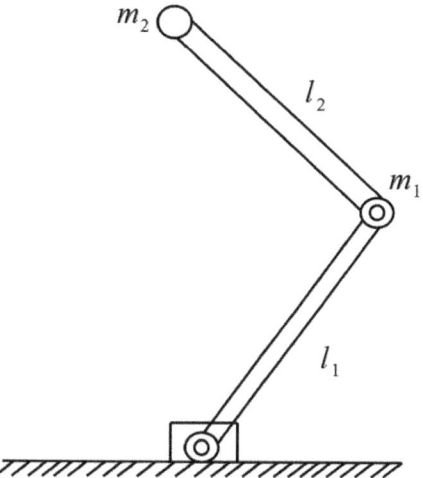

Figure 3. Two-link manipulator.

The Hamilton equations of the proposed robot are calculated using Equation (48). Therefore, these equations are written as follows:

$$\dot{p}_1 = \tau_1 + \mathcal{G}_1^T s_1 + \mathcal{G}_2^T s_1 - \mathcal{P}_1^T \left[s_1, N_1^{-1}\mathcal{P}_1\right] - \mathcal{P}_2^T \left[s_1, N_1^{-1}\mathcal{P}_1\right] \quad (65)$$

$$\dot{p}_2 = \tau_2 + \mathcal{G}_2^T s_2 - \mathcal{P}_2^T \left[s_2, N_2^{-1}\mathcal{P}_2\right] \quad (66)$$

Now, to illustrate the behavior of the previous system with the Theorem 1 is necessary to apply Equation (49). Therefore, the system can be written as:

$$\dot{p}_1 = K_1 sign(S_1) + K_{S_1} S_1 - \frac{\partial \mathcal{H}(\theta, p, t)}{\partial p_1} \quad (67)$$

$$\dot{p}_2 = K_2 sign(S_2) + K_{S_2} S_2 - \frac{\partial \mathcal{H}(\theta, p, t)}{\partial p_2} \quad (68)$$

where:

$$\begin{aligned} S_1 &= \tilde{\theta}_1 + \tilde{p}_1 \\ S_2 &= \tilde{\theta}_2 + \tilde{p}_2 \end{aligned} \quad (69)$$

On the other hand, the behavior of the robot with the Theorem 2 can be written as:

$$\dot{p}_1 = K_{p_1}\tilde{\theta}_1 + K_{v1}\tilde{p}_1 + \dot{p}_{d1} \quad (70)$$

$$\dot{p}_2 = K_{p_2}\tilde{\theta}_2 + K_{v2}\tilde{p}_2 + \dot{p}_{d2} \quad (71)$$

Comparison

In the same way as the previous example, to simulate the results of the example, it is necessary to implement the parameters in Table 3. However, in this example, the robot has two DoFs. Therefore, the system has two laws of control, where the constant values and equations are chosen as Table 4 (the gains were calculated using [40]). The simulations were performed using Euler's integration method, with a step size of 0.01 s. The initial conditions were selected as $\theta_1(0) = \theta_2(0) = 0°$, $p_1(0) = p_2(0) = 0\ kg\frac{m}{s}$ and the desired values as $\theta_{d1} = 175°, \theta_{d2} = 45°$. Hence, Figures 4 and 5 illustrate the results.

Table 3. Parameters of the robot.

Parameter	Value	Unit
m_1, m_2	0.25	kg
l_1, l_2	2	m
g	9.81	$\frac{m}{s^2}$

Table 4. Feedback controllers.

Law of Control	Law of Control	Gains
Theorem 1	See Equation (49)	$K_1 = K_2 = 1; K_{S1} = K_{S2} = 10$
Theorem 2	See Equation (55)	$K_{p_1} = K_{p_2} = 25; K_{v1} = K_{v2} = 25$
PD	$\tau = K_p\, e(t) + K_v \frac{de(t)}{dt}$	$K_p = K_v = \begin{bmatrix} 25 & 0 \\ 0 & 25 \end{bmatrix}$
PID	$\tau = K_p\, e(t) + K_I \int e(t)dt + K_v \frac{de(t)}{dt}$	$K_p = K_v = \begin{bmatrix} 25 & 0 \\ 0 & 25 \end{bmatrix}, K_I = \begin{bmatrix} 15 & 0 \\ 0 & 15 \end{bmatrix}$

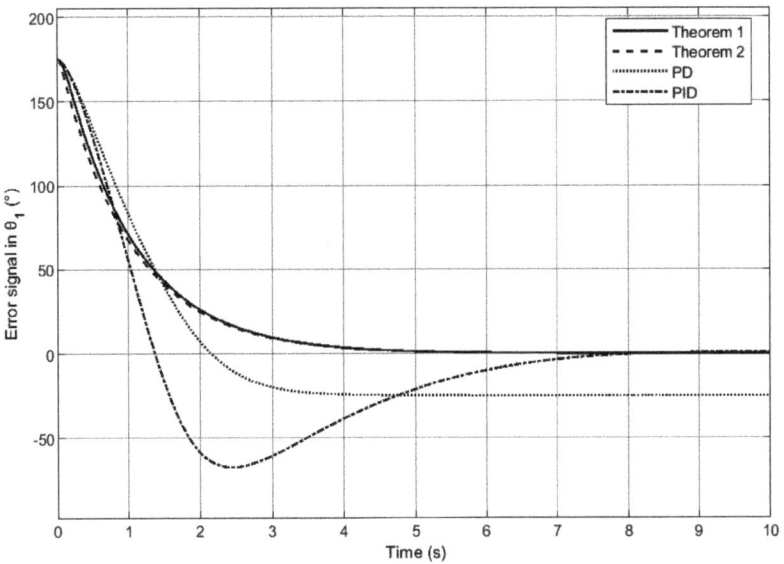

Figure 4. Error signals with diverse controllers in θ_1 for a two degrees-of-freedom robot.

In this example, the efficiency of the algorithm is proved instead of the traditional techniques. The dynamic equations are computed in an iterative form and are easy to develop, which is an advantage for new researchers in the robotic field. On the other hand, in accordance with the simulations, the controllers are faster than the typical laws of control in the industry and they are easy to program in hardware.

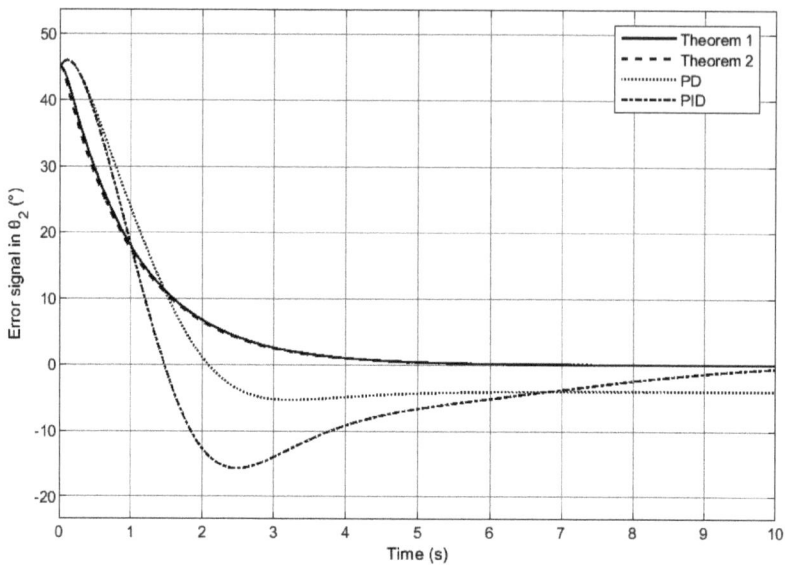

Figure 5. Error signals with diverse controllers in θ_2 for a two degrees-of-freedom robot.

6. Conclusions and Future Work

In the present article, the capacity of the proposed method for the modeling and control of robots in phase space is demonstrated. The dynamic equations, in phase space, of an articulated robot can be developed easily and iteratively (which cause it to be easy to program) using the suggested technique. In the examples, it is clearly seen that, with a few simple steps, the equations of motion of the system can be computed; otherwise, when using the traditional method, it is necessary to develop the Euler–Lagrange or Newton–Euler Equations (in addition, the kinematic model should be contemplated before) to later use the Legendre transform; this causes it to be a long and tedious process for new researchers in the field. Talking about the controllers, it is observed how easy it is to build controllers using the screw theory, such as the dynamic equations, where the control laws are obtained iteratively with a few steps. In the simulation, it was shown that the proposed controllers have a better performance than traditional techniques in phase space. Thus, it is illustrated that this technique can be used for the dynamic model and its control in the phase space.

On the other hand, this paper only contemplates the dynamic equations of the robot and its controller. However, the perturbations, unknown parameters, or other external elements are not added to the algorithm. Thus, the previous analysis and the dynamic equations of more complex robots will be taken into account for future work.

Author Contributions: Conceptualization, J.A.M.-H.; data curation, R.L.-P.; formal analysis, A.E.R.-M. and R.L.-P.; funding acquisition, R.B.-A.; investigation, J.A.M.-H.; methodology, J.A.M.-H.; project administration, J.A.M.-H. and R.L.-P.; resources, A.E.R.-M. and R.B.-A.; software, J.A.M.-H. and A.E.R.-M.; supervision, J.A.M.-H. and A.E.R.-M.; validation, R.L.-P. and R.B.-A.; visualization, A.E.R.-M. and R.B.-A.; writing—original draft, J.A.M.-H.; writing—review and editing, J.A.M.-H. and R.L.-P. All authors have read and agreed to the published version of the manuscript.

Funding: This research received no external funding.

Informed Consent Statement: Not applicable.

Data Availability Statement: Not applicable.

Conflicts of Interest: The authors declare no conflict of interest.

Appendix A

Appendix A.1. Robot Dynamics Using Screw Theory

The Lagrangian is written as:

$$\mathcal{L}(\theta, \dot{\theta}, t) = \sum_{j=1}^{n} \frac{1}{2} V_j^T N_j V_j - \tilde{g}^T \tilde{c}_j \tag{A1}$$

Using the Euler–Lagrange equation $\left(\tau_i = \frac{d}{dt}\left(\frac{\partial \mathcal{L}(\theta,\dot{\theta},t)}{\partial \dot{\theta}_i}\right) - \frac{\partial \mathcal{L}(\theta,\dot{\theta},t)}{\partial \theta_i}\right)$. Hence:

$$\frac{\partial \mathcal{L}(\theta, \dot{\theta}, t)}{\partial \dot{\theta}_i} = \frac{\partial \left(\sum_{j=1}^{n} \frac{1}{2} V_j^T N_j V_j - \tilde{g}^T \tilde{c}_j\right)}{\partial \dot{\theta}_i} \tag{A2}$$

Here, $V_j = s_j \dot{\theta}_j$:

$$\frac{\partial \mathcal{L}(\theta, \dot{\theta}, t)}{\partial \dot{\theta}_i} = \frac{\partial \left(\sum_{j=1}^{n} \frac{1}{2} \left((s_j \dot{\theta}_j)^T N_j s_j \dot{\theta}_j\right) - \tilde{g}^T \tilde{c}_j\right)}{\partial \dot{\theta}_i} \tag{A3}$$

Therefore:

$$\frac{\partial \mathcal{L}(\theta, \dot{\theta}, t)}{\partial \dot{\theta}_i} = \sum_{j=i}^{n} s_i^T N_j V_j \tag{A4}$$

Now, differentiating with respect to time:

$$\frac{d}{dt}\left(\frac{\partial \mathcal{L}(\theta, \dot{\theta}, t)}{\partial \dot{\theta}_i}\right) = \sum_{j=i}^{n} \frac{d}{dt}\left(s_i^T N_j V_j\right) \tag{A5}$$

$$\frac{d}{dt}\left(\frac{\partial \mathcal{L}(\theta, \dot{\theta}, t)}{\partial \dot{\theta}_i}\right) = \sum_{j=i}^{n} \frac{d}{dt}\left(s_i^T\right) N_j V_j + s_i^T \frac{d}{dt}(N_j) V_j + s_i^T N_j \frac{d}{dt}(V_j) \tag{A6}$$

$$\frac{d}{dt}\left(\frac{\partial \mathcal{L}(\theta, \dot{\theta}, t)}{\partial \dot{\theta}_i}\right) = \sum_{j=i}^{n} V_i^T N_j ad(V_i) s_i - s_i^T ad^T(V_j) N_j V_j - s_i^T N_j ad(V_j) V_j + s_i^T N_j \dot{V}_j \tag{A7}$$

$$\frac{d}{dt}\left(\frac{\partial \mathcal{L}(\theta, \dot{\theta}, t)}{\partial \dot{\theta}_i}\right) = \sum_{j=i}^{n} V_j^T N_j [V_i, s_i] + s_i^T \{V_j, N_j V_j\} - s_i^T N_j [V_j, V_j] + s_i^T N_j \dot{V}_j \tag{A8}$$

where $\{V_j, N_j V_j\}$ represent the co-bracket. Considering $\{V_2, N_2 V_2\}^T s_1 = V_2^T N_2 [s_1, V_2]$:

$$\frac{d}{dt}\left(\frac{\partial \mathcal{L}(\theta, \dot{\theta}, t)}{\partial \dot{\theta}_i}\right) = \sum_{j=i}^{n} \dot{V}_j^T N_j s_i + V_j^T N_j [s_i, V_j] + V_j^T N_j [V_i, s_i] \tag{A9}$$

On the other hand:

$$\frac{\partial \mathcal{L}(\theta, \dot{\theta}, t)}{\partial \theta_i} = \frac{\partial \left(\sum_{j=1}^{n} \frac{1}{2} V_j^T N_j V_j - \tilde{g}^T \tilde{c}_j\right)}{\partial \theta_i} \tag{A10}$$

$$\frac{\partial \mathcal{L}(\theta, \dot{\theta}, t)}{\partial \theta_i} = \sum_{j=1}^{n} \frac{1}{2} \frac{\partial V_j^T}{\partial \theta_i} N_j V_j + V_j^T \frac{\partial N_j}{\partial \theta_i} V_j + V_j^T N_j \frac{\partial V_j}{\partial \theta_i} - \frac{\partial \tilde{g}^T \tilde{c}_j}{\partial \theta_i} \tag{A11}$$

$$\frac{\partial \mathcal{L}(\theta, \dot{\theta}, t)}{\partial \theta_i} = \sum_{j=i}^{n} V_j^T N_j ad(s_i)(V_j - V_i) + s_i^T \mathcal{G}_j - \frac{1}{2}\left(V_j^T ad^T(s_i) N_j V_j + V_j N_j ad(s_i) V_j\right) \tag{A12}$$

$$\frac{\partial \mathcal{L}(\theta, \dot{\theta}, t)}{\partial \theta_i} = \sum_{j=i}^{n} V_j^T N_j [s_i, V_j - V_i] + s_i^T \mathcal{G}_j - \frac{1}{2}\left(V_j N_j [s_i, V_j] - V_j^T \{s_i, N_j V_j\}\right) \tag{A13}$$

$$\frac{\partial \mathcal{L}(\theta,\dot{\theta},t)}{\partial \theta_i} = \sum_{j=i}^{n} V_j^T N_j [s_i, V_j - V_i] + s_i^T \mathcal{G}_j + V_j^T N_j [V_j, s_i] \qquad (A14)$$

$$\frac{\partial \mathcal{L}(\theta,\dot{\theta},t)}{\partial \dot\theta_i} = \sum_{j=i}^{n} \mathcal{G}_j^T s_i - V_j^T N_j [s_i, V_i] \qquad (A15)$$

Finally, applying Equations (A9) and (A15) into the Euler–Lagrange equation:

$$\tau_i = \sum_{j=i}^{n} \dot{V}_j^T N_j s_i + V_j^T N_j [s_i, V_j] - \mathcal{G}_j^T s_i \qquad (A16)$$

Appendix A.2. Hamilton's Equations Using Screw Theory

Hamilton's equation in Equation (44) can be easily computed using Equation (A15). Thus, it can be illustrated by:

$$\frac{\partial \mathcal{H}(\theta,p,t)}{\partial \theta_i} = \sum_{j=i}^{n} \mathcal{P}_j^T \left[s_i, N_i^{-1} \mathcal{P}_i \right] - \mathcal{G}_j^T s_i \qquad (A17)$$

In addition to the foregoing, Hamilton's equation in Equation (45) can be computed using Equation (A17):

$$\dot{p}_i = \tau_i + \sum_{j=i}^{n} \mathcal{G}_j^T s_i - \mathcal{P}_j^T \left[s_i, N_i^{-1} \mathcal{P}_i \right] \qquad (A18)$$

References

1. Goldstein, H. *Classical Mechanics*; Addison-Wesley: Boston, MA, USA, 1980.
2. Taylor, J. *Classical Mechanics*; G—Reference, Information and Interdisciplinary Subjects Series; University Science Books: Melville, NY, USA, 2005.
3. Peymani, E.; Fossen, T.I. A Lagrangian framework to incorporate positional and velocity constraints to achieve path-following control. In Proceedings of the 2011 50th IEEE Conference on Decision and Control and European Control Conference, Orlando, FL, USA, 12–15 December 2011; pp. 3940–3945. [CrossRef]
4. Arimoto, S. *Control Theory of Non-Linear Mechanical Systems: A Passivity-Based and Circuit-Theoretic Approach*; Oxford Engineering Science Series; Clarendon Press: Oxford, UK, 1996.
5. Záda, V.; Belda, K. Mathematical modeling of industrial robots based on Hamiltonian mechanics. In Proceedings of the 2016 17th International Carpathian Control Conference (ICCC), High Tatras, Slovakia, 29 May–1 June 2016; pp. 813–818. [CrossRef]
6. Chi, J.; Yu, H.; Yu, J. Hybrid Tracking Control of 2-DOF SCARA Robot via Port-Controlled Hamiltonian and Backstepping. *IEEE Access* **2018**, *6*, 17354–17360. [CrossRef]
7. Záda, V. Exponentially stable tracking control in terms of Hamiltonian mechanics. In Proceedings of the 2017 18th International Carpathian Control Conference (ICCC),Sinaia, Romania, 28–31 May 2017; pp. 483–487. [CrossRef]
8. Hestenes, D. Hamiltonian Mechanics with Geometric Calculus. In *Proceedings of the Spinors, Twistors, Clifford Algebras and Quantum Deformations*; Oziewicz, Z., Jancewicz, B., Borowiec, A., Eds.; Springer: Dordrecht, The Netherlands, 1993; pp. 203–214.
9. Bayro-Corrochano, E.; Zamora-Esquivel, J. Differential and inverse kinematics of robot devices using conformal geometric algebra. *Robotica* **2007**, *25*, 43–61. [CrossRef]
10. Dahab, E.A.E. A formulation of Hamiltonian mechanics using geometric algebra. *Adv. Appl. Clifford Algebr.* **2000**, *10*, 217–223. [CrossRef]
11. Bayro-Corrochano, E.; Medrano-Hermosillo, J.; Osuna-González, G.; Uriostegui-Legorreta, U. Newton–Euler modeling and Hamiltonians for robot control in the geometric algebra. *Robotica* **2022**, *40*, 4031–4055. [CrossRef]
12. Huang, Z.; Li, Q.; Ding, H. *Basics of Screw Theory*; Springer: Berlin, Germany, 2013; pp. 1–16. [CrossRef]
13. Müller, A. Screw Theory–A forgotten Tool in Multibody Dynamics. *PAMM* **2017**, *17*, 809–810. [CrossRef]
14. Ball, R. *A Treatise on the Theory of Screws*; Cambridge Mathematical Library; Cambridge University Press: Cambridge, UK, 1998.
15. Toscano, G.S.; Simas, H.; Castelan, E.B.; Martins, D. A new kinetostatic model for humanoid robots using screw theory. *Robotica* **2018**, *36*, 570–587. [CrossRef]
16. Hunt, K.H. Special configurations of robot-arms via screw theory. *Robotica* **1986**, *4*, 171–179. [CrossRef]
17. Selig, J.M. *Geometric Fundamentals of Robotics (Monographs in Computer Science)*; Springer: Berlin/Heidelberg, Germany, 2004.
18. Lynch, K.; Park, F. *Modern Robotics: Mechanics, Planning, and Control*; Cambridge Univeristy Press: Cambridge, UK, 2017.

19. Yi, B.J.; Kim, W.K. Screw-Based Kinematic Modeling and Geometric Analysis of Planar Mobile Robots. In Proceedings of the 2007 International Conference on Mechatronics and Automation, Harbin, China, 5–8 August 2007; pp. 1734–1739. [CrossRef]
20. Medrano-Hermosillo, J.A.; Lozoya-Ponce, R.; Ramírez-Quintana, J.; Baray-Arana, R. Forward Kinematics Analysis of 6-DoF Articulated Robot using Screw Theory and Geometric Algebra. In Proceedings of the 2022 XXIV Robotics Mexican Congress (COMRob), Mineral de la Reforma/State of Hidalgo, Mexico, 9–11 November 2022; pp. 1–6. [CrossRef]
21. Zou, Y.; Zhang, A.; Zhang, Q.; Zhang, B.; Wu, X.; Qin, T. Design and Experimental Research of 3-RRS Parallel Ankle Rehabilitation Robot. *Micromachines* **2022**, *13*, 950. [CrossRef] [PubMed]
22. Sun, T.; Lian, B.; Yang, S.; Song, Y. Kinematic Calibration of Serial and Parallel Robots Based on Finite and Instantaneous Screw Theory. *IEEE Trans. Robot.* **2020**, *36*, 816–834. [CrossRef]
23. Liang, Z.; Meng, S.; Changkun, D. Accuracy analysis of SCARA industrial robot based on screw theory. In Proceedings of the 2011 IEEE International Conference on Computer Science and Automation Engineering, Shanghai, China, 10–12 June 2011; Volume 3, pp. 40–46. [CrossRef]
24. Huang, Y.; Liao, Q.; Wei, S.; Guo, L. Research on Dynamics of a Bicycle Robot with Front-Wheel Drive by Using Kane Equations Based on Screw Theory. In Proceedings of the 2010 International Conference on Artificial Intelligence and Computational Intelligence, Sanya, China, 23–24 October 2010; Volume 1, pp. 546–551. [CrossRef]
25. Selig, J.M.; McAree, P.R. Constrained robot dynamics I: Serial robots with end-effector constraints. *J. Robot. Syst.* **1999**, *16*, 471–486. [CrossRef]
26. Cheng, J.; Bi, S.; Yuan, C.; Cai, Y.; Yao, Y.; Zhang, L. Dynamic Modeling Method of Multibody System of 6-DOF Robot Based on Screw Theory. *Machines* **2022**, *10*, 499. [CrossRef]
27. Qin, Q.; Gao, G. Screw Dynamic Modeling and Novel Composite Error-Based Second-order Sliding Mode Dynamic Control for a Bilaterally Symmetrical Hybrid Robot. *Robotica* **2021**, *39*, 1264–1280. [CrossRef]
28. Abaunza, H.; Chandra, R.; Özgür, E.; Ramón, J.A.C.; Mezouar, Y. Kinematic screws and dual quaternion based motion controllers. *Control Eng. Pract.* **2022**, *128*, 105325. . [CrossRef]
29. Bayro-Corrochano, E. *Geometric Algebra Applications Vol. I: Computer Vision, Graphics and Neurocomputing*; Springer International Publishing: Berlin/Heidelberg, Germany, 2018.
30. Bayro-Corrochano, E. A Survey on Quaternion Algebra and Geometric Algebra Applications in Engineering and Computer Science 1995–2020. *IEEE Access* **2021**, *9*, 104326–104355. [CrossRef]
31. Ji, P.; Li, C.; Ma, F. Sliding Mode Control of Manipulator Based on Improved Reaching Law and Sliding Surface. *Mathematics* **2022**, *10*, 1935. [CrossRef]
32. Hestenes, D.; Sobczyk, G. *Clifford Algebra to Geometric Calculus: A Unified Language for Mathematics and Physics*; Fundamental Theories of Physics; Springer: Dordrecht, The Netherlands, 1987.
33. Perwass, C. *Geometric Algebra with Applications in Engineering*; Springer: Berlin, Germany, 2009; Volume 4. [CrossRef]
34. Lee, J. Velocity workspace analysis for multiple arm robot systems. *Robotica* **2001**, *19*, 581–591. [CrossRef]
35. Siciliano, B.; Sciavicco, L.; Villani, L.; Oriolo, G. *Robotics: Modelling, Planning and Control*; Advanced Textbooks in Control and Signal Processing; Springer: London, UK, 2010.
36. Craig, J. *Introduction to Robotics, Global Edition*; Pearson Education Limited: London, UK, 2021.
37. Selig, J.; Ding, X. A screw theory of static beams. In Proceedings of the 2001 IEEE/RSJ International Conference on Intelligent Robots and Systems. Expanding the Societal Role of Robotics in the the Next Millennium (Cat. No.01CH37180), Maui, HI, USA, 29 October–3 November 2001; Volume 1, pp. 312–317. [CrossRef]
38. Utkin, V.I. *Sliding Modes in Control and Optimization*; Springer Science & Business Media: Berlin/Heidelberg, Germany, 1992.
39. Khalil, H. *Nonlinear Systems*; Pearson Education; Prentice Hall: Kent, OH, USA, 2002.
40. Kelly, R. A tuning procedure for stable PID control of robot manipulators. *Robotica* **1995**, *13*, 141–148. [CrossRef]

Disclaimer/Publisher's Note: The statements, opinions and data contained in all publications are solely those of the individual author(s) and contributor(s) and not of MDPI and/or the editor(s). MDPI and/or the editor(s) disclaim responsibility for any injury to people or property resulting from any ideas, methods, instructions or products referred to in the content.

Article

Modern Dimensional Analysis-Based Heat Transfer Analysis: Normalized Heat Transfer Curves

Ioan Száva [1,*], Sorin Vlase [1,2,*], Ildikó-Renáta Száva [1], Gábor Turzó [3], Violeta Mihaela Munteanu [1], Teofil Gălățanu [1], Zsolt Asztalos [1] and Botond-Pál Gálfi [1]

[1] Department of Mechanical Engineering, Transylvania University of Brasov, B-dul Eroilor 29, 500036 Brasov, Romania
[2] Romanian Academy of Technical Sciences, B-dul Dacia 26, 030167 Bucharest, Romania
[3] Veiki Energia, Research and Design in Heat-Technology Co., Ltd., 30923 Budapest, Hungary
* Correspondence: eet@unitbv.ro (I.S.); svlase@unitbv.ro (S.V.)

Abstract: In this contribution, the authors continued their initial study on the efficiency of the analysis of experimentally obtained temperature curves, in order to determine some basic parameters that are as simple and reliable as possible, such as "m", the heat transfer coefficient. After the brief review of the previous results, on which the present article is based, the authors offered a brief argumentation of the importance of dimensional methods, especially the one called modern dimensional analysis, in these theoretical-experimental investigations regarding the propagation of the thermal field of structural elements with solid sections, and especially with tubular-rectangular sections. It could be concluded that modern experimental investigations mostly follow the behavior of models attached to the initial structures, i.e., prototypes, because there are clear advantages in this process of forecasting the behavior of the prototype based on the measurement results obtained on the attached model.

Keywords: experimentally obtained temperature distribution law; relative temperature curves; m parameter's variation laws; 2D steel structural elements; testing bench; reduced-scale models

MSC: 74S05

1. Introduction

It is well known that the structural elements of civil and industrial buildings must be protected against the unwanted action of fires. Thus, with the occurrence of fires, goods and human beings must be provided with sufficiently large time intervals for evacuation, which directly depends on the fire resistance of the structural elements. This, in turn, is decisively influenced by the way in which they were protected (for example with layers of thermoprotective paints, also called intumescent, etc.), and by the way in which the thermal flow introduced by the fire propagates along the respective structural element.

The previous results of the authors' investigations [1–3], as well as those presented below, facilitate the mastery of this heat flow propagation process along the structural elements.

In a previous paper [3], the authors performed, on an original electric stand [1], a series of experimental investigations of great finesse. The elements subjected to the tests were bars made of steel S275JO, EN 10025:2005, having a full circular section, with a diameter of $d = 0.02$ m and made in different lengths $l = (0.050; 0.100; 0.150; 0.200)$ m.

The bars were electrically heated at one end to achieve nominal temperatures of $t_{O,n} = (100; 400)$ °C. The stand also allowed the positioning of the bars with an angle $\alpha_g = 0°$ or $90°$ from the vertical direction during the experiments.

The bars were equipped with a sufficient number of thermo-couples (FPA15P-type, Ahlborn GmbH, Holzkirchen, Germany), fixed in specially made bores of 0.002 m diameter, which ensured the monitoring of the propagation of the thermal field along them.

In fact, this was the focus of the authors' thorough analysis, i.e., the correlation between $\alpha_n(z)$, m, $\lambda(z)$, as well as its accurate validation. Finally, the authors obtained for each analyzed case one single particular value of "m" along the entire bar.

It should also be emphasized that, based on the curves obtained experimentally under strictly metrological conditions, in [1–3], the magnitudes of the constants (c_1, c_2, m) could be determined, which are essential elements in the analytical description of the propagation law (1).

Also, the authors proposed an easier, and at the same time, more efficient approach to establishing these constants (c_1, c_2, m) using the curve-fitting method, where approximation curves of at most order III of the real temperature distribution ensured the same precision as the classical approach based on the laborious (and quite difficult) analysis of the theoretical exponential law. It was also possible to highlight the fact that, with the increase in temperature, this precision of the curve-fitting method increases, even surpassing the classic, exponential one.

Another research direction of the work [3] consisted in the desire of the authors to verify if the hypothesis also remains valid in the case of tubular section bars. In this case, they were made of rectangular tubular bars of steel S355J2, EN 10025:2005. More precisely, they were square pipes, of different lengths, provided with sets of FPA15P-type thermo-couples and subjected to thermal regimes similar to those previously mentioned. According to the authors' knowledge, such investigations, with the aim of verifying the condition of bars having a tubular section, have not been carried out before; at least, we had no knowledge from the specialized literature.

In this way, the authors offered the comparative, effectively measured, thermal distribution laws, with respect to the massive circular (0.016 m in diameter by 0.240 m in length, and 0.020 m in diameter by 0.200 m length), as well as square tubular (0.040 × 0.040 × 0.005 m by 0.400 m in length) cross-sectional straight bars, having $\alpha_g = 0°$ and $\alpha_g = 90°$, respectively, in angular positioning with respect to the vertical direction, heated at their lower end to nominal temperatures of $t_{O,n} = 100\,°C$ and $t_{O,n} = 400\,°C$.

These comparative diagrams point out for the engineers involved in fire-protection analysis the importance of the length in the thermal calculi and, based on this, the fire-protecting coating thickness value, too.

The authors proposed a generalized curve, by plotting the relative t_ψ [%] thermal curve, i.e., monitoring the remaining percentage of the nominal $t_{O,n}$ temperature (considered to represent 100%). These relative t_ψ [%] thermal curves were plotted for the same initial conditions, and based on the obtained results, several useful conclusions were drawn. One can mention that, based on these relative t_ψ [%] curves, precisely the same temperature fields were restored in every analyzed case.

The authors also found the very important fact, that in the case of the tubular cross-sectional bars, the $m = const.$ hypothesis for the whole length of the bar is not valid. The hypothesis is valid (can be applied) only for the smallest, constitutive intervals of these tubular bars. In conclusion, the experimentally obtained greater gradients of the thermal distribution law for these tubular cross-sectional bars can be described or drawn up using these "m"-values corresponding to the smallest constitutive intervals.

One other proposed parameter was the so-called compared $\Delta t_\psi = 100 - t_\psi$ [%] temperature loss (the percentages of the lost temperatures), which offers a clearer image on the temperature-loss phenomenon.

Based on their graphical images, the increase in the lost Δt_ψ [%] for the same reference length of ℓ [m] was stated, together with the increase in the bar's total length; this phenomenon was much greater for the horizontally placed bars ($\alpha_g = 90°$), than the vertically positioned one ($\alpha_g = 0°$).

This new parameter assures the most accurate evaluation of the bar's behaviour, having different effective lengths, with respect to the temperature: i.e., its reduction, as well as its propagation along the bars.

Based on the aforementioned strategy, the authors performed thorough analytical calculi of the "m" parameter along these square tubular cross-sectional straight bars for several nominal temperatures: $t_{O,n} = 50$; 100; 200; 300; 400; and $500\,°C$.

Using these results, the authors established that an adequate description of the obtained "m"-curves can be obtained by dividing the whole length of the bar into a minimum of three intervals, i.e.: $\ell_I \in [(0\ldots 0.05) \cdot \ell]$; $\ell_{II} \in [(0.05\ldots 0.10) \cdot \ell]$, and $\ell_{III} \in [(0.10\ldots 1.00) \cdot \ell]$. These intervals give different gradients and cannot be analyzed together.

The authors, similarly with the t_ψ [%] curve, proposed a new parameter, i.e., *the relative m_ψ [%] curve*, which monitors the remaining percentage of the initial value (for $z = 0$) of "m" along the bars' length, considered to represent 100%.

In the same manner, the authors offered a polynomial approach, using a curve-fitting method, both for the global m_ψ [%] curves, as well as for their segmental parts, corresponding to those three separate (detached) intervals.

From this previous contribution [3], as conclusions on m_ψ [%], one can mention the following:

- The greatest gradient for the m_ψ [%] is on the first interval ℓ_I, where the obtained gradient is 100 %, that will decrease to 62.3 %; on the second interval ℓ_{II}, there will be a decrease from 62.3 % to 57 %, as well as on the third interval ℓ_{III}, which will decrease from 57 % to 36.8 %;
- Taking into consideration that ℓ_{III} represents, in fact, 90 % of the whole bar length ℓ, the corresponding gradient correlated with its real length is very small;
- For other $t_{O,n}$ nominal temperatures, the mentioned calculi of m_ψ [%] can be performed in a similar manner, which can assure, without difficult analytical calculi, that predictable values for the "m" parameter are obtained;
- In the authors' opinion, these new practical approaches to the temperature distribution law can be applied successfully in the thermal analysis of 2D and 3D structures, in the first stage on reduced scale models, involving the results of the modern dimensional analysis (MDA) (analyzed briefly in the following), as well as in real-scale structures;
- The performed analytical calculi offer a useful tool for fire safety engineers to predict both the heat transfer along the steel structural elements and their load bearing capacity.

The study of structural elements subjected to fire took a new direction with the implementation of dimensional methods in these analyses [4–41].

Starting from the geometric analogy (GA), continuing with the theory of similitude (TS), along with classical dimensional analysis (CDA), the researchers, specialized in problems of preventing the effects of fire, replaced the experimental study carried out directly on the real elements (called prototypes) [39,40,42–65], with that performed on models (usually reduced to scale) [1,2,66–69].

The experimental results obtained on these models could later be transferred to real structural elements based on the relationships provided by the above-mentioned dimensional methods. Thus, the specialists were able to predict the behavior of the prototype based on the measurements made on the model, which obviously represented experiments carried out in much more advantageous conditions in terms of price, cost, working time, specialized personnel, and the equipment involved.

On the advantages and limits of these methods, the authors of this paper made a detailed synthesis of the works [70–74], of which the most significant can be mentioned:

- GA works only with a limited number of laws, based on the identification of points, angles and homologous surfaces of the prototype, in accordance with the related model;
- TS provides an extension of these laws, but can also only be applied to a number of particular cases;
- CDA, although theoretically it would be the ideal method of approach, presents several other shortcomings, such as:

- o The deduction of the model law (ML) is based on the processing of a limited number of differential equations related to the phenomenon;
- o This processing is unfortunately quite arbitrary, non-unitary, and its efficiency depends to a large extent on the user's experience, usually consisting of grouping some terms of the equations involved, or identifying adimensional groups from the same constitutive equations, in order to obtain dimensionless expressions;
- o It requires deep knowledge of higher mathematics, but also of the field of the respective phenomenon;
- o Only in particular cases can it provide the complete set of dimensionless variables, based on which the ML is later defined;
- o The method, not being unitary in approach, is not easily applicable to ordinary researchers, remaining accessible only to a narrow segment of established specialists.

As is well known, both TS and CDA operate with a set of dimensionless variables π_j, $j = 1, 2, \ldots, n$, from which the ML will ultimately result.

Also, the number of dimensionless expressions, which can thus be obtained from a limited number of differential equations related to the phenomenon, will also be limited. This is why CDA cannot provide, except in very particular cases, the full set of the ML through these dimensionless variables.

In order to eliminate these shortcomings, as well as to make dimensional analysis an accessible and effective method for ordinary researchers, Th. Szirtes developed a new approach, which gave rise to the so-called modern dimensional analysis (MDA) [75,76].

Among the indisputable advantages of MDA, the following can be highlighted:

- The method is unitary, simple and accessible to any researcher;
- It does not require thorough knowledge in the field, but only that all the parameters are taken into account, which can in a certain way have an influence on the respective phenomenon;
- The parameters, which have no influence on the phenomenon, are automatically removed from the protocol;
- The complete set of dimensionless variables is always provided, and consequently also the complete ML;
- The developed method is very flexible, allowing, based on the ML deduced for the general case, customizations to be made in order to simplify and optimize the model, as well as the related experiments;
- MDA allows choosing at will the set of variables that define the protocol of experiments on the model, but also the model itself.

MDA was also successfully applied by the authors of this paper, among others, in the analysis of the stressed-strained states of the reticular structures in constructions [77], but also in the detailed study of the thermal field propagation phenomenon [70–73,78], for those tracking the simulated effect of fires on original stands designed and made by them [2,47,72,78,79].

One might ask, why did the authors use the MDA in these investigations?

The reason was that only the further application of such research to firm and reliable laws such as those provided by MDA can ensure a firm correlation between the behavior of a prototype and its associated model.

Thus, if much simpler, safe and repeatable investigations are desired to be carried out on the associated model and to form a solid basis in predicting the behavior of the prototype, then this safe method, i.e., MDA, must be involved.

Consequently, the authors, in their previous works [70,72,78,79], proposed and performed the validation of the model law deduced not only for the case of the solid circular section bar, but also for the one with tubular-rectangular section, with the implicit and obvious particular case of the tubular-square section.

Based on the ML deduced for the rectangular-tubular section, the authors performed a thorough validation study regarding the thermal regimes of a prototype, which was the column segment of a real pillar in an industrial hall, using models reduced to scales of 1:2; 1:4 and 1:10.

In the following, the major aspects of these experimental investigations, which were the basis for establishing the thermal propagation curves along the tested structural elements, are briefly presented.

As will be seen below, the analysis of these thermal curves through a new lens allowed a much more efficient approach, which is in fact the main purpose of this work.

2. Materials and Methods

In order to carry out these theoretical-experimental investigations, for the first time the authors designed an original electrical stand [2,71,72,79]. This stand, with a high-performance electronic control, ensures precise monitoring and control of the heating of structural elements, made either on a natural scale or on a reduced scale.

The ML, deduced for the case of structural elements with tubular-rectangular sections [73], was validated based on a significant number of experimental measurements, both on the analyzed prototype and on the associated models, made at 1:2, 1:4, and 1:10 scales [2,71,72,80].

According to the works [2,71,72,78], the scheme of these structural elements, as well as the location of the temperature sensors, which were PT100-420 thermoresistors with 150 mm long terminals, having a working temperature between -70 and $+500\ °C$, are shown in Figures 1–3, and Table 1. The thermoresistors were fixed to the structural elements with the help of M3 screws in precisely positioned threaded holes.

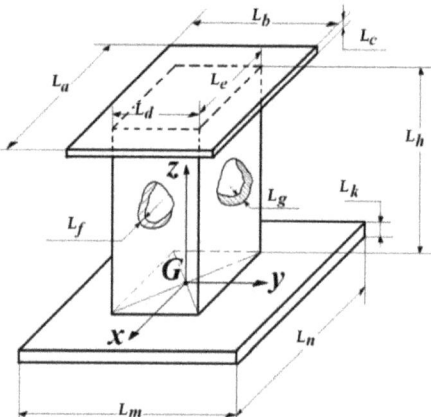

Figure 1. Dimensions of the column segment [2,71,72,78].

The geometric similarity is respected in all of them, accepting the same scales of all dimensions of 1:1, 1:2, and 1:4.

The upper closing plate, with the dimensions $(L_a \times L_b)$, substitutes the rest of the column, and the lower one, with the dimensions $(L_m \times L_n)$, assures a perfect and unitary placement of all the elements tested on the test stand.

Table 1. Principal dimensions of the column segment presented in Figure 1 [2,71,72,78].

	Prototype, at Scale 1:1	Model I, at Scale 1:2	Model II, at Scale 1:4
		Dimensions, in m	
L_a	0.370	0.185	0.0925
L_b	0.370	0.185	0.0925
L_c	0.006	0.003	0.0015
L_d	0.350	0.175	0.0875
L_e	0.350	0.175	0.0875
L_f	0.016	0.008	0.004
L_g	0.016	0.008	0.004
L_h	0.400	0.200	0.100
L_k	0.010	0.005	0.0025
L_m	0.450	0.450	0.450
L_n	0.450	0.450	0.450

The structural element (1) from Figure 2, is placed by translation on the upper area of the truncated pyramid-shaped dome (2); this dome rests on the rigid frame (3) and on the supporting legs (4).

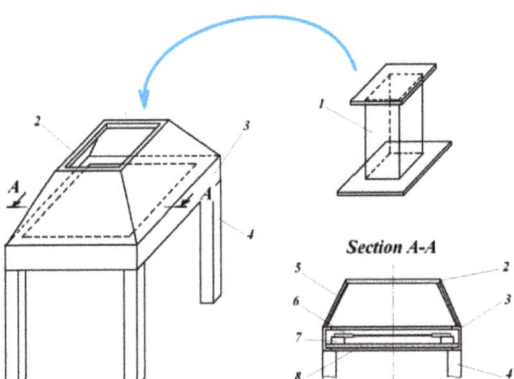

Figure 2. The assembled stand [2,71,72,78].

During experimental investigations, the free surface of the laying board with dimensions ($L_m \times L_n$), shown in Figure 1, is covered with a thermal insulation blanket. As an illustration of the degree of thermal insulation, it can be mentioned that at the nominal heating temperature of $t_{o,nom} = 600\ °C$ for the tested structural elements, around the support frame (3) and the truncated pyramid (2), the temperature did not exceed (45...50) $°C$. In section A–A the heating elements (6) are shown, consisting of twelve silite rods, each four connected in series for the three phases of the industrial power supply at 380 V. These silite rods, placed on chamotte bricks (7), rest on a thermal insulation layer (8) of ceramic fiber 0.0254 m thick. A similar insulation (5), provided for the lateral sidewalls of the truncated pyramid (2), assures an efficient thermal insulation of the test bench (see Table 2).

Table 2. Principal coordinates of the temperature measuring points [2,71,72,78].

Prototype, at Scale 1:1	Model I, at Scale 1:2	Model II, at Scale 1:4	Model III, at Scale 1:10
	Coordinates $z(j)$ in m		
0.020	0.020	0.020	0.015
0.110	0.060	0.055	0.030
0.200	0.105	0.090	0.045
0.290	0.150		0.060
0.380	0.190		0.100
			0.200
			0.400
			0.460
			0.495

A thermo-couple was always placed at the coordinate level $z(0)$, which also ensured the implicit control of the nominal temperature $t_{O,nom}$ $[°C]$.

The important fact should be mentioned that, at the time of carrying out the tests on the first three elements, i.e., on the prototype and the models made at the scales of 1:2 and 1:4, the results of the theoretical-experimental investigations carried out on the first tubular structural elements, synthesized, were not yet known in our previous article [3].

As mentioned in Section 1, these investigations, reproduced in the work [3], demonstrated the fact that, in the case of tubular sections, the hypothesis $m = const.$ is valid only on constitutive areas of the length of the bar, which is why the respective bar must be divided into at least three subintervals, for which, subsequently, this assumption will be respected individually.

The tests on the last model reduced to the scale of 1:10 were carried out after the completion of the theoretical-experimental investigations presented in the authors' previous work [3], which is why it was already possible here to take into account this important conclusion regarding the validity of the hypothesis $m = const.$ on subintervals.

Figure 3 shows the mounting on the aforementioned testing bench of the thin tubular-rectangular tested specimen (frame column), manufactured at 1:10 scale [71,72,78,79].

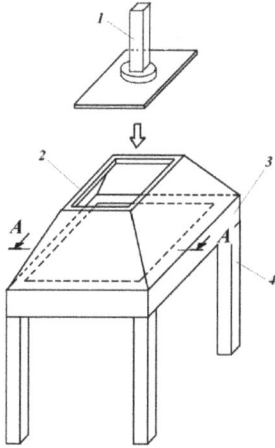

Figure 3. Heating stand, together with the tested 1:10 scale pillar model.

The dimensions of this reduced scale model are 0.030 × 0.030 × 0.0015 m, and its height is 0.5 m. This model presents on its lower end a steel cylindrical part with diameter $d = 0.105$ m and height $h = 0.015$ m, by means of an intermediate 0.080 × 0.080 × 0.003 m steel plate (Figure 4).

The significant thermal inertia of this cylindrical part assures the corresponding heat transfer from the testing bench to the reduced-scale tubular model.

A 0.025 m thick heat-insulation open cylinder, with 0.45 m diameter and 0.65 m height, disposed around the tested element, eliminates the undesirable influence of an accidental current of air from the lab. The radius of this heat-insulation cylinder is comparable, at the reduced scale of 1:10, with the half-distance between the columns.

Figure 4. The lower end of the thin-walled tested element (column): 1—cylinder; 2—intermediate plate; 3—tested element (column).

The thermal protection of the elements subjected to the tests was carried out with the help of solvent-based intumescent paint (Interchar 404, from International Marine and Protective Coatings), applied with a thickness of 1.2 mm.

The thermal regimes imposed on the first three elements, i.e., of the prototype and the models reduced to the 1:2 and 1:4 scale, were at the nominal temperatures $t_{0,nom} = (100, 200, 300, 400, 450, 500)$ °C, and the nominal temperatures for the element made at the 1:10 scale, were $t_{0,nom} = (100, 200, 300, 400, 450, 500, 600)$ °C.

The protocol of these heatings, i.e., their evolution over time, for both thermally unprotected and thermally protected elements, according to the paper [71], is shown in Figures 5–12. Here, for the thermoresistors located at different heights, their indications were specified, i.e., the temperatures stabilized at their level, corresponding to the imposed nominal temperatures $t_{0,nom}$ [°C].

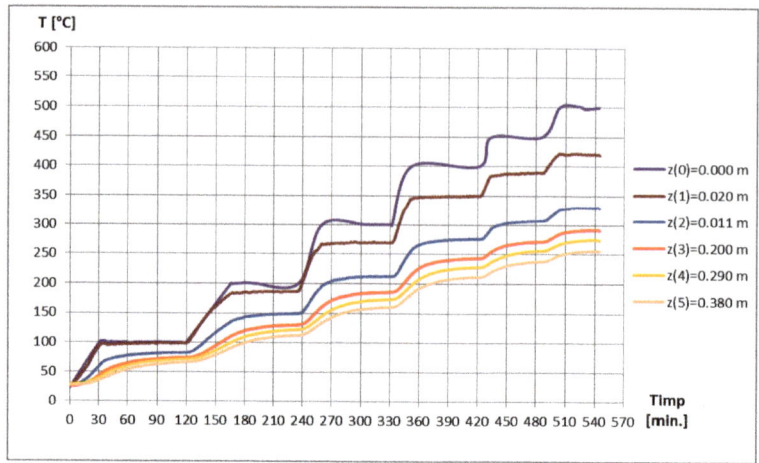

Figure 5. Time evolution of the temperature in the unpainted prototype.

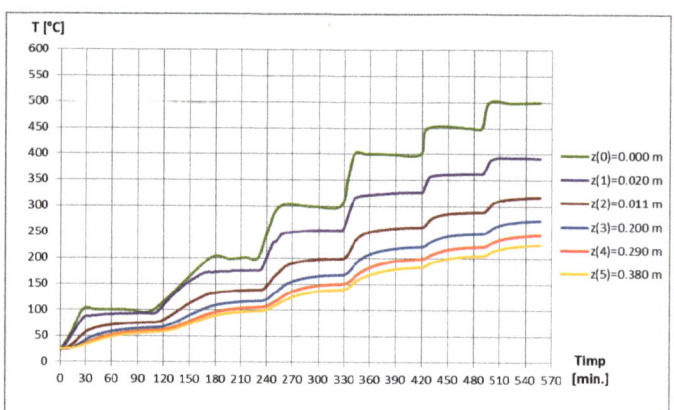

Figure 6. Time evolution of the temperature in the painted prototype.

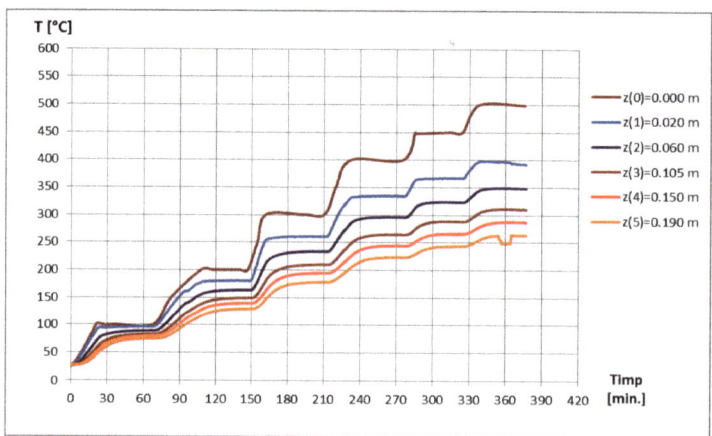

Figure 7. Time evolution of the temperature of the unpainted 1:2 scale model.

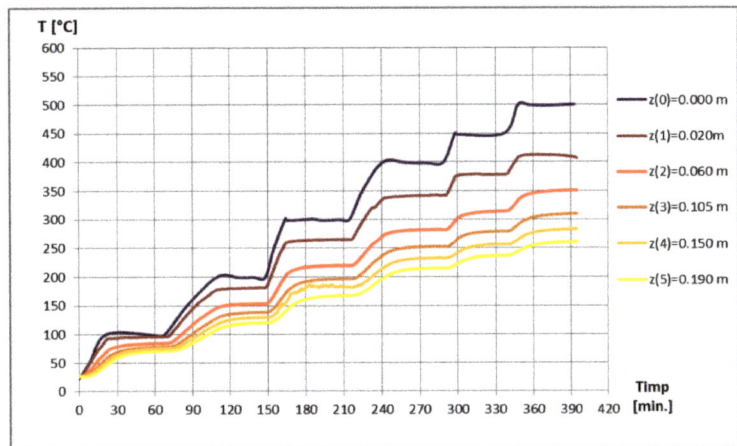

Figure 8. Time evolution of the temperature of the painted 1:2 scale model.

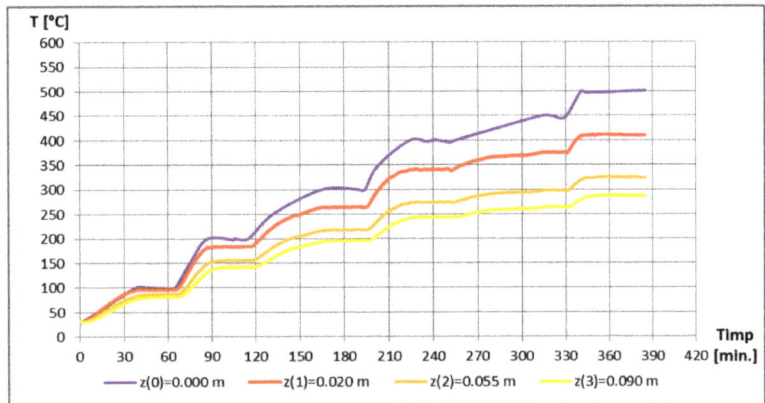

Figure 9. Time evolution of the temperature of the unpainted 1:4 scale model.

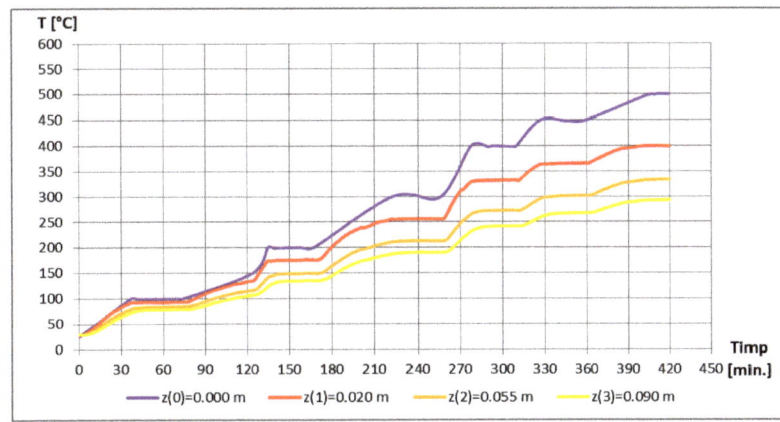

Figure 10. Time evolution of the temperature of the painted 1:4 scale model.

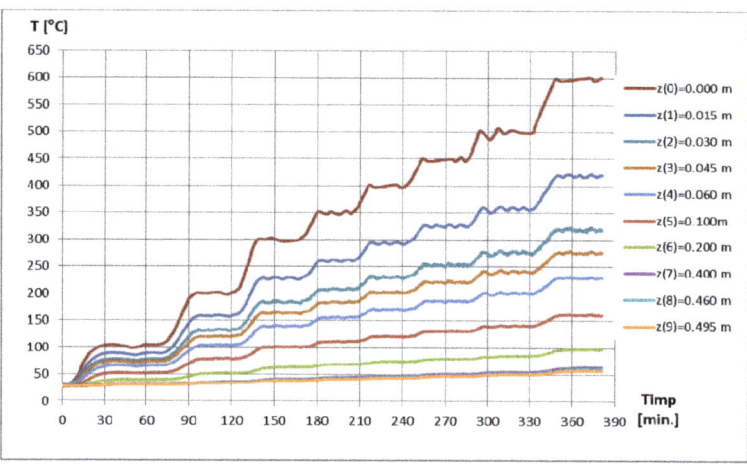

Figure 11. Time evolution of the temperature of the unpainted 1:10 scale model.

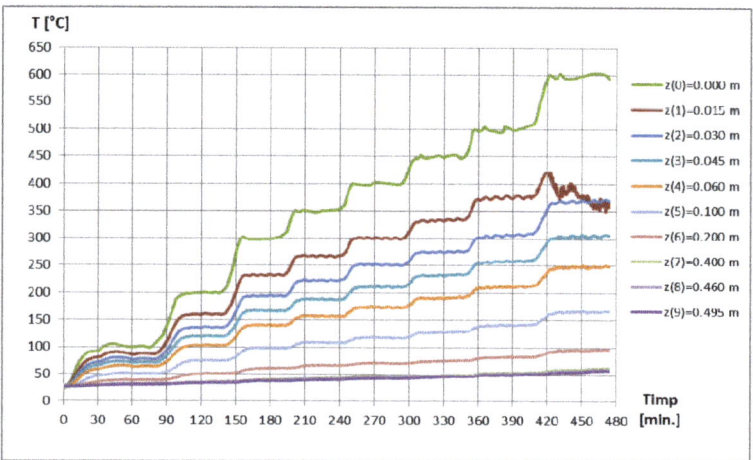

Figure 12. Time evolution of the temperature of the painted 1:10 scale model.

It can be seen that, at the end of each heating step, there is a temperature stabilization level; the monitoring of the temperatures along the elements subjected to the tests was carried out only after the completion of the respective stabilization cycle.

3. Results

In Figures 13–18, the results of monitoring the thermal field with the help of thermoresistors mounted on these structural elements are provided (see [71]).

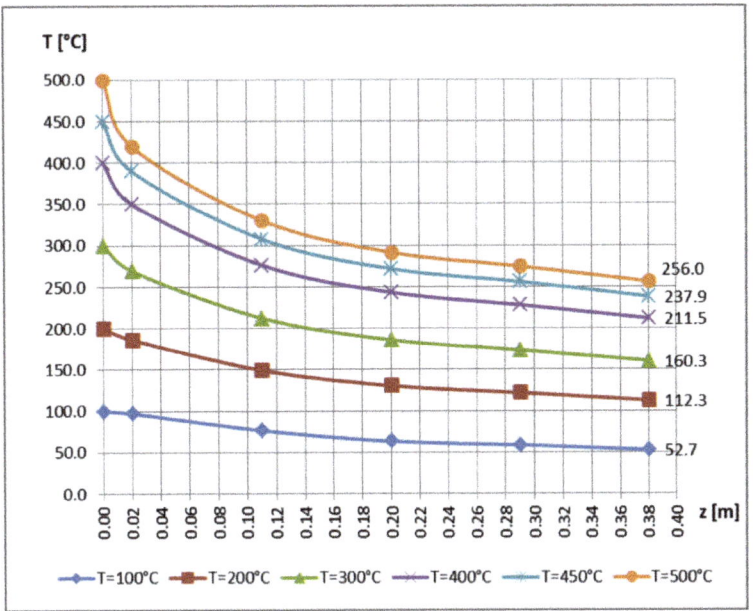

Figure 13. Temperature variation along the unpainted prototype.

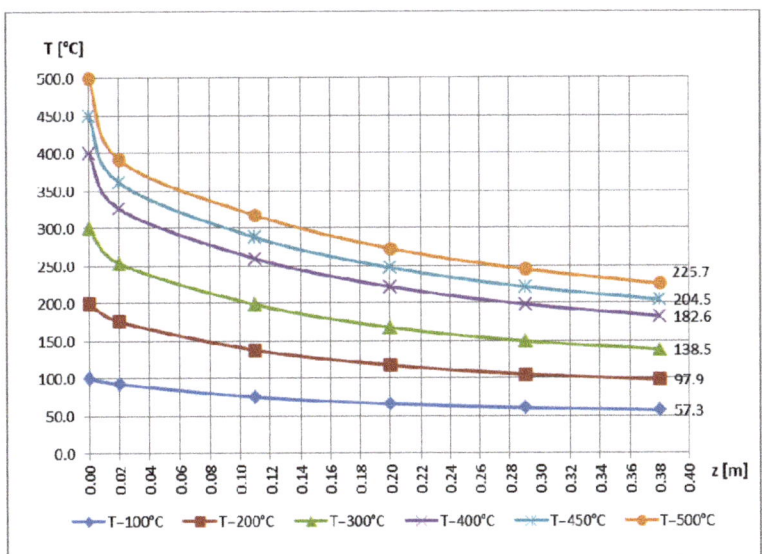

Figure 14. Temperature variation along the painted prototype.

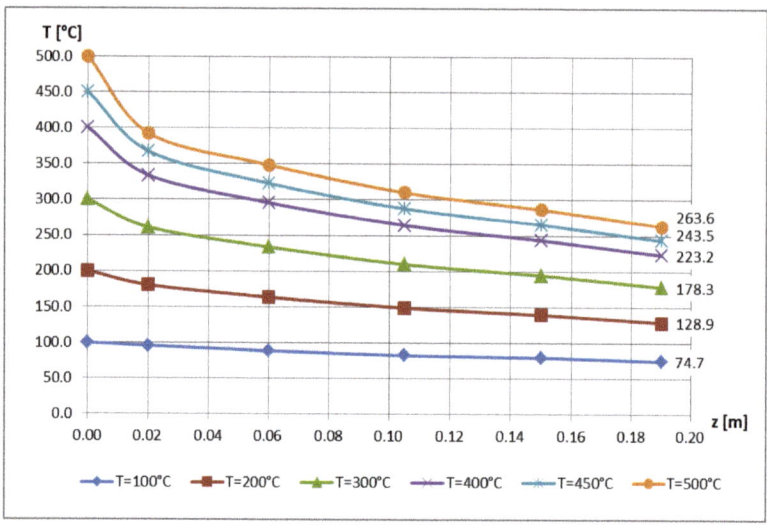

Figure 15. Temperature variation along the unpainted 1:2 scale model.

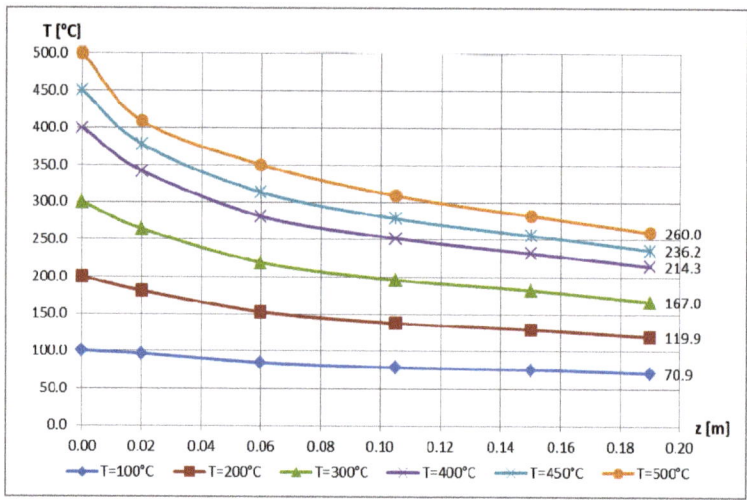

Figure 16. Temperature variation along the painted 1:2 scale model.

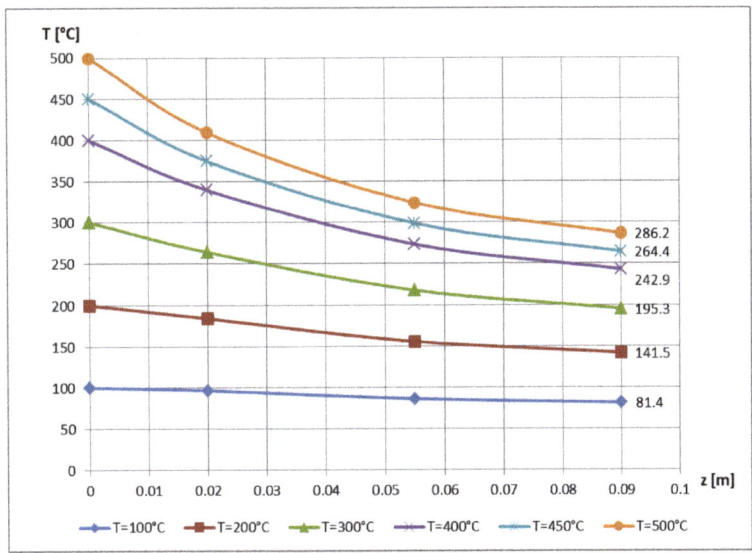

Figure 17. Temperature variation along the unpainted 1:4 scale model.

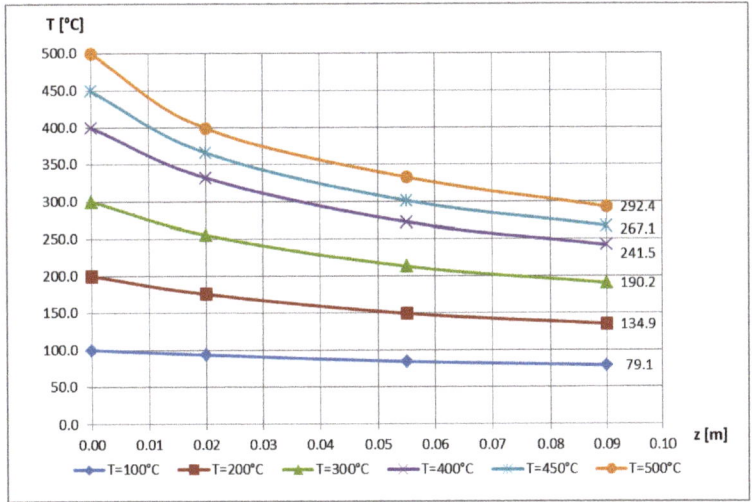

Figure 18. Temperature variation along the painted 1:4 scale model.

In Figures 19 and 20 it can be seen that the thermoresistor, located at a distance of $z = 0.015$ m, presented a deficiency in operation, which is why its last recording could not be taken into consideration during the subsequent processing of the data.

It should also be mentioned that the last structural element, made at a scale of 1:10, actually represented the model attached to the entire pillar.

Starting from this fact, and taking into account the results obtained and presented in the work [2], we proceeded to divide the curves related to this model reduced to a scale of 1:10 into three intervals, according to those in Section 1, i.e., $\ell_I \in [(0\ldots0.05) \cdot \ell] = [0\ldots0.03]$ m; $\ell_{II} \in [(0.05\ldots0.10) \cdot \ell] = [0.03\ldots0.06]$ m, and $\ell_{III} \in [(0.10\ldots1.00) \cdot \ell] = [0.06\ldots0.50]$ m.

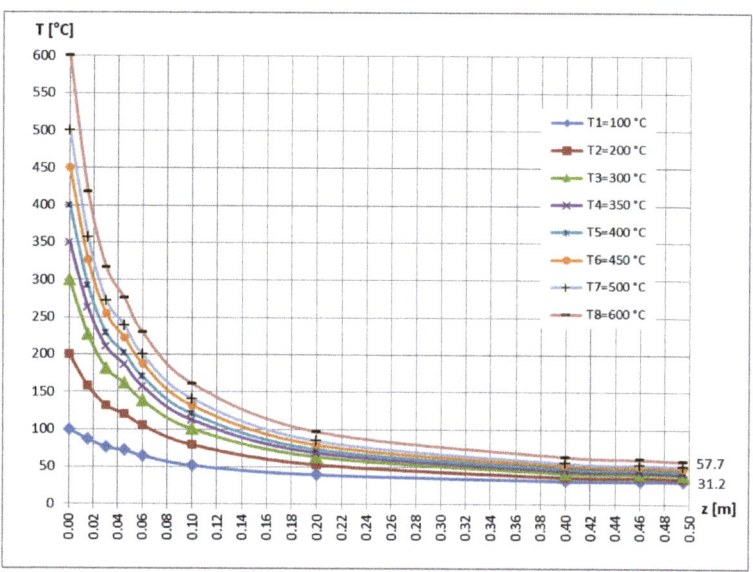

Figure 19. Temperature variation along the unpainted pole, made at 1:10 scale.

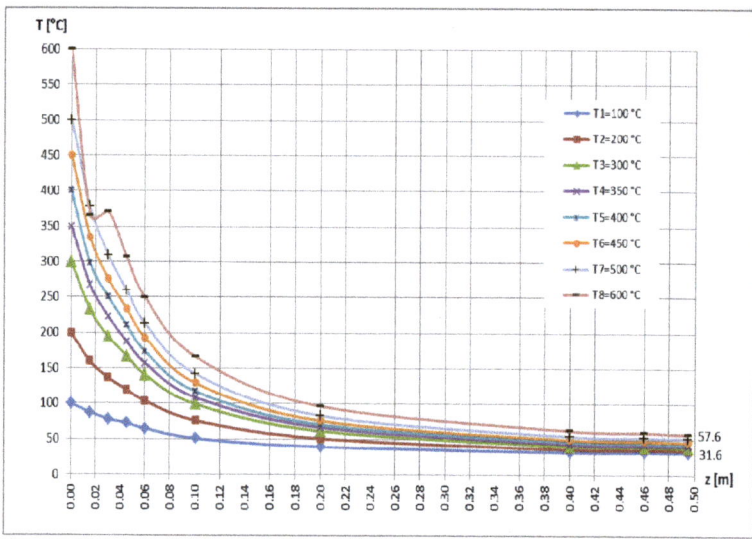

Figure 20. Temperature variation along the painted pole, made at 1:10 scale.

Later, based on this subdivision, the respective curves obtained through experimental measurements could be approximated each time with minimum degree polynomial functions; these results are analyzed in Section 4.

Figure 21a–c show these new intervals related to the curves in Figure 19, and in Figure 22a–c, those corresponding to the curves in Figure 20.

At first glance, the curves in Figures 21c and 22c would show strong gradients of temperature variation, but if one carefully follows the z(m) scale, one notices that, in fact, these lengths are much larger than at the first two sets of diagrams (Figures 21a,b and 22a,b); consequently, these last intervals actually show very smooth changes in temperatures on the portion The faulty behavior of the above-mentioned thermoresistor can also be seen on Figure 22a; here, in fact, the processing of the initial curve from Figure 20 was carried out.

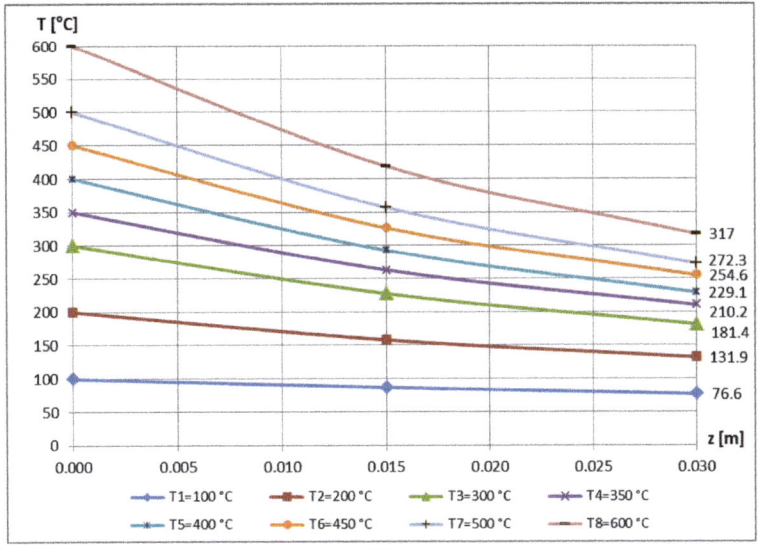

(a)

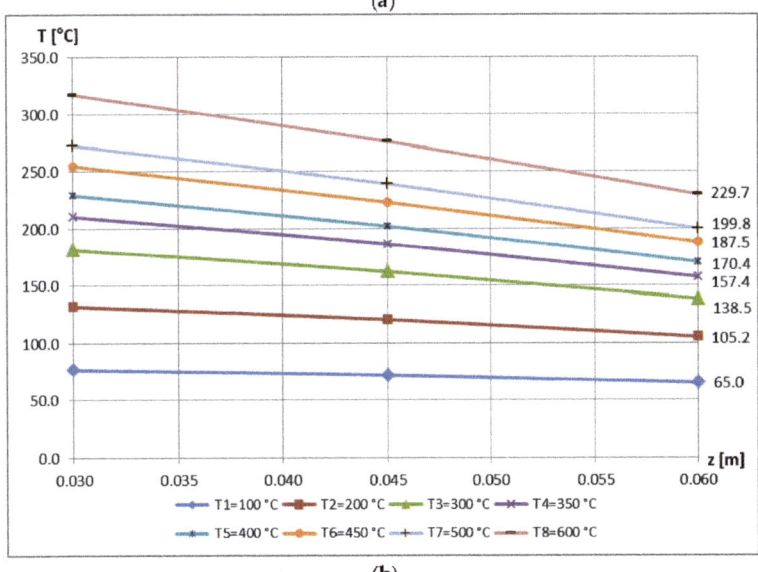

(b)

Figure 21. *Cont.*

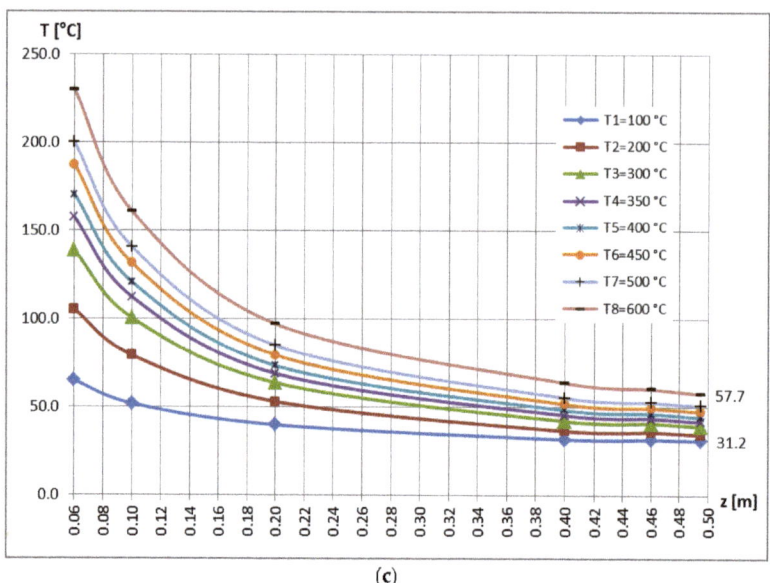

(c)

Figure 21. Variation of temperature along the intervals of the unpainted base, made at a scale of 1:10, according to Figure 19: (**a**) ℓ_I; (**b**) ℓ_{II}; (**c**) ℓ_{III} [71].

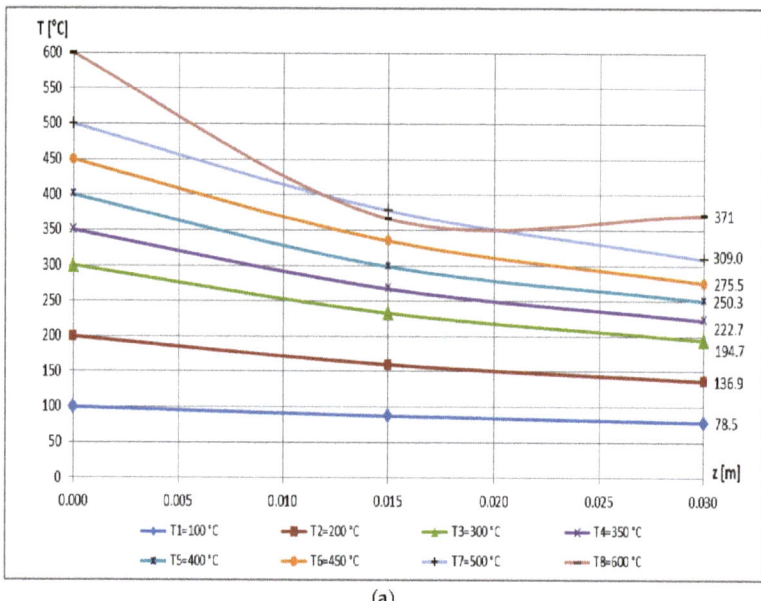

(a)

Figure 22. *Cont.*

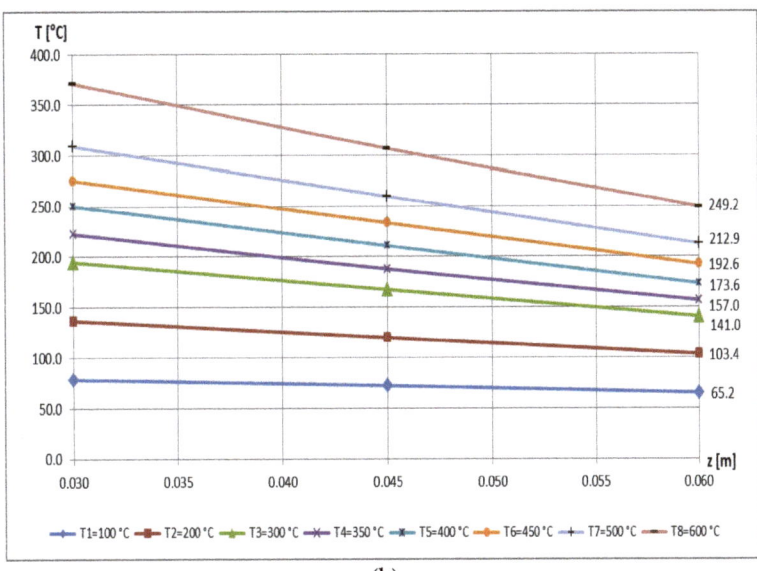

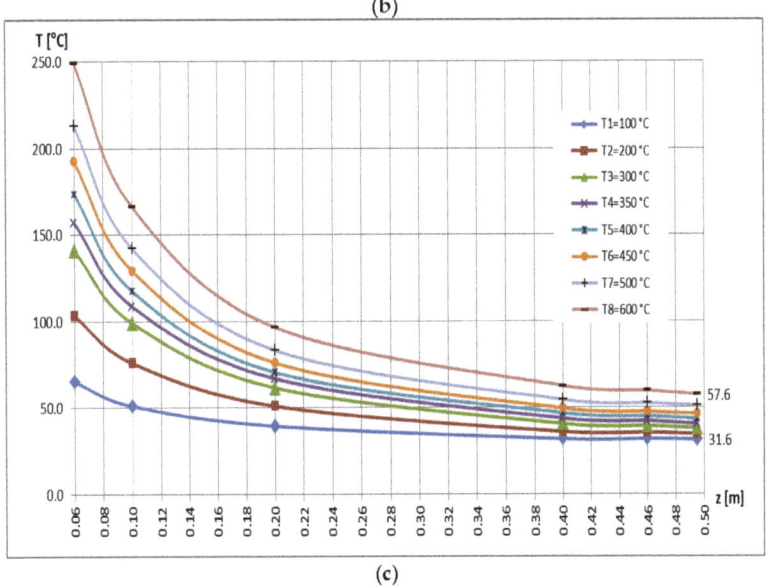

Figure 22. Variation of temperature along the intervals of the painted pillar, made on a scale of 1:10, according to Figure 20: (**a**) ℓ_I; (**b**) ℓ_{II}; (**c**) ℓ_{III} [71].

4. Discussion

In the previous paper [3], the classical, exponential, and the polynomial approach to temperature variation curves, curves obtained based on rigorous measurements, was presented.

New parameters were proposed, namely: the relative thermal curve t_ψ [%] as well as the compared temperature loss $\Delta t_\psi = 100 - t_\psi$ [%] (the percentages of the lost temperatures). Also, also in the work [2] a more effective methodology for establishing the "m"

parameter was proposed, but also the proposal of a new parameter, i.e., the relative curve m_ψ [%].

These results, as mentioned before, also facilitate the calculation of the heat transfer coefficient α_n, which, as is well known, is a major objective of these analyses.

The authors performed high-accuracy metrological measurements of the involved heat/temperature sensors' accuracy, namely, of the PT 100-type thermoresistors. In Figure 23 the original testing device of these thermoresistors' accuracy is shown. From the literature, it is a well-known fact that the thermo-couples have, in practice, high-accuracy sensors, up to class 0.1. Because the involved PT 100 thermoresistors present a lower accuracy, the authors first performed a comparative analysis of them with such a calibrated thermo-couple.

A steel disc, with a 105 mm diameter and a height of 15 mm, manufactured from the same quality steel as the associated elements in the described experiments from the present contribution, was designed with a central hole with a 2 mm diameter (destined for the thermo-couple fixing) and with three other M3 screws disposed symmetrically for the PT 100 thermoresistors. By applying the same thermo-charging (heating them up to the same temperatures as the involved sensors in the described experiments), their own calibration curves were drawn up with respect to the thermo-couple's indication, as well as a probable (global) calibration curve, i.e., with their mean values. Consequently, by this preliminary calibration, the thermal deviation of the involved PTs was stated with respect to the real indicated values (by means of a high-accuracy thermo-couple). All collected data during the experiments mentioned in the paper were corrected, taking into consideration the obtained thermal deviation.

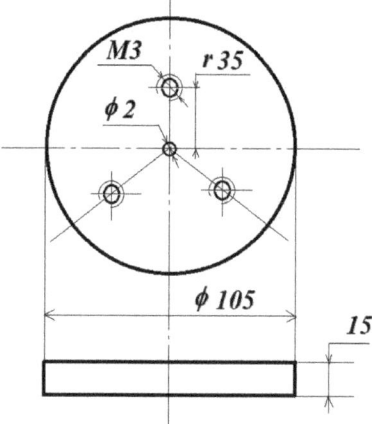

Figure 23. The testing device of the comparative accuracies (dimensions are in mm).

One other supplementary approach to the measurements' uncertainty consisted in performing a metrological evaluation for each channel of the involved data acquisition chain, starting from the thermoresistor, a LABJACK 9 acquisition device, up to the laptop.

In this way, different high-accuracy (class 0.1) electrical resistors substituted each PT in order to obtain for the whole thermal interval (up to 600 °C) the corresponding electrical signals for all involved channels. Based on these indications a second re-calibration of the collected electrical signals from each PT became possible.

One can conclude that this re-calibration was performed the first time by the above-mentioned comparative measurements of the calibrated thermo-couple vs. three PT 100 thermoresistors, and afterwards, based on these electrical resistors' indications.

In the authors' opinion, the obtained data can be considered acceptable from the point of view of metrological accuracy, as well as uncertainty.

To obtain a more comprehensive (more general) approach, the authors propose introducing a percentage length L_ψ [%] instead of the effective length z(m); this new length considers the value of 100% of the size of the quota z_{max}. With the help of this new parameter, Figure 24 shows the curves related to the nominal temperature $t_{0,nom} = 400\,°C$ for the first three unpainted structural elements (not thermally protected), i.e., the prototype, and the models reduced to the scales of 1:2 and 1:4; these curves are extracted from Figure 13, Figure 15, Figure 17 respectively, and analyzed with the percentage length L_ψ [%].

Similarly, in Figure 25 the related curves of the same structural elements are shown, but thermally protected, i.e., painted; these resulted by extracting data from from Figure 14, Figure 16, Figure 18 respectively, and analyzed with the help of L_ψ [%].

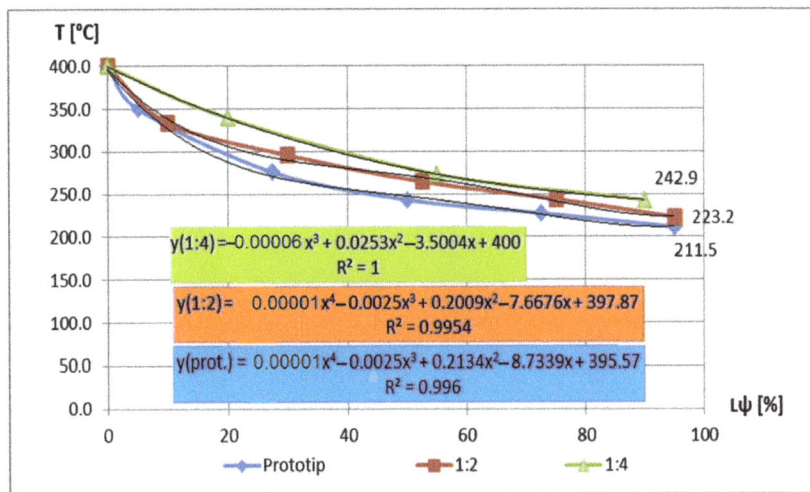

Figure 24. The three segments of unpainted columns, at 400 °C [71].

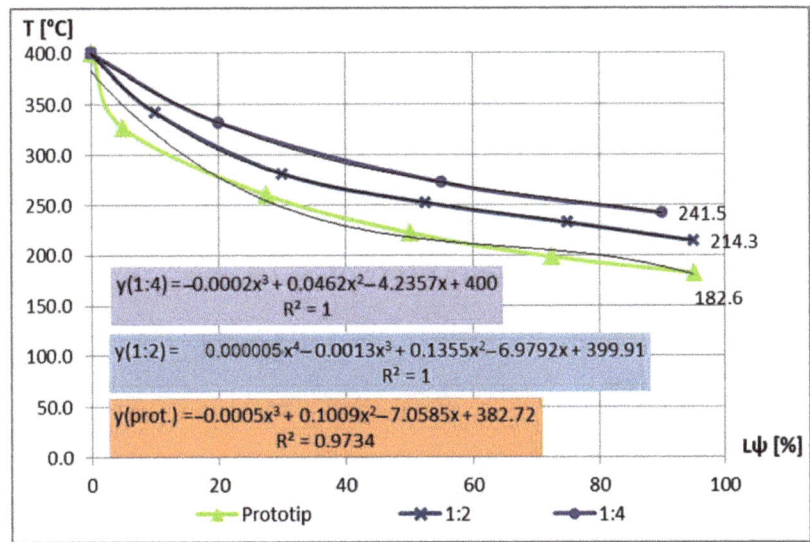

Figure 25. The three segments of painted columns, at 400 °C [71].

One can notice a very similar allure of the curves rendered within the same figure, although their sizes and volumes were very different. In the same figures, the approximation polynomial curves are also mentioned, of the order IV at most, but with a very good correlation factor R^2.

A similar approach in the case of the pillar reduced to a scale of 1:10 led to obtaining the curves in Figure 26, according to Figure 19, and its more precise analysis of the subintervals, corresponding to the nominal temperatures of $t_{0,nom} = 400\ °C$ and $t_{0,nom} = 500\ °C$, shown in Figures 27–29. It can be noted that the change in the degree of the approximation polynomial functions with the analyzed subinterval depends on the gradient of the initial temperature curves.

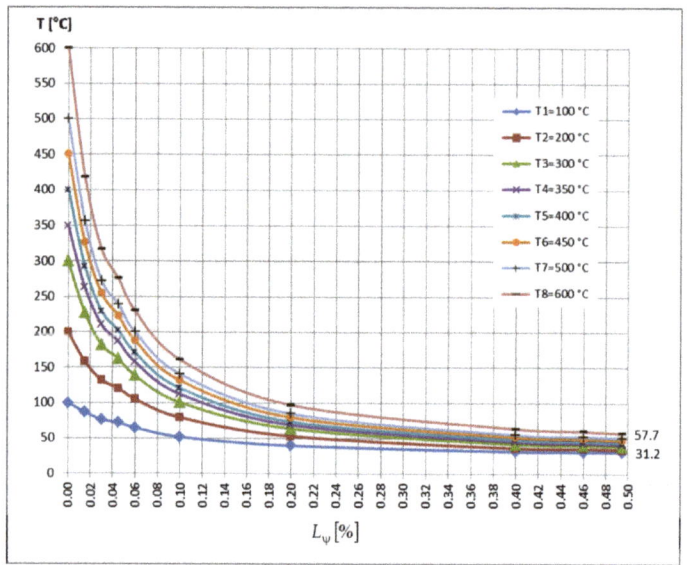

Figure 26. Temperature variation along the unpainted pole, made at 1:10 scale.

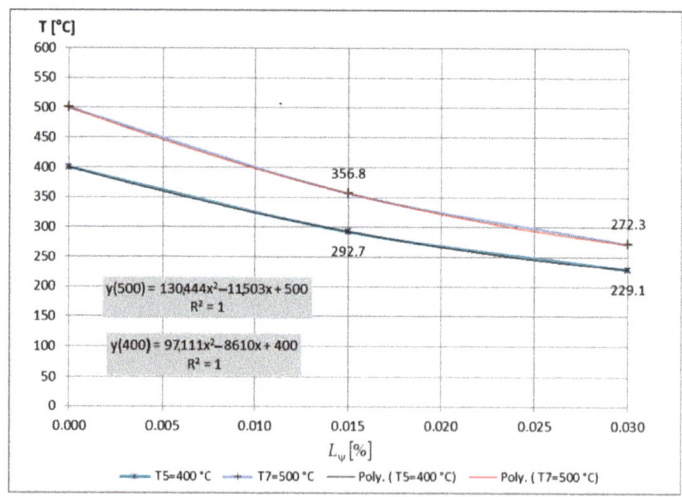

Figure 27. Variation of temperatures along the painted pole, made at 1:10 scale; the first interval in Figure 26.

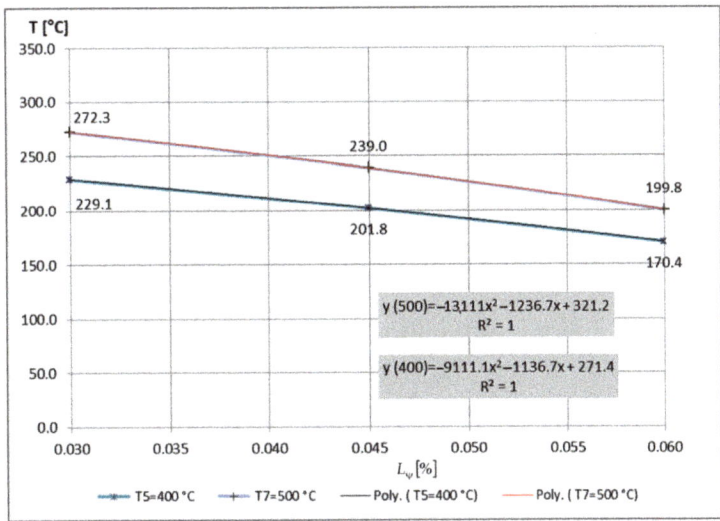

Figure 28. Variation of temperatures along the unpainted pole, made at 1:10 scale; the second interval in Figure 26.

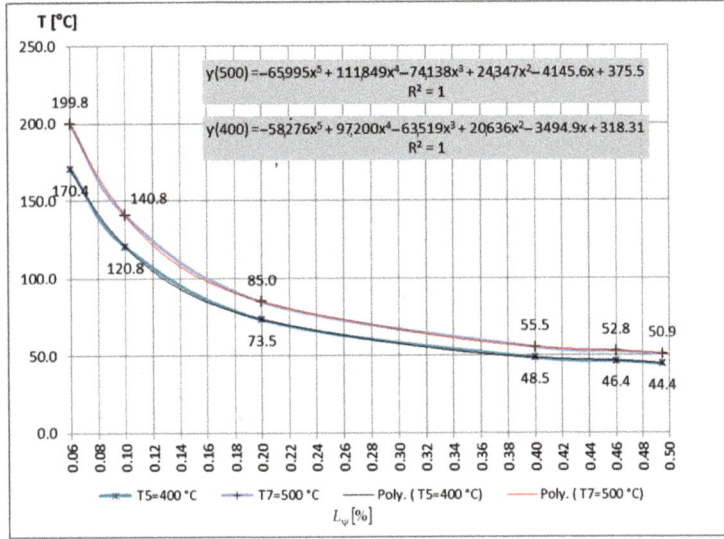

Figure 29. Variation of temperatures along the painted pole, made at 1:10 scale; the third interval in Figure 27.

If on the first subinterval, related to ℓ_I, the gradient is too strong, then one can use an additional division of it into two other units in order not to excessively increase the degree of the approximation polynomial, but also to keep a better correlation factor as R^2.

A similar analysis for the painted 1:10 scale pillar is shown in Figure 30, according to Figure 20, and its more precise analysis of the subintervals, corresponding to the same nominal temperatures of $t_{0,nom} = 400\ °C$ and $t_{0,nom} = 500\ °C$, is shown in Figures 31–33.

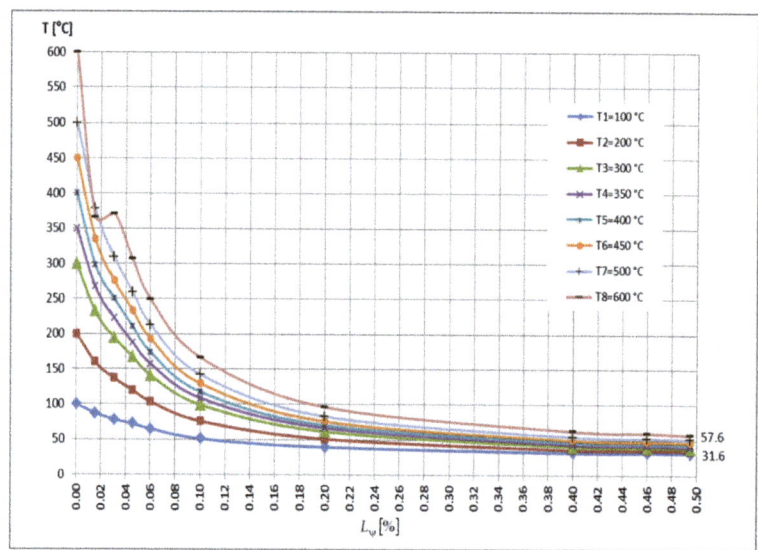

Figure 30. Temperature variation along the painted pillar, made at 1:10 scale.

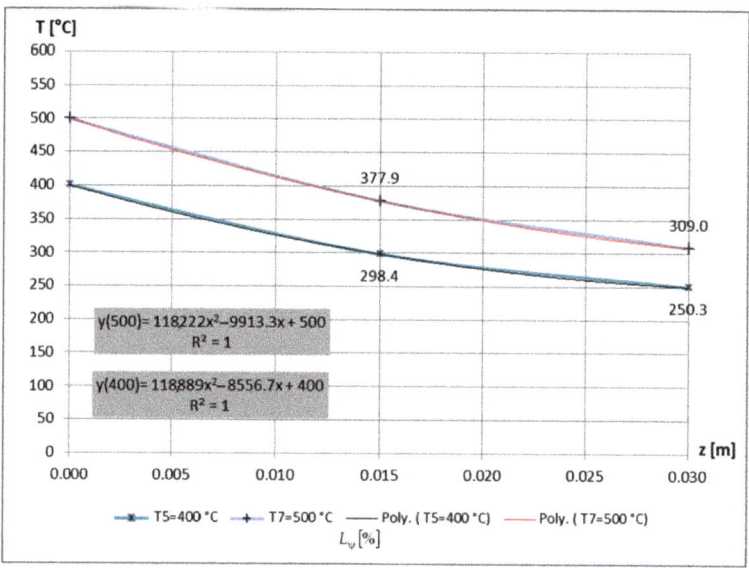

Figure 31. Temperature variation along the painted pole, made at 1:10 scale, for the first interval in Figure 30.

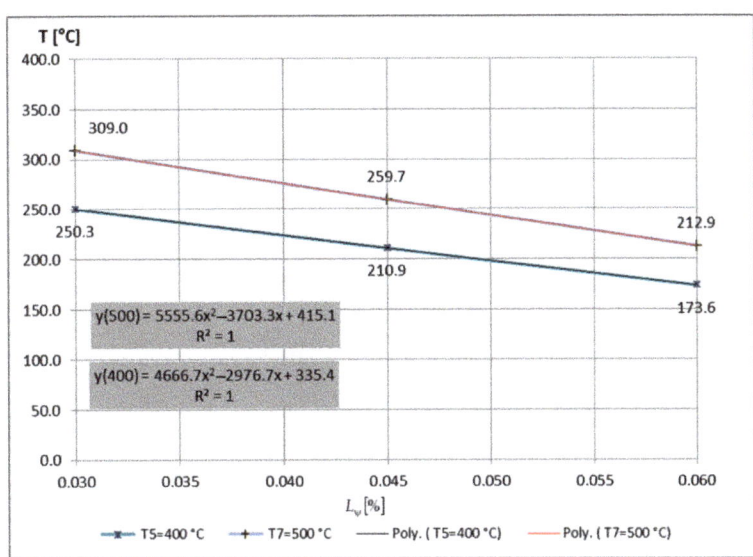

Figure 32. Variation of temperatures along the painted pole, made at a scale of 1:10, on the second interval in Figure 30.

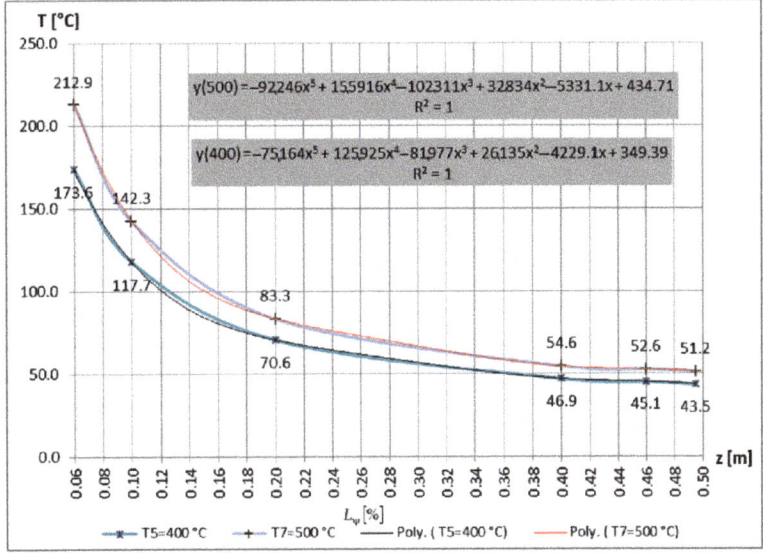

Figure 33. Variation of temperatures along the painted pole, made on a scale of 1:10, on the third interval in Figure 30.

If we switch to the use of dimensionless curves $T_\psi - L_\psi$, then it will be possible to highlight the net advantage of this new approach, because curves with very similar, practically identical slopes will be obtained, which will allow the form of templates or nomograms intended for preliminary calculations to be used in in further research. The explanation could also consist in the fact that differences of the order of a few tens of degrees will not lead to significant deviations of these curves (since we are talking about percentages of temperatures in the order of hundreds of degrees), even if their nominal temperatures are different.

Next, the authors illustrate the efficiency and net advantage of this new dimensionless approach.

Thus, in Figures 34–39, the curves analyzed in Figures 13–18 are reproduced, but in dimensionless representation.

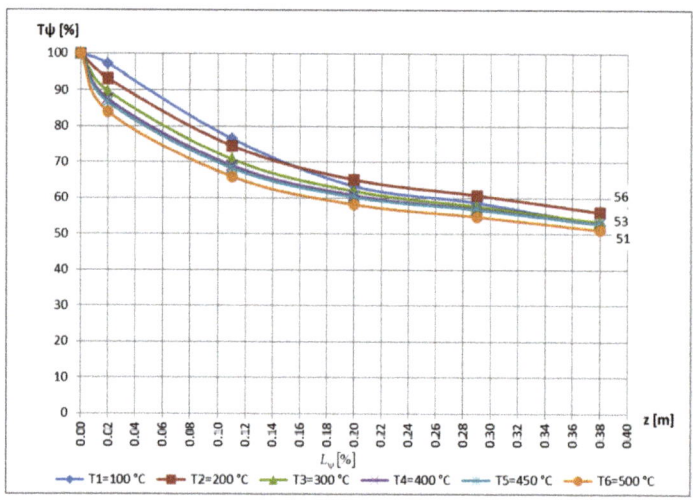

Figure 34. Variation of temperatures along the unpainted prototype, in dimensionless representation.

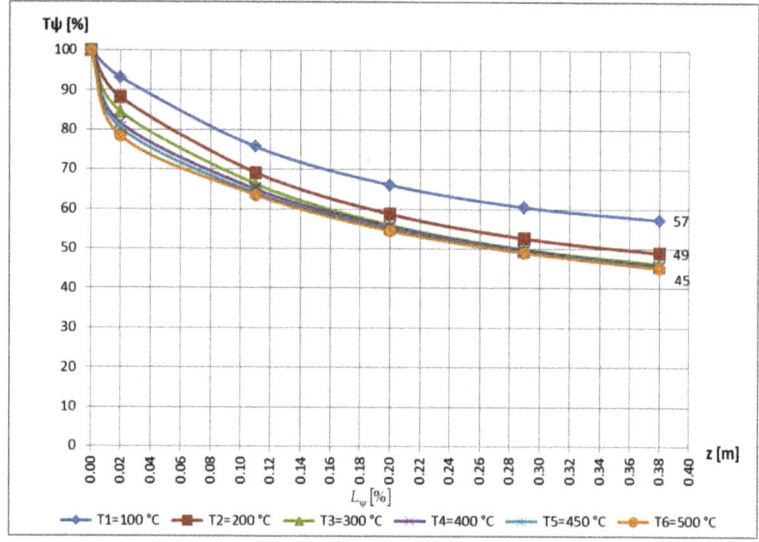

Figure 35. Variation of temperatures along the painted prototype, in dimensionless representation.

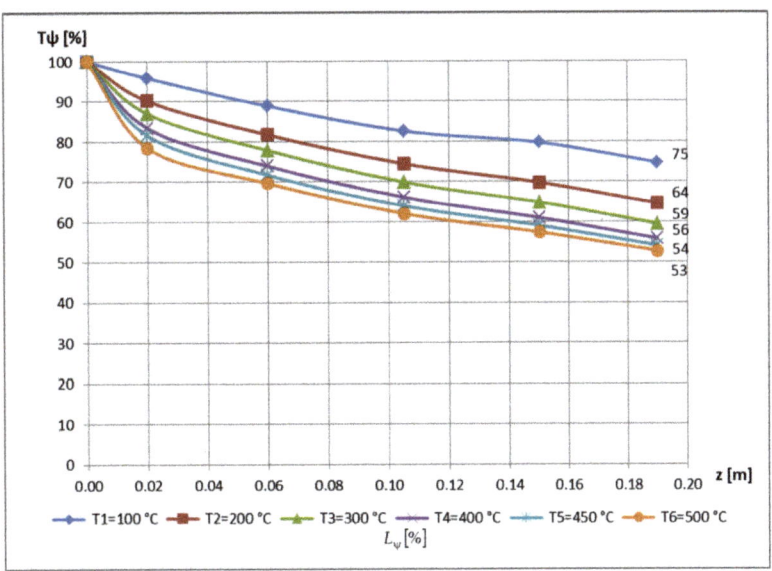

Figure 36. Variation of temperatures along the unpainted 1:2 scale model.

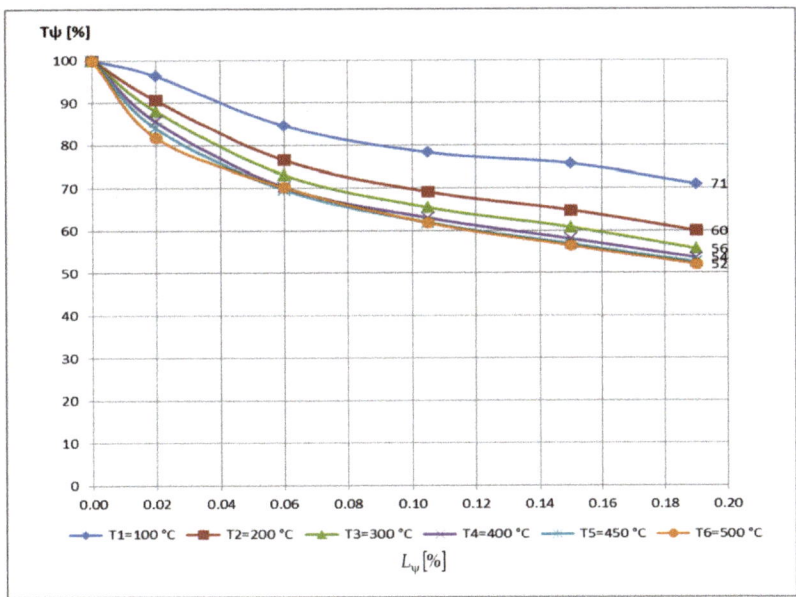

Figure 37. Variation of temperatures along the painted 1:2 scale model.

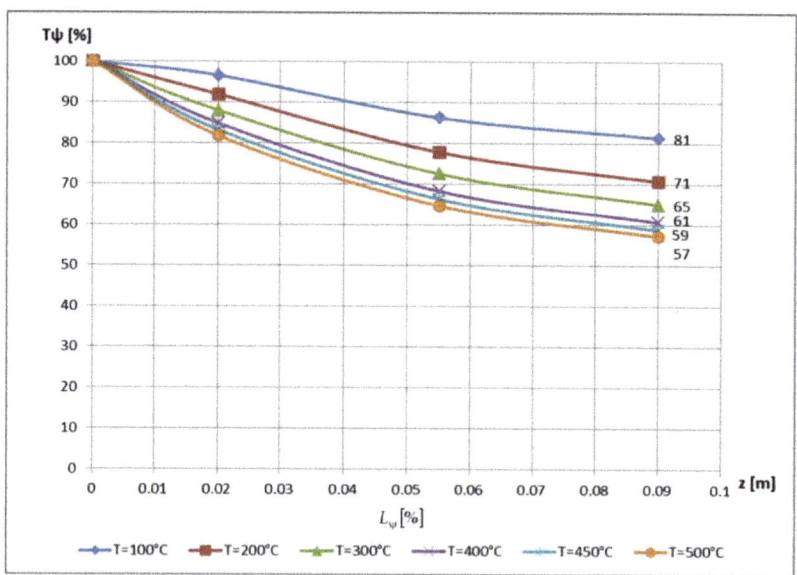

Figure 38. Variation of temperatures along the unpainted 1:4 scale model.

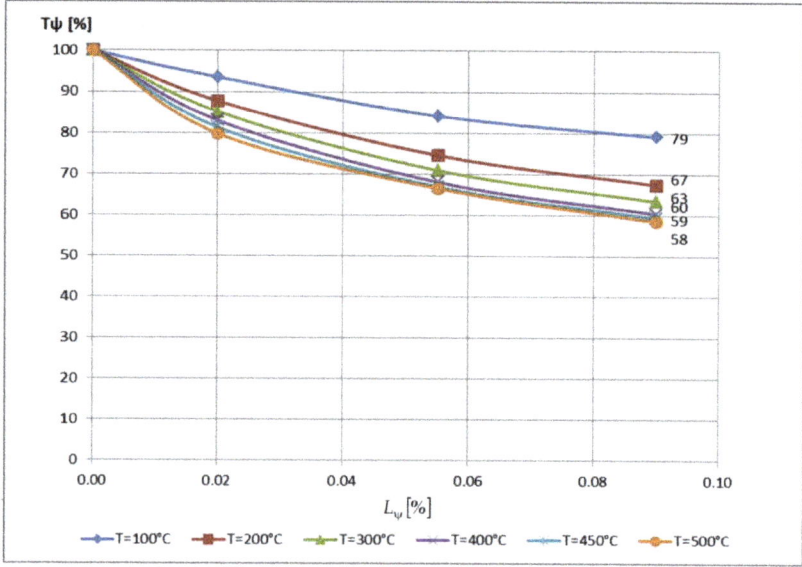

Figure 39. Variation of temperatures along the painted 1:4 scale model.

This very similar behavior of these structural elements, also observable in the above-mentioned figures, justifies the use of a single dimensionless curve $T_\psi - L_\psi$, as a weighted average of them, which will be of great use in an evaluation of the behavior of the structures with the help of MDA.

In this way, as mentioned in Section 3, the testing of these structural elements was carried out with the assurance of a thermal similarity, i.e., reaching identical temperatures in the homologous points of the structures. The most important homologous points from a thermal point of view were the measurement points at the base, near the upper end of the respective structural element.

In this new approach, those reported in Figures 24 and 25 will take the forms shown in Figures 40 and 41, respectively.

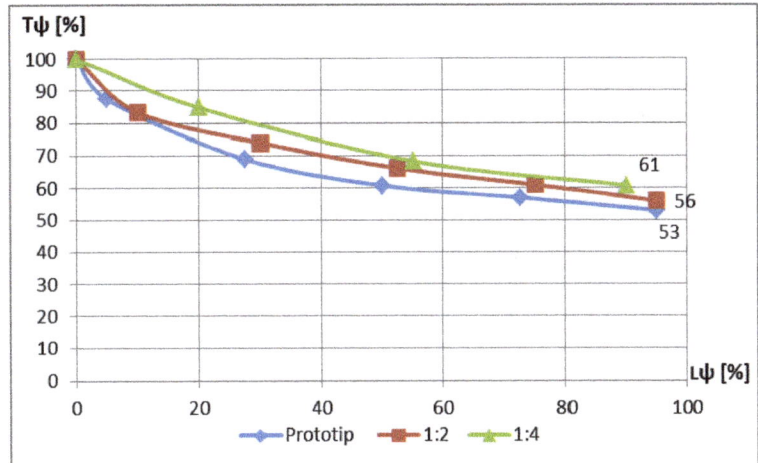

Figure 40. The three segments of unpainted pillars, at 400 °C, in dimensionless coordinate system.

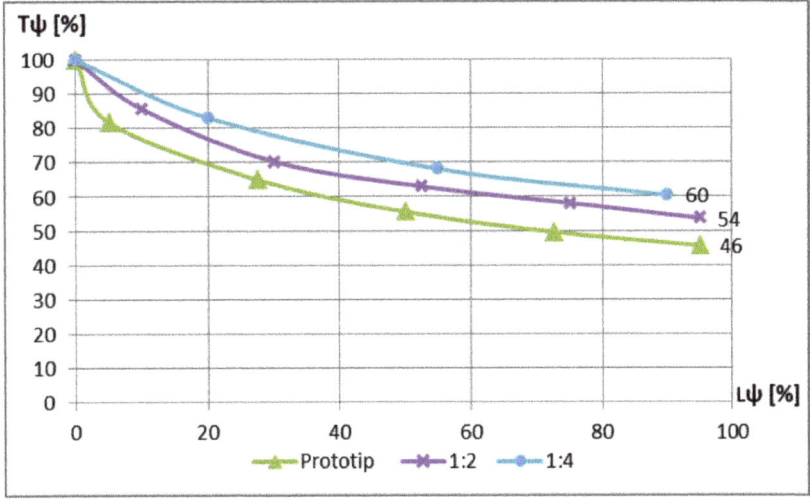

Figure 41. The three segments of painted pillars, at 400 °C, in dimensionless coordinate system.

Similarly, for the pillar made on a scale of 1:10, the diagrams in Figures 26 and 27 will take on the shapes shown in Figures 42 and 43, respectively.

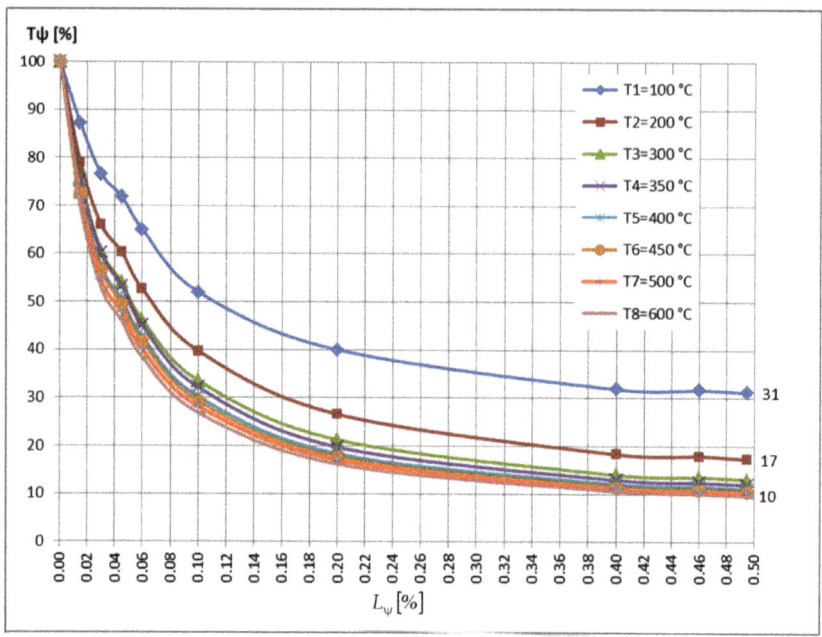

Figure 42. Variation of temperatures along the unpainted pole, in dimensionless representation.

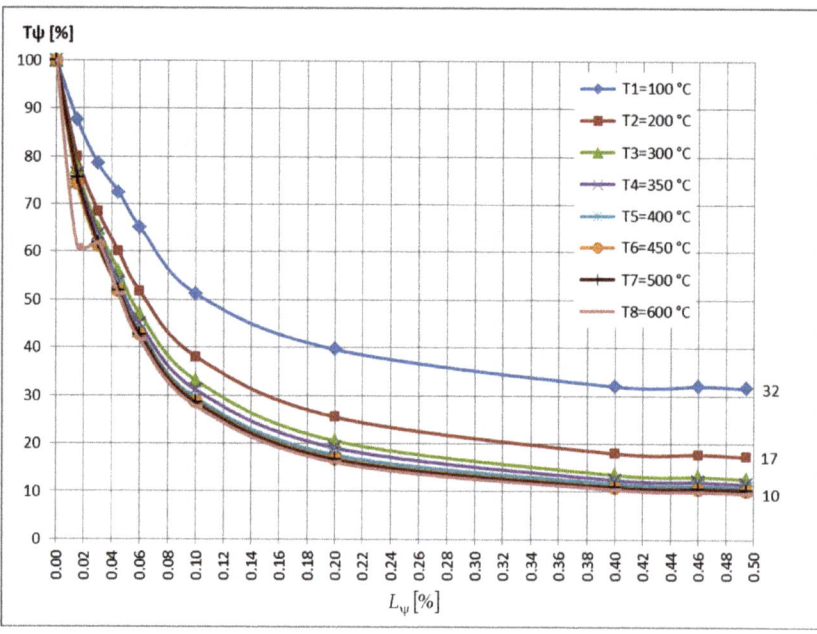

Figure 43. Temperature variation along the painted pole, in dimensionless representation.

It can be observed that, even if the thermal responses of the structural element are reproduced at eight nominal temperatures, starting from $t_{0,nom} = 300\,°C$, practically all the curves will overlap, which justifies the idea of using a single dimensionless curve $T_\psi - L_\psi$, as a weighted average of them; the polynomial function, which will approximate it, will serve to perform subsequent calculations.

Obviously, further dividing this representative curve into three subdivisions will give the researcher the possibility of a much more accurate polynomial approximation.

Once this global curve, or even the individual dimensionless curves $T_\psi - L_\psi$ are obtained, the strategy for determining the value of the "m" parameter and its variation law along the structural element $m(z)$ becomes unitary and particularly efficient; in the paper [71] this new approach is detailed.

5. Conclusions

Both the original electrical stand and the results of the investigations carried out with its help were presented, in order to monitor the behavior of a real structural element (a pillar of an existing industrial hall), as well as of some models attached to it, made at different scales (1:2; 1:4; 1:10), all followed in the stabilized thermal regimes. These results were materialized in a series of temperature variation diagrams along the respective structural elements.

Based on these diagrams, the authors went on to illustrate the new approach to diagram analysis, using some normalization steps, gradually moving to dimensionless curves and replacing those resulting from experimental measurements with approximation curves (made using the "curve-fitting" method).

The thermoprotective layer, used in engineering applications, represented a shield in front of the heat flow and prevented the transfer of heat between the structure and the surrounding environment.

The authors express their hope that this new approach, with the help of dimensionless curves $T_\psi - L_\psi$, due to its simplicity and efficiency argued in this article, will be implemented as soon as possible in the thermal study of structural elements subjected to fires by specialists in the field.

The obtained results support the methodology studied by the authors considering the application of MDA to hit transfer phenomena. In this way, measurements made on a scale model, which can be studied in the laboratory, allow quick conclusions to be drawn regarding the behavior of the real model.

In this sense, either the individual curves $T_\psi - L_\psi$ or their representative curve, as their weighted average, can be of great use to specialists and can also serve as a starting point in the creation of nomogram-type databases, related to quick preliminary calculations.

The approach of the easier establishment of the "m" parameter along the structural element and the heat transfer coefficient α_n based on it, essential elements in any analysis of the fire resistance of resistance structures, is also not without importance.

Among the goals pursued by the authors in the near future is even the creation of a database, taking into account first the requirements of the domestic industry, but later also of international companies.

Another future objective would be to carry out some numerical simulations, based on the obtained experimental results, that would validate some pertinent numerical models useful to specialists in the field.

Author Contributions: Conceptualization, I.S. and S.V.; methodology, I.S., I.-R.S. and G.T.; software, Z.A. and B.-P.G.; validation, I.S. and S.V.; formal analysis, I.S. and S.V.; investigation, I.S., S.V., I.-R.S., G.T., V.M.M., T.G., Z.A. and B.-P.G.; resources, I.S. and B.-P.G.; data curation, I.-R.S., G.T., V.M.M. and T.G.; writing—original draft preparation, I.S.; writing—review and editing, I.S. and S.V.; visualization, I.S., S.V., I.-R.S., G.T., V.M.M., T.G., Z.A. and B.-P.G.; supervision, I.S. and S.V.; project administration, I.S.; funding acquisition, I.S. and S.V. All authors have read and agreed to the published version of the manuscript.

Funding: This research received no external funding. The APC was funded by Transylvania University of Brasov.

Data Availability Statement: Not applicable.

Acknowledgments: The authors express their sincere thanks to the ISI-Sys Company of Kassel, Germany for the loan of the VIC-3D optical system, and to the Correlated Solutions Company, USA for the related software.

Conflicts of Interest: The authors declare no conflict of interest.

References

1. Turzó, G. Temperature distribution along a straight bar sticking out from a heated plane surface and the heat flow transmitted by this bar (I)-Theoretical Approach. *Ann. Fac. Eng. Hunedoara-Int. J. Eng.* **2016**, *14*, 49–53.
2. Turzó, G.; Száva, I.R.; Gálfi, B.P.; Száva, I.; Vlase, S.; Hota, H. Temperature Distribution of the Straigth Bar, fixed into a Heated Plane Surface. *Fire Mater.* **2018**, *42*, 202–212. [CrossRef]
3. Turzó, G.; Száva, I.R.; Dancsó, S.; Száva, I.; Vlase, S.; Munteanu, V.; Gălățanu, T.; Asztalos, Z. A New Approach in Heat Transfer Analysis: Reduced-Scale Straight Bars with Massive and Square-Tubular Cross-Sections. *Mathematics* **2022**, *10*, 3680. [CrossRef]
4. Baker, W.; Westine, P.S.; Dodge, F.T. *Similarity Methods in Engineering Dynamics*; Elsevier: Amsterdam, The Netherlands, 1991.
5. Barenblatt, G.I. *Dimensional Analysis*; Gordon and Breach: New York, NY, USA, 1987.
6. Barr, D.I.H. Consolidation of Basics of Dimensional Analysis. *J. Eng. Mech.-ASCE* **1984**, *110*, 1357–1376. [CrossRef]
7. Bejan, A. *Convection Heat Transfer*; John Wiley & Sons: Hoboken, NJ, USA, 2013.
8. Bhaskar, R.; Nigam, A. Qualitative Physics using Dimensional Analysis. *Artif. Intell.* **1990**, *45*, 73–111. [CrossRef]
9. Bridgeman, P.W. *Dimensional Analysis*; Yale University Press: New Haven, CT, USA, 1922; (Reissued in paperbound in 1963).
10. Buckingham, E. On Physically Similar Systems. *Phys. Rev.* **1914**, *4*, 345. [CrossRef]
11. Canagaratna, S.G. Is dimensional analysis the best we have to offer. *J. Chem. Educ.* **1993**, *70*, 40–43. [CrossRef]
12. Carabogdan, G.I.; Badea, A.; Brătianu, C.; Mușatescu, V. *Methods of Analysis of Thermal Energy Processes and Systems*; Technical Publishing House: Bucharest, Romania, 1989. (In Romanian)
13. Carinena, J.F.; Santander, M. Dimensional Analysis. *Adv. Electron. Electron Phys.* **1988**, *72*, 181–258.
14. Carlson, D.E. Some New Results in Dimensional Analysis. *Arch. Ration. Mech. Anal.* **1978**, *68*, 191–210. [CrossRef]
15. Carslaw, H.S.; Jaeger, J.C. *Conduction of Heat in Solid*, 2nd ed.; Oxford Science Publications: New York, NY, USA, 1986.
16. Chen, W.K. Algebraic Theory of Dimensional Analysis. *J. Frankl. Inst.* **1971**, *292*, 403–409. [CrossRef]
17. Coyle, R.G.; Ballicolay, B. Concepts and Software for Dimensional Analysis in Modelling. *IEEE Trans. Syst. Man Cybern.* **1984**, *14*, 478–487. [CrossRef]
18. Fourier, J. *Theorie Analytique de la Chaleur*; Firmin Didot: Paris, France, 1822. (In French)
19. Gibbings, J.C. Dimensional Analysis. *J. Phys. A-Math. Gen.* **1980**, *13*, 75–89. [CrossRef]
20. Gibbings, J.C. A Logic of Dimensional Analysis. *J. Phys. A-Math. Gen.* **1982**, *15*, 1991–2002. [CrossRef]
21. Incropera, F.P.; DeWitt, D.P.; Bergman, T.L.; Lavine, A.S. *Fundamentals of Heat and Mass Transfer*; John Wiley & Sons Ltd.: Chichester, UK, 2002.
22. Jofre, L.; del Rosario, Z.R.; Iaccarino, G. Data-driven dimensional analysis of heat transfer in irradiated particle-laden turbulent flow. *Int. J. Multiph. Flow* **2020**, *125*, 103198. [CrossRef]
23. Környey, T. *Heat Transfer*; Műegyetemi Kiadó: Budapest, Hungary, 1999. (In Hungarian)
24. Langhaar, H.L. *Dimensional Analysis and Theory of Models*; John Wiley & Sons Ltd.: New York, NY, USA, 1951.
25. Martins, R.D.A. The Origin of Dimensional Analysis. *J. Frankl. Inst.* **1981**, *311*, 331–337. [CrossRef]
26. Nakla, M. On fluid-to-fluid modeling of film boiling heat transfer using dimensional analysis. *Int. J. Multiph. Flow* **2011**, *37*, 229–234. [CrossRef]
27. Nezhad, A.H.; Shamsoddini, R. Numerical Three-Dimensional Analysis of the Mechanism of Flow and Heat Transfer in a Vortex Tube. *Therm. Sci.* **2009**, *13*, 183–196. [CrossRef]
28. Pankhurst, R.C. *Dimensional Analysis and Scale Factor*; Chapman & Hall Ltd.: London, UK, 1964.
29. Quintier, G.J. *Fundamentals of Fire Phenomena*; John Wiley & Sons: New York, NY, USA, 2006.
30. Remillard, W.J. Applying Dimensional Analysis. *Am. J. Phys.* **1983**, *51*, 137–140. [CrossRef]
31. Romberg, G. Contribution to Dimensional Analysis. *Inginieur Arch.* **1985**, *55*, 401–412. [CrossRef]
32. Schnittger, J.R. Dimensional Analysis in Design. *Journal of Vibration, Accoustic. Stress Reliab. Des.-Trans. ASME* **1988**, *110*, 401–407. [CrossRef]
33. Sedov, I.L. *Similarity and Dimensional Methods in Mechanics*; MIR Publisher: Moscow, Russia, 1982.
34. de Silva, V.P. Determination of the temperature of thermally unprotected steel members under fire situations considerations on the section factor. *Lat. Am. J. Solids Struct.* **2006**, *3*, 113–125.
35. Szekeres, P. Mathematical Foundations of Dimensional Analysis and the Question of Fundamental Units. *Int. J. Theor. Phys.* **1978**, *17*, 957–974. [CrossRef]
36. Șova, S.; Șova, D. *Thermotecnics*; Transilvania University Press: Brașov, Romania, 2001; Volume II.
37. Șova, D. *Heat Engineering*; Transilvania University Press: Brasov, Romania, 2006; ISBN 9789736357664.
38. Șova, D. *Applied Thermodynamics*; Transilvania University Press: Brasov, Romania, 2015; ISBN 9786061907144.
39. Ștefănescu, D.; Marinescu, M.; Dănescu, A. *Heat Transfer in Technique*; Tehnică: București, Romania, 1982; Volume I.
40. VDI. *VDI-Wärmeatlas*, 7th ed.; Verein Deutscher Ingenieure: Düsseldorf, Germany, 1994.

41. Zierep, J. *Similarity Laws and Modelling*; Marcel Dekker: New York, NY, USA, 1971.
42. Aglan, A.A.; Redwood, R.G. Strain-Hardening Analysis of Beams with 2 WEB- Rectangular Holes. *Arab. J. Sci. Eng.* **1987**, *12*, 37–45.
43. Al-Homoud, M.S. Performance characteristics and practical applications of common building thermal insulation materials. *Build. Environ.* **2005**, *40*, 353–366. [CrossRef]
44. Bączkiewicz, J.; Malaska, M.; Pajunen, S.; Heinisuo, M. Experimental and numerical study on temperature distribution of square hollow section joints. *J. Constr. Steel Res.* **2018**, *142*, 31–43. [CrossRef]
45. Bailey, C. Indicative fire tests to investigate the behaviour of cellular beams protected with intumescent coatings. *Fire Saf. J.* **2004**, *39*, 689–709. [CrossRef]
46. Ferraz, G.; Santiago, A.; Rodrigues, J.P.; Barata, P. Thermal Analysis of Hollow Steel Columns Exposed to Localized Fires. *Fire Technol.* **2016**, *52*, 663–681. [CrossRef]
47. Franssen, J.-M. Calculation of temperature in fire-exposed bare steel structures: Comparison between ENV 1993-1-2 and EN 1993-1-2. *Fire Saf. J.* **2006**, *41*, 139–143. [CrossRef]
48. Franssen, J.-M.; Real, P.V. *Fire Design of Steel Structures, ECCS Eurocode Design Manuals, ECCS-European Convention for Constructional Steelwork*; Ernst & Sohn: Berlin, Germany, 2010.
49. Gao, F.; Guan, X.-Q.; Zhu, H.P.; Liu, X.-N. Fire resistance behaviour of tubular T-joints reinforced with collar plates. *J. Constr. Steel Res.* **2015**, *115*, 106–120. [CrossRef]
50. Ghojel, J.I.; Wong, M.B. Heat transfer model for unprotected steel members in a standard compartment fire with participating medium. *J. Constr. Steel Res.* **2005**, *61*, 825–833. [CrossRef]
51. Xiao, B.Q.; Li, Y.P.; Long, G.B. A Fractal Model of Power-Law Fluid through Charged Fibrous Porous Media by using the Fractional-Derivative Theory. *FRACTALS- Complex Geom. Patterns Scaling Nat. Soc.* **2022**, *30*, 2250072. [CrossRef]
52. Xiao, B.Q.; Fang, J.; Long, G.B.; Tao, Y.Z.; Huang, Z.J. Analysis of Thermal Conductivity of Damaged Tree-Like Bifurcation Network with Fractal Roughened Surfaces. *FRACTALS-Complex Geom. Patterns Scaling Nat. Soc.* **2022**, *30*, 2250104. [CrossRef]
53. Long, G.; Liu, Y.; Xu, W.; Zhou, P.; Zhou, J.; Xu, G.; Xiao, B. Analysis of Crack Problems in Multilayered Elastic Medium by a Consecutive Stiffness Method. *Mathematics* **2022**, *10*, 4403. [CrossRef]
54. Kado, B.; Mohammad, S.; Lee, Y.H.; Shek, P.N.; Ab Kadir, M.A. Temperature Analysis of Steel Hollow Column Exposed to Standard Fire. *J. Struct. Technol.* **2018**, *3*, 1–8.
55. Khan, M.A.; Shah, I.A.; Rizvi, Z.; Ahmad, J. A numerical study on the validation of thermal formulations towards the behaviours of RC beams. *Sci. Mater. Today Proc.* **2019**, *17*, 227–234. [CrossRef]
56. Krishnamoorthy, R.R.; Bailey, C.G. Temperature distribution of intumescent coated steel framed connection at elevated temperature. In Proceedings of the Nordic Steel Construction Conference '09, Malmo, Sweden, 2–4 September 2009; Swedish Institute of Steel Construction: Stockholm, Sweden, 2009; Publication 181, Volume I, pp. 572–579.
57. Lawson, R.M. Fire engineering design of steel and composite Buildings. *J. Constr. Steel Res.* **2001**, *57*, 1233–1247. [CrossRef]
58. Levac, M.L.J.; Soliman, H.M.; Ormiston, S.J. Three-dimensional analysis of fluid flow and heat transfer in single- and two-layered micro-channel heat sinks. *Heat Mass Transf.* **2011**, *47*, 1375–1383. [CrossRef]
59. Noack, J.; Rolfes, R.; Tessmer, J. New layerwise theories and finite elements for efficient thermal analysis of hybrid structures. *Comput. Struct.* **2003**, *81*, 2525–2538. [CrossRef]
60. Papadopoulos, A.M. State of the art in thermal insulation materials and aims for future developments. *Energy Build.* **2005**, *37*, 77–86. [CrossRef]
61. Tafreshi, A.M.; Di Marzo, M. Foams and gels as temperature protection agents. *Fire Saf. J.* **1999**, *33*, 295–305. [CrossRef]
62. Yang, K.-C.; Chen, S.J.; Lin, C.-C.; Lee, H.-H. Experimental study on local buckling of fire-resisting steel columns under fire load. *J. Constr. Steel Res.* **2005**, *61*, 553–565. [CrossRef]
63. Yang, J.; Shao, Y.B.; Chen, C. Experimental study on fire resistance of square hollow section (SHS) tubular T-joint under axial compression. *Adv. Steel Constr.* **2014**, *10*, 72–84.
64. Wong, M.B.; Ghojel, J.I. Sensitivity analysis of heat transfer formulations for insulated structural steel components Fire. *Saf. J.* **2003**, *38*, 187–201. [CrossRef]
65. Vlase, S.; Teodorescu-Draghicescu, H.; Calin, M.R.; Scutaru, M.L. Advanced Polylite composite laminate material behavior to tensile stress on weft direction. *J. Optoelectron. Adv. Mater.* **2022**, *14*, 658–663.
66. Alshqirate, A.A.Z.S.; Tarawneh, M.; Hammad, M. Dimensional Analysis and Empirical Correlations for Heat Transfer and Pressure Drop in Condensation and Evaporation Processes of Flow Inside Micropipes: Case Study with Carbon Dioxide (CO_2). *J. Braz. Soc. Mech. Sci. Eng.* **2012**, *34*, 89–96.
67. Andreozzi, A.; Bianco, N.; Musto, M.; Rotondo, G. Scaled models in the analysis of fire-structure interaction. In Proceedings of the 33rd UIT (Italian Union of Thermo-Fluid-Dynamics) Heat Transfer Conference, L'Aquila, Italy, 22–24 June 2015; IOP: Bristol, UK, 2015; Volume 655, p. 012053. [CrossRef]
68. He, S.-B.; Shao, Y.-B.; Zhang, H.-Y.; Wang, Q. Parametric study on performance of circular tubular K-joints at elevated temperature. *Fire Saf. J.* **2015**, *71*, 174–186. [CrossRef]
69. Illan, F.; Viedma, A. Experimental study on pressure drop and heat transfer in pipelines for brine based ice slurry Part II: Dimensional analysis and rheological Model. *Int. J. Refrig.-Rev. Int. Du Froid* **2009**, *32*, 1024–1031. [CrossRef]

70. Gálfi, B.-P.; Száva, I.; Șova, D.; Vlase, S. Thermal Scaling of Transient Heat Transfer in a Round Cladded Rod with Modern Dimensional Analysis. *Mathematics* **2021**, *9*, 1875. [CrossRef]
71. Munteanu (Száva), I.R. Investigation Concerning Temperature Field Propagation along Reduced Scale Modelled Metal Structures. Ph.D. Thesis, Transilvania University of Brasov, Brasov, Romania, 2018.
72. Száva, I.R.; Șova, D.; Dani, P.; Élesztős, P.; Száva, I.; Vlase, S. Experimental Validation of Model Heat Transfer in Rectangular Hole Beams Using Modern Dimensional Analysis. *Mathematics* **2022**, *10*, 409. [CrossRef]
73. Șova, D.; Száva, I.R.; Jármai, K.; Száva, I.; Vlase, S. Modern method to analyze the Heat Transfer in a Symmetric Metallic Beam with Hole. *Symmetry* **2022**, *14*, 769. [CrossRef]
74. Trif, I.; Asztalos, Z.; Kiss, I.; Élesztős, P.; Száva, I.; Popa, G. Implementation of the Modern Dimensional Analysis in Engineering Problems; Basic Theoretical Layouts. *Ann. Fac. Eng. Hunedoara* **2019**, *17*, 73–76.
75. Szirtes, T. The Fine Art of Modelling. *SPAR J. Eng. Technol.* **1992**, *1*, 37.
76. Szirtes, T. *Applied Dimensional Analysis and Modelling*; McGraw-Hill: Toronto, ON, Canada, 1998.
77. Száva, I.; Szirtes, T.; Dani, P. An Application of Dimensional Model Theory in the Determination of the Deformation of a Structure. *Eng. Mech.* **2006**, *13*, 31–39.
78. Száva, R.I.; Száva, I.; Vlase, S.; Gálfi, P.B.; Jármai, K.; Gălăţanu, T.; Popa, G.; Asztalos, Z. Modern Dimensional Analysis-Based Steel Column' Heat Transfer Evaluation using Multiple Experiments. *Symmetry* **2022**, *14*, 1952. [CrossRef]
79. Dani, P.; Száva, I.R.; Kiss, I.; Száva, I.; Popa, G. Principle Schema of an Original Full-, and Reduced-Scale Testing Bench, Destined to Fire Protection Investigations. *Ann. Fac. Eng. Hunedoara-Int. J. Eng.* **2018**, *16*, 149–152.
80. Gálfi, B.P.; Száva, R.I.; Száva, I.; Vlase, S.; Gălăţanu, T.; Jármai, K.; Asztalos, Z.; Popa, G. Modern Dimensional Analysis based on Fire-Protected Steel Members' Analysis using Multiple Experiments. *Fire* **2022**, *5*, 210. [CrossRef]

Disclaimer/Publisher's Note: The statements, opinions and data contained in all publications are solely those of the individual author(s) and contributor(s) and not of MDPI and/or the editor(s). MDPI and/or the editor(s) disclaim responsibility for any injury to people or property resulting from any ideas, methods, instructions or products referred to in the content.

Article

A Posteriori Error Estimators for the Quasi-Newtonian Stokes Problem with a General Boundary Condition

Omar El Moutea [1], Lahcen El Ouadefli [2], Abdeslam El Akkad [2,3], Nadia Nakbi [3], Ahmed Elkhalfi [2], Maria Luminita Scutaru [4,*] and Sorin Vlase [4,5]

[1] Laboratory of Mathematics and Applications, ENS, Hassan II University Casablanca, Casablanca 20000, Morocco
[2] Mechanical Engineering Laboratory, Faculty of Science and Technology, University Sidi Mohammed Ben Abdellah, B.P. 30000 Route Imouzzer, Fez 30000, Morocco
[3] Département de Mathématiques, Centre Regional des Métiers d'Education et de Formation de Fès Meknès (CRMEF Fès-Meknès), Rue de Koweit 49, Ville Nouvelle, Fez 30050, Morocco
[4] Department of Mechanical Engineering, Faculty of Mechanical Engineering, Transylvania University of Brasov, B-dul Eroilor 29, 500036 Brasov, Romania
[5] Romanian Academy of Technical Sciences, B-dul Dacia 26, 030167 Bucharest, Romania
* Correspondence: lscutaru@unitbv.ro

Abstract: In this paper, we approach two nonlinear differential equations applied in fluid mechanics by finite element methods (FEM). Our objective is to approach the solution to these problems; the first one is the "*p*-Laplacian" problem and the second one is the "Quasi-Newtonian Stokes" problem with a general boundary condition. To study and analyze our solutions, we introduce the a posteriori error indicator; this technique allows us to control the error, and each is shown the equivalent between the true and the a posterior errors estimators. The performance of the finite element method by this type of general boundary condition is presented via different numerical simulations.

Keywords: a posteriori error estimation; FEM; Laplacian operator; quasi-Newtonian flows problem

MSC: 65N30; 65N15; 65G99; 76D07; 76D99

1. Introduction

One of the important objectives of numerical studies of differential problems is: to have a "realistic simulation"; for this, many researchers have concentrated on controlling the error by using the adaptive finite element methods (FEM) meshes. The adaptive meshes provide effective means of optimizing calculation with reasonable results; "the meshes are automatically modified by enhancing the scope of their applications". The error estimation technique provides an assessment of the accuracy of the solutions obtained by the finite element solvers, see [1,2] for more precise details. These techniques can efficiently offer certain flow features (stagnation, reattachment points, and recirculation eddies, with small velocity magnitudes). Generally, this technique is based on a posteriori local error estimation, see [3].

Nonlinear differential equations are used to model complex problems in the sciences and engineering. Many studies have been developed to simplify these complex models. Among these models, we mention the "*p*-Laplacian" equation and the "Quasi-Newtonian Stokes" system. These nonlinear equations have had more attention in recent years, and one of the important domains using these equations is the glaciology domain. These equations model the dynamics of ice sheets or glaciers, see [4], and the evolution of glacier geometry, see [5,6]. Another application in the biological domain is the common use for blood flows, see [7] for details.

One of the important domains that uses these equations is fluid mechanics. For example, to model "viscoelastic" fluids we use the "Quasi-Newtonian Stokes" method, see [8] for more details. This quasi-Newtonian law was first proposed by Carreau et al. in [9]; a popular extension to the Carreau law is studied by Yasuda et al. in [10] and a closely related model, the Cross law, is investigated by Cross in [11]. The well-posedness of these problems is established in these papers [12,13]. Much mathematical modeling for complex fluids and numerical algorithms are applied to solve linear/nonlinear equations, see [14]. The fully non-linear elliptic problems in divergence form by using a mixed finite volume scheme are studied in [15]; the discontinuous Galerkin approximation was considered in [5] and the hybrid high-order scheme was studied in [16]. The paper where the authors studied the comportment of solutions of some non–linear diffusion problems and in the boundary–layer flow of a pseudo-plastic fluid is given [17]. The a posteriori error estimator for elliptic partial differential equations by using finite elements is presented in [18] and proves some (elliptic) a posteriori error estimators. The p-Laplacian problem is studied by using a FEM method in many papers, see [19–22] for details. In [23,24], the authors analyzed a posteriori error estimators for quasi-Newtonian problems with a homogeneous Dirichlet boundary condition. There are at least as many relevant references over the past 30 years on the quasi-Newtonian Stokes problem concerning the posterior estimate and its use in adaptivity; there were important developments in the Chinese [25–27], German [28–30], and French [31,32] schools for flow fluid in complex porous media using new boundary conditions [33] and combined mixed finite element [34].

This paper is organized as follows: in Section 2 and in order to study the p-Laplacian problem with the new boundary condition, we introduce some useful notations, state our main assumptions regarding the modeling equations, and following a finite element discretization, we calculate error estimators with respect to the true error. Section 3 contains the description of our second problem (quasi-Newtonian system) which is discretized by a mixed finite element scheme. The a posteriori error estimator is developed in terms of the Residus of variational formulas with respect to the real error. Section 4 presents two numerical examples using a velocity angle error indicator.

The authors propose the study of two nonlinear differential equations that have applications in fluid mechanics, using FEM. These problems are studied in two steps, within the "p-Laplacian" problem, and then solving the "Quasi-Newtonian Stokes" problem imposing a general boundary condition. To study and analyze our solutions, an a posteriori error indicator will be introduced. In this way, there is the possibility to control the error at each step and compare the calculated error with the a posteriori error. The obtained results are supported by several numerical simulations that we considered significant for the presentation of the research.

2. Approximation of p-Laplacian Equation by Finite Element Method

The section aims to study the p-Laplacian equation with a nonhomogeneous Robin boundary condition; we use FEM to approximate this model. To analyze the error, we use the a postriori estimates for the Dirichlet boundary condition, see [17,24,35]. First of all, we recall some useful properties of generalized nonlinear diffusion problems and we investigate the existence/uniqueness of the solution. Let Ω be an open-bounded (connected) subset of $\mathbb{R}^d$ ($d = 2, 3$) whose boundary $\Gamma = \partial \Omega$, and let $\beta \in \mathbb{N}^*$ with conjugate $\beta' = \frac{\beta}{\beta+1}$.

2.1. Results of the p-Laplacian Operator

We consider the generalized nonlinear diffusion problem, defined by

$$-\nabla \cdot \varphi(x, \nabla u(x)) = f(x) \text{ in } \Omega, \tag{1}$$

where the flux $\varphi : \Omega \times \mathbb{R}^2 \to \mathbb{R}^2$ is assumed to satisfy the following assumptions:

There exist two positive constants C_1, C_2, and two functions $b_1 \in L^1(\Omega)$ and $b_2 \in L^{\beta'}(\Omega)$ such that

$$\begin{cases} (\varphi(x,y) - \varphi(x,z), y - z) > 0, & (H_1) \\ (\varphi(x,y), y) \geq C_1 |y|^\beta - b_1(x), & (H_2) \\ \varphi(x,y) \leq C_2 |y|^{\beta-1} - b_2(x), & (H_3) \end{cases}$$

for all $x, y, z \in \Omega$ with $y \neq z$.

Under these assumptions the problem (1) has a unique solution $u \in W^{1,\beta}(\Omega)$, and the functional $u \mapsto -\mathrm{div}(\varphi(\cdot, \nabla u(\cdot)))$ is a Leray–Lions operator which satisfies

$$u \in \left(L^\beta(\Omega)\right)^2 \mapsto \varphi(\cdot, \nabla u(\cdot)) \in \left(L^{\beta'}(\Omega)\right)^2.$$

The p-Laplacian equation is defined by

$$-\nabla \cdot a(\nabla u) = f \text{ in } \Omega, \tag{2}$$

where the vector field $a(\zeta) = |\zeta|^{\beta-2}\zeta$ and $\beta \in \mathbb{N}^*$.

The p-Laplacian equation is a nonlinear diffusion problem. Now, we recall some key lemmas useful to prove the monotonicity and continuity properties of such operators, see [12,20].

Let $z = (z_1, z_2) \in \mathbb{R}^2$ and let us define the following operator

$$A(\cdot) : u \in V \to A(u) = -\nabla\left(|\nabla u|^{\beta-2} \nabla u\right) \in V',$$

where space V depends on the boundary condition and V' its dual. In order to prove the ellipticity of the problem, we need the following lemma.

Lemma 1. *For all $y, z \in \mathbb{R}^2$, we have*

$$\begin{cases} \left(|z|^{\beta-2}z - |y|^{\beta-2}y, z - y\right) \geq \alpha |z - y|^{\beta-1} \text{ if } \beta \geq 2, \\ (|z| + |y|)^{2-\beta}\left(|z|^{\beta-2}z - |y|^{\beta-2}y, z - y\right) \geq \alpha |z - y|^2 \text{ if } 1 < \beta \leq 2, \end{cases}$$

where $\alpha > 0$ is independent of y and z.

Proof. See [12]. □

Proposition 2 (Ellipticity). *For all $u, v \in V$, we have the following ellipticity properties*

$$\begin{cases} (A(u) - A(v), u - v) \geq \alpha ||u - v||^\beta & \text{if } \beta \geq 2, \\ (||u|| + ||v||)^{2-\beta}(A(u) - A(v), u - v) \geq \alpha ||u - v||^2 & \text{if } 1 < \beta \leq 2, \end{cases} \tag{3}$$

Proof. A direct consequence Lemma 2.1 from [12] for a detailed proof. □

To proof the continuity property, it needs the following lemma,

Lemma 3. *For all $y, z \in \mathbb{R}^2$, we have*

$$\begin{cases} \left||z|^{\beta-2}z - |y|^{\beta-2}y\right| \leq \alpha |z - y|(|z| + |y|)^{\beta-2} & \text{if } \beta \geq 2, \\ \left||z|^{\beta-2}z - |y|^{\beta-2}y\right| \leq \alpha |z - y|^{\beta-1} & \text{if } 1 < \beta \leq 2, \end{cases}$$

where $\alpha > 0$ is independent of y and z.

Proof. See [12]. □

Proposition 4 (Continuity). *For all $u, v \in V$, we have the following continuity properties*

$$\begin{cases} ||A(u) - A(v)||_* \leq \alpha ||u - v||(||u|| + ||v||)^{\beta-2} & \text{if} \quad \beta \geq 2, \\ ||A(u) - A(v)||_* \leq \alpha ||u - v||^{\beta-1} & \text{if} \quad 1 < \beta \leq 2, \end{cases} \quad (4)$$

here $\alpha > 0$, independent to u and v.

Proof. A (direct) consequence of the lemma 2.1, see also [12] for a detailed proof. □

2.2. *Mathematical Problem*

The practical applications of the p-Laplacian equations [4,5,36] have previously been mentioned; which, proved useful in a wide range of applications. For example, glacier dynamics are an important topic in engineering and hydrology. Thus, the ice flow is assumed to be an incompressible fluid with nonlinear viscosity. Next, let us consider the problem of the model

$$-\nabla \cdot a(\nabla u) = f \text{ in } \Omega, \quad (5)$$

with $a(\zeta) = |\zeta|^{\beta-2}\zeta$ and $f \in L^{\beta'}(\Omega)$. Note that if $\beta = 2$, it coincides with the linear Laplacian operator, i.e., $A = -\Delta$.

This equation can then be carried with the following new boundary conditions

$$\begin{cases} \alpha(u)u + \left(|\nabla u|^{\beta-2}\nabla u\right) \cdot n = g & \text{on } \Gamma_{ND}, \\ u = 0 & \text{on } \Gamma_D, \end{cases} \quad (6)$$

where $\alpha \in L^\infty(\Gamma)$ ($\alpha > 0$) and $g \in W^{1-\frac{1}{\beta},\beta}(\partial\Omega)$.

Theorem 1. *The problems (5) and (6) have a unique solution $u \in W^{1,\beta}(\Omega)$.*

Proof. The proof is a consequence of ellipticity–continuity assumptions on the operator A. □

The systems (5) and (6) are equivalent to a minimization problem (see [12,13]) defined by: find $u \in V$ such that

$$J(v) \leq J(u), \forall v \in V, \quad (7)$$

where

$$J(u) = \frac{1}{\beta}\int_\Omega |\nabla u|^\beta + \frac{1}{2}\int_{\Gamma_{ND}} \alpha|u|^2 - \int_\Omega fv - \int_{\Gamma_{ND}} gv, \quad (8)$$

for all $v \in V$.

The function J is continuous, strictly convex, and differentiable operator with $\lim_{||v|| \to \infty} J(v) = +\infty$; it results, see [37], that J is Gateaux differentiable and (7) admits a unique solution characterized by its variational formulation: find $u \in V$ such that

$$\int_\Omega \left(|\nabla u|^{\beta-2}\nabla u\right)\nabla v + \int_{\Gamma_{ND}} \alpha uv = \int_\Omega fv + \int_{\Gamma_{ND}} gv, \quad (9)$$

for all $v \in V$.

Now, in order to analyze the finite element approximation of the problem (9), we consider a regular mesh T_h, $h > 0$, of the domain Ω. For any element $T \in T_h$, we define: ω_T the set of elements share at least one edge with T; $\tilde{\omega}_T$ the set of all elements sharing at least one vertex with T; $\varepsilon(T)$ the set of edges of T; h_T the diameter of the simplex T; and

$h = \max_{T \in T_h} h_T$. Respectively, for edge elements $E \in \partial T$ with $T \in T_h$: ω_E is the set of elements sharing at least one edge with E; $\widetilde{\omega}_E$ the set of all elements sharing at least one vertex with E; and h_E the diameter of a face E of T. Let $\varepsilon_h = \bigcup_{T \in T_h} \varepsilon(T)$ designate the set of all edges; hence, one can divide it into interior and exterior edges such that $\varepsilon_h = \varepsilon_{h,\Gamma} \cup \varepsilon_{h,\Omega}$ with

$$\varepsilon_{h,\Omega} = \{E \in \varepsilon_h : E \subset \Omega\}, \ \varepsilon_{h,\Gamma} = \{E \in \varepsilon_h : E \subset \Gamma\}.$$

Let $V_h \subset V = W^{1,\beta}(\Omega)$, the finite dimensional spaces associated to regular partition of Ω, and a discrete weak formulation is defined using finite dimensional spaces as: find the vector $u_h \in V_h$ such that

$$\int_\Omega \left(|\nabla u_h|^{\beta-2} \nabla u_h\right) \nabla v_h + \int_\Gamma \alpha u_h v_h = \int_\Omega f v_h + \int_\Gamma g v_h, \qquad (10)$$

for all $v_h \in V_h$.

2.3. A Posteriori Error Estimator

We illustrate the proposed technique with results of the a posteriori error estimation for the p-Laplacian problem. Denoting u the solution of (5) and (6) and u_h the approched solution of (10). Our aim is to estimate the velocity error $e = u - u_h \in V$ by using some important results.

Lemma 6. *There is a constant $C > 0$ for all the elements $K \in T_h$ and $v \in W^{1,\beta}(\Omega)$, such that*

$$h_T \|v\|_{0,\beta,\partial K}^\beta \leq C\left(\|v\|_{0,\beta,K}^\beta + \|v\|_{1,\beta,K}^\beta\right), \qquad (11)$$

Proof. See [24]. □

Lemma 7 (Clement interpolation estimate). *There is a constant $C > 0$, for any $K \in T_h$ and for all $E \in \partial K$, let $v \in V$ and π_h the operator of the interpolation of discontinuous functions defined by Clement satisfying*

$$\|v - \pi_h v\|_{0,\beta,K} \leq C h_K^{1-m} \sum_{K' \in S_K} \|v\|_{0,\beta,\widetilde{\omega}_{K'}} \qquad (12)$$

for all $v \in H^1(S_K)$, and $m = 0$ or 1.

Where $S_K = \bigcup\{K', K \cap K' \neq \varnothing\}$. In particular, for v_h, is the quasi-interpolant of v defined by averaging as in

$$\|v - v_h\|_{0,\beta,K} \leq C h_k^{1-m} |v|_{1,\beta,\widetilde{\omega}_{K'}} \qquad (13)$$

with $m = 0$ or 1.

Proof. See [12,24]. □

The residual error estimator $R : V \mapsto \mathbb{R}$ is given by

$$\langle R, v \rangle = \int_\Omega |\nabla u_h|^{\beta-2} \nabla u_h \nabla v + \int_\Gamma \alpha u_h v - \int_\Omega fv - \int_\Gamma gv, \qquad (14)$$

By applying the Green formula, we obtain

$$\begin{aligned}
\langle R, v \rangle &= \sum_{K \in T_h} \left\{ \int_K |\nabla u_h|^{\beta-2} \nabla u_h \nabla v + \int_{\Gamma \cap K} \alpha u_h v - \int_K fv - \int_{\Gamma \cap K} gv \right\} \\
&= \sum_{K \in T_h} \left\{ \int_K \left(-\nabla \cdot \left(|\nabla u_h|^{\beta-2} \nabla u_h\right) - f\right) v + \int_{\partial K} |\nabla u_h|^{\beta-2} \nabla u_h \cdot nv + \int_{\Gamma \cap K} \alpha u_h v + |\nabla u_h|^{\beta-2} \nabla u_h \cdot nv - gv \right\} \\
&= \sum_{K \in T_h} \left\{ \int_K \left(-\nabla \cdot \left(|\nabla u_h|^{\beta-2} \nabla u_h\right) - f\right) v + \sum_{l \in \partial K} \int_l |\nabla u_h|^{\beta-2} \nabla u_h \cdot nv + \sum_{l \in \Gamma \cap \partial K} \int_l \left(\alpha u_h + |\nabla u_h|^{\beta-2} \nabla u_h \cdot n - g\right) v \right\}.
\end{aligned} \qquad (15)$$

Because $R, v_h = 0$ for all $v_h \in V_h$, we use the interpolation operator π_h to obtain

$$\langle R, v \rangle = \sum_{K \in T_h} \left\{ \int_K \left(-\nabla \cdot \left(|\nabla u_h|^{\beta-2} \nabla u_h \right) - f \right)(v - \pi_h v) + \sum_{l \in \partial K} \int_l |\nabla u_h|^{\beta-2} \nabla u_h \cdot n(v - \pi_h v) \right. \\ \left. + \sum_{l \in \Gamma \cap \partial K} \int_l \left(\alpha u_h + |\nabla u_h|^{\beta-2} \nabla u_h \cdot n - g \right)(v - \pi_h v) \right\} \quad (16)$$

and

$$\langle R, v \rangle \leq \sum_{K \in T_h} \left\{ \int_K \left| -\nabla \cdot \left(|\nabla u_h|^{\beta-2} \nabla u_h \right) - f \right|_{0,\beta',K} |v - \pi_h v|_{0,\beta,K} + \sum_{l \in \partial K} \int_l \left| |\nabla u_h|^{\beta-2} \nabla u_h \cdot n \right|_{0,\beta',l} |v - \pi_h v|_{0,\beta,l} \right. \\ \left. + \sum_{l \in \Gamma \cap \partial K} \int_l \left| \alpha u_h + |\nabla u_h|^{\beta-2} \nabla u_h \cdot n - g \right|_{0,\beta',l} |v - \pi_h v|_{0,\beta,l} \right\}. \quad (17)$$

So, by (12), we get

$$\langle R, v \rangle \leq C \sum_{K \in T_h} h_K \left| -\nabla \cdot \left(|\nabla u_h|^{\beta-2} \nabla u_h \right) - f \right|_{0,\beta',K} \cdot \|v\|_{1,\beta,K} + \sum_{K \in T_h} \left\{ C \sum_{l \in \partial K} \left| \left[|\nabla u_h|^{\beta-2} \nabla u_h \cdot n \right] \right|_{0,\beta',l} \cdot |v - \pi_h v|_{0,\beta,l} \right. \\ \left. + C \sum_{l \in \Gamma \cap \partial K} \left| \alpha u_h + |\nabla u_h|^{\beta-2} \nabla u_h \cdot n - g \right|_{0,\beta',l} \cdot |v - \pi_h v|_{0,\beta,l} \right\}. \quad (18)$$

For the first term of the second member, we have

$$I_1 = \sum_{K \in T_h} h_K \left| -\nabla \cdot \left(|\nabla u_h|^{\beta-2} \nabla u_h \right) - f \right|_{0,\beta',K} \cdot \|v\|_{1,\beta,K} \leq C \left(\sum_{K \in T_h} h_K^{\beta'} \left| -\nabla \cdot \left(|\nabla u_h|^{\beta-2} \nabla u_h \right) - f \right|_{0,\beta',K}^{\beta'} \right)^{\frac{1}{\beta'}} \|v\|_{1,\beta,K}. \quad (19)$$

Now, we increase the second term as follows

$$\begin{aligned} I_2 &= \sum_{l \in \partial K} \left| \left[|\nabla u_h|^{\beta-2} \nabla u_h \cdot n \right] \right|_{0,\beta',l} \cdot |v - \pi_h v|_{0,\beta,l} \\ &= \sum_{l \in \partial K} h_l^{\frac{1}{\beta'}} \left| \left[|\nabla u_h|^{\beta-2} \nabla u_h \cdot n \right] \right|_{0,\beta',l} \cdot h_l^{-\frac{1}{\beta'}} |v - \pi_h v|_{0,\beta,l} \\ &\leq \left(\sum_{l \in \partial K} h_l \left| \left[|\nabla u_h|^{\beta-2} \nabla u_h \cdot n \right] \right|_{0,\beta',l}^{\beta'} \right)^{\frac{1}{\beta'}} \times \left(\sum_{l \in \partial K} h_l^{-\frac{\beta}{\beta'}} |v - \pi_h v|_{0,\beta,l}^{\beta} \right)^{\frac{1}{\beta}}. \end{aligned} \quad (20)$$

Using (11), we have

$$\begin{aligned} \sum_{l \in \partial K} h_l^{-\frac{\beta}{\beta'}} |v - \pi_h v|_{0,\beta,l}^{\beta} &\leq C \sum_{K \in T_h} h_K^{-\frac{\beta}{\beta'}} |v - \pi_h v|_{0,\beta,\partial K}^{\beta} \\ &\leq C \sum_{K \in T_h} h_K^{-(1+\frac{\beta}{\beta'})} \left(|v - \pi_h v|_{0,\beta,\partial K}^{\beta} + h_K^{\beta} |v - \pi_h v|_{1,\beta,K}^{\beta} \right) \\ &\leq C \sum_{K \in T_h} h_K^{-(1+\frac{\beta}{\beta'})} \left(h_K^{\beta} |v|_{1,\beta,K}^{\beta} + h_K^{\beta} |v|_{1,\beta,K}^{\beta} \right). \end{aligned} \quad (21)$$

As $1 + \frac{\beta}{\beta'} = \beta$, it implies that

$$\begin{aligned} I_2 &\leq \sum_{l \in \partial K} \left| \left[|\nabla u_h|^{\beta-2} \nabla u_h \cdot n \right] \right|_{0,\beta',l} \cdot |v - \pi_h v|_{0,\beta,l} \\ &\leq C \left(\sum_{l \in \partial K} h_l \left| \left[|\nabla u_h|^{\beta-2} \nabla u_h \cdot n \right] \right|_{0,\beta',l}^{\beta'} \right)^{\frac{1}{\beta'}} \times |v|_{1,\beta,\Omega}. \end{aligned} \quad (22)$$

Now, it is simple to increase the third term as follows

$$I_3 = \sum_{l \in \Gamma \cap \partial K} h_l^{\frac{1}{\beta'}} \left| \alpha u_h v + |\nabla u_h|^{\beta-2} \nabla u_h \cdot nv - g \right|_{0,\beta',l} \cdot h_l^{-\frac{1}{\beta'}} \left| v - \pi_h v \right|_{0,\beta,l}$$

$$\leq \left(\sum_{l \in \Gamma \cap \partial K} h_l \left| \alpha u_h + |\nabla u_h|^{\beta-2} \nabla u_h \cdot n - g \right|_{0,\beta',l}^{\beta'} \right)^{\frac{1}{\beta'}} \times \left(\sum_{l \in \partial K} h_l^{-\frac{\beta}{\beta'}} \left| v - \pi_h v \right|_{0,\beta,l}^{\beta} \right)^{\frac{1}{\beta}} \quad (23)$$

$$\leq \left(\sum_{l \in \Gamma \cap \partial K} h_l \left| \alpha u_h + |\nabla u_h|^{\beta-2} \nabla u_h \cdot n - g \right|_{0,\beta',l}^{\beta'} \right)^{\frac{1}{\beta'}} \times |v|_{1,\beta,\Omega}.$$

Hence, by combining (19), (22), and (23) we get

$$\langle R, v \rangle \leq C \left\{ \left(\sum_{K \in T_h} h_K \left| \nabla \cdot \left(|\nabla u_h|^{\beta-2} \nabla u_h \right) + f \right|_{0,\beta',K}^{\beta'} \right)^{\frac{1}{\beta'}} + \left(\sum_{l \in \partial K} h_l \left| \left[|\nabla u_h|^{\beta-2} \nabla u_h \cdot n \right]_l \right|_{0,\beta',l}^{\beta} \right)^{\frac{1}{\beta'}} \right.$$

$$\left. + C \left(\sum_{l \in \Gamma \cap \partial K} h_l \left| \alpha u_h + |\nabla u_h|^{\beta-2} \nabla u_h \cdot n - g \right|_{0,\beta',l}^{\beta'} \right)^{\frac{1}{\beta'}} \right\} \|v\|. \quad (24)$$

As $a^{\frac{1}{\beta'}} + b^{\frac{1}{\beta'}} \leq 2^{\frac{1}{\beta}}(a+b)^{\frac{1}{\beta'}}$ for a and $b \geq 0$, we have the following estimate

$$\|R\|_* = \|A(u) - A(u_h)\|_* \leq \left(C \sum_{K \in T_h} \eta_K^{\beta'} \right)^{\frac{1}{\beta'}},$$

with the contribution element of η_K, the residual error estimator is given by

$$\eta_K^{\beta'} = h_K^{\beta'} \|R_K\|_{0,\beta',K}^{\beta'} + \sum_{l \in \partial K} h_l \|R_l\|_{0,\beta',l}^{\beta'}, \quad (25)$$

his components are given by

$$R_K = \left\{ \nabla \cdot \left(|\nabla u_h|^{\beta-2} \nabla u_h \right) + f \right\}_{K'} \quad (26)$$

and

$$R_l = \begin{cases} \frac{1}{2} \left[|\nabla u_h|^{\beta-2} \nabla u_h \cdot n \right]_l & \text{if } l \in \varepsilon_{h,\Omega}, \\ \alpha(u_h) u_h + |\nabla u_h|^{\beta-2} \nabla u_h \cdot n - g & \text{if } l \in \varepsilon_{h,\Gamma}. \end{cases} \quad (27)$$

where $[\cdot]_l$ is the jump of the derivative of u_h over the interior edge $l = T \cap S$, defined by

$$\left[|\nabla u_h|^{\beta-2} \nabla u_h \cdot n \right]_l = \left(\left(|\nabla u_h|^{\beta-2} \nabla u_h \cdot n \right) \Big|_T - \left(|\nabla u_h|^{\beta-2} \nabla u_h \cdot n \right) \Big|_S \right) \vec{n}_{E,T}. \quad (28)$$

It remains to connect $\|R\|_*$ and $\|u - u_h\|$, which uses a coercivity property of the operator $A : V \mapsto W^{-1,\beta'}$ for $\beta \in \,]1,2[$, where we have

$$\langle A(u) - A(v), u - v \rangle \geq C \frac{\|u - v\|^2}{(\|u\| + \|v\|)^{2-\beta}}, \quad (29)$$

for all $u, v \in W^{1,\beta}(\Omega)$, where C is a constant that does not depend on either u or v. By taking $v = 0$, in (29), with u as the solution of problem (5), we get (since $A(0) = 0$)

$$\langle A(u), u \rangle \geq \alpha \|u\|^{\beta}.$$

As $A(u) = f$, then $\alpha \|u\|^{\beta} \leq f, u \leq \|f\|_{W^{-1,\beta'}(\Omega)} \cdot \|u\|$, which implies (since the injection of $L^{\beta'}(\Omega)$ in $W^{-1,\beta'}(\Omega)$ is continuous)

$$\|u\| \leq \left(\frac{1}{C} \|f\|_{W^{-1,\beta'}(\Omega)} \right)^{\frac{1}{\beta-1}} \leq C \left(\|f\|_{L^{\beta'}(\Omega)} \right)^{\frac{1}{\beta-1}}.$$

Similarly, for u_h, we have

$$(\|u\| + \|u_h\|)^{2-\beta} \le C\left(\|f\|_{L^{\beta'}(\Omega)}\right)^{\frac{2-\beta}{\beta-1}}. \tag{30}$$

Finally, from (19), (22), and (23), we obtain the following result.

Theorem 8. *For any mixed finite element approximation defined on regular grids T_h, the residual estimator satisfies*

$$\|e\| \le C\left(\sum_{K \in T_h} \eta_K^{\beta'}\right)^{\frac{1}{\beta'}},$$

where C is independent of β, Ω, a, and f.

Proof of Theorem 8. A direct consequence of these inequalities (15) to (29). □

Remark 9. *Some remarks are in order: for $\beta \ge 2$, we obtain*

$$\|e\| \le C\left(\sum_{K \in T_h} \eta_K^{\beta'}\right)^{\frac{1}{\beta}}$$

where C is independent of u and f, in this case and instead of (29), we have

$$\langle A(u) - A(v), u - v \rangle \ge \alpha \|u - v\|^\beta,$$

$\forall u, v \in W^{1,\beta}(\Omega)$.

This result also holds for stable (and unstable) mixed approximations defined on a regular triangulation.

3. Approximation of Quasi-Newtonian Stokes Problem by Finite Element Method

In reality, the comportment of fluids is more complex; this type of fluid is modeled by nonlinear operators or tensors. Let us start this part with some definitions of fluid that we will treat. The type of fluid that is more important is modeled by a nonlinear operator; the problem is the quasi-Newtonian Stokes flow. For many details on the different models and algorithms solving these problems, see [14].

3.1. Definition of Quasi-Newtonian Stokes Problem

We denote by u the velocity vector, p the pressure, σ the stress tensor, $D(u)$ the symmetric gradient of the velocity vector, and f the external forces.

Definition 1 (Quasi-Newtonian fluid)**.** *The fluid is said to be quasi-Newtonian when there exists a positive function $\mu : \mathbb{R}^+ \mapsto \mathbb{R}^+$ called the "viscosity" function, such that the stress deviator σ is expressed as*

$$\sigma = -p\mathbb{I} + 2\mu\left(|2D(u)|^2\right)D(u). \tag{31}$$

There are two classical laws of quasi-Newtonian Stokes problems, the first one is the "Carreau law viscosity" and the second one is the "power law viscosity".

Definition 2 (Carreau law viscosity)**.** *The Carreau law expresses the viscosity as*

$$\mu(s) = \mu_\infty + (\mu_0 - \mu_\infty)(1 + \lambda s)^{\frac{-1+n}{2}}, \forall s \in \mathbb{R}^+, \tag{32}$$

where $\mu_0, \mu_\infty, \lambda, n \in \mathbb{R}^{+*}$ are given real constants satisfying $\mu_0 \geq \mu_\infty$ when $n \leq 1$ and $\mu_0 \leq \mu_\infty$ when $n \geq 1$.

The Figure 1 presents Carreau law viscosity for $n < 1$ and for $n > 1$. We can see that under simplification conditions, the Carreau law viscosity can be rewritten as power law viscosity defined by

$$\mu(\zeta) = K\zeta^{\frac{-1+n}{2}}, \quad \forall \zeta \in \mathbb{R}, \tag{33}$$

where K and $n \in \mathbb{R}^{+*}$.

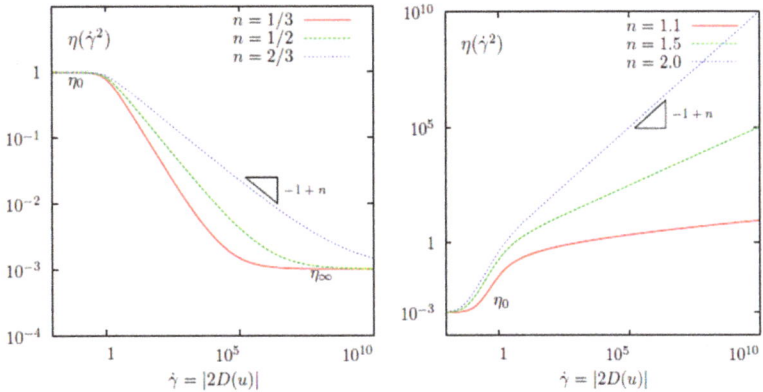

Figure 1. Quasi-Newtonian fluid flow, Carreau law viscosity for $n < 1$ (**left**) and $n > 1$ (**right**).

Note that, when $n = 1$, both the power law and Carreau law are reduced to a Newtonian fluid model with constant viscosity. When $n < 1$, the viscosity is decreasing with the shear rate and the fluid is said to be "shear thinning" or "pseudoplastic". The tensor norm and the shear rate are defined as follows (see [14], Definition 1.9 for more precise details).

Definition 3 (Tensor norm). *The following tensor norm is defined as*

$$|\tau|^2 = \frac{\tau : \tau}{2} = \frac{1}{2}\sum_{i=1}^{3}\sum_{j=1}^{3}\tau_{i,j}^2, \quad \forall \tau \in \mathbb{R}^{3\times 3}. \tag{34}$$

Definition 4 (Shear rate). *The shear rate, denoted by $\dot{\gamma}$, is defined by*

$$\dot{\gamma} = |2D(u)|.$$

Note that, the stress tensor σ in Newtonian fluid flow is "generally" defined by $\sigma = -p\mathbb{I} + 2\mu D(u)$, where μ is the fluid viscosity (a bound function).

3.2. Mathematical Problem

To simplify this study, the stationary case where the flow is incompressible remains; hence, we neglect the inertia term which will allow us to focus on the nonlinearity of results (from the viscosity law). The governing system can be written as

$$\begin{cases} -\mathrm{div}(2\mu(|2D(u)|_2)D(u)) + \nabla p = f \text{ in } \Omega, \\ \mathrm{div}\, u = 0 \text{ in } \Omega, \end{cases} \tag{35}$$

where $f \in X'$, we define the general boundary condition $C_{a,\mu}$ by

$$C_{a,\mu} : a(u)u + \left(2\mu\left(|2D(u)|^2\right)D(u) - pI\right) \cdot n = g \text{ on } \Gamma, \qquad (36)$$

where $g \in \Gamma$ and $a(u)$ are a bounded function defined in the boundary.

The existence and unique solution (u, p) of the problem (35) and (36) is defined in the product space $X \times M$ with $X = \left(H^1(\Omega)\right)^2$ and $M = L^2(\Omega)$. The operator $A = 2\mu\left(|2D(u)|^2\right)D(u) : X \mapsto X'$, appearing in (35), satisfies the following two propositions.

Proposition 10. *For all $u, v \in X$, we have*

$$\langle A(u) - A(v), u - v \rangle \geq C(u, v)\|u - v\|^2, \qquad (37)$$

where

$$C(u,v) = \left\{\alpha_1 + \alpha_2(\|u\| + \|v\|)^{2-\beta}\right\}^{-1},$$

with $\alpha_1, \alpha_2 > 0$.

Proposition 11. *For all u, v in X and all $\beta > 1$, there exists a positive constant $C > 0$ such that*

$$\|A(u) - A(v)\|_{X'} \leq C(u,v)\|u - v\|_X. \qquad (38)$$

Proof of Proposition 10 and 11. See [38]. □

It should be noted that conditions (37) and (38) are satisfied for a fluid with a power law viscosity, see, e.g., [12,39]. For the existence and uniqueness of the solution, we refer to the works [17,40] by Baranger and Najib. The variational formulation to the problem (35) and (36) is equivalent to: find $(u, p) \in X \times M$ such that

$$\begin{cases} \langle A(u), v \rangle + \langle Bv, p \rangle = \langle f, v \rangle, \\ \langle Bu, q \rangle = \langle g, q \rangle, \end{cases} \qquad (39)$$

for all $(v, q) \in X \times M$, where

$$\langle A(u), v \rangle = \int_\Omega \left(2\eta\left(|2D(u)|^2\right) : D(u)\right)D(v)dx + \int_\Gamma auvd\gamma(x), \qquad (40)$$

and

$$\langle Bv, q \rangle = \int_\Omega q \operatorname{div}(v). \qquad (41)$$

Theorem 12. *The problem (39) has a unique solution $(u, p) \in X \times M$ if and only if (40) has a unique solution and B is surjective satisfying the inf-sup condition.*

Proof. See [17,41]. □

The functional spaces X and M are Hilbert spaces, then (u, p) (resp. (U, P)) is a solution of problem (39) associated to the couple (f, g) (resp. (F, G)) such that

$$\|u - U\| + \|p - P\| \leq C(\|f - F\|_* + |g - G|_*),$$

where C is a positive constant, see [42] for more details.

We have to describe the discrete approximation problem corresponding to (39)–(41) by using notations of Section 2; to this aim, we define the finite element spaces $(X_h, M_h) \subset$

(X, M), where the discrete approximation of the quasi-Newtonian flow problem (with $C_{a,\mu}$ boundary condition) can be equivalently written as: find $(u_h, p_h) \in X_h, M_h$ such that

$$\begin{cases} \int_\Omega \left(2\mu|2D(u_h)|^2\right) D(u_h) : D(v_h) + p_h v_h d + \int_\Gamma \alpha u_h v_h d\gamma = \int_\Omega fv dx + \int_\Gamma gv_h d\gamma, x \\ \int_\Omega q_h \operatorname{div} u_h \, dx = 0, \end{cases} \qquad (42)$$

for all $(v_h, q_h) \in X_h \times M_h$.

Under properties (3.2) and (3.2), and assuming the inf-sup condition is satisfied in the discrete approximation problem (42), we obtain one solution, $(u_h, p_h) \in X_h \times M_h$.

3.3. A Posteriori Error Estimator

A posteriori error indicator and residual error for quasi-Newtonian problems with Dirichlet and Newman boundary conditions are developed in these papers [17,24,35]. Based on these results, one can adapt their estimates to the case of our problem (42); by using the notation $\mu_h = 2\mu|2D(u_h)|^2$, we get

$$\langle R, v \rangle = \sum_{K \in T_h} \int_K \operatorname{div}\left(2\mu|2D(u_h)|^2\right) D(u_h) D(v) - \sum_{K \in T_h} \int_K p_h \operatorname{div} v - \sum_{K \in T_h} \int_K fv + \sum_{K \in T_h} \int_{\partial K \cap \Gamma} \alpha u_h v + \sum_{K \in T_h} \int_{\partial K \cap \Gamma} gv. \quad (43)$$

From Green's formula, and for any element K, we obtain

$$\begin{aligned} \langle R, v \rangle &= \sum_{K \in T_h} \left(\int_K (A(u_h) + \nabla p_h - f)v + \int_{\partial K} (\mu_h D(u_h)n - p_h n)v + \int_{\partial K \cap \Gamma} \alpha u_h v + \int_{\partial K \cap \Gamma} gv \right) \\ &= \sum_{K \in T_h} \left(\int_K (A(u_h) + \nabla p_h - f)v + \int_{\partial K} (\mu_h D(u_h)n - p_h n)v + \int_{\partial K \cap \Gamma} \alpha u_h v + (\mu_h D(u_h)n - p_h n)v - gv \right) \\ &= \sum_{K \in T_h} \left(\int_K (A(u_h) + \nabla p_h - f)v + \sum_{l \in \varepsilon_h} \int_l (\mu_h D(u_h)n - p_h n)v + \sum_{l \in \varepsilon_\Gamma} \int_l \alpha u_h v + (\mu_h D(u_h)n - p_h n)v - gv \right) \end{aligned}$$

where ε_Γ is the set of all edges of all elements T_h divided into interior and exterior edges $\varepsilon_h = \varepsilon_{h,\Gamma} \cup \varepsilon_{h,\Omega}$ with $\varepsilon_{h,\Omega} = \{E \in \varepsilon_h : E \subset \Omega\}$ and $\varepsilon_{h,\Gamma} = \{E \in \varepsilon_h : E \subset \Gamma\}$. As $\langle R, v_h \rangle = 0$ for all $v_h \in X_h$, and for $v_h = \pi_h v$, we get

$$\begin{aligned} \langle R, v \rangle = \langle R, v - \pi_h v \rangle &= \sum_{K \in T_h} \int_K (A(u_h) + \nabla p_h - f)(v - \pi_h v) \\ &+ \sum_{l \in \varepsilon_h} \int_l (\mu_h D(u_h)n - p_h n)(v - \pi_h v) \\ &+ \sum_{l \in \varepsilon_\Gamma} \int_l (\alpha u_h + (\mu_h D(u_h)n - p_h n) - g)(v - \pi_h v). \end{aligned} \qquad (44)$$

Hence

$$\langle R, v \rangle \le \sum_{K \in T_h} |A(u_h) + \nabla p_h - f|_{0,K} |v - \pi_h v|_{0,K} + \sum_{l \in \varepsilon_h} |\mu_h D(u_h)n - p_h n|_{0,l} |v - \pi_h v|_{0,l} \\ + \sum_{l \in \varepsilon_\Gamma} |\alpha u_h + (\mu_h D(u_h)n - p_h n) - g|_{0,l} |v - \pi_h v|_{0,l}. \qquad (45)$$

In order to deal with the three terms of the right-hand side, we write

$$\sum_{K \in T_h} |A(u_h) + \nabla p_h - f|_{0,K} |v - \pi_h v|_{0,K} \le \left(\sum_{K \in T_h} h_K^2 |A(u_h) + \nabla p_h - f|_{0,K}^2 \right)^{\frac{1}{2}} \left(\sum_{K \in T_h} h_K^{-2} |v - \pi_h v|_{0,K}^2 \right)^{\frac{1}{2}} \qquad (46)$$

we use Lemma 3 (when $m = 0$) to obtain

$$\sum_{K \in T_h} |A(u_h) + \nabla p_h - f|_{0,K} |v - \pi_h v|_{0,K} \leq \left(\sum_{K \in T_h} h_K^2 |A(u_h) + \nabla p_h - f|_{0,K}^2 \right)^{\frac{1}{2}} \|v\|. \quad (47)$$

Defining the vector s

$$s = |\mu_h D(u_h) n - p_h n|_{0,l} = |[\sigma(u_h, p_h) n]_l|_{0,l} = |[\sigma^h n]_l|_{0,l},$$

the second term of the right-hand side is rewritten as

$$\sum_{l \in \varepsilon_h} s |v - \pi_h v|_{0,l} \leq \left(\sum_{l \in \varepsilon_h} h_l |s|^2 \right)^{\frac{1}{2}} \left(\sum_{l \in \varepsilon_h} h_l^{-1} |v - \pi_h v|_{0,l}^2 \right)^{\frac{1}{2}}. \quad (48)$$

Observe that

$$\left(\sum_{K \in T_h} \sum_{l \in \varepsilon_h} h_l^{-1} |v - \pi_h v|_{0,l}^2 \right)^{\frac{1}{2}} \leq \left(\sum_{K \in T_h} C h_K^{-1} |v - \pi_h v|_{0,l}^2 \right)^{\frac{1}{2}}$$

$$= C \left(\sum_{K \in T_h} h_K^{-1} |v - \pi_h v|_{0,l}^2 \right)^{\frac{1}{2}}, \quad (49)$$

then, one can use lemma 3 (with $\beta = 2$) to get

$$\left(\sum_{K \in T_h} \sum_{l \in \varepsilon_h} h_l^{-1} |v - \pi_h v|_{0,l}^2 \right)^{\frac{1}{2}} \leq C \left(\sum_{K \in T_h} h_K^{-2} |v - \pi_h v|_{0,K}^2 + \sum_{K \in T_h} h_K^2 |v - \pi_h v|_{1,K}^2 \right)^{\frac{1}{2}}$$

$$\leq C \left(\sum_{K \in T_h} |v|_{1,K}^2 \right)^{\frac{1}{2}} = C \|v\|. \quad (50)$$

Thus, the second term of (45) is increased by

$$C \left(\sum_{l \in \varepsilon_h} |[\sigma(u_h, p_h) n]_l|_{0,l}^2 \right)^{\frac{1}{2}} \|v\|.$$

To treat the last term of (45), we write §

$$\sum_{l \in \varepsilon_h} |\alpha u_h + s - g|_{0,l} |v - \pi_h v|_{0,l} \leq \left(\sum_{l \in \varepsilon_h} h_l |\alpha u_h + s - g|^2 \right)^{\frac{1}{2}} \left(\sum_{l \in \varepsilon_h} h_l^{-1} |v - \pi_h v|_{0,l}^2 \right)^{\frac{1}{2}},$$

by using lemma 3 and (50), the last term of (45) is increased by

$$C \left(\sum_{l \in \varepsilon_h} |[(\alpha u_h + \sigma(u_h, p_h) - g) n]_l|_{0,l}^2 \right)^{\frac{1}{2}} \|v\|. \quad (51)$$

Finally, we conclude

$$\langle R, v \rangle \leq C \left(\sum_{K \in T_h} h_K^2 |A(u_h) + \nabla p_h - f|_{0,K}^2 \right)^{\frac{1}{2}} \|v\| + C \left(\sum_{l \in \varepsilon_h} |[\sigma(u_h, p_h) n]_l|_{0,l}^2 \right)^{\frac{1}{2}} \|v\|$$

$$+ C \left(\sum_{l \in \varepsilon_h} |[(\alpha u_h + \sigma(u_h, p_h) - g) n]_l|_{0,l}^2 \right)^{\frac{1}{2}} \|v\|, \quad (52)$$

where

$$\|R\|_* \leq C\left(\sum_{K\in T_h} h_K^2 |A(u_h) + \nabla p_h - f|_{0,K}^2\right)^{\frac{1}{2}} + C\left(\sum_{l\in\varepsilon_h} |[\sigma(u_h,p_h)n]_l|_{0,l}^2\right)^{\frac{1}{2}} \qquad (53)$$

$$+ C\left(\sum_{l\in\varepsilon_h} |[(\alpha u_h + \sigma(u_h,p_h)) - g)n]_l|_{0,l}^2\right)^{\frac{1}{2}}.$$

Finally, from (47), (50), and (51) we obtain the following result:

Theorem 13. *There exists a constant C (independent of h) such that*

$$\|u - u_h\| + \|p - p_h\| \leq C\left(\sum_{K\in T_h} \eta(K)^2\right)^{\frac{1}{2}} \qquad (54)$$

where

$$\eta(K) = h_K^2 |A(u_h) + \nabla p_h - f|_{0,K}^2 + \sum_{l\in\varepsilon_h \cap K} |[\sigma(u_h,p_h)n]_l|_{0,l}^2$$
$$+ \sum_{l\in\varepsilon_\Gamma \cap K} |[(\alpha u_h + \sigma(u_h,p_h)) - g)n]_l|_{0,l}^2 + |\mathrm{div}\, u_h|_{0,K}^2. \qquad (55)$$

Proof of Theorem 13. A direct consequence of these inequalities (43) to (53). □

Remark. *For more complex models where the dependence of the viscosity with respect to the second invariant is more strongly nonlinear (for example Carreau law with $\mu_\infty = 0$ or power law), we should use both methods of Sections 2 and 3 and a nonlinear version of Theorem 3.3, in [43].*

These systems are written as a big matrix (his component is nonlinear). In these simulations, we used the GMRES (GMRES is a generalized minimal residual algorithm applied to solve nonsymmetric linear systems, see [31,41,42] for more details.) algorithm to accelerate simulation.

4. Numerical Simulations

To conclude this paper, and in order to see the performance of the finite element method for the nonlinear equations, two different numerical simulations are represented: the first one uses the finite element software package "IFISS toolbox " (IFISS software library is an algorithm executed under MATLAB for the interactive numerical study of differential equations for incompressible flow problems) to solve the Navier–Stokes equations with different rectangular discretization sizes of meshes (16×16, 32×32, 64×64, 128×128, 256×256) and multiple elements (Q_1–Q_1, Q_1–P_0, Q_2–Q_1 and Q_2–P_1); while the second one, uses the engineering simulation software "COMSOL Multiphysics software (COMSOL Multiphysics is a cross-platform finite element analysis, solver, and multi-physics simulation software. It allows conventional physics-based user interfaces and coupled systems of partial differential equations (PDEs)". Inspired by the model defined in this paper [44] (applied in a porous media), we consider a "nonlinear Brinkman equation" with an inhomogeneous boundary condition, where the change of the parameter represents the change of the velocity field u and the pressure p in a different figure.

4.1. Fist Experience

We consider a Poiseuille (the Poiseuille flow problem is a steady horizontal flow in a channel driven by a pressure difference between the two ends) channel flow solution with an analytic solution of the Navier–Stokes equations as $u = (1 - y^2, 0)$ and $p = -2\nu x$, see [45,46] for more details. Where the boundary conditions are of Dirichlet or Neumann type on all the boundary—the inflow boundary is considered in the part $[x = -1, -1 < y < 1]$—a no-flow Dirichlet condition, $u = 0$, is applied on the characteristic boundaries $y = \{-1, 1\}$ and an outflow condition is considered in the rest of the boundary (i.e., $[x = 1, -1 < y < 1]$). Figures 2–5 represent the uniform streamline and the pressure associated with, respectively, 16×16 and 256×256 in cases Q_1–Q_1, Q_1–P_0, Q_2–Q_1 and Q_2–P_1 mixed approximation.

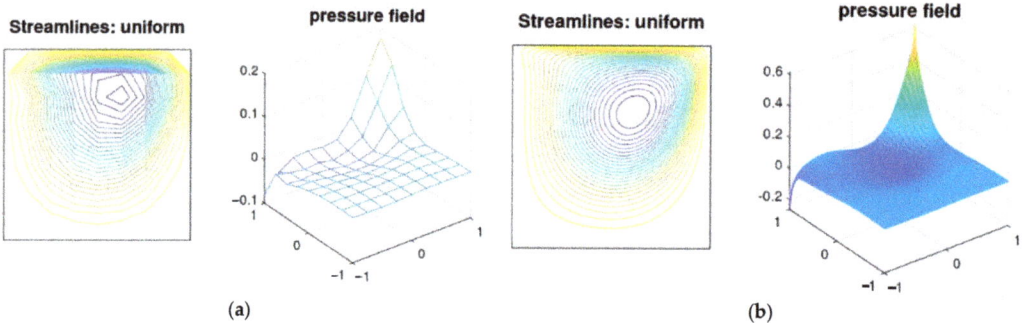

Figure 2. Equally distributed streamline plot associated with a 16×16 and 256×256 square grid, Q_1–Q_1 approximation. (**a**) 16×16 elements; (**b**) 256×256 elements.

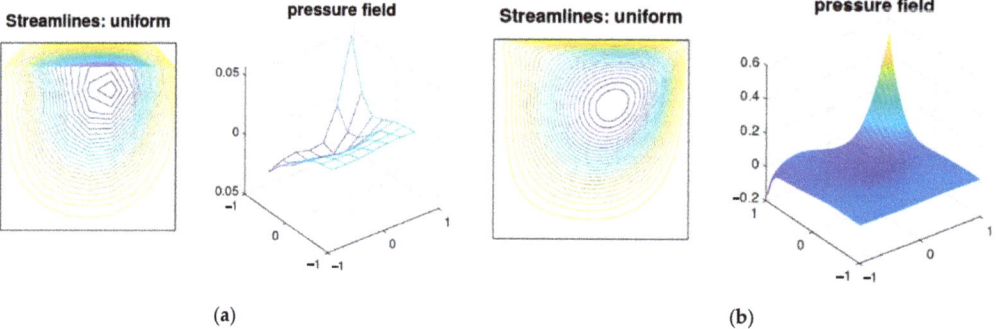

Figure 3. Equally distributed streamline plot associated with a 16×16 and 256×256 square grid, Q_1–P_0 approximation. (**a**) 16×16 elements; (**b**) 256×256 elements.

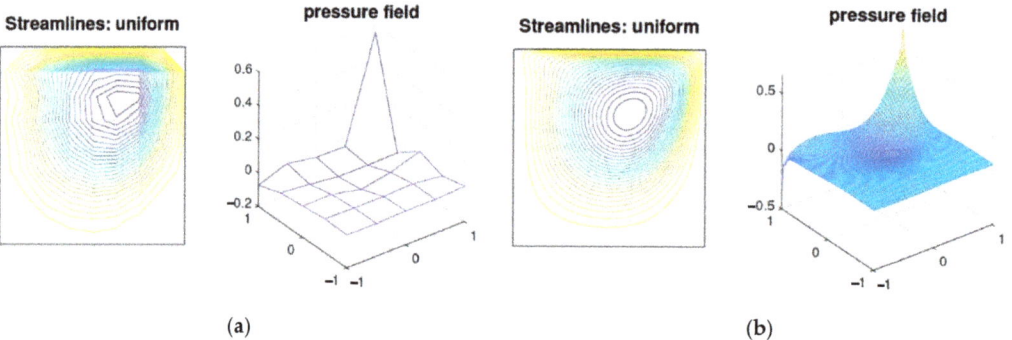

Figure 4. Equally distributed streamline plot associated with a 16×16 and 256×256 square grid, Q_2–Q_1 approximation. (**a**) 16×16 elements; (**b**) 256×256 elements.

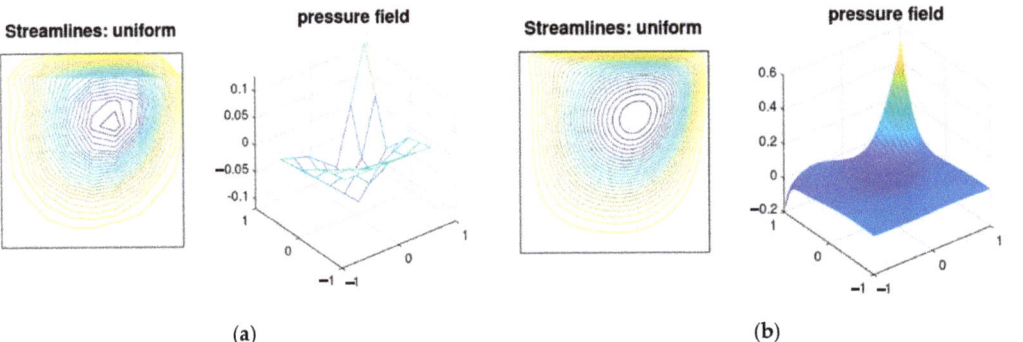

Figure 5. Equally distributed streamline plot associated with a 16×16 and 256×256 square grid, Q_2–P_1 approximation. (**a**) 16×16 elements; (**b**) 256×256 elements.

Figures 6–9 represent the errors, associated with a 16×16 and a 256×256 uniform square grid with a different element, Q_1–Q_1, Q_1–P_0, Q_2–Q_1, and Q_2–P_1.

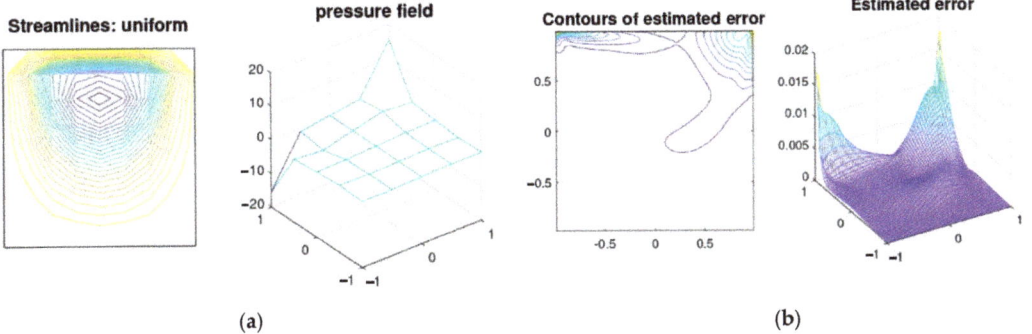

Figure 6. Error associated with a 16×16 and a 256×256 square grid, Q_1–Q_1 approximation. (**a**) 16×16 elements; (**b**) 256×256 elements.

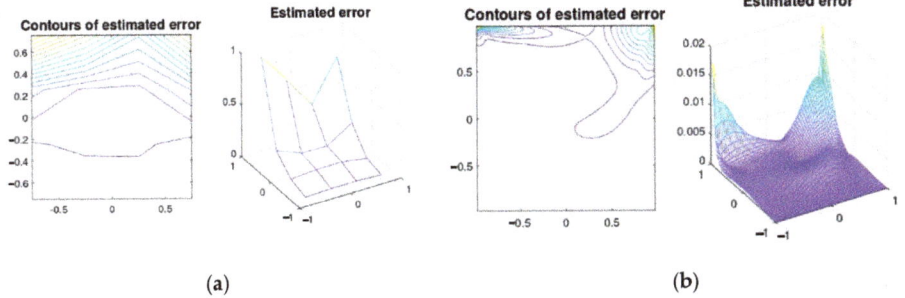

Figure 7. Error associated with a 16×16 and a 256×256 square grid, Q_1–P_0 approximation. (**a**) 16×16 elements; (**b**) 256×256 elements.

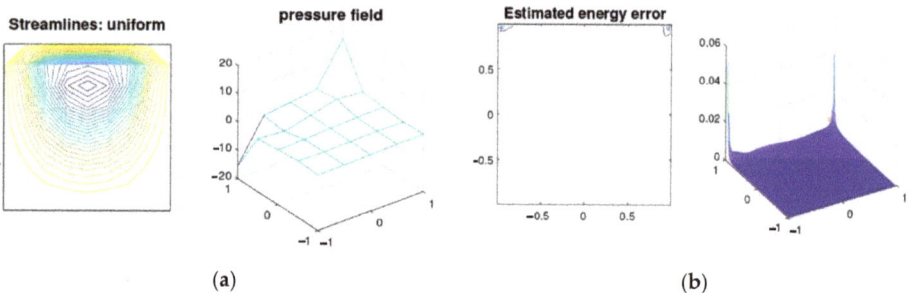

(a)   (b)

Figure 8. Error associated with a 16 × 16 and a 256 × 256 square grid, Q_2–Q_1 approximation. (**a**) 16 × 16 elements; (**b**) 256 × 256 elements.

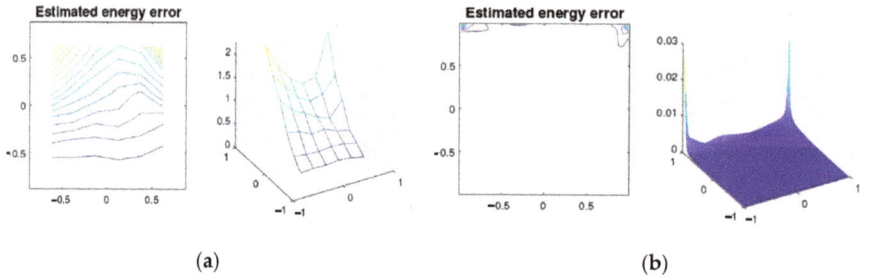

(a)   (b)

Figure 9. Error associated with a 16 × 16 and a 256 × 256 square grid, Q_2–P_1 approximation. (**a**) 16 × 16 elements; (**b**) 256 × 256 elements.

In the previous figures, we can notice that the results are well-presented if we take the mesh to be very small.

Table 1 represents the residual error estimator η, the estimated velocity divergence error $\|\nabla \cdot \overleftarrow{u}_h\|_{0,\Omega}$, and the Stokes solution residual η_S for difference discretization (16 × 16, 32 × 32, 64 × 64, 128 × 128, and 256 × 256) in these elements, cases Q_1–Q_1, Q_1–P_0, Q_2–Q_1 and Q_2–P_1 mixed approximations.

Table 1. Residual error estimator, estimated velocity divergence error, and Stokes solution residual for 16 × 16, 32 × 32, 64 × 64, 128 × 128, and 256 × 256.

Elements	Errors	Number of Girds				
		16 × 16	32 × 32	64 × 64	128 × 128	256 × 256
Q_1–Q_1	η	5.86×10^0	1.34×10^0	9.99×10^{-1}	8.38×10^{-1}	2.37×10^{-1}
	$\|\nabla \cdot \overleftarrow{u}_h\|_{0,\Omega}$	8.77×10^{-2}	2.22×10^{-2}	5.65×10^{-3}	1.47×10^{-3}	3.92×10^{-4}
	η_S	4.22×10^0	1.75×10^0	9.43×10^{-1}	5.58×10^{-1}	3.26×10^{-1}
Q_1–P_0	η	5.98×10^0	1.90×10^0	1.28×10^0	9.93×10^{-1}	2.47×10^{-1}
	$\|\nabla \cdot \overleftarrow{u}_h\|_{0,\Omega}$	1.29×10^{-1}	4.09×10^{-2}	1.35×10^{-2}	7.39×10^{-3}	1.00×10^{-3}
	η_S	1.11×10^1	3.90×10^0	1.45×10^0	1.65×10^0	3.51×10^{-1}
Q_2–Q_1	η	5.36×10^0	2.05×10^0	6.09×10^{-1}	2.25×10^{-1}	1.02×10^{-1}
	$\|\nabla \cdot \overleftarrow{u}_h\|_{0,\Omega}$	1.05×10^{-1}	3.23×10^{-2}	6.06×10^{-3}	1.31×10^{-3}	3.2×10^{-4}
	η_S	3.24×10^0	2.14×10^0	1.30×10^0	7.61×10^{-1}	4.29×10^{-1}
Q_2–P_1	η	5.36×10^0	1.67×10^0	4.92×10^{-1}	1.55×10^{-1}	6.14×10^{-2}
	$\|\nabla \cdot \overleftarrow{u}_h\|_{0,\Omega}$	1.07×10^{-1}	1.28×10^0	5.25×10^{-3}	1.23×10^{-3}	3.03×10^{-4}
	η_S	2.70×10^0	6.09×10^{-1}	1.21×10^0	7.18×10^{-1}	4.09×10^{-1}

A good way to explore the capabilities of this method is to see the convergence time. Table 2 presents the solve time of finite element methods with different discretization and elements.

Table 2. Solve time of finite element methods for 16×16, 32×32, 64×64, 128×128, and 256×256.

Elements	16×16	32×32	64×64	128×128	256×256
Q_1-Q_1	1.71×10^{-1} s	2.08×10^{-1} s	8.75×10^{-1} s	3.78×10^{0} s	1.99×10^{1} s
Q_1-P_0	8.24×10^{-2} s	3.58×10^{-1} s	3.69×10^{-1} s	5.53×10^{0} s	2.42×10^{1} s
Q_2-Q_1	3.19×10^{-2} s	1.88×10^{-1} s	1.30×10^{0} s	6.55×10^{0} s	2.66×10^{1} s
Q_2-P_1	1.69×10^{-1} s	1.88×10^{0} s	5.33×10^{0} s	3.25×10^{1} s	5.66×10^{1} s

4.2. Second Experience

The second experience comes from the second example (pore–scale flow experiments) defined by Sirivithayapakorn and Keller in [44] to model the transport of colloids in saturated porous media, and by Auset and Keller in [47] to control the dispersion of colloids. Inspired by the same model examples, and considering the new boundary conditions, the domain covers [0.640 µm × 0.320 µm], see Figure 10. The flow in the pores does not penetrate the solid grains and the inlet fluid pressure is known as $p = 0.715\ Pa$, see Figure 10, and assumes that the boundary is changed at the outlet. Top and bottom boundaries are modeled by $\alpha(u)u + (-pI + K) \cdot n = f$, where the change of the parameter $\alpha(u)$ represents the change of the velocity field and the pressure in the figures. The primary zone of interest is the rectangular region with an upper-left corner at $(0,0)$ and lower-right coordinates at [581.6 µm × 265.0 µm].

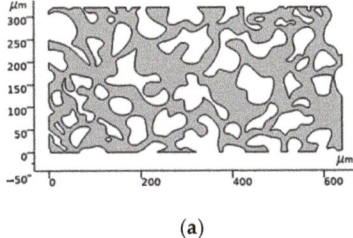
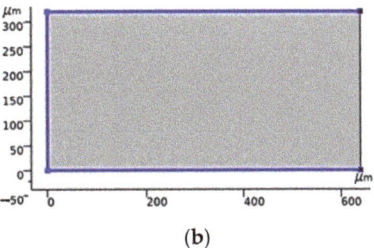

(a)   (b)

Figure 10. Geometry and boundary conditions of the reservoir (the color code is blue for 0 and red for 1). (**a**) Geometry of the reservoir; (**b**) boundary conditions of the reservoir.

Instead of solving for the creeping flow in the channels, the incompressible, stationary Brinkman equations are used, with the Stokes—Brinkman assumptions used next. Figure 11 shows the reservoir and localization of the boundary conditions. Figures 11 and 12 represent the velocity and pressure of the model defined for these simulations. We use the finite element method to approach the unknown functions (pressure and velocity), change the value of μ in the boundary condition to see the comportment of the fluid in the reservoir, and take the two cases $\mu \gg 1$ and $\mu \ll 1$.

In this simulation, we can see the difference between Figures 11 and 12: the distribution of the lines is modified when the parameter is changed. For this, in modeling the linear or nonlinear problems, we can count on this boundary condition, i.e., we can treat complex boundary conditions. This method, "the finite element method", remains valid in our case to solve these types of problems.

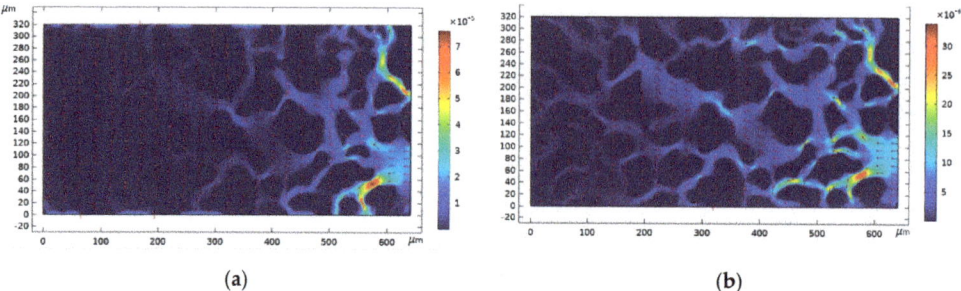

Figure 11. The velocity field calculated by the Brinkman equations. (**a**) $\mu = 10^{-3}$; (**b**) $\mu = 10^{6}$.

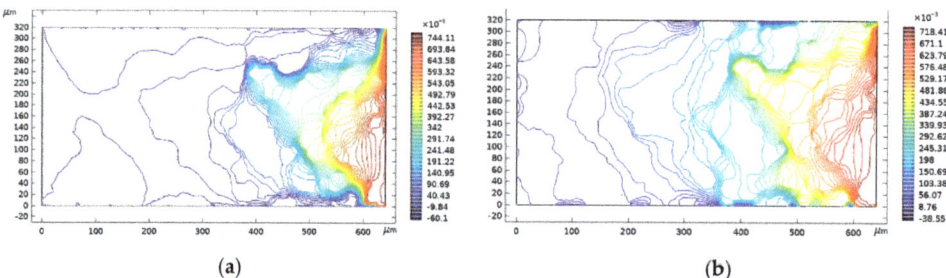

Figure 12. The pressure calculated by the Brinkman equations. (**a**) $\mu = 10^{-3}$; (**b**) $\mu = 10^{6}$.

5. Conclusions & Perspectives

In this paper, we studied two nonlinear differential equations, the "p-Laplacian" problem and the "Quasi-Newtonian Stokes" problem. This model is applied in many domains, for example in fluid mechanics, and we approach these models with a general boundary condition using the finite element method (FEM). For the theoretical study, we introduced the a posteriori error indicator to control the errors. The performance of this method is presented via different numerical simulations. From these perspectives, we can apply the $P1/P1$ Bubble method to approach this model for the study of the element, see [48] for a linear Brinkman model. Another problem that we can treat is to couple this model (quasi-Newtonian Stokes problem (35)) with Darcy's law, see [49] for how the authors use the finite element methods to approach the coupled Darcy—Stokes problem. Another model which we can choose for permeability is a tensor in the equation and in the boundary condition for the quasi-Newtonian Stokes problem in (35) and (36) (i.e., we can choose a more complex model), see for example [50–53] applied to the linear model.

Author Contributions: Conceptualization, O.E.M., L.E.O., A.E.A. and A.E.; Methodology, O.E.M., L.E.O., A.E.A., N.N., M.L.S. and S.V.; Software, N.N.; Validation, O.E.M., A.E.A., A.E and S.V.; Formal analysis, L.E.O., A.E., M.L.S. and S.V.; Investigation, O.E.M., L.E.O., A.E.A., N.N. and A.E.; Resources, O.E.M. and A.E.A.; Data curation, L.E.O., N.N. and A.E.; Writing—original draft, O.E.M., L.E.O. and A.E.; Writing—review & editing, A.E.A., M.L.S. and S.V.; Visualization, M.L.S. and S.V.; Supervision, A.E.A.; Project administration, O.E.M., A.E. and M.L.S.; Funding acquisition, S.V. All authors have read and agreed to the published version of the manuscript.

Funding: The APC was founded by Transilvania University of Brasov.

Data Availability Statement: Not applicable.

Acknowledgments: Finally, the authors would like to thank all the authors in the bibliography who allow us to do this work.

Conflicts of Interest: The authors declare no conflict of interest.

References

1. Babuka, I.; Strouboulis, T.; Upadhyay, C.S.; Gangaraj, S.K.; Copps, K. Validation of a-posteriori error estimators by numerical approach. *Int. J. Numer. Methods Eng.* **1994**, *37*, 1073–1123. [CrossRef]
2. Zhu, J.Z. A-posteriori error estimation-the relationship between different procedures. *Comput. Methods Appl. Mech. Eng.* **1997**, *150*, 411–422. [CrossRef]
3. Baker, T.J. Mesh adaptation strategies for problems in fluid dynamics. *Finite Elem. Anal. Des.* **1997**, *25*, 243–273. [CrossRef]
4. Greve, R.; Blatter, H. *Dynamics of Ice Sheets and Glaciers*; Springer: Berlin/Heidelberg, Germany, 2009.
5. Pralong, A.; Funk, M. A level-set method for modeling the evolution of glacier geometry. *J. Glaciol.* **2004**, *50*, 485–491. [CrossRef]
6. Pralong, A.; Funk, M. Dynamic damage model of crevasse opening and application to glacier calving. *J. Geophys.* **2005**, *110*, B01309. [CrossRef]
7. Abraham, F.; Behr, M.; Heinkenschloss, M. Shape optimization in unsteady blood flow: A numerical study of non-Newtonian effects. *Comput. Meth. Biomech. Biomed.* **2005**, *8*, 201–212. [CrossRef] [PubMed]
8. Baranger, J.; Sandri, D. Finite element approximation of viscoelastic fluid flow: Existence of approximate solutions and error bounds Part I. discontinuous constraints. *Numer. Math.* **1992**, *63*, 13–27. [CrossRef]
9. Carreau, P.J.; MacDonald, I.F.; Bird, R.B. A nonlinear viscoelastic model for polymer solutions and melts (II). *Chem. Eng. Sci* **1968**, *23*, 901–911. [CrossRef]
10. Yasuda, K.Y.; Armstrong, R.C.; Cohen, R.E. Shear flow properties of concentrated solutions of linear and star branched polystyrenes. *Rheol. Acta* **1981**, *20*, 163–178. [CrossRef]
11. Cross, M.M. Rheology of non-Newtonian fluids: A new flow equation for pseudoplastic systems. *J. Colloid Sci.* **1965**, *20*, 417–437. [CrossRef]
12. Glowinski, R.; Marrocco, A. Sur l'approximation par éléments finis d'ordre 1 et la résolution par pénalisation-dualité d'une classe de problèmes de Dirichlet non linéaires. *RAIRO Anal. Numérique* **1975**, *R–2*, 41–76. [CrossRef]
13. Ciarlet, P.G. *The Finite Element Method for Elliptic Problems*; SIAM Society for Industrial and Applied Mathematics: Philadelphia, PA, USA, 1978.
14. Saramito, P. *Complex Fluids Modeling and Algorithms*; Springer: Cham, Swtzerland, 2016.
15. Droniou, J. Finite volume schemes for fully non-linear elliptic equations in divergence form. *ESAIM Math. Model. Numer. Anal.* **2006**, *40*, 1069–1100. [CrossRef]
16. Di Pietro, D.A.; Droniou, J. A hybrid high-order method for Leray-Lions elliptic equations on general meshes. *Math. Comp.* **2017**, *86*, 2159–2191. [CrossRef]
17. Atkinson, C.; Jones, C.W. Similarity solutions in some non-linear diffusion problems and in boundary-layer flow of a pseudo-plastic fluid. *Quart. J. Mech. Appl. Math.* **1974**, *27*, 193–211. [CrossRef]
18. Bank, R.E.; Weiser, A. Some a posteriori error estimators for elliptic partial differential equations. *Math. Comput.* **1985**, *44*, 283–301. [CrossRef]
19. Barrett, J.W.; Liu, W.B. Finite element approximation of the parabolic p-Laplacian. *SIAM J. Numer. Anal.* **1994**, *31*, 413–428. [CrossRef]
20. Liu, W.B.; Barrett, J.W. A remark on the regularity of the solutions of the p-Laplacian and its application to their finite element approximation. *J. Math. Anal. Appl.* **1993**, *178*, 470–487. [CrossRef]
21. Liu, W.B.; Barrett, J.W. A further remark on the regularity of the solutions of the p-Laplacian and its applications to their finite element approximation. *Nonlinear Anal.* **1993**, *21*, 379–387. [CrossRef]
22. Barrett, J.W.; Liu, W.B. Finite element approximation of the p-Laplacian. *Math. Comput.* **1993**, *61*, 523–537. [CrossRef]
23. Philip, J.R. N-diffusion. *Aust. J. Phys.* **1961**, *14*, 1–13. [CrossRef]
24. Baranger, J.; El Amri, H. Estimateurs a posteriori d'erreurs pour le calcul adaptatif d'écoulements Quasi-newtoniens. *RAIRO Modél. Math. Anal. Numér.* **1991**, *25*, 31–48. [CrossRef]
25. Bi, C.; Wang, C.; Lin, Y. A posteriori error estimates of hp-discontinuous Galerkin method for strongly nonlinear elliptic problems. *Comput. Methods Appl. Mech. Eng.* **2015**, *297*, 140–166. [CrossRef]
26. Liu, W.; Yan, N. Quasi-norm local error estimators for p-Laplacian. *SIAM J. Numer. Anal.* **2001**, *39*, 100–127. [CrossRef]
27. Liu, W.; Yan, N. On quasi-norm interpolation error estimation and a posteriori error estimates for p-Laplacian. *SIAM J. Numer. Anal.* **2002**, *40*, 1870–1895. [CrossRef]
28. Verfürth, R. A posteriori error estimates for nonlinear problems, Finite element discretizations of elliptic equations. *Math. Comput.* **1994**, *62*, 445–475. [CrossRef]
29. Verfürth, R. A posteriori error estimates for nonlinear problems. Finite element discretizations of elliptic equations. *ESAIM Math. Model. Numer. Anal.* **1998**, *32*, 817–842. [CrossRef]
30. Veeser, A. Convergent adaptive finite elements for the nonlinear Laplacian. *Numer. Math.* **2002**, *92*, 743–770. [CrossRef]
31. Carstensen, C.; Liu, W.; Yan, N. A posteriori FE error control for p-Laplacian by gradient recovery in quasi-norm. *Math. Comput.* **2006**, *75*, 1599–1616. [CrossRef]
32. Endtmayer, B.; Langer, U.; Wick, T. Multigoal-oriented error estimates for non-linear problems. *J. Numer. Math.* **2019**, *27*, 215–236. [CrossRef]
33. EL-Moutea, O.; EL-Amri, H.; EL-Akkad, A. Mixed finite element method for flow of fluid in complex porous media with a new boundary condition. *Comput. Sci.* **2020**, *15*, 413–431.

34. EL-Moutea, O.; EL-Amri, H. Combined Mixed Finite Element and Nonconforming Finite Volume Methods For Flow And Transport In Porous Media. *Analysis* **2021**, *41*, 123–144. [CrossRef]
35. Barrett, J.W.; Liu, W.B. Quasi-norm error bounds for the finite element approximation of a non-Newtonian flow. *Numer. Math.* **1994**, *68*, 437–456. [CrossRef]
36. Glowinski, R.; Rappaz, J. Approximation of a nonlinear elliptic problem arising in a non-Newtonian fluid flow model in glaciology. *M2AN Math. Model. Numer. Anal.* **2003**, *37*, 175–186. [CrossRef]
37. Dautray, R.; Lions, J.L. *Mathematical Analysis and Numerical Methods for Science and Technology*; Springer: Berlin/Heidelberg, Germany, 2000.
38. Georget, P. Contribution à L'étude des Equations de Stokes à Viscosité Variable. Ph.D. Thesis, Université de Lyon I, Saint-Étienne, France, 1985.
39. Oden, J.T. *Qualitative Methods in Nonlinear Mechanics*; Prentice Hall, Inc. Englewood Cliffs: Hoboken, NJ, USA, 1986.
40. Najib, K. Analyse Numérique de Modèles d'Écoulements Quasi-Newtoniens. Ph.D. Thesis, Université de Lyon I, Saint-Étienne, France, 1988.
41. Barreet, J.W.; Liu, W.B. Finite element error analysis of a Quasi-Newtonian flow obeying the Carreau or power law. *Numer. Math.* **1993**, *64*, 433–453. [CrossRef]
42. Scheurer, B. Existence et approximation de points selles pour certains problèmes non linéaires. *RAIRO Anal. Numérique* **1977**, *11*, 369–400. [CrossRef]
43. Baranger, J.; El Amri, H. A posteriori error estimators for mixed finite element approximation of some Quasi-newtonian flows. In Proceedings of the an Innovative Finite Element Methods 1989, Rio de Janeiro, Brazil, 27 November–1 December 1989.
44. Sirivithayapakorn, S.; Keller, A. Transport of Colloids in Saturated Porous Media: A Pore-scale Observation of the Size Exclusion Effect and Colloid Acceleration. *Water Resour. Res.* **2003**, *39*, 1109. [CrossRef]
45. Elman, H.C.; Ramage, A.; Silvester, D.J. Algorithm 866: IFISS, a Matlab toolbox for modelling incompressible flow. *ACM Trans. Math. Softw. TOMS* **2007**, *33*, 14-es. [CrossRef]
46. Silvester, D.; Elman, H.; Ramage, A. *Incompressible Flow and Iterative Solver Software (IFISS), Version 3.2*; University of Manchester: Manchester, UK, 2012.
47. Auset, M.; Keller, A. Pore-scale Processes that Control Dispersion of Colloids in Saturated Porous Media. *Water Resour.* **2004**, *40*, W03503. [CrossRef]
48. El Ouadefli, L.; El Akkad, A.; El Moutea, O.; Moustabchir, H.; Elkhalfi, A.; Luminița Scutaru, M.; Muntean, R. Numerical simulation for Brinkman system with varied permeability tensor. *Mathematics* **2022**, *10*, 3242. [CrossRef]
49. EL Moutea, O.; EL Amri, H.; EL Akkad, A. Finite Element Method for the Stokes–Darcy Problem with a New Boundary Condition. *Numer. Anal. Appl.* **2020**, *13*, 136–151. [CrossRef]
50. Elakkad, A.; Elkhalfi, A.; Guessous, N. An a posteriori error estimate for mixed finite element approximations of the Navier-Stokes equations. *J. Korean Math. Soc.* **2011**, *48*, 529–550. [CrossRef]
51. El Fakkoussi, S.; Moustabchir, H.; Elkhalfi, A.; Pruncu, C.I. Computation of the stress intensity factor KI for external longitudinal semi-elliptic cracks in the pipelines by FEM and XFEM methods. *Int. J. Interact. Des. Manuf.* **2019**, *13*, 545–555. [CrossRef]
52. Koubaiti, O.; Elkhalfi, A.; El-Mekkaoui, J.; Mastorakis, N. Solving the problem of constraints due to Dirichlet boundary conditions in the context of the mini element method. *Int. J. Mech.* **2020**, *14*, 12–22.
53. Montassir, S.; Yakoubi, K.; Moustabchir, H.; Elkhalfi, A.; Rajak, D.; Pruncu, C. Analysis of crack behaviour in pipeline system using FAD diagram based on numerical simulation under XFEM. *Appl. Sci.* **2020**, *10*, 6329. [CrossRef]

Disclaimer/Publisher's Note: The statements, opinions and data contained in all publications are solely those of the individual author(s) and contributor(s) and not of MDPI and/or the editor(s). MDPI and/or the editor(s) disclaim responsibility for any injury to people or property resulting from any ideas, methods, instructions or products referred to in the content.

Article

Mathematical Model for Fault Handling of Singular Nonlinear Time-Varying Delay Systems Based on T-S Fuzzy Model

Jianing Cao and Hua Chen *

College of Science, China University of Petroleum (East China), Qingdao 266580, China; 2009010413@s.upc.edu.cn
* Correspondence: chenhua@upc.edu.cn

Abstract: In this paper, a mathematical model based on the T-S fuzzy model is proposed to solve the fault estimation (FE) and fault-tolerant control (FTC) problem for singular nonlinear time-varying delay (TVD) systems with sensor fault. TVD is is extremely difficult to solve and the Laplace transform is devised to build an equal system free of TVD. Additionally, the sensor fault is changed to actuator fault by the developed coordinate transformation. A fuzzy learning fault estimator is first built to estimate the detailed sensor fault information. Then, a PI FTC scheme is suggested aiming at minimizing the damage caused by the fault. Simulation results from multiple faults reveal that the FE and FTC algorithms are able to estimate the fault and guarantee the system performance properly.

Keywords: T-S fuzzy model; time-varying delay; singular systems; sensor fault; FE; FTC

MSC: 93C10; 93C42; 93C43

1. Introduction

Singular systems, also known as generalized systems, are more complex systems than general systems, consisting of faster-changing differential systems and slower-changing algebraic equations [1–3]. There are still many unsolved problems waiting to be studied, and the study of singular systems is very meaningful. The stability analysis and PD controller design methods for nonlinear singular systems are given in [4]. Reference [5] provides the design of a predictive sliding mode controller for the control of singular systems. Meanwhile, nonlinear problems are widely found in real systems [6–8]. The reference in [9] constructs an explicit controller for systems with stochastic nonlinearities to make the closed-loop system globally bounded. The neuro-fuzzy and state feedback control scheme for the problem of nonlinear control systems is presented in [10]. For fuzzy control, the selection of the membership function is very important. In [11], a membership function of interval type-2 is given and relies on the characteristics of the function for an analytical approach to analyze the system stability. An enhanced membership function transformation method is proposed in [12] to approximate the membership function, and stability analysis of a polynomial fuzzy system is performed. The problem of time delay has also received the attention of researchers [13,14]. Reference [15] presents a consistency analysis of a system with a distributed delay adopted PI controller. A nonlinear mixed reaction diffusion dynamics model for prostate cancer cells with time delay is given in [16], and the properties of the positive solutions of the model are investigated. Therefore, the problem addressed in this paper is a very worthy research direction.

When a fault occurs in a normal system, the output of the system can be severely affected or even destroy the system directly, so fault estimation algorithms should be proposed to obtain fault information for subsequent processing [17,18]. Firstly, for the data-based fault estimation aspect, a multi-scale bidirectional diversity-entropy-based FE algorithm is addressed in [19] to improve the extraction of nonlinear dynamic fault features. Various adaptive principal component analysis methods are proposed in [20] to perform early fault detection by comparing their monitoring metrics. There are also algorithms

Citation: Cao, J.; Chen, H. Mathematical Model for Fault Handling of Singular Nonlinear Time-Varying Delay Systems Based on T-S Fuzzy Model. *Mathematics* 2023, 11, 2547. https://doi.org/10.3390/math11112547

Academic Editors: Maria Luminița Scutaru and Catalin I. Pruncu

Received: 27 April 2023
Revised: 26 May 2023
Accepted: 29 May 2023
Published: 1 June 2023

Copyright: © 2023 by the authors. Licensee MDPI, Basel, Switzerland. This article is an open access article distributed under the terms and conditions of the Creative Commons Attribution (CC BY) license (https://creativecommons.org/licenses/by/4.0/).

that perform fault estimation by monitoring changes in the system model through an estimator [21–23]. In [24], a memory-state feedback control algorithm is designed for time-delay interval type-2 T-S fuzzy systems to mitigate the effects of external disturbances and actuator fault. A time-based sliding mode estimator for a quadrotor UAS with multiple actuator faults is suggested in [25] and the output residuals are applied in the estimation algorithm. Tests demonstrate that the algorithm is able to identify multiple faults even under the influence of perturbations. In [26], a reduced-order estimation observer is developed for an uncertain system and equipped with an online adaptive FE method, which is capable of identifying multiple faults simultaneously. In addition, a batch-type least squares projection method is constructed to measure the degree of the faults. Multiple fault detection methods based on directed unknown input observers are designed in [27] for networked control systems and validated in power systems. However, the FE research results of singular systems are relatively few.

Once the fault information is acquired, control algorithms are needed to mitigate the effects of the fault [28,29]. Reference [30] addresses the problem that bounded nonlinear systems are affected by sensor and link fault, and proposes a distributed state estimation and active FTC scheme to ensure the stable operation of the communication. An output feedback FTC scheme is suggested in [31] for nonlinear uncertain systems with multiple faults. In [32], a data-driven distributed formation FTC method is developed for quadrotors with nonlinearity, uncertainty, and multiple faults. A data-based distributed iterative FTC method is designed in [33] for multi-input systems, which does not require all the system information, reduces the computational burden, and the simulation verifies the performance of the algorithm. However, there has been relatively little focus on the research of FTC algorithms for generalized delay systems.

In this paper, a mathematical model for the FE and FTC of singular nonlinear TVD systems with sensor fault is addressed based on a T-S fuzzy model. The T-S fuzzy model is implemented to approach the system's nonlinear dynamics. A Laplace transform method is devised to construct an equivalent system without explicit TVD. The sensor fault is changed to actuator fault by the developed coordinate transformation. A fuzzy learning fault estimator is built to estimate the detailed sensor fault information. When the system output drifts away to the expected value, a PI FTC scheme is suggested with the aim of reducing the damage of the fault. Simulation results from multiple faults indicate that the FE and FTC algorithms are capable of estimating the fault and guaranteeing the system performance appropriately.

Among the main contributions of this paper are

1. The nonlinear dynamics is approached through a T-S fuzzy model, Laplace transform is adopted to tackle the TVD issue, and coordinate transformation is utilized to simplify the sensor fault handling challenge.
2. A novel fuzzy learning fault estimator is addressed to capture detailed fault information.
3. A fuzzy PI FTC scheme is introduced to mitigate the impact of fault on system performance to the maximum extent possible.

This paper is structured as follows: In Section 2, the system T-S fuzzy modelling is presented. In Section 3, the coordinate transformation algorithms and the design of a fuzzy learning fault estimator are given. A PI FTC controller is introduced in Section 4. Next, some examples of comparative simulations are provided in Section 5. Eventually, Section 6 presents the conclusion.

2. Model Description

The T-S fuzzy model is the most powerful tool to process system nonlinearity, so the T-S fuzzy system is deployed to approach the system dynamics in this paper. The T-S model is characterized via IF-THEN fuzzy rules, and under each rule is a linear subsystem whose set represents an approximation of the nonlinear system. The ith fuzzy rule for a class of singular nonlinear systems is represented as

rule i: IF $\zeta_1(k)$ is δ_{i1}, $\zeta_2(k)$ is δ_{i2}, ..., and $\zeta_{\kappa_1}(k)$ is $\delta_{i\kappa_1}$, THEN

$$E\dot{x}(t) = A_i x(t) + B_i u(t-\tau) + N_i d(t),$$
$$y(t) = D_i x(t) + S_i f_s(t). \tag{1}$$

where $x(t)$, $u(t)$, $y(t)$ denote the state vector, control input vector, and output vector, respectively. Matrices A_i, B_i, D_i, N_i, S_i represent the system parameters with the required dimensions. The TVD τ obeys the exponential distribution of parameter α. $f_s(t)$ denotes the vector of possible sensor fault. $\|d(t)\| \leq K_d$ is bounded extraneous noise. $\zeta_j(k)(j = 1,2,\ldots,\kappa_1)$ is the antecedent variable, $\delta_{ij}(i = 1,2,\ldots,\kappa_2; j = 1,2,\ldots,\kappa_1)$ is the vague collection, characterized with the membership function, and κ_1 and κ_2 are the number of If-Then rules and the antecedent variables.

Assumption 1 ([34]). *The system is regular, namely, $|sE - A| \neq 0$.*

Assumption 2 ([35]). *The system is pulseless, i.e., $rankE = \deg|sE - A|$.*

Assumption 3. *For fault f_s, the condition is satisfied $\|f_s\| \leq K_f$ with unknown positive scalar K_f.*

When assumptions 1 and 2 hold, there are two non-singular matrices and so that the following formula is established:

$$\Psi_1 E \Psi_2 = \begin{bmatrix} I_p & 0 \\ 0 & 0 \end{bmatrix}, \Psi_1 A \Psi_2 = \begin{bmatrix} A^1 & 0 \\ 0 & I_{n-p} \end{bmatrix},$$
$$\Psi_1 B = \begin{bmatrix} B^1 \\ B^2 \end{bmatrix}, \Psi_1 N = \begin{bmatrix} N^1 \\ N^2 \end{bmatrix}, D\Psi_2 = \begin{bmatrix} D^1 & D^2 \end{bmatrix}. \tag{2}$$

where $\Psi_1, \Psi_2 \in R^{n \times n}$, $A^1 \in R^{p \times p}$, I_i is i-dimensional unit matrix, then System (1) can be transformed by coordinate transformation $\begin{bmatrix} x_1(t) \\ x_2(t) \end{bmatrix} = \Psi_2^{-1} x(t)$ as

rule i: IF $\zeta_1(k)$ is δ_{i1}, $\zeta_2(k)$ is δ_{i2}, ..., and $\zeta_{\kappa_1}(k)$ is $\delta_{i\kappa_2}$, THEN

$$\Psi_1 E \Psi_2 \begin{bmatrix} \dot{x}_1(t) \\ \dot{x}_2(t) \end{bmatrix} = \Psi_1 A_i \Psi_2 \begin{bmatrix} x_1(t) \\ x_2(t) \end{bmatrix} + \Psi_1 B_i u(t-\tau) + \Psi_1 N_i d(t),$$
$$y(t) = D_i \Psi_2 \begin{bmatrix} x_1(t) \\ x_2(t) \end{bmatrix} + S_i f_s(t). \tag{3}$$

By plugging the block matrix from (2) into the above equation, the following can be obtained:

rule i: IF $\zeta_1(k)$ is δ_{i1}, $\zeta_2(k)$ is δ_{i2}, ..., and $\zeta_{\kappa_1}(k)$ is $\delta_{i\kappa_2}$, THEN

$$\dot{x}_1(t) = A_i^1 x_1(t) + B_i^1 u(t-\tau) + N_i^1 d(t),$$
$$x_2(t) = -B_i^2 u(t-\tau) - N_i^2 d(t),$$
$$y(t) = D_i^1 x_1(t) + D_i^2 x_2(t) + S_i f_s(t). \tag{4}$$

By fusing the local models guided by all IF-THEN rule through fuzzy blending, the global fuzzy model below is obtained:

$$\begin{aligned}\dot{x}_1(t) &= \sum_{i=1}^{\kappa_2} \hbar_i(\zeta(t))[A_i^1 x_1(t) + B_i^1 u(t-\tau) + N_i^1 d(t)],\\ \dot{x}_2(t) &= \sum_{i=1}^{\kappa_2} \hbar_i(\zeta(t))[-B_i^2 u(t-\tau) - N_i^2 d(t)], \\ y(t) &= \sum_{i=1}^{\kappa_2} \hbar_i(\zeta(t))[D_i^1 x_1(t) + D_i^2 x_2(t) + S_i f_s(t)].\end{aligned} \quad (5)$$

where $\zeta(k) = [\zeta_1(k), \zeta_2(k), \ldots, \zeta_{\kappa_2}(k)]$, $\omega_i(\zeta(k)) = \prod_{j=1}^{\kappa_2} \delta_{ij}(\zeta_j(k)) > 0$, $\hbar_i(\zeta(k)) = \frac{\omega_i(\zeta(k))}{\sum_{i=1}^{\kappa_2} \omega_i(\zeta(k))} > 0$, $\sum_{i=1}^{q} \hbar_i(\zeta(k)) = 1$.

Lemma 1. *For real matrices X, Y, the following inequality holds [31]:*

$$X^T Y + Y^T X \leq X^T X + Y^T Y. \quad (6)$$

3. Fault Estimation

The system is affected by both sensor fault and TVD, which are very difficult to handle directly. Two transformation methods are presented below to deal with sensor fault and TVD.

Introducing a new state variable

$$\dot{x}_s = -A_s x_s(t) + A_s y(t). \quad (7)$$

where A_s is a Hurwitz matrix.

The new system structure is represented below

$$\begin{aligned}\dot{x}_{s1}(t) &= \sum_{i=1}^{\kappa_2} \hbar_i(\zeta(t))[A_i^s x_{s1}(t) + B_i^s u(t-\tau) + S_i^s f_s(t) + N_i^s d(t)],\\ y_{s1}(t) &= \sum_{i=1}^{\kappa_2} \hbar_i(\zeta(t))[D_i^s x_{s1}(t)],\end{aligned} \quad (8)$$

where $x_{s1}(t) = \begin{bmatrix} x_1(t) \\ x_s(t) \end{bmatrix}$, $A_i^s = \begin{bmatrix} A_i^1 & 0 \\ A_s D_1^s & -A_s \end{bmatrix}$, $B_i^s = \begin{bmatrix} B_i^1 \\ -A_s D_2^s B_i^2 \end{bmatrix}$, $S_i^s = \begin{bmatrix} 0 \\ A_s S \end{bmatrix}$, $D_i^s = \begin{bmatrix} 0 & I_p \end{bmatrix}$.

After the above conversion, the sensor fault is transformed into actuator fault, which is convenient for subsequent processing.

To deal with TVD, the Laplace transform is used to solve the delays and convert System (8) into an equivalent system without significant delays. The delay module in this paper satisfies the exponential distribution function and yields the following results:

$$F_T(t) = 1 - e^{-\alpha t}. \quad (9)$$

The probability density function (PDF) of the exponential distribution is $f(\alpha, t) = \alpha e^{-\alpha t}$, and taking the Laplace transform on the PDF yields

$$F_T(s) = \int_0^\infty \alpha e^{-\alpha \tau} e^{-s\tau} d\tau = \frac{\alpha}{\alpha + s}. \quad (10)$$

The expected value of the output response of a random delay block is equivalent to the Laplace transform of the phase-synchronized signal with the same sampling period [36], and it leads to

$$E[u(t-\tau)] = L^{-1}\left\{\frac{\alpha}{\alpha + s} u(s)\right\}. \quad (11)$$

Furthermore,
$$x_{s2}(t) = \frac{\alpha}{\alpha+s}u(s). \quad (12)$$

Then the following system is available:
$$\dot{x}_{s2}(t) = -\alpha x_{s2}(t) + \alpha u(t). \quad (13)$$

Merging Systems (8) and (13), the novel system model is given below:
$$\begin{aligned}\dot{\bar{x}}(t) &= \sum_{i=1}^{\kappa_2}\hbar_i(\zeta(t))[\bar{A}_i\bar{x}(t)+\bar{B}_iu(t)+\bar{S}_if_s(t)+\bar{N}_id(t)],\\ \bar{y}(t) &= \sum_{i=1}^{\kappa_2}\hbar_i(\zeta(t))[\bar{D}_i\bar{x}(t)],\end{aligned} \quad (14)$$

where $\bar{x} = \begin{bmatrix} x_{s1} \\ x_{s2} \end{bmatrix}, \bar{A}_i = \begin{bmatrix} A_i^s & B_i^s \\ 0 & -\alpha \end{bmatrix}, \bar{B}_i = \begin{bmatrix} 0 \\ \alpha \end{bmatrix}, \bar{S}_i = \begin{bmatrix} S_i^s \\ 0 \end{bmatrix}, \bar{N}_i = \begin{bmatrix} N_i^s \\ 0 \end{bmatrix}, \bar{D}_i = \begin{bmatrix} D_i^s & 0 \end{bmatrix}$.

After the above transformation, the system has been transformed into a system without significant time delay affected by actuator fault. To estimate detailed fault information, the structure of the fuzzy learning fault estimator is given below:

$$\begin{aligned}\dot{\hat{x}}(t) &= \sum_{i=1}^{\kappa_2}\hbar_i(\zeta(t))[\bar{A}_i\hat{x}(t)+\bar{B}_iu(t)+\bar{S}_iZ(t)+G_i\varepsilon(t)],\\ \hat{y}(t) &= \sum_{i=1}^{\kappa_2}\hbar_i(\zeta(t))[\bar{D}_i\hat{x}(t)],\\ Z(t) &= \sum_{i=1}^{\kappa_2}\hbar_i(\zeta(t))[K_{1i}Z(t-\tau)+K_{2i}\varepsilon(t-\tau)],\\ \dot{\hat{f}}_s(t) &= WZ(t),\end{aligned} \quad (15)$$

where $\hat{x}(t)$ and $\hat{f}_s(t)$ are the estimated state and sensor fault, $\varepsilon(t) = \bar{y}(t) - \hat{y}(t)$ is the residual signal, and G_i, K_{1i}, K_{2i} are gain matrices remaining undetermined.

The estimated error is specified below:
$$\begin{aligned}\bar{e}_x(t) &= \bar{x}(t) - \hat{x}(t),\\ e_{fs}(t) &= f_s(t) - \hat{f}_s(t).\end{aligned} \quad (16)$$

Combining System (14) and the learning estimator (15), the estimation error system is gained below:
$$\dot{\bar{e}}_x(t) = \sum_{i=1}^{\kappa_2}\hbar_i(\zeta(t))[(\bar{A}_i - G_i\bar{D}_i)\bar{e}_x(t) + \bar{S}_if_s(t) - \bar{S}_iZ(t) + \bar{N}_id(t)]. \quad (17)$$

Theorem 1. *For System (14) and the learning estimator (15), the error system (17) is considered convergent when there exist positive definite symmetric matrices (PDSMs) P_1, R_1 and $K_{1i}, K_{2i} > 0$ to make the following inequalities valid:*

$$\begin{aligned}(\bar{A}_i - G_i\bar{D}_i)^T P_1 + P_1(\bar{A}_i - G_i\bar{D}_i) + R_1 + P_1\bar{S}_i\bar{S}_i^T P_1 + Q_1 &\leq 0,\\ 0 < (6+3\sigma)K_{1i}^T K_{1i} &\leq I,\\ 0 < (6+3\sigma)(K_{2i}\bar{D})^T(K_{2i}\bar{D}) &\leq R_1.\end{aligned} \quad (18)$$

Proof. The following is a definition of the Lyapunov function:
$$\Lambda_1(t) = \bar{e}_x^T(t)P_1\bar{e}_x(t) + \int_{t-\tau}^t \bar{e}_x^T(\varsigma)R_1\bar{e}_x(\varsigma)d\varsigma + \int_{t-\tau}^t Z^T(\varsigma)Z(\varsigma)d\varsigma, \quad (19)$$

The derivative of $\Lambda_1(t)$ yields

$$\dot{\Lambda}_1(t) \leq \sum_{i=1}^{\kappa_2} \hbar_i(\zeta(t)) \sum_{j=1}^{\kappa_2} \hbar_j(\zeta(t))[\bar{e}_x^T(t)(P_1(\bar{A}_i - G_i\bar{D}_j) \\
+ (\bar{A}_i - G_i\bar{D}_j)^T P_1)\bar{e}_x(t) + 2\bar{e}_x^T(t)P_1\bar{S}_i f(t) \\
- 2\bar{e}_x^T(t)P_1\bar{S}_i Z(t) + 2\bar{e}_x^T(t)P_1\bar{N}_i d(t) + \bar{e}_x^T(t)R_1\bar{e}_x(t) \\
- \bar{e}_x^T(t-\tau)R_1\bar{e}_x(t-\tau) + Z^T(t)Z(t) - Z^T(t-\tau)Z(t-\tau)], \quad (20)$$

For the learning estimator (15), the following inequalities are established:

$$2Z^T(t)Z(t) \leq \sum_{i=1}^{\kappa_2} \hbar_i(\zeta(t)) \sum_{j=1}^{\kappa_2} \hbar_j(\zeta(t))[2Z^T(t-\tau)K_{1i}^T K_{1i} Z(t-\tau) \\
+ Z^T(t-\tau)K_{1i}^T K_{1i} Z(t-\tau) + \bar{e}_x^T(t-\tau)(K_{2i}\bar{D}_j)^T(K_{2i}\bar{D}_j)\bar{e}_x(t-\tau) \\
+ Z^T(t-\tau)K_{1i}^T K_{1i} Z(t-\tau) + \bar{e}_x^T(t-\tau)(K_{2i}\bar{D}_j)^T(K_{2i}\bar{D}_j)\bar{e}_x(t-\tau) \\
+ Z^T(t-\tau)K_{1i}^T K_{1i} Z(t-\tau) + 2\bar{e}_x^T(t-\tau)(K_{2i}\bar{D}_j)^T(K_{2i}\bar{D}_j)\bar{e}_x(t-\tau) \\
+ \bar{e}_x^T(t-\tau)(K_{2i}\bar{D}_j)^T(K_{2i}\bar{D}_j)\bar{e}_x(t-\tau) + Z^T(t-\tau)K_{1i}^T K_{1i} Z(t-\tau) \\
+ \bar{e}_x^T(t-\tau)(K_{2i}\bar{D}_j)^T(K_{2i}\bar{D}_j)\bar{e}_x(t-\tau)] \\
= \sum_{i=1}^{\kappa_2} \hbar_i(\zeta(t)) \sum_{j=1}^{\kappa_2} \hbar_j(\zeta(t))[6Z^T(t-\tau)K_{1i}^T K_{1i} Z(t-\tau) \\
+ 6\bar{e}_x^T(t-\tau)(K_{2i}\bar{D}_j)^T(K_{2i}\bar{D}_j)\bar{e}_x(t-\tau)], \quad (21)$$

Using Lemma 1, one can obtain

$$2\bar{e}_x^T(t)P_1\bar{S}_i Z(t) \leq \bar{e}_x^T(t)P_1\bar{S}_i\bar{S}_i^T P_1\bar{e}_x(t) + Z^T(t)Z(t), \\
2\bar{e}_x^T(t)P_1\bar{N}_i d(t) \leq \bar{e}_x^T(t)P_1\bar{N}_i\bar{N}_i^T P_1\bar{e}_x(t) + d^T(t)d(t), \quad (22)$$

Substituting the above equation into Formula (20) and rearranging yields

$$\dot{\Lambda}_1(t) \leq \sum_{i=1}^{\kappa_2} \hbar_i(\zeta(t)) \sum_{j=1}^{\kappa_2} \hbar_j(\zeta(t))[\bar{e}_x^T(t)(P_1(\bar{A}_i - G_i\bar{D}_j) + (\bar{A}_i - G_i\bar{D}_j)^T P_1)\bar{e}_x(t) \\
+ \bar{e}_x^T(t)P_1\bar{S}_i\bar{S}_i^T P_1\bar{e}_x(t) + 2K_f^2 + \bar{e}_x^T(t)P_1\bar{S}_i\bar{S}_i^T P_1\bar{e}_x(t) + \sigma Z^T(t)Z(t) \\
+ \bar{e}_x^T(t)P_1\bar{N}_i\bar{N}_i^T P_1\bar{e}_x(t) + 2K_d^2 + 2Z^T(t)Z(t) - \sigma Z^T(t)Z(t) \\
- \bar{e}_x^T(t-\tau)R_1\bar{e}_x(t-\tau) - Z^T(t-\tau)Z(t-\tau)] \\
\leq \sum_{i=1}^{\kappa_2} \hbar_i(\zeta(t)) \sum_{j=1}^{\kappa_2} \hbar_j(\zeta(t))[\bar{e}_x^T(t)(P_1(\bar{A}_i - G_i\bar{D}_j) + (\bar{A}_i - G_i\bar{D}_j)^T P_1 + R_1 \\
+ 2P_1\bar{S}_i\bar{S}_i^T P_1 + P_1\bar{N}_i\bar{N}_i^T P)\bar{e}_x(t) + 2K_f^2 + 2K_d^2 \\
+ (6+3\sigma)Z^T(t-\tau)K_{1i}^T K_{1i} Z(t-\tau) \\
+ (6+3\sigma)\bar{e}_x^T(t-\tau)(K_{2i}\bar{D}_j)^T(K_{2i}\bar{D}_j)\bar{e}_x(t-\tau) \\
- \bar{e}_x^T(t-\tau)R_1\bar{e}_x(t-\tau) - \sigma Z^T(t)Z(t) - Z^T(t-\tau)Z(t-\tau)] \\
= \sum_{i=1}^{\kappa_2} \hbar_i(\zeta(t)) \sum_{j=1}^{\kappa_2} \hbar_j(\zeta(t))[\bar{e}_x^T(t)(P_1(\bar{A}_i - G_i\bar{D}_j) + (\bar{A}_i - G_i\bar{D}_j)^T P_1 + R_1 \\
+ 2P_1\bar{S}_i\bar{S}_i^T P_1 + P_1\bar{N}_i\bar{N}_i^T P)\bar{e}_x(t) + 2K_f^2 + 2K_d^2 \\
+ Z^T(t-\tau)\big((6+3\sigma)K_{1i}^T K_{1i} - I\big)Z(t-\tau) \\
+ \bar{e}_x^T(t-\tau)\big((6+3\sigma)(K_{2i}\bar{D}_j)^T(K_{2i}\bar{D}_j) - R_1\big)\bar{e}_x(t-\tau) - \sigma Z^T(t)Z(t)], \quad (23)$$

When Theorem 1 holds, the following result is obtained:

$$\dot{\Lambda}_1(t) \leq \sum_{i=1}^{\kappa_2} \hbar_i(\zeta(t)) \sum_{j=1}^{\kappa_2} \hbar_j(\zeta(t))[\bar{e}_x^T(t)(P_1(\bar{A}_i - G_i\bar{D}_j) + (\bar{A}_i - G_i\bar{D}_j)^T P_1 + R_1 \\
+ 2P_1\bar{S}_i\bar{S}_i^T P_1 + P_1\bar{N}_i\bar{N}_i^T P)\bar{e}_x(t) + 2K_f^2 + 2K_d^2 - \sigma Z^T(t)Z(t)] \\
= \sum_{i=1}^{\kappa_2} \hbar_i(\zeta(t)) \sum_{j=1}^{\kappa_2} \hbar_j(\zeta(t))[\varphi^T(t)Q_1\varphi(t) + 2K_f^2 + 2K_d^2] \quad (24) \\
\leq \sum_{i=1}^{\kappa_2} \hbar_i(\zeta(t)) \sum_{j=1}^{\kappa_2} \hbar_j(\zeta(t))[-\lambda_{min}(Q_1)\|\varphi(t)\|^2 + 2K_f^2 + 2K_d^2],$$

where $\lambda_{min}(\cdot)$ represents the minimum eigenvalue of the matrix.

Therefore, when Theorem 1 and $\|\varphi(t)\| > \sqrt{2 \frac{K_f^2 + 2K_d^2}{-\lambda_{min}(Q_1)}}$ are satisfied, then $\dot{\Lambda}_1(t) < 0$. Depending on the Lyapunov theory, the error system (17) is convergent. □

4. Fault-Tolerant Control

System performance is severely affected when fault is not handled in a timely manner, so when fault information is obtained through the designed fuzzy learning estimator, a fault-tolerant control algorithm needs to be designed to compensate for fault to the maximum extent possible to ensure that expected output is followed even with fault. In this paper, a fault-tolerant controller is constructed based on a PI control strategy.

A new state variable is introduced as follows:

$$\omega(t) = [\tilde{x}^T(t), \int_0^t (\tilde{y}(\varsigma) - y_c)^T d\varsigma]^T. \tag{25}$$

where y_c is a reference output.

The corresponding estimation error of $\omega(t)$ is defined as

$$e_\omega(t) = \omega(t) - \hat{\omega}(t) = \begin{bmatrix} \tilde{x}(t) \\ \int_0^t (\tilde{y}(\varsigma) - y_c) d\varsigma \end{bmatrix} - \begin{bmatrix} \hat{x}(t) \\ \int_0^t (\hat{y}(\varsigma) - y_c) d\varsigma \end{bmatrix}. \tag{26}$$

On the basis of system (14), the new dynamic system is expressed as

$$\dot{\omega}(t) = \sum_{i=1}^{\kappa_2} \hbar_i(\zeta(t)) [\tilde{A}_i \omega(t) + \tilde{B}_i u(t) + \tilde{S}_i f_s(t) + \tilde{N}_i d(t) - \tilde{I} y_c], \tag{27}$$

where $\tilde{A}_i = \begin{bmatrix} \bar{A}_i & 0 \\ \bar{D}_i & 0 \end{bmatrix}, \tilde{B}_i = \begin{bmatrix} \bar{B}_i \\ 0 \end{bmatrix}, \tilde{S}_i = \begin{bmatrix} \bar{S}_i \\ 0 \end{bmatrix}, \tilde{N}_i = \begin{bmatrix} \bar{N}_i \\ 0 \end{bmatrix}, \tilde{I} = \begin{bmatrix} 0 \\ I \end{bmatrix}$

To ensure that the system output continues tracking the intended output when fault occurs, the PI compensating controller is provided below:

$$\begin{aligned} u(t) &= \sum_{i=1}^{\kappa_2} \hbar_i(\zeta(t)) \tilde{B}_i^p \left[G_{Pi} \hat{x}(t) + G_{Ii} \int_0^t (\hat{y}(\tau) - y_c) d\tau - \hat{f}_s(t) \right] \\ &= \sum_{i=1}^{\kappa_2} \hbar_i(\zeta(t)) \tilde{B}_i^p \left\{ \begin{bmatrix} G_{Pi} & G_{Ii} \end{bmatrix} \begin{bmatrix} \hat{x}(t) \\ \int_0^t (\hat{y}(\tau) - y_c) d\tau \end{bmatrix} - \hat{f}_s(t) \right\} \\ &= \sum_{i=1}^{\kappa_2} \hbar_i(\zeta(t)) \tilde{B}_i^p \left[G_{PI} \hat{\omega}(t) - \hat{f}_s(t) \right], \end{aligned} \tag{28}$$

where $\tilde{B}^p$ is the pseudo inverse of matrix $\tilde{B}$, and $G_{PI} = \begin{bmatrix} G_{Pi} & G_{Ii} \end{bmatrix}$ is the pending controller gain.

The error system yields the following results:

$$\begin{aligned} \dot{e}_\omega(t) &= \dot{\omega}(t) - \dot{\hat{\omega}}(t) \\ &= \sum_{i=1}^{\kappa_2} \hbar_i(\zeta(t)) [(\tilde{A}_i + \tilde{B}_i G_{PI}) \omega(t) + (\tilde{S}_i - \tilde{B}_i) f_s(t) + \tilde{N}_i d(t) - \tilde{I} y_c] \\ &\quad - [(\tilde{A}_i + \tilde{B}_i G_{PI}) \hat{\omega}(t) + (\tilde{S}_i - \tilde{B}_i) \hat{f}_s(t) - \tilde{I} y_c] \\ &= \sum_{i=1}^{\kappa_2} \hbar_i(\zeta(t)) [(\tilde{A}_i + \tilde{B}_i G_{PI}) e_\omega(t) + (\tilde{S}_i - \tilde{B}_i) e_{fs}(t)]. \end{aligned} \tag{29}$$

Theorem 2. *The convergence of the closed-loop dynamical system (29) is guaranteed when there exist G_{PI}, PDSM P_2 and Q_2 to make the following inequality hold:*

$$(\tilde{A}_i + \tilde{B}_i G_{PI})^T P_2 + P_2 (\tilde{A}_i + \tilde{B}_i G_{PI}) + P_2 (\tilde{S}_i - \tilde{B}_i)(\tilde{S}_i - \tilde{B}_i)^T P_2 + Q_2 \leq 0. \tag{30}$$

Proof. The Lyapunov function is defined below:

$$\Lambda_2(t) = e_\omega^T(t) P_2 e_\omega(t), \tag{31}$$

Taking the interval derivative of $\Lambda_2(t)$ and employing Lemma 1, this leads to

$$\begin{aligned}
\dot{\Lambda}_2(t) &= \sum_{i=1}^{\kappa_2} \hbar_i(\zeta(t))((\tilde{A}_i + \tilde{B}_i G_{PI}) e_\omega(t) + (\tilde{S}_i - \tilde{B}_i) e_{fs}(t))^T P_2 e_\omega(t) \\
&+ \sum_{i=1}^{\kappa_2} \hbar_i(\zeta(t)) e_\omega^T(t) P_2((\tilde{A}_i + \tilde{B}_i G_{PI}) e_\omega(t) + (\tilde{S}_i - \tilde{B}_i) e_{fs}(t)) \\
&= \sum_{i=1}^{\kappa_2} \hbar_i(\zeta(t)) \{ e_\omega^T(t)((\tilde{A}_i + \tilde{B}_i G_{PI})^T P_2 + P_2(\tilde{A}_i + \tilde{B}_i G_{PI})) e_\omega(t) \\
&+ 2 e_\omega^T(t) P_2(\tilde{S}_i - \tilde{B}_i) e_{fs}(t) \\
&\leq \sum_{i=1}^{\kappa_2} \hbar_i(\zeta(t)) e_\omega^T(t)((\tilde{A}_i + \tilde{B}_i G_{PI})^T P_2 + P_2(\tilde{A}_i + \tilde{B}_i G_{PI})) e_\omega(t) \\
&+ e_\omega^T(t) P_2(\tilde{S}_i - \tilde{B}_i)(\tilde{S}_i - \tilde{B}_i)^T P_2 e_\omega(t) + e_{fs}^T(t) e_{fs}(t) \\
&\leq \sum_{i=1}^{q} \hbar_i(\xi(t)) e_\omega^T(t)((\tilde{A}_i + \tilde{B}_i G_{PI})^T P_2 + P_2(\tilde{A}_i + \tilde{B}_i G_{PI}) \\
&+ P_2(\tilde{S}_i - \tilde{B}_i)(\tilde{S}_i - \tilde{B}_i)^T P_2) e_\omega(t) + 2 K_f^2 \\
&= \sum_{i=1}^{\kappa_2} \hbar_i(\zeta(t)) e_\omega^T(t) Q_2 e_\omega(t) + 2 K_f^2 \\
&\leq \sum_{i=1}^{\kappa_2} \hbar_i(\zeta(t)) [-\lambda_{min}(Q_2) \|e_\omega(t)\|^2 + 2 K_f^2],
\end{aligned} \tag{32}$$

Thus, in case Theorem 2 and $\|e_\omega(t)\| \geq K_f \sqrt{\frac{2}{-\lambda_{min}(Q_2)}}$ are valid, it is evident that $\dot{\Lambda}_2 < 0$, which implies that System (29) is stable. □

5. Simulation and Discussion

In this paper, MATLAB software was applied for simulation verification. To verify the efficacy of the suggested FE and FTC schemes, some simulation procedures are given and the desired results are presented.

The parameter matrix of the initial system is given below:

$$E = \begin{bmatrix} 1 & 0 & 0 \\ 0 & 1 & 0 \\ 0 & 0 & 0 \end{bmatrix}, A_1 = \begin{bmatrix} -2 & 1 & 0 \\ 3 & -2.8 & 0 \\ -0.7 & 0.5 & -1 \end{bmatrix}, A_2 = \begin{bmatrix} -2.3 & 0.95 & 0 \\ 1 & -3.08 & 0 \\ -0.16 & 1.06 & -1.51 \end{bmatrix},$$

$$B_1 = \begin{bmatrix} 0.15 \\ 0.3 \\ 0.21 \end{bmatrix}, B_2 = \begin{bmatrix} 0.21 \\ 0.29 \\ 0.15 \end{bmatrix}, N_1 = \begin{bmatrix} 1.2 \\ 0.9 \\ 0.5 \end{bmatrix}, N_2 = \begin{bmatrix} 0.5 \\ 1.6 \\ 0.1 \end{bmatrix}, D_1 = \begin{bmatrix} 1 & 0.2 & 0 \\ 0.5 & -1 & 1 \end{bmatrix},$$

$$D_2 = \begin{bmatrix} -0.5 & 0.1 & -0.2 \\ 0.1 & 1 & 0.6 \end{bmatrix}, S_1 = \begin{bmatrix} 0.3 \\ 1 \end{bmatrix}, S_2 = \begin{bmatrix} 0.5 \\ 1 \end{bmatrix}.$$

To validate the algorithm, the TVD module is set to satisfy an exponential distribution whose rate parameter is $\alpha = 10$. In this paper, the coupling between the TVD and the system is reduced, so the TVD is relatively independent, and the initial state of the TVD has very little influence on the system, so the initial state of time delay is taken as 0.05.

The following two types of sensor faults are given:

Constant fault:

$$f_s(t) = \begin{cases} 0 & 0 \leq t < 120 \\ 0.7 & 120 \leq t < 300 \end{cases},$$

Time-varying fault:

$$f_s(t) = \begin{cases} 0 & 0 \leq t < 120 \\ 0.2 \sin(0.05t) + 0.4 & 120 \leq t < 300 \end{cases}.$$

The intended output is given as $y_c = [1.2, 4.6]$. By solving the inequalities in Theorems 1 and 2, the FE and FTC parameters are obtained below:

$$K_{11} = 0.29, K_{21} = \begin{bmatrix} -5.5 & -0.04 & 0.02 & 0.5 \end{bmatrix},$$
$$K_{12} = 0.53, K_{22} = \begin{bmatrix} -3.8 & 0.15 & 0.6 & 0.09 \end{bmatrix},$$
$$G_{P1} = \begin{bmatrix} -0.366 & 0.453 & -0.648 & 0.048 \end{bmatrix},$$
$$G_{P2} = \begin{bmatrix} 0.109 & -0.043 & 0.214 & -0.513 \end{bmatrix},$$
$$G_{I1} = \begin{bmatrix} -0.371 & 0.266 & 0.012 & 0.743 \end{bmatrix},$$
$$G_{I2} = \begin{bmatrix} -1.292 & -0.021 & 0.125 & -1.503 \end{bmatrix}.$$

Regarding a constant fault, the residual signal depicted in Figure 1 displays a noticeable variation at 120 s, indicating the occurrence of the fault at that moment. The results of FE in Figure 2 demonstrate that sensor fault is effectively estimated quite well. The proposed FE algorithm is highly effective for constant fault. The FTC result is depicted in Figure 3. Obviously, the system output deviates from the target output at 120 s. Nevertheless, by adopting the FTC method suggested in Section 4, the system output can continue tracking the intended output. To illustrate the comparison, Figure 4 depicts the system output without FTC, indicating that the system is not well controlled and its performance is seriously affected.

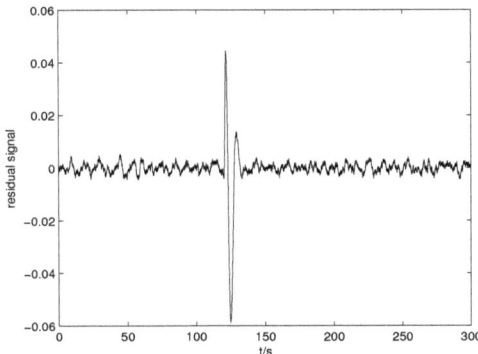

Figure 1. Residual signal of constant fault.

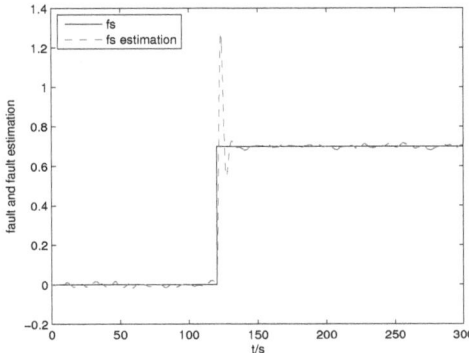

Figure 2. Sensor fault and its estimation of constant fault.

To more comprehensively verify the algorithm's feasibility, simulation results for time-varying fault are displayed in Figures 5–8. The residual signal in Figure 5 additionally confirms that the fault occurred at 120 s. The FE algorithm can accurately track the changes in the time-varying fault, as evident from the FE results in Figure 6. When detailed fault information is obtained, applying the designed controller, the system output results displayed in Figure 7 show that system output tracking of the expected output can be ensured even in the event of fault, thus maintaining system performance. The results in Figure 8 without FTC reveal that the system output failed to track the desired output.

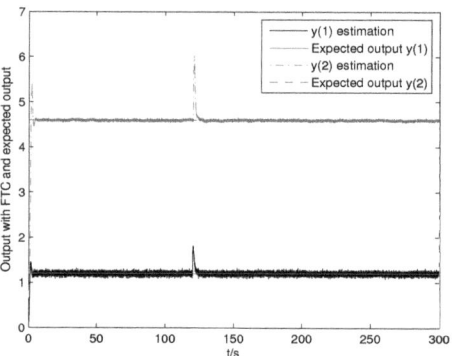

Figure 3. The system output with FTC of constant fault.

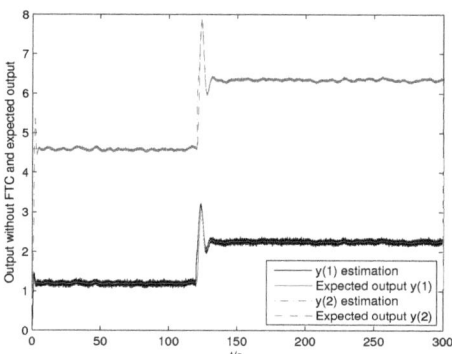

Figure 4. The system output without FTC of constant fault.

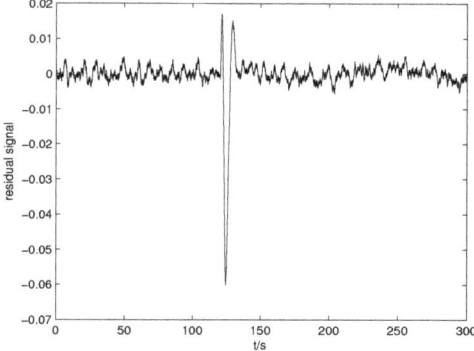

Figure 5. Residual signal of time-varying fault.

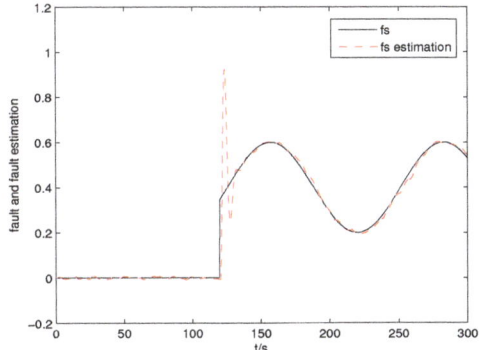

Figure 6. Sensor fault and its estimation of time-varying fault.

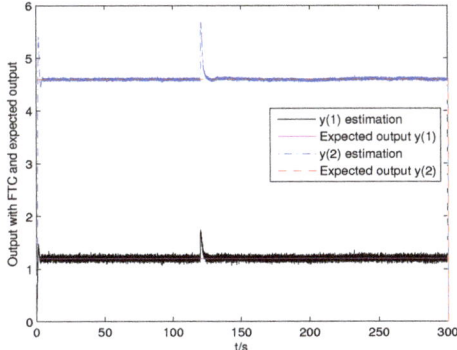

Figure 7. The system output with FTC of time-varying fault.

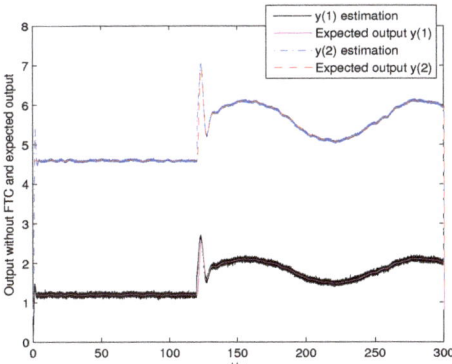

Figure 8. The system output without FTC of time-varying fault.

Therefore, for different types of faults, the algorithm designed in this paper yields very good results.

6. Conclusions

In this paper, the mathematical modelling problem for the FE and FTC of singular nonlinear TVD systems with sensor fault is solved based on the T-S fuzzy model. The

Laplace transform is utilized to build an equal system free of TVD to solve the TVD issue. The coordinate transformation is developed to change sensor fault to actuator fault for processing. A fuzzy learning fault estimator is built to estimate sensor fault. As shown in the results in Figures 2 and 6, the fault estimation error at steady state is much less than 0.01 for constant or time-varying faults, indicating that the fault diagnosis algorithm has a good estimation effect. When fault occurs, the PI-compensated FTC is engineered to decrease the possible effect of the fault. The simulation results show that the error of the system output before and after the fault is less than 0.3 when adopting the FTC algorithm designed in this paper, but the error of the system output before and after the fault is generally greater than 1 when there is no FTC algorithm. The algorithm of this paper has good results for both constant and time-varying faults. Singular systems are widely available in power grid systems, chemical processes, satellite attitude control systems, etc. The algorithms in this paper provide solutions for fault handling in these systems.

Further research may include research on mathematical models for the fault handling of singularly uncertain systems, singularly switching systems, and their applications.

Author Contributions: Conceptualization, J.C. and H.C.; Methodology, J.C.; Software, J.C.; Validation, J.C. and H.C.; Formal Analysis, J.C.; Investigation, J.C.; Resources, J.C.; Data Curation, J.C.; Writing—Original Draft Preparation, J.C.; Writing—Review and Editing, H.C.; Visualization, J.C.; Supervision, H.C.; Project Administration, H.C. All authors have read and agreed to the published version of the manuscript.

Funding: This work was supported by the Major Scientific and Technological Projects of CNPC (ZD2019-184-001).

Data Availability Statement: Not applicable.

Conflicts of Interest: The authors declare that they have no conflicts of interest.

References

1. Jin, Z.; Zhang, Q.; Ren, J. The approximation of the T-S fuzzy model for a class of nonlinear singular systems with impulses. *Neural Comput. Appl.* **2020**, *32*, 10387–10401. [CrossRef]
2. Chen, G.; Zheng, M.; Yang, S.; Li, L. Admissibility analysis of a sampled-data singular system based on the input delay approach. *Complexity* **2022**, *2022*, 3151620. [CrossRef]
3. Phat, V.; Sau, N. Exponential stabilisation of positive singular linear discrete-time delay systems with bounded control. *IET Control Theory Appl.* **2019**, *13*, 905–911. [CrossRef]
4. Khoshnevisan, L.; Liu, X. Fractional order predictive sliding-mode control for a class of nonlinear input-delay systems: Singular and non-singular approach. *Int. J. Syst. Sci.* **2019**, *50*, 2424–2436. [CrossRef]
5. Ku, C.; Chang, W.; Tsai, M.; Lee, Y. Observer-based proportional derivative fuzzy control for singular Takagi-Sugeno fuzzy systems. *Inf. Sci.* **2021**, *570*, 815–830. [CrossRef]
6. Chen, M.; Chen, C. Robust nonlinear observer for lipschitz nonlinear systems subject to disturbances. *IEEE Trans. Autom. Control* **2007**, *52*, 2365–2369. [CrossRef]
7. Yao, L.; Li, L. Minimum rational entropy fault tolerant control for non-Gaussian singular stochastic distribution control systems using T-S fuzzy modelling. *Int. J. Syst. Sci.* **2018**, *49*, 2900–2911.
8. Jian, H.; Feng, S.; Wang, L. Sign-changing solutions of critical quasilinear Kirchhoff-Schrodinger-Poisson system with logarithmic nonlinearity. *AIMS Math.* **2023**, *8*, 8580–8609. [CrossRef]
9. Li, G.; Chen, Y. Controller design for stochastic nonlinear systems with matched conditions. *J. Syst. Eng. Electron.* **2018**, *29*, 160–165. [CrossRef]
10. Gil, P.; Oliveira, T.; Palma, L. Adaptive neuro-fuzzy control for discrete-time nonaffine nonlinear systems. *IEEE Trans. Fuzzy Syst.* **2019**, *27*, 1602–1615. [CrossRef]
11. Chen, M.; Lam, H.; Xiao, B.; Xuan, C. Membership-function-dependent control design and stability analysis of interval type-2 sampled-data fuzzy-model-based control system. *IEEE Trans. Fuzzy Syst.* **2022**, *30*, 1614–1623. [CrossRef]
12. Xie, W.; Sang, S.; Lam, H.; Zhang, J. A polynomial membership function approach for stability analysis of fuzzy systems. *IEEE Trans. Fuzzy Syst.* **2021**, *29*, 2077–2087. [CrossRef]
13. Youssef, T.; Chadli, M.; Karimi, H.; Wang, R. Actuator and sensor faults estimation based on proportional integral observer for T-S fuzzy model. *J. Frankl. Inst.* **2017**, *354*, 2524–2542. [CrossRef]
14. Zhang, X.; Han, Q.; Zhang, B. An overview and deep investigation on sampled-data-based event-triggered control and filtering for networked systems. *IEEE Trans. Ind. Inform.* **2017**, *13*, 4–16. [CrossRef]

15. Ma, Q.; Xu, S. Consensus switching of second-order multiagent systems with time delay. *IEEE Trans. Cybern.* **2022**, *52*, 3349–3353. [CrossRef]
16. Zhao, K. Attractor of a nonlinear hybrid reaction–diffusion model of neuroendocrine transdifferentiation of human prostate cancer cells with time-lags. *AIMS Math.* **2023**, *8*, 14426–14448. [CrossRef]
17. Yan, S.; Sun, W.; He, F.; Yao, J. Adaptive fault detection and isolation for active suspension systems with model uncertainties. *IEEE Trans. Reliab.* **2019**, *68*, 927–937. [CrossRef]
18. Zhang, Q. Adaptive Kalman filter for actuator fault diagnosis. *Automatica* **2018**, *93*, 333–342. [CrossRef]
19. Ke, Y.; Song, E.; Chen, Y.; Yao, C.; Ning, Y. Multiscale bidirectional diversity entropy for diesel injector fault-type diagnosis and fault degree diagnosis. *IEEE Trans. Instrum. Meas.* **2022**, *71*, 6503410. [CrossRef]
20. Michalski, M.; Souza, G. Comparing PCA-based fault detection methods for dynamic processes with correlated and Non-Gaussian variables. *Expert Syst. Appl.* **2022**, *207*, 117989. [CrossRef]
21. Gao, C.; Zhao, Q.; Duan, G. Robust actuator fault diagnosis scheme for satellite attitude control systems. *J. Frankl. Inst.* **2013**, *350*, 2560–2580. [CrossRef]
22. Gu, Y.; Yang, G. Fault detection for discrete-time Lipschitz non-linear systems in finite-frequency domain. *IET Control Theory Appl.* **2017**, *11*, 2177–2186. [CrossRef]
23. Sakthivel, R.; Kavikumar, R.; Mohammadzadeh, A.; Kwon, O.; Kaviarasan, B. Fault estimation for mode-dependent it2 fuzzy systems with quantized output signals. *IEEE Trans. Fuzzy Syst.* **2021**, *29*, 198–309. [CrossRef]
24. Kavikumar, R.; Sakthivel, R.; Kwon, O.; Kaviarasan, B. Faulty actuator-based control synthesis for interval type-2 fuzzy systems via memory state feedback approach. *Int. J. Syst. Sci.* **2020**, *51*, 2958–2981. [CrossRef]
25. Falcon, R.; Rios, H.; Dzul, A. A robust fault diagnosis for quad-rotors: A sliding-mode observer approach. *IEEE-ASME Trans. Mechatron.* **2022**, *27*, 4487–4496. [CrossRef]
26. Tutsoy, Q.; Asadi, D.; Ahmadi, K.; Nabavi-Chashmi, S. Robust reduced order thau observer with the adaptive fault estimator for the unmanned air vehicles. *IEEE Trans. Veh. Technol.* **2023**, *72*, 1601–1610. [CrossRef]
27. Khan, A.A.; Khan, A.; Iqbal, N.; Mustafa, G.; Abbasi, M.; Mahmood, A. Design of a computationally efficient observer-based distributed fault detection and isolation scheme in second-order networked control systems. *ISA Trans.* **2022**, *128*, 229–241. [CrossRef]
28. Hwang, K.; Yoon, K. Fault-tolerant design process of spoke-type IPM motor considering irreversible demagnetization of PM in integrated electric brake system. *IEEE Trans. Magn.* **2022**, *58*, 8206809. [CrossRef]
29. Zhao, X.; Zong, Q.; Tian, B.; Liu, W. Integrated fault estimation and fault-tolerant tracking control for lipschitz nonlinear multiagent systems. *IEEE Trans. Cybern.* **2020**, *50*, 678–688. [CrossRef]
30. Gao, M.; Niu, Y.; Sheng, L. Distributed fault-tolerant state estimation for a class of nonlinear systems over sensor networks with sensor faults and random link failures. *IEEE Syst. J.* **2022**, *16*, 6328–6337. [CrossRef]
31. Sun, S.; Zhang, H.; Wang, Y.; Cai, Y. Dynamic output feedback-based fault-tolerant control design for T-S fuzzy systems with model uncertainties. *ISA Trans.* **2018**, *81*, 32–45. [CrossRef] [PubMed]
32. Zhao, W.; Liu, H.; Wan, Y. Data-driven fault-tolerant formation control for nonlinear quadrotors under multiple simultaneous actuator faults. *Syst. Control Lett.* **2021**, *15*, 105063. [CrossRef]
33. Wei, Q.; Li, H.; Li, T.; Wang, F. A novel data-based fault-tolerant control method for multicontroller linear systems via distributed policy iteration. *IEEE Trans. Syst. Man Cybern.-Syst.* **2022**, in press. [CrossRef]
34. Dai, L. *Singular Control Systems*; Springer: Berlin/Heidelberg, Germany, 1989.
35. Masubuchi, I.; Kamitane, Y.; Ohara, A.; Suda, N. H_∞ control for descriptor systems: A matrix inequalities approach. *Automatica* **1997**, *33*, 669–673. [CrossRef]
36. Zhou, J.; Wang, Z.; Wang, J.; Zhu, H. A frequency domain method for stochastic time delay. In Proceedings of the 36th Chinese Control Conference, Dalian, China, 26–28 July 2017; pp. 7944–7949.

Disclaimer/Publisher's Note: The statements, opinions and data contained in all publications are solely those of the individual author(s) and contributor(s) and not of MDPI and/or the editor(s). MDPI and/or the editor(s) disclaim responsibility for any injury to people or property resulting from any ideas, methods, instructions or products referred to in the content.

MDPI
St. Alban-Anlage 66
4052 Basel
Switzerland
www.mdpi.com

Mathematics Editorial Office
E-mail: mathematics@mdpi.com
www.mdpi.com/journal/mathematics

Disclaimer/Publisher's Note: The statements, opinions and data contained in all publications are solely those of the individual author(s) and contributor(s) and not of MDPI and/or the editor(s). MDPI and/or the editor(s) disclaim responsibility for any injury to people or property resulting from any ideas, methods, instructions or products referred to in the content.

www.ingramcontent.com/pod-product-compliance
Lightning Source LLC
LaVergne TN
LVHW070407100526
838202LV00014B/1408